The Revolution of 1688 in England

REVOLUTIONS IN THE MODERN WORLD

General Editor: JACK P. GREENE, Johns Hopkins University

J. R. Jones

Professor of English History in the University of East Anglia

The Revolution of

1688 in England

 W · W · Norton & Company · Inc · NEW YORK

Library of Congress Cataloging in Publication Data
Jones, James Rees.
    The Revolution of 1688 in England.
    (Revolutions in the modern world)
    Bibliography: p.
    1. Great Britain—History—Revolution of 1688.
I. Title
DA452.J63   1973   942.06'8   73-4726
ISBN 0-393-05459-4
ISBN 0-393-09998-9 (pbk.)

1 2 3 4 5 6 7 8 9 0

To Sheila, Peter and Deborah

Contents

M A P

The Low Countries in 1688

Preface

THE REACTION OF MOST professional historians and many intelligent students, on learning that I was engaged in this study, was to wonder whether there was sufficient scope to justify a new study of the Revolution of 1688 which has traditionally been given the title of the Glorious Revolution. They assumed that the general lines of interpretation established well over a century ago by T. B. Macaulay were still valid, and had stood the test of subsequent research, so that a few factual amendments, or minor modifications of his judgements, were the most that a new study could expect to achieve. Indeed there would have been little point in writing a new account of the Revolution of 1688 along orthodox lines. The justification for this book is that it is in part an essay in historical revisionism, with an interpretation which is provocatively and designedly different from that which most historians have accepted. In order to achieve this, I have tried to detach myself entirely from Macaulay's finely written and still potent work, by disregarding what seem to me to be his basic and fundamentally erroneous assumptions: that James II's defeat and the collapse of his policies, and the success of the Revolution and the Revolution Settlement, were all historically inevitable. In order to elaborate this argument, a substantial historiographical section has been included in the Introduction. It may also be noticed that the footnotes contain no references whatsoever to his *History* as a source; this is quite deliberate.

Secondly, this book is intended to draw the attention of readers and students away from the over-crowded, over-emphasized and heavily worked period of the 'English Revolution' of the mid-seventeenth century, to the still neglected topics and problems of the period after 1660. It is my thesis that the events of the 1640s and 1650s had not been decisive or conclusive, that the major constitutional and political issues were still open and undecided in James's time, and that the victory of parliament, representative government and the common law was by no means pre-determined or inevitable. In this book I argue that James had intelligible reasons for adopting the policies which he tried to implement, and that not only he but his opponents believed that they had a good chance of success. These policies and their effects are examined in detail, but there are some aspects of the events leading up to the Revolution where it has been possible only to put questions, and frame hypotheses. Full answers to these questions must await further research, for instance on the personnel and politics of the army, on James's economic policies and his relations with the commercial and financial sections, on French influences in Britain and British attitudes towards France and French systems (the subject to which I hope to turn in a future book), and, above all, on politics in the municipalities – in my view the key feature of late seventeenth-century politics, and the one that differentiates them from those of the early Stuart period.

After much thought, and with reluctance, it has been considered necessary, so as to keep this study to a manageable length, to omit any detailed consideration of James II's policies and the Revolution in Scotland, Ireland and the North American colonies. While it can be said that these were essentially peripheral areas, and that all the major decisions were made in England, nevertheless it must be stressed that the events of 1687–90 were of decisive importance for the future development of all three.

The short bibliography, mostly of recent works, is intended as a guide to further reading. The older and primary sources used in this study appear in the footnotes, fully described either on their first mention or in the list of abbreviations.

Dates are given in Old Style (with the year beginning on 1 January) when they refer to events in Britain, in New Style when they refer to continental Europe. Where confusion might arise, both dates are given.

The use of the words 'the Revolution' should be taken as refer-ring to 1688; purely for purposes of differentiation, the 'English Revolution' should be read as meaning the events of 1640–60.

I am greatly indebted to the criticisms and suggestions made by Professor Jack P. Greene, the general editor of this series, and by Donald S. Lamm, vice-president of W. W. Norton and Company, Inc. I wish also to acknowledge helpful suggestions made by John Miller of Caius College, Cambridge, Mr S. Groen-veld of the University of Leiden, and Mr K. I. Milne of the Univer-sity of East Anglia. Above all else, I am grateful for the patience which my own family have shown throughout the period while this book has been in progress.

University of East Anglia   J. R. JONES

Principal Personages

AILESBURY, Earl of. Friend of Charles II, remained loyal to James and went into voluntary exile; wrote *Memoirs*.

BARRILLON, Paul. French ambassador since 1677. A central figure at court, personally intimate with James and his queen, who tended to see things through their eyes and those of the Catholic faction.

BATH, Marquis of. Lord lieutenant and dominant election manager in Cornwall and Devon; a firm Anglican.

BEAUFORT, Duke of. Lord lieutenant and magnate in Gloucestershire, Wales and Herefordshire; of unimpeachable loyalty but his influence was being eroded by inertia and incompetence.

BENTINCK, Willem. William's chief confidant and servant, employed on every type of political task; created Earl of Portland in 1689.

BRENT, Robert. Catholic lawyer and confidential agent; James's chief electoral organiser, 1687–8.

BUTLER, Sir Nicholas. Humble origins, customs commissioner; after conversion to Catholicism was made a privy councillor; electoral agent.

BURNET, Gilbert. In exile in Holland, 1686–8; indiscreet and opinionated, especially in his *History*, but an important influence on Mary, if not William; made Bishop of Salisbury, 1689.

CARE, Henry. Journalist; had been heavily fined for Whig pamphleteering, but in 1686 switched to support James and his toleration policies, becoming a Catholic.

CARLINGFORD, Earl of. Catholic soldier and diplomat; virtually a French auxiliary while envoy at Vienna 1688–9; killed at the Boyne, 1690.

CARSTARES, William. William's trusted adviser and confidential agent for Scottish affairs.

CASTLEMAINE, Earl of. Generally despised husband of Charles II's first titled mistress. Disastrously inept as ambassador to the Vatican, 1687.

CHURCHILL, John. Later Duke of Marlborough; second in command of the army, he owed his rise to James's favour but his stubborn Protestantism was endangering his position by 1688; defected to William.

CITTERS, Aernout Van. Ambassador in England for the States-General from 1680; observant, and trusted by William.

CLARENDON, second Earl of. Son of the historian; recalled as Lord Lieutenant of Ireland, 1687. Leading Anglican. Surprisingly joined William in 1688, later a non-juror.

COLCHESTER, Lord. Heir of Lord Rivers, former Whig exclusionist. Army officer and plotter.

COMPTON, Henry. Bishop of London; aristocratic and ambitious clerical politician, but also one of the few leading Anglicans to take an active interest in European Protestantism. One of the Seven who invited William.

CORNBURY, Lord. Clarendon's heir; army officer, defected to William.

CREWE, Nathaniel. Bishop of Durham, 1674–1721, unscrupulous time-server, in James's favour but rallied to William after the Revolution.

CUTTS, John. Former friend of Monmouth's. Colonel in Dutch service 1688, later lieutenant-general. Nicknamed the 'Salamander'.

D'ALBEVILLE, Ignatius White. James's surprise appointment as envoy at the Hague, 1687–8; disreputable, despised and obtuse.

DANBY, Earl of. Later Marquis of Carmarthen and Duke of Leeds. Former lord treasurer, the most experienced political fixer and manager. Yorkshire magnate. Had arranged William's marriage to Mary in 1677. One of the Seven who invited William.

DARTMOUTH, Earl of. Naval officer, personal friend of James, commanded fleet against invasion 1688, but refused to ship the infant Prince of Wales to France.

D'AVAUX, Count. French ambassador at the Hague, 1678–88; ruthless, astute and observant, but his *Memoirs* are in part a self-justification.

DELAMERE, Lord. Whig firebrand, who had tried to help Monmouth in 1685. Honest and determined but a poor chancellor of the exchequer, 1689–90. Influential in the north west. Created Earl of Warrington, 1690.

DEVONSHIRE, Earl of. Former Whig; fined for court incident by James; one of the Seven; influential in north midlands.

DIJKVELT, Evaraard van Weede. Dutch soldier and diplomat, one of William's most trusted servants.

DOVER, Earl of. Newly created Catholic peer, privy councillor and Treasury lord, alleged to be using offices primarily for corrupt gain.

FAGEL, Gaspar. William's trusted collaborator as Pensionary of Holland; as important and burdened as Bentinck; died 15 December 1688.

FEVERSHAM, Earl of. Officer and diplomat of French birth, Turenne's nephew, naturalised 1665, a Protestant; James's trusted servant for twenty-five years; commanded army in 1685 and 1688.

FÜRSTENBERG, Bishop of Strasbourg. French diplomatic agent and candidate for electorate of Cologne; Cardinal 1686.

GEORGE, Prince. Anne's devoted husband, but otherwise unimportant and neglected.

GODOLPHIN, Sidney. Future lord treasurer. Treasury lord 1679, commissioner 1687; remained with James in 1688 although he had supported exclusion in 1680 and was a long-standing correspondent of William.

GRAFTON, Duke of. Ambitious naval officer, son of Charles II; favoured William. Killed in capture of Cork, 1690.

GUY, Henry. Secretary to the Treasury, 1679–88, and parliamentary manager.

HALIFAX, Marquis of. Politician and political writer; the 'Trimmer'. Opposed Exclusion, lord privy seal, 1682–5, 1689–90; lord president February–October 1685. Speaker of House of Lords, 1689–90.

HAMPDEN, John. Grandson of the celebrated opponent of Charles I; in France, 1682, convicted of treason but bought a pardon 1685–6; radical Whig. Suicide 1696.

HAMPDEN, Richard. Father of above. Senior radical Whig, manager in convention, treasury commissioner 1689, chancellor of the exchequer, 1690–95.

HERBERT, Arthur. Naval officer dismissed by James in 1687. Commanded the invasion fleet in 1688; defeated off Beachy Head, 1690. Created Earl of Torrington.

HERBERT, Edward. Younger brother. Chief justice who opposed James over Magdalen College case, but went into exile with him.

HUTTON, John. Mary's Scottish physician; one of the chief managers of William's English and Scottish correspondence.

JEFFREYS, George. Created Lord Wem, 1685. Lord chancellor, September 1685. His name a by-word for judicial infamy but in practice *the* scapegoat because of his friendlessness. An alcoholic. Died in the Tower, 1689.

JOHNSTONE, James. Son of Covenanter Archibald Johnstone of Warriston, important secret agent for William in England. Envoy to Berlin, 1689; secretary of state for Scotland, 1692–6.

LANGSTON, Thomas. Lieutenant-colonel, agent for William in the army.

LOUVOIS, The French war minister, who influenced Louis towards aggressive and direct policies.

LOVELACE, Lord. Aggressive Whig peer. Arrested November 1688 at Cirencester while rallying to William.

LUMLEY, Lord. One of the Seven who invited William; converted to Protestantism, 1687; north country magnate; 1690 created Earl of Scarborough.

MELFORT, Earl of. Able and thrusting, but unreliable and unpopular minister; ruled Scotland for James with his brother the Earl of Perth. A Catholic extremist.

MIDDLETON, second Earl of. Secretary of state, 1684–8, and later in exile at St-Germain. A moderate, but with little influence on James.

MONMOUTH, Duke of. Charles II's favourite son; disgraced in 1679 but never out of hopes of recovering his father's favour. In Holland 1684–5. Invaded 1685, proclaimed himself king. Defeated and executed.

MORDAUNT, Lord. Later the 'great' Earl of Peterborough and Earl of Monmouth. First exile to suggest an invasion to William; 1689 privy councillor and Treasury lord. An extreme Whig in 1689–91, later an extreme and erratic Tory.

NEWCASTLE, Duke of. Pompous, self-important, but incompetent north-country magnate and multiple lord lieutenant.

NOSWORTHY, Edward. Former Whig extremist who began to invade Bath's west-country constituencies as a political manipulator, 1688.

NOTTINGHAM, Earl of. Anglican and constitutionalist, influential in politics, 1672–1716. Refused to participate in the Revolution, but secretary of state, 1689–93.

ORMONDE, second Duke of. Later a Jacobite, but in 1688 hurriedly elected Chancellor of Oxford University so as to prevent James installing a Catholic; army plotter.

PENN, William. The Quaker; trusted friend of James and champion of toleration, tried to obtain William's and Mary's approval, 1686.

PETRE, Edward. Ambitious and well-connected Jesuit and politician; cast as the villain by contemporaries, very little is in fact known of his influence on James. Fled to France, 1688.

POWLE, Henry. Former Whig exclusionist; chairman of 1688 Assembly and Speaker of Convention, 1689–90.

PRESTON, Lord. Envoy to France, 1682–5; parliamentary manager 1685, replaced Sunderland as lord president, October 1688. Jacobite, arrested 1689 and 1690.

QUEEN MARY of Modena. James's second wife. A fervent Catholic whose marriage had been arranged by Louis. Never lost hope of a restoration after 1688, but her intransigence hampered her son's chances.

RIVERS, James. Secret agent for William, travelling between England and Holland.

ROCHESTER, Earl of. Not the poet (died 1680) but the first Earl of Clarendon's second son. Tory and Anglican leader. Treasury lord, 1679–85; lord president, 1684; lord treasurer, 1685–7.

RUSSELL, Edward. Naval officer; friend of James but disaffected after execution of his cousin Lord William Russell in 1683. One of the Seven who invited William, and confidential agent; admiral, treasurer of navy, and Earl of Orford after the revolution.

SANCROFT, William. Archbishop of Canterbury from 1678. Scrupulous, pious and largely non-political. Refused to serve on Ecclesiastical Commission under James, or take any part in public life after his flight. Suspended August 1689, deprived February 1690.

SAWYER, Sir Robert. Prosecuting counsel in trials of Whigs, 1683 and London charter; attorney-general until December 1687. Defence counsel for the Seven Bishops.

SEYMOUR, Edward. Ambitious and aggressive Tory politician; firm Anglican; speaker 1673, opposed Exclusion and James's policies in 1685. Treasury lord, 1691–4.

SHAFTESBURY, Earl of. Author of Exclusion and leader of the first Whigs; had died in Amsterdam, January 1683.

SHARP, John. Chaplain to James; Dean of Norwich; sermon led to Compton's prosecution. 1691–1714 Archbishop of York and ecclesiastical adviser to Queen Anne.

SHREWSBURY, Earl of. Dismissed as lord lieutenant and colonel by James, 1687. One of the Seven who invited William; secretary of state, 1689–90. Able, but periodical aversion to politics. Lord treasurer, 1714.

SIDNEY, Henry. Soldier, diplomat and playboy; younger brother of Algernon, uncle to Sunderland and possibly lover of Lady Sunderland. Envoy to Holland, 1679–85.

William's most intimate English adviser, created Earl of Romney 1694, secretary of state, 1690–91

SKELTON, Bevil. Envoy to Holland, 1685–6; to France, 1686–8; recalled for suggesting the D'Avaux memorandum September 1688. Hated by William.

SPEKE, Hugh. Whig propagandist and agent for William in 1688, son of a prominent Whig, his brother had been executed in 1685.

STRICKLAND, Sir Roger. Catholic admiral, commanded fleet until September 1688, then vice-admiral to Dartmouth.

SUNDERLAND, Earl of. Secretary of state, 1679–81 (dismissed for supporting Exclusion) and 1683–5. President of council 1685 to October 1688, when dismissed by James as part of his policy of concessions. Fled to Holland, returned 1691. Private adviser to William; lord chamberlain, 1697.

TEMPLE, Sir William. Diplomat and writer; adviser to William but refused secretaryship of state, 1679 and 1689.

TITUS, Silas. Whig exclusionist, made privy councillor by James 1688, which he accepted to ensure repayment of debts owing him from crown.

TREVOR, Sir John. Cousin and rival to Jeffreys. Speaker 1685 and 1690–95 (removed for taking bribes) and master of the rolls; privy councillor, 1688.

TURNER, Francis. Chaplain to James, by whose favour he became Bishop of Ely 1684; prospective archbishop of Canterbury, able and masterful. Suspended 1689, active Jacobite, but had been one of the Seven Bishops prosecuted in 1688.

TYRCONNEL, Earl of. Irish Catholic soldier and courtier, long-standing associate of James. Earl 1685, lieutenant-general 1686, lord deputy 1687. Died at Limerick just before its surrender, 1691.

WADE, Nathaniel. Former Whig agent, invaded with Monmouth. Turned King's evidence and became electoral organiser for James.

WHARTON, Thomas. Able and aggressive Whig, later Junta leader. Part-author of hit song of the Revolution, *Lilliburlero*, a doggerel verse deriding the Irish.

WILDMAN, John. Elderly radical, former Leveller and Whig. In exile in Holland, 1685–8. Postmaster, 1689–91.

WILLIAMS, William. Lawyer and Whig, personal rival to Jeffreys. Speaker 1680–81, heavily fined for a libel on James. Solicitor-general, 1687–8, prosecuting the Seven Bishops. Created baronet by James. Helped draft Bill of Rights, 1689.

ZUYLESTEIN, Willem. Dutch officer and William's confidential agent. Major-general in invading army 1688. Created Earl of Rochford, 1695.

The Revolution of 1688 in England

ONE **_Introduction_**

SUPERFICIALLY THE REVOLUTION OF 1688 can be seen as perhaps the most rapidly executed of all revolutions, with the decisive action and changes concentrated into a few weeks: William landed at Torbay on 5 November, James fled to France on 23 December, and the crown was offered to William and Mary on 13 February 1689. But the speed and bloodlessness of the Revolution in England, the near unanimity of the formerly hostile Whig and Tory parties in support of the main parts of the Settlement, are all the more remarkable when set (as they must be) against the background of chronic political crisis, instability and lack of mutual trust which characterized the period after the Restoration.

The Restoration of the monarchy and the old order in 1660 had been hopefully intended to obliterate the divisions, enmities and aberrations caused by the civil wars and the military tyranny of the Commonwealth. In practice its total and lamentable failure was quickly apparent to everyone. From the first the political atmosphere was polluted by corruption, cynical opportunism and constant, deadly faction fighting. Fundamental questions remained unsettled about the balance of the constitution and the distribution of power between king, Lords, Commons, the Church and the electors. Clarendon, Charles II's first chief minister, tried to govern in the traditional way but when he fell from power in 1667 the king actually encouraged the final attack. Similarly, Charles made no attempt to save the members of the cabal, the composite ministry which attempted in 1670–73 to introduce governmental absolutism and religious toleration, even though this left him temporarily dependent on parliament. The cabal's policies were simply abandoned, indeed the new minister Danby switched to a diametrically opposite policy of coercive Anglicanism as an aid to building up working majorities in both Houses of Parliament. For five years he succeeded in carrying on government, but at the price of provoking suspicions that the independence of Parliament was being subverted. Pressures built up which exploded in the Popish Plot, an outburst of hysteria at the end of 1678 caused by elaborate stories of a Catholic plot to murder Charles so as to bring his Catholic brother to the throne. This hysteria, and the authentic evidence of close links between the court and Louis XIV, was ruthlessly exploited by Shaftesbury during the Exclusion Crisis of 1678–81, which took its title from the bill excluding James from the succession. This bill split the nation and excited almost universal political consciousness. In favour were the first Whigs, a formidably organized and aggressive party, who dominated three general elections in 1679 and 1681. The Tories rallied to defend the crown and the legitimate succession, and regarded themselves as playing a decisive and irreplaceable part in defeating the Whigs and blocking Exclusion.

The defeat of the Whig challenge, at the Oxford Parliament of March 1681, was followed by a period of prolonged repression, not of calm. Shaftesbury was unsuccessfully prosecuted for treason, but the Whig hold on London and many other corporate towns was destroyed, and the dissenters were subject to the most prolonged persecution of the Restoration period. Some Whigs reacted by contemplating violence. In 1683 many of their surviving leaders were accused of planning a rebellion, and a radical section was charged with plotting to kill Charles and James (the Rye House Plot). Executions followed, with many others of those implicated having to take refuge abroad, in the United Provinces. In 1685 rebellion actually occurred. Monmouth invaded the west country, raised an army in three weeks from rank and file Whigs, and denounced James as the murderer of Charles. His defeat was followed by severe repression and left James in a stronger position than any of his Stuart predecessors.

After a period of such turbulence and crisis most of the political nation (the minority that actively participated in politics and administration) would have cheerfully acquiesced in James's possession of such strength. But the Tories who now monopolized offices were not ready to accept the further demands which James made at the end of 1685, over the strength of the army and the eligibility of Catholics for offices, which they interpreted as tending towards absolutism. There followed, in 1687 and early 1688, a total realignment of political alliances. James appealed to his old enemies, the Whigs and the dissenters, and purged his former Tory allies from offices. He concentrated on the systematic preparation of general elections, abandoning his campaign to pack a collaborationist Parliament only at the end of September 1688, on the eve of William's invasion. Not until then did James realize his danger. His belated defensive preparations included discarding the agents whom he had employed and discarding the policies which had provoked opposition, but his only real chance of defeating William was through the use of his navy and army. When these failed him, James's position collapsed within a month. Defections by officers made the army unserviceable. This allowed the nobility and gentry to assemble, armed, in several provincial capitals, to declare for William and a free Parliament. Deserted by his daughter Anne, and finding that his most intimate advisers were already preparing to seek refuge in France, James broke down psychologically. He sent his wife and baby son to safety in France. On 10 December he set out to follow them, leaving London secretly while he was still engaged in discussions with his councillors and before the emissaries sent to William had had a chance of reporting. In Kent James was intercepted by a vigilante group of fishermen and brought back, a virtual captive. James found London unexpectedly sympathetic, largely because of the fears aroused by serious anti-Catholic riots, but he made no effort to resume the initiative. He thought only of reaching France, but his second and successful flight (on the 23rd) was so obviously facilitated by

William that later Jacobite propagandists used it to show that William had aimed throughout at usurping the English throne.

James calculated that his departure would create a constitutional and governmental vacuum. William's followers would break up into hostile factions and there could be a re-emergence of the formerly bitter divisions into Whigs and Tories. This did not happen on a significant scale. A permanent constitutional settlement was accomplished with comparatively little delay or difficulty and unity was preserved. At Christmas an assembly of peers and former MPs asked William to take over the provisional administration of government and to issue letters for parliamentary elections. These elections were held without disorder. The Convention Parliament (one which had not been elected on the basis of writs issued by a king) met on 22 January 1689. Despite the preference of many peers and MPs for a regency, which would leave James with the empty title of king but give actual control of government to William, or alternatively for the latter's wife Mary to become queen, with William actually controlling government, there was little persistent opposition to the solution finally adopted. This was to offer the throne jointly to William and Mary, a settlement contrary to strict constitutional law. Its wide and ready acceptance was largely due to the urgent need for a quick solution, since James's adherents were active in Scotland and controlled most of Ireland, and also to the accompaniment of the offer to William and Mary with a statute embodying and safeguarding religion and liberties, the celebrated Bill of Rights. Religious toleration was also enacted for most dissenters, the army was brought under parliamentary control by the Mutiny Act, and the terms of the financial settlement ensured that all future sovereigns would have no option but to govern in cooperation with Parliament.

The speed with which this constitutional settlement was concluded is perhaps less surprising than its long-term success. None of its architects could have predicted its effectiveness in securing the liberties, religion, property and independence of the nation, after so many previous attempts had failed. Despite the ease with which the Revolution had been accomplished, the success of the Settlement was not inevitable. By describing it as such, the classic

Whig historians writing in the nineteenth century distorted its real meaning and significance.

Nineteenth-century English historians had no doubt that the Revolution of 1688 was Glorious, and the most important single event in the development of modern Britain. Today it is totally overshadowed by the English Revolution of the mid-seventeenth century, and as a subject it is comparatively neglected. This is shown by the fact that after a hundred and twenty years Macaulay is still the principal authority, despite the obsolescence of the type of questions which he asked, and his blatant historical partiality, which stemmed from his active participation in the battles which political liberalism was fighting in his lifetime. Because of his mastery of the sources, Macaulay is still an overpowering figure, and he has largely dominated the three historians who have recently published studies of the Revolution. Ashley's and Carswell's studies contain some interesting new points of detail, and provide more detached and balanced judgements, but the approach is still exclusively political and the interpretation broadly similar.[1] The third study, by Pinkham, is much more derivative, since it attempts what is in effect a direct refutation of Macaulay.[2]

By following Macaulay's approach none of these studies can hope to convince present-day students and readers that the Revolution was anything more than a mere postscript to the English Revolution, or that it provides an intrinsically important subject for study, offering opportunities for investigation and research. In reviewing Maurice Ashley's book in the *Observer,* John Kenyon confidently asserted : 'Every other revolution in the sixteenth and seventeenth centuries, in England and Europe, can be given a social or economic interpretation . . . only the Glorious Revolution remains exclusively a political or a religious event.' Such a statement deters modern historians who see no value in one-dimensional history, but it is the thesis of this study that social factors must be taken into account if the Revolution is to be understood. Furthermore it is suggested that there can be seen the out-

---

[1] M. Ashley, *The Glorious Revolution of 1688* (1966); J. Carswell, *The Descent on England* (1969).
[2] L. Pinkham, *William III and the Respectable Revolution* (1954).

lines of several sets of questions requiring research, including several in the fields of economic and local history.

Today everyone in Britain and the United States is in a sense a residuary beneficiary of the Revolution, although we can at present take this for granted since the issues involved now form the accepted bases of our institutions and societies. All Liberals and Marxists have a vested interest in seeing the Revolution as one of the stages in the process of historical changes which produced the world in which we live. Only very old-fashioned Catholics now share the values and principles which James II held. Consequently 1688 provides a very clear example of the dictum that 'history is the propaganda of the victors'. William has always been (rightly) seen as the centrepiece; James has been neglected or caricatured. As a result the policies which he followed have been misrepresented or totally dismissed, without being subject to serious examination or analysis. While remembering that James failed, this study is based on the thesis that the Revolution cannot be understood or its significance appreciated unless James's policies are systematically examined, in the context of the way in which Restoration politics worked, and of contemporary developments in Europe.

All historians of the Revolution have been more than usually influenced in their interpretation by the political considerations of their own time. Henry Hallam and T. B. Macaulay (and G. M. Trevelyan later) were committed by their belief that the Revolution had laid the basis for liberal parliamentary government and religious freedom. For them the English (or rather Puritan) Revolution had been diverted from its original, sane and moderate principles, and had ended in military tyranny and fanaticism. Like the French Revolution it became a destructive force, producing an abrupt and violent break with the past. This was a development incompatible with the element of continuity which these historians saw as the key to the development of English liberties, whereas the Revolution enshrined this principle. The Revolution was a praiseworthy paradox, a revolution with little violence (in England at least) and few victims. William was the greater man because, like George Washington, he did not succumb to the temptations of power. James was foolish and misled. Eighteenth-

century historians (even David Hume) had seen him as wicked
or false, but Hallam and Macaulay could not share their attitude;
they disapproved of James's Catholic principles, but they disapproved even more strongly of blind anti-papist prejudice, because
they had to fight it in the opponents of Catholic Emancipation
in the 1820s.

More historiographically interesting are the French writers, who
from Benjamin Constant in 1799 to the Boulangists in the late
1880s were drawing parallels between France in their own time
and seventeenth-century England.[3] Many were looking for a
French General Monk to restore the monarchy. Guizot turned to
English history to try to find the answer to the question of how to
restore political unity and stability after a period of revolutions
and recurrent crises.[4] By studying the ways in which William and
the architects of the Revolution settlement had achieved a solution,
appropriate policies could be formulated for use in France.
Guizot's glorification of William, and the claim that lessons
drawn from English seventeenth-century history were applicable,
led Marx to pronounce on the Revolution, and his polemical depre-
ciation of its importance has contributed to the current Marxist
interpretation of the Revolution as no more than a palace *coup*.
Marx saw William as the servant of the bourgeoisie, the instrument
which it used to consolidate its power, and (unbelievably) as the
agent of foreign policies based on commercial interest.[5] But
actual conclusions on seventeenth-century English history were
not Marx's purpose in writing; his arguments were to refute
Guizot's hopes, to show that nothing could save bourgeois France
from the approaching proletarian revolution. Just as no Monk
ever appeared, so in Marx's view there could be no halting of the
irresistible processes that had started in France in 1789 but
in England in 1640.

Most recent historians have seen little to interest them in the
Revolution, whereas the English Revolution seems to offer far more
numerous and rewarding subjects for investigation and discussion.

---

[3] B. Constant, *Des Suites de la contre-révolution de 1660 en Angleterre* (1798–9).
[4] F. P. Guizot, *Pourquoi la révolution d'Angleterre a-t-elle réussi? Discours sur l'histoire
de la révolution d'Angleterre* (1850).
[5] K. Marx and F. Engels, *On Britain* (1962), pp. 345, 347–8.

Sixteen hundred and eighty-eight is seen as a postscript, confirming what had been done earlier but adding little that was new or important. It is assumed that it was a conservative *coup,* the work of a small and self-interested elite; in one historian's view, an aristocratic revolution.[6] This was also the interpretation of the now unimportant neo-Jacobite writers. James appealed to Catholics like Hilaire Belloc and M. V. Hay as the defender of both the old faith and of the old hierarchical order of society (in which view they were wrong).[7] He fell a victim to the rapacious, money-minded aristocracy and bourgeoisie. Hard, cold and calculating, William first helped them destroy James, and then exploit and degrade the people of England. Pinkham's study is a variation on this theme, with William caricatured as just a cunning plotter. Her study, valuable chiefly as a manual of erroneous historical interpretation, totally ignores or misrepresents the contexts of English politics and the European situation.

Today it would seem that the Revolution has insufficient current political relevance to engage our prejudices or passions. This study is intended as a reinterpretation, an exercise in historical revisionism based, not on any mass of unused material but on discarding accepted views and unexamined assumptions. A new set of questions is formulated and asked. If the approach is influenced by a response to our contemporary situation, it is in the emphasis given to the practical and manipulative aspects of Restoration politics. Politicians of the Restoration period were primarily skilled political operators and organizers of propaganda, for whom political ideals were a luxury, faced as they were by the hard demands of endlessly changing day-to-day problems. Political manoeuvring, polemical pamphleteering, the techniques of electoral organization and political management were what current politics demanded, and it is these aspects that are emphasized here, not the political theory of Locke or the theoretical bases of policies of religious toleration.

The first part of this reinterpretation is to claim that the Revolution must be put into the context of contemporary English

[6] J. P. Kenyon, *The Nobility in the Revolution of 1688* (1963).
[7] H. Belloc, *James the Second* (1928); M. V. Hay, *The Enigma of James II* (1938).

politics. It is no use assuming that there was a structure of politics similar to that of the eighteenth century. Equally the context of the Revolution was dissimilar from that of the English Revolution, whose influence on the men of the generation that lived after 1660 was strongly negative; they were appalled at what had happened, thought they knew why it had happened, and were determined that it should not happen again.

Secondly, it is necessary to take James's policies seriously, because they were based on political realities. This applies particularly to his central policy – the campaign to pack Parliament. Unless this is attempted it is impossible to understand the force, and extent, of the reaction which these policies provoked.

Thirdly, an attempt is made to relate James's political and religious policies to the social as well as the political position in the localities, and especially in the towns. It is claimed that the basic importance of municipal politics is one of the key characteristics of politics after 1660, differentiating them from those of the period before 1640. If slogans are permissible, 'municipalize' is what those undertaking research in the period should be urged to do.[8] Fourthly, in examining these policies a social dimension appears. James allied with the urban middle classes against the landowning aristocracy and gentry. His switch of alliances from Tory to Whig could have become more than a change of political partners; with time it could have resulted in the emergence of a synthetic ruling class to replace the traditional associates of the crown in government.

Fifthly, an examination of the methods which James used in his campaign to pack Parliament, and in his attempt to mobilize the support he expected to gain from toleration, shows that these were methods formerly used by Shaftesbury during the Exclusion Crisis. Superficially at least James can be seen as his only successor. In fact this was only a technical imitation, concerned with methods. James's ultimate objective consisted of establishing some form of

[8] Analyses are needed of the relation between politics in the municipalities and developments in the Long Parliament, and of the changes in the franchise and representation suggested and attempted during the Commonwealth. Similarly, research is needed on the possible link between the position in the boroughs resulting from James's policies, and the Triennial Act of 1694.

absolutism. Those historians who have said that Charles I's fate made this impossible, or even unthinkable, ignore developments in contemporary Europe.[9] James's policies were realistic in the context of the general development and extensions of systems of absolutist power and government, principally in France, but also in Sweden, Denmark, and many German states.

Finally, William's invasion needs to be related to the other contemporary instances of foreign intervention in English politics, by France, the Dutch, and even Spain. There is a sharp contrast between the 1640s, when Britain was effectively insulated from a Europe torn by a prolonged series of wars, and the way in which the hostility between William and Louis extended into English politics the lines of division that existed between their opposing camps. English politics became a secondary theatre of the wars, and on three occasions of internal stalemate (in 1673 and 1681 as well as in 1688) foreign intervention proved to be the decisive factor.

Historians should be cautious before comparing the Revolution with other revolutions, such as the French or American. Well-founded comparisons require countries, or periods, with approximately similar social structures, economic organization and governmental institutions. This means seventeenth-century France and the United Provinces. James's hopes of success owed more to contemporary developments in France than to the example of his father. Only one of the major policies that Charles had inherited from the Tudors (the Ecclesiastical Commission) was revived by James. He and his ministers were far more strongly influenced by Louis XIV's methods and their results. In England James lacked the time to make substantial progress towards establishing absolutism, and the opposition which he provoked led to the Revolution. But in Scotland, Ireland and the North American colonies he was able to go a long way. It is vital to understand that in 1688 James was in some ways a dynamic innovator. Among his opponents were those who represented what were known as 'country' opinions and interests. They were mostly landed gentry

---

[9] For example, B. Moore, *Social Origins of Dictatorship and Democracy* (1967), p. 17.

without experience of central office-holding who, with their descendants, were to remain obstinately attached to the same fixed views, principles and prejudices for more than another half century. They thought of themselves as men of honesty and consistency, as defenders of the constitution against ministerial corruption and illegalities. From the governmental point of view they were self-interested defenders of privileges, who obstructed effective administration by their behaviour in Parliament – particularly over matters of finance and taxation – and who also wished to perpetuate their predominant influence within the counties. It was this last reason that led James to try to make himself independent of them in 1667–8. As a result the 'country' 𝕏 gentry helped William during the Revolution. Disillusionment soon followed. Most soon came to believe that the new government was still using the old methods, so that by the mid-1690s they were opposing William and his ministers (former Whigs though they were, by then, for the most part) for corruption and unconstitutional behaviour. Their intransigent and persistent refusal to recognize changing political realities, especially the financial demands created by the nine years war, and their total suspicion of the executive, made them a largely negative political force.

Another section among James's opponents consisted of members of the great aristocracy, Benjamin Disraeli's 'Venetian oligarchy', magnates who believed that they had a prescribed right to share in the conduct of government, at the centre as well as in the counties. In the latter case there is an obvious, if general, parallel with France, where Richelieu, Mazarin and Louis dispensed with the greater aristocracy, but English society was not constituted in such a way that James could follow their example in using the middle nobility against the great; only the Scottish and Irish aristocracy (many of whom had served in France) fell into this category. Similarly, while it can be said that the army was governmentally the most advanced of James's institutions, he lacked the time to follow the example of the rulers of France, or Frederick William in Brandenburg-Prussia, by extending into other fields the methods used in military administration, or by militarizing his entire administration.

In claiming that James was being realistic in seeking the collaboration of the urban middle class against the landowning classes, this is true mainly in terms of parliamentary and electoral politics. It is in this area alone that officials can be found who resemble *intendants* – in the persons of Brent, Butler and the itinerant electoral agents. But in the long term James's alliance with the urban middle class was not likely to prove sufficiently strong to enable him to relegate his opponents to a position of permanent subordination and political impotence. Although many towns were expanding at this time, and their economies and societies becoming increasingly diversified, only London dominated the surrounding rural areas and country landowners in the way that the cities of Holland did. Even more important is the fact that the urban middle class were often less commercially oriented and money-minded than a section of the aristocracy and gentry. Many of the latter (again with the exception of London), had more and better opportunities for large-scale investment, in the form of market-farming, mining, rural industries and suburban real estate, than did townsmen.

Furthermore the commercial class, because of the nature of its business activities and the composition of its assets, was not generally in a position yet to play the same kind of dominating role in politics as did the regent class in Holland. Business management was still usually personal, absorbing too much time. Wealth still largely consisted of stock in trade, and so was vulnerable to changes in commodity prices, overseas trading conditions and consumer demand. Secure and profitable outlets for investment did not compare with those that existed in Holland from the 1620s. Land purchases locked up capital, meant lower returns and led, if on a large scale, to absorption into the landed class. Only with the establishment of the Bank of England can a permanent and increasingly influential monied interest be said to have become an important social and political factor. Before 1696, and certainly in James's reign, royal bankers were in the same desperately vulnerable position as clients of the crown as the French *financiers*. More generally, as has recently been demonstrated, commercial wealth at this time lacked staying power; it was often transient, and could not yet be regarded as offering a serious challenge to the landowning interest.[10]

Nevertheless James's attempt to use the urban middle class as a replacement for the landowning class should make historians hesitate before sweepingly describing the Revolution as a bourgeois revolution. Strictly speaking it was exactly the opposite. Moreover, there is another aspect, which is in sharp contrast to the situation in rural England in the sixteenth and early seventeenth centuries; the absence of acute tension between the landowning classes and their social inferiors. James was attempting to exploit the friction which often existed between towns and the gentry of the surrounding countryside. In some cases this appears to have had economic causes, but more often it derived from the local political struggles of the civil war and the Commonwealth, about which we as yet know comparatively little. But it is significant that in 1687–8 the aristocracy and gentry did not face a challenge in the countryside itself. With the exception of some county elections during the Exclusion Crisis, and possibly Monmouth's rebellion, there is very little evidence of rural radicalism during this period, and rural dissenters were less politically minded than their urban counterparts.[11] Apparently there was no widespread tension in the countryside for James's agents to exploit, so that they concentrated on using the tensions and divisions that certainly did exist in the towns.

Another sweeping generalization which needs to be scrutinized is the postulation of a causal connection between the Revolution (or the English Revolution for that matter) and the Industrial Revolution. It is entirely incorrect to think of William as any more concerned with commercial interests in England after 1688 than in the United Provinces before. The nine years war, in which he deliberately involved Britain for diplomatic and political reasons, had a seriously adverse effect on the economy as a whole and on trading interests in particular. By contrast throughout his career, as Duke of York as well as king, James

[10] *Ibid.*, pp. 8–9, 14–15. R. Grassby, 'English Merchant Capitalism in the late Seventeenth Century', *Past and Present*, 46.
[11] We need a breakdown of Monmouth's captured supporters, by occupation and place of residence.

had far closer connections with commercial interests. He had consistently sponsored mercantilist policies, although like Louis XIV's minister, Colbert, he was interested in expanding trade and national prosperity as means towards achieving greater power, not as ends in themselves. However, it has to be added that the whole subject of James's relations with mercantile and financial interests, the significance of his association with Josiah Childe and John Friend, the relation of business to court and political groups, still needs detailed research.[12] But it can be said that there is at present no evidence to suggest that James's policies – especially after his break with the Tories – were antagonistic to, or obstructive of, economic expansion and prosperity. His policies of toleration were advocated on the specific ground that they would free business and individual enterprise from arbitrary clerical interference, and royal propagandists pointed to the economic advantages which the Dutch derived from toleration.

In this, as well as in two other respects, there are in my view valid parallels with the Dutch Revolution. Those who fought most resolutely for Dutch independence – the Calvinist militants, the sea-beggars, the urban poor and petite bourgeoisie – did not turn out to be its beneficiaries. Similarly, many of the smaller country gentry who defied James felt betrayed after 1688 by the way in which government was conducted, and by adverse economic conditions – hence the bitterness of 'country' opposition under William and Anne. Secondly, what was defeated in both countries was an apparently more modern and efficient system of government, based on a professional bureaucracy, centralization and the subordination of all classes to the sovereign. Instead anomalies were perpetuated; municipal and provincial autonomy, representative institutions that were used by sectional interests and foreign powers for their own purposes. In the localities and at the centre, government was directed by amateurs, although governmental functions were becoming more complex and onerous. The experts were used as subordinates. They functioned under the amateurs, who retained overall

[12] W. Letwin, *Sir Josiah Childe: merchant economist* (1959).

control, whereas in France, Scandinavia and the Empire the trend was in the opposite direction. In the seventeenth-century United Provinces, as in eighteenth-century England, an army could not be dispensed with, but it was feared as a possible political menace and was often deliberately allowed to run down for this reason. Foreign policy became subject to a constant tug of war between those who believed that it should concentrate on furthering economic interests and those (Frederick Henry, William II, William III, George I and George II) who were suspected of trying to follow an unnecessarily aggressive and essentially personal or dynastic policy.

The contention of this study, then, is that on examination, and after setting them in the context of the way in which Restoration politics worked, James's policies were realistic. They failed, but it needed William's invasion to wreck them, and Englishmen were generally alarmed enough to believe that only such an invasion could ensure their failure. Secondly, attention is drawn to the importance of municipal politics since they were the key to success in parliamentary elections, and to the need for further research into the composition of groups in municipal politics. Thirdly, the strength and advantages which James derived from the army are a reminder that he was trying (with certain variations due to conditions in England) to emulate most European sovereigns by making himself independent of his subjects, using the contemporarily fashionable and effective methods of absolutism.

TWO *The Working of Politics*

THROUGHOUT THE RESTORATION PERIOD political affairs revolved around two centres, and of these the court at
Whitehall was more continuously important than the
Parliament at Westminster. All ministers and aspirants to office
had to walk on these two legs, and found that the task of securing
their position at court, and undermining that of rivals there, was
more complex and time-consuming than parliamentary work.
Unlike its post-Revolutionary successors, the late Stuart court was
both the main accepted centre of fashionable social life and the
focal point of politics and administration. Its characteristics
reflected the uncertainties and ambiguities of contemporary life
and manners. Just as the Palace of Whitehall ('large but not
magnificent' in Grammont's words) was an undistinguished
jumble of courts, galleries, halls and suites built at different
times, and in various styles and materials, unimpressive by
comparison with the Louvre or Versailles, so its life and ways
were more casual than those of Louix XIV's court. Except on a
few formal occasions, there was little elaborate ceremonial. The
Court at Whitehall formed what was in effect a rambling village,
one of several on the edge of London and Westminster, with

an open street running through its centre. It was not insulated from ordinary metropolitan life, nor was it highly regimented or subject to the immediately effective control of the king. Whitehall was in no way the centre of the cultural life of the capital, since neither Charles nor James made any systematic attempt to encourage and patronize the arts.

The informality with which Charles, James and their courtiers lived is attractive to modern tastes, which find the rigid protocol and complex etiquette of Versailles repellent and stifling. However in practical terms this informality made life much more difficult for courtiers. At Versailles every act and word of the king was intentional and regulated; the meaning could be immediately and accurately interpreted by the experienced courtier. In contrast, nobody knew where they stood with Charles, who generally permitted familiar and even offensive behaviour but who could also suddenly and unexpectedly assert himself. Consequently the successful courtier was one who could predict how the king would behave under any particular set of circumstances. James was more predictable, and introduced a degree of protocol into court life, but he again was difficult to manage because of his obstinacy, and it was equally hazardous to try to divine his intentions.

In addition, Charles and James, by their way of life, blurred the distinction between public and private matters. Both encouraged circles of personal confidants or cronies, often excluding and embarrassing, and sometimes actually endangering their official servants. Both allowed themselves to be used and exploited, James because he was stupid and imperceptive, Charles because he was cynical and indifferent. It is most significant that William, after his accession, made little effort to maintain a court on the former model. He was accustomed to a very much smaller court, more in the nature of a household or personal entourage, and neither he nor Mary was capable of manipulating the English court for the furtherance of their very definite and specific policies. Both reacted strongly against what they condemned as its worldliness, falsity, immorality and lack of religion.[1] They lacked the personality and will (and William

[1] R. Doebner, *Memoirs of Mary Queen of England* (1886), pp. 11, 17.

the time and physical energy) to play the role which Charles had enjoyed and James accepted, so that after 1688 politics became far more polycentric. Appropriately most of Whitehall disappeared in the fires of 1691 and 1698, and there were other than financial reasons why the palace was never rebuilt.

Whitehall contained a permanent population of more than two thousand, a total which can be divided into several different categories, not all of them mutually exclusive. A basic division was that between unimportant menial servants and those who held offices of honour. Among the latter, two separate groups can be suggested; one, official, between those with offices in the central executive and those holding positions in the household.[2] The other is a personal division, between the men of pleasure and those of business. Of course the latter group were the ones who really mattered politically, but there were many men (and women) of pleasure who enjoyed political influence through their personal intimacy with Charles and James. It was they who created the general atmosphere of indolence and frivolity which so suited Charles and tempted James, with their trivial talk and by their gaming, horseracing, drinking and whoring. By these diversions they often seriously impeded the transaction of governmental business. Moreover, they were as greedy for grants, pensions and offices as men of serious political or administrative importance, and by the frequency and closeness of their connections with the king often much better placed to obtain them. Ministers neglected such men, whom Essex described as 'the little people', at their peril.[3] Even if the part which they played in contriving Clarendon's fall has been exaggerated, they were still a real threat to the position of ministers. For instance, Danby and Halifax were both ill-equipped to deal with this type of intriguer, or more generally for this kind of social life. Danby relied on money, for example spending very large sums on the Duchess of Portsmouth, the only one of the royal mistresses who had real political ambitions.

[2] There is no study of the court of this period; as models for one: G. Aylmer, *The King's Servants* (1961), and J. M. Beattie, *The English Court in the Reign of George I* (1967). Editions of the contemporary directory, E. Chamberlayne's *Angliae Notitia*, appeared in 1684 and 1687.

[3] O. Airy (ed.), *Essex Papers* (1890), I, 272.

In any court system access (and particularly secret access) to the ruler is of the greatest importance. No minister under Charles or James could ever be confident that he controlled it, or even knew whom the king was seeing, whose private advice he was taking, what promises he was making. Attempts to get such information cost ministers much time and worry and this element of uncertainty poses problems for the historian. We can never know the full 'secret history' of Whitehall, although several unreliable books were published after 1688 to satisfy public curiosity on the subject; apart from Grammont we have no equivalent to the French court chroniclers Saint-Simon, de Sourches and Dangeau. But there are enough references to hint at the influence possessed by such 'little people' as Tom Elliott (groom of the bedchamber), William Chiffinch (who controlled the backstairs), Edward Progers (chief pimp to Charles), Edward Coleman (James's ill-fated secretary) and Ralph Sheldon, confidant during the crisis of 1688.

Other groups of courtiers were equally detested, particularly the permanently large French and Irish contingents at Whitehall. Apart from the ambassador the former group was not as dangerous as was thought. Many were menial servants. Several were voluntary expatriates or exiles – the philosopher Saint Evremond and Mazarin's niece Hortense Mancini in the first category, the disgraced courtier Lauzun in the second. Nevertheless the number increased during James's reign, and in 1688 a number of volunteers began to arrive in order to support him against either rebellion or invasion. Probably the most valuable French asset lay in the influence and network of contacts possessed by ambassador Paul Barrillon (1677–88), although the events of the Revolution were to show that his knowledge and contacts did not extend far outside the court.[4] The Irish Catholic interest was in reality a more serious danger to English and Protestant interests. A number of Catholic or crypto-Catholic courtiers were always present in Whitehall, despite intermittently enforced bans on

---

[4] The most important of Barrillon's despatches are in the PRO (Baschet transcripts, 31/3), but those from 7 June 1688 must be seen in the Archives du Ministère des Affaires Etrangères; CPA, 165, 166, 167.

Catholics.[5] They worked as lobbyists and the most powerful interest, that of the Talbot family connection of Catholic Anglo-Irish, had associations with James that originated before the Restoration. Many of the Irish also possessed contacts with France. Their activities extended to Whitehall all the tensions of Irish politics, since their chief objectives were toleration for the Catholic majority and the reversal of the Irish land settlement which had punished nearly all Catholic landowners, whether innocent or not, for the rebellion of 1641. As James was to discover in 1688–9, some of the most powerful interests in the English political nation were either directly involved in Irish land and affairs themselves, or were closely associated with the Irish Protestant ascendancy. Irish office-holders, from the lord lieutenant downwards, always had reason to fear that rivals at court were attempting to supplant them, but the presence in James's court of prominent Catholic activists added a new fear – which was to be confirmed by the developments of 1687–8 – that the basic principle of subordinating Ireland to England was being abandoned.

James's court also contained a number of English and Scottish Catholics, among them several recent converts. This presence was a reflection of the social composition of the Catholic minority, with its relatively strong representation among the aristocracy and wealthier landowning gentry, but it aggravated both fears of Catholicism and suspicion of the court. The argument that the Catholics constituted only a tiny minority in England was discounted by their concentration at the centre of political influence. The obvious fact that the atmosphere of the court was congenial to Catholics revived the charges that had been so persuasive in John Pym's time, when he had led the Long Parliament against Charles 1. It was popularly believed to be the spearhead of the Catholic offensive, and conversions of courtiers were interpreted as being the result of a calculated campaign to get possession of the key offices of power.

In practice, as well as in constitutional theory, the king acted

[5] *CSPD*, 1686–7, pp. 67–8. A bill was to be prepared authorising them to live at court: Baschet, Barrillon 4 February 1686.

as the working centre of politics and administration. His central power was that of patronage. Charles, and James until the birth of the prince, consciously maintained a balance in their appointments to the chief offices, preventing any single group from achieving a dominant position, and would never permit minor offices to be filled exclusively by the nominees of a single minister or faction. This principle explains the retention of Halifax in 1682-5 and of George Jeffreys in 1687-8, when they had lost both immediate usefulness and the king's confidence. Arlington was retained after 1675 to show Danby that he did not monopolize power, while Sunderland was kept on in 1685-6 as a check on Rochester and the Anglican interest.

Charles and James both participated personally in the actual transaction of government business, but their interest could never be relied on. James's main concern centred on the navy, with which he had been associated since 1660, but during his reign he gave more time and personal attention to the development and training of the army. Both kings personally directed foreign policy for short periods, Charles in 1668-70, James in 1685 and in the weeks after Sunderland's dismissal, but normally they delegated control to ministers. Royal attendance at council and its committees varied considerably and unpredictably. Ministers never knew when the king would assert himself by intervening to upset their calculations, but they correctly assumed that Charles was unwilling, and James incompetent, to undertake the crushing daily burden of routine work which enabled Louis XIV in France to control every important aspect of government and make every major decision personally. More disturbing was their knowledge that ministers could not rely on royal protection or active support if their position should begin to weaken. Historians have generally emphasized the attacks made on ministers by the parliamentary opposition, but the picture is not quite so simple as has usually been assumed. Charles certainly abandoned his first principal minister Clarendon in 1667, and he left the cabal ministers to defend themselves in 1673 as best they could, but he acted much more forcefully in his last years, while James always believed that ministers should be defended against threats coming from outside the court. Both came to see that action was needed when the prestige and rights of the crown were involved. Charles repulsed ferocious Whig attacks on his ministers at the end of the 1680–1 session, and James resisted the Commons pressure to remove all Catholic officers in the second session of 1685.[6] The more insidious (and common) threats were those which came from colleagues and subordinates. Made under cover, these were never easy to counter, especially as both kings usually showed themselves indifferent in such cases.

Between 1667 and 1688 the court lived in what may best be described as a Hobbesian state of nature. Every minister or courtier feared his fellows. All, including those at the top, had constantly to battle for survival. Ministers were the major predators fighting for the chief rewards, with a train of jackals scavenging behind them, followers who could not afford to be delicate in their tastes. Moreover, this state of perpetual war within the court was superimposed on that between the 'ins' and 'outs'. Friends turned into enemies frequently and unexpectedly, all alliances and groupings were very temporary. The famous cabal was by no means unique or exceptional in its character and operations.[7] All ministries were composite. There was no sense of unity or collective responsibility, all were constantly disturbed by intrigue and manoeuvres. Clarendon's administration, for instance, not only included the separate Monk interest but, from 1662, the group associated with the Earl of Arlington, whose main objective was to subvert Clarendon's power. Similarly with Clarendon's son Rochester; in 1685 he was incontestably the leading minister, but he proved unable to prevent the Earl of Sunderland's power increasing until Rochester's Anglican interest was almost completely ousted from court.[8] In turn, by 1688 Sunderland's leading position was coming under threat from Father Petre and Lord Melfort, the leaders of the extreme Catholic party. The waning of his influence, and the collapse of both Catholic and Protestant reversionary interests with the birth of the prince, left him with no option but

[6] *CJ*, ix, 756.
[7] See M. Lee, *The Cabal* (1965).
[8] Addit., 34512, f.56.

to declare himself a Catholic convert.[9] This retrieved his position at court and Sunderland could then calculate that the calling of Parliament in November would restore his primacy. The preparatory work for the general elections was being done by men under his supervision, who would be able to act as managers, whereas the extremist Catholics were likely to have negligible influence at least in the Commons. The assembly of Parliament would change the whole character of politics, and only Sunderland at this time could expect to operate from a position of influence in Whitehall and at Westminster.

Another complicating factor was added by the connections which existed between groups and personalities at court and those in the localities. These worked both ways. A minister could become involved in local feuds and so increase the number of his enemies, or alternatively local enmities could import into the court an entirely extraneous set of differences – as in James's reign with the struggles between Scottish factions. A minister had also to be prepared to deal with externally organized pressure groups working at court through agents or professional intermediaries. Dissenters and Catholics worked by this means, but the most potent outside influences were those exerted by foreign states, which maintained a network of agents and contacts at court. French influence was repeatedly of decisive importance – destroying Danby in 1678, blocking the Whigs in 1681 and undermining Rochester in 1686. During Charles's reign Dutch contacts, by contrast, were mainly with opposition groups outside the court; during the first two years of James's reign they were primarily concerned with fostering the reversionary interests at court. More active and aggressive intervention did not begin until after Dijkvelt's reconnaissance mission in the summer of 1687. The activities of a further category of pressure groups – those representing economic interests – form a subject which has yet to be fully researched, but there are indications that they had considerable influence. This seems to have been the case particularly with the East India Company, enjoying a monopoly trading position, which led its internal politics

[9] Addit., 34510, f.137. J. P. Kenyon, *Robert Spencer, Earl of Sunderland* (1958), pp. 197–8.

to become interwoven with those of court and Parliament. Moreover, the company's notably able and aggressive governor, Josiah Childe, became an ardent and active supporter of James's policies.

Of course most of these characteristics are to be found operating in the courts of other periods, but several factors made the late Stuart court particularly fluid and competitive. In an institution centering on the king, the personalities of Charles and James were important. Secondly it must be remembered that the older and middle generations of the 1680s had lived through the revolutions of the civil wars and the Commonwealth. They had seen the old order collapse, many had had to exist as poverty-stricken exiles, all had at one time or another been displaced in power and public life by those whom they despised as social inferiors. Small wonder, then, that while the sun shone they should try to satisfy their ambitions and appetites, for the future was unusually uncertain. However, the most significant factor working at this time was the fluidity and mobility that existed within the political nation. At no time were there such opportunities and prospects for its members, provided that they were within the general categories of the upper, governing classes – and this meant not only the nobility and major landowners, but also minor gentry, wealthy merchants, bankers and lawyers, and the higher Anglican clergy. By comparison with the reign of Elizabeth, or the eighteenth century, the upper sections of society were not so rigidly hierarchical and there were fewer impediments, either of status or finance, to impede able and ruthless men who aspired to the top positions. Many ministers rose from relatively obscure (though not humble) positions as private men – Lord Clifford, Danby, Jeffreys, Charles Montague were outstanding examples – although it is clear that in the long term society in general was becoming more stratified and it was increasingly difficult for the poor, or underprivileged and unconnected, to break into the governing classes, despite individual exceptions like Stephen Fox, paymaster general and Treasury commissioner.

The mobility that existed within the political nation created acute problems for ministers in their relations with subordinates and clients. In rising from relative obscurity many of them first used, and then ruthlessly discarded, the patrons to whom they owed their first advances in office; Clifford was originally Arlington's client, Danby the Duke of Buckingham's. Then in turn they had to face subordinates playing the same game. Danby was hardly installed as treasurer when he detected an intrigue for his ruin by his newly appointed chancellor of the exchequer.[10] Shaftesbury found his leadership of the first Whigs challenged by Ralph Montague, whom he had treated as no more than a subordinate.[11] Jeffreys, after climbing to the chancellorship by a career of unlimited and exhausting service-ability, was threatened by equally unscrupulous lawyers in his fellow Welshmen, John Trevor and William Williams. So every minister lived in the knowledge that power-hungry rivals were watching to exploit any mistake or any sign of the withdrawal of royal confidence.

Without exaggeration it is possible to enumerate at least twenty-five politicians in the period 1660 to 1688 who were ready and (at least in their own eyes) qualified to take over as chief minister, and there were nearly as many serious contenders for each of the other principal offices.[12] Moreover, this was to create serious difficulties for William in 1689, since a high proportion of these aspirants were still alive, and vociferous in pressing their claims on him. But it would be a distortion to conclude that a lack of scruples, naked ambition and such an arbitrary factor as royal favour were all that were needed to gain and retain office. Particularly in the key offices ability and expert knowledge were also indispensable.[13] Clifford was the most ambitious and absolutist minister of the period, and the

[10] E. M. Thompson (ed.), *Hatton Correspondence* (1878), i, 122.

[11] J. R. Jones, *The First Whigs* (1961), pp. 151–4.

[12] Monk, the first and second Earls of Clarendon, Bristol, Clifford, Arlington, Buckingham, Shaftesbury, Rochester, Danby, Essex, Seymour, Sunderland, Halifax, Godolphin, Melfort, Ralph Montagu, Sir William Jones, Lord William Russell, Sir William Coventry, Sir Richard Temple, Dover, Arundel of Wardour, Duncomb and Radnor.

[13] A new study of Restoration finance has been prepared, but not yet published, by Douglas Chandaman. See S. B. Baxter, *The Development of the Treasury, 1660–1702* (1957).

one who rose fastest, but his lack of financial ability and his consequent readiness to take short cuts doomed him and his policies, whereas skill and knowledge in financial matters account for Danby's long tenure, and also for the meteoric rise of Charles Montague after the Revolution. Another perhaps obvious point is relevant. Any successful minister had literally to devote himself to his work and duties, no easy task in the enervating and distracting atmosphere of the court. Indolence as well as irresponsibility made Buckingham incredible as a chief minister, while under James, Dover's laziness and Jeffreys's illness relegated them to a secondary place in terms of influence.

Ministerial duties were varied as well as time-consuming; in addition to actual administration the higher offices also entailed attendance on the king in person. This requirement differentiated them from the hierarchy of professional administrators that was developing in these years. Such men would now be called civil servants, but although they were acting as departmental heads rather than as independent politicians, men like Samuel Pepys, William Blathwayt, William Bridgeman, and Henry Guy sat in the Commons to protect their official interests, explain policies and justify requests for money. They possessed little initiative in policy matters and few had enough self-confidence or standing to make an independent figure at court (Guy is an exception here). As the business of government became more complex this type of official became more numerous and a hierarchy of government servants with a defined differentiation of duties began to emerge, a development which gained impetus from the extension of governmental functions which the post-Revolutionary involvement in the European wars necessitated. However, even then such functionaries possessed little importance in terms of political power.[14] The only group which can be compared with *intendants* on the French model was the small unit of electoral agents and organizers which was engaged, under Robert Brent and Sir Nicholas Butler, in the campaign to manage parliamentary elections in 1687–8 by systematic regulation of the boroughs and electoral preparation. Sunderland and Jeffreys were nominally responsible for the

[14] G. A. Jacobsen, *William Blathwayt* (1932), pp. 2–4, 14–19, and chapter xii.

work, but these men were the real directors and would have been strongly placed had Parliament met in November 1688, as James planned.

Clifford was the first politician fully to realize and exploit the fact that power in politics depended primarily on possession of the Treasury. As commissioner, and then as treasurer, he pioneered the techniques of manipulation and management that were to be developed more successfully by Danby in 1673–8 and, in more sophisticated forms, were to form the basis of most eighteenth-century ministerial interests. There is no need to describe these techniques in detail, which centred on making systematic use of all patronage possibilities, but it is necessary to emphasize how very dissimilar conditions were from those that came into existence after 1688. A treasurer faced very different fiscal problems; there was no funded debt or Bank of England and no regular direct taxation. One of his main objectives was to achieve fiscal independence, to end reliance on parliamentary grants, and in this respect it is almost impossible to overstate the value of the financial settlement which Rochester obtained for James at the beginning of his reign. After 1681 Charles had been able to maintain a rather precarious financial independence, but James was not troubled by the anxieties that had plagued his father and brother – although it is evident that even his preparations aimed at the repulse of William's invasion would in any case have plunged him into insolvency, and forced him to seek new parliamentary grants. From a political point of view Rochester succeeded too well, and made himself expendable. Another vital difference from the eighteenth-century position was that patronage had to be exercised more with a view to building up influence at court than in the more intermittent task of managing Parliament. Something closely resembling a spoils system came into operation whenever a treasurer was dismissed – notably and extensively when Danby and Rochester fell. Disruptive as this might be of administrative continuity and experience, it had the very significant side-effect of preventing the development of a proprietorial class of office-holders such as existed in most European countries.[15] Although never formal-

15 *Ibid.*, pp. 4, 6.

ized, a trend in this direction can be detected, particularly through the system of making (or selling) grants of office in reversion, that is in succession after the death or retirement of the holder.

Theoretically the highest office was still that of chancellor, but Clarendon's failure and fall revealed its limitations as a power base. Only in extraordinary circumstances, such as those of 1660, when all appointments, grants and pardons needed sealing, did the chancellor have anything approaching decisive power. Nevertheless, his control of the judiciary and the administration of justice, remembering that the law courts were inseparably connected with politics at this time, together with his patronage powers within the Church, made the chancellor (or lord keeper) a central figure. During James's reign, when the effective enforcement and extension of the powers of the royal prerogative depended directly on the legal opinions and judgements which Jeffreys procured from the judicial bench, he played a key role. Jeffreys was responsible for the technically complex operations against the municipal and company charters, the issuing of pardons and dispensations, the conduct of political trials, the maintenance of discipline in the army through court martial proceedings against deserters, and the enforcement of royal policies in religion through his presidency of the Court of Ecclesiastical Commission. Technical skill and achievements enabled Jeffreys to hold on to his offices, despite illness and the persistent attacks of the Catholic ministers on him for his Anglicanism. But, despite the popular myth, and the ferocious attacks made on him during 1687–8, Jeffreys never belonged to the group of ministers who actually made policy.[16]

The importance and influence of the other great offices of state depended on what their holders tried to make of them. For example, both Rochester (in 1684) and Halifax (in 1685) were 'kicked upstairs' into what was regarded as the honorific but uninfluential office of lord president of the council. Yet this was the position which Shaftesbury held briefly at the height of his influence in 1679, and which served Sunderland during the

[16] PWA, 2103, 2122b; Addit., 34487, ff. 8, 13; See G. W. Keeton, *Lord Chancellor Jeffreys and the Stuart Cause* (1965).

years 1686–8 when he was incontestably James's leading minister. Similarly, the influence of the two secretaries of state varied according to the social status and personal ambitions of the holder. Some, like Arlington and Sunderland, used the office to formulate foreign policies, and as a base for the advancement of their own interests in terms of domestic politics. Other secretaries were minor, secondary figures, dependents of leading ministers, or mere clerks like Sir Joseph Williamson (1674–8) and Sir William Trumbull, who executed decisions made by others without their being consulted. Personality also determined the amount of influence exerted by holders of such purely court offices as lord steward, master of the robes and groom of the stole. Some were satisfied with the prestige and perquisites, some used their positions blatantly to make money out of the petitioners and others who wanted access to the king, but a few were active politicians themselves.

In general the Stuart court, representing the top segment of society, formed a privileged enclave set apart from the mass of the nation. But during Charles's reign it was never entirely insulated. His casual attitudes and the lack of protocol permitted a surprisingly wide range of unimportant people to enter or attach themselves, including such proverbially obscure people as north country knights and Welsh squires, as well as an indiscriminate collection of adventurers and crooks. By comparison, James's court gained in respectability and orderliness, but became increasingly isolated. The influence exerted by the queen, Mary of Modena, was a principal reason for these developments. She played a much more active role on behalf of Catholics than had Charles's queen, and she was identified with the French interest in the popular view, her marriage in 1673 having been arranged by French diplomatic initiatives.[17] After the banishment of Catherine Sedley in 1686 her influence over James strengthened, and in a permanent form, since it was connected with his change to the deep personal piety and rigorous repentance that was later to colour the entire life of the exiled court at St-Germain. In the autumn of 1687 Mary's pregnancy, and the suspiciously confident predictions of a male heir to oust the heretics Mary

[17] Grey, ii, 182, 189–96, 214–15.

and Anne from the succession, converted the queen into *the* key person at court, as the immediate movement of courtiers towards her demonstrated. James's health and life-expectancy were poor; a regency now became a probability and, living in hope, Mary had already qualified herself to act in this capacity by taking part in the coronation in 1685, despite her strong prejudices against the heretic bishops who officiated.[18] As the French examples of Marie de Medici and Anne had shown, a queen regent had effective power within her grasp if she wished to take it.

Under Mary's influence, James did something to cleanse and reorganize the court. It became simpler and less extravagant – over 200 servants were dismissed in 1685. James also revived the old practice of 'progresses' in which he showed himself to the people in a series of provincial tours. Deputations, at first from Tory loyalists, but in 1687–8 mainly from dissenters and the new members of municipal corporations, were welcomed at Whitehall. But in practice James's policies emptied the court of many of its long-serving inhabitants. Unlike Charles he never forgot, and rarely forgave, disobedience or obstruction of his wishes, but insisted on unswerving loyalty from his servants. Courtiers were subject to personal pressure from James; in 1686 he canvassed them systematically to get pledges of support for the repeal of the tests and penal laws, dismissing those who refused, and this pressure was repeated in 1687–8. Many were also pressed to become Catholics. As a result, widespread purges took place, and unofficial provincial gentry were deterred from coming to court for fear of coming under pressure.

These purges of the traditional Tory loyalists changed the social as well as the political character of the court. This was now no longer an accurate reflection of the composition, interests and views of the predominant sections of the political nation. The mass refusals to collaborate, and the insufficiency of Catholic replacements for those who had been purged, left James with no option but to employ almost any person of some standing or ability who volunteered to collaborate. So loyalists were replaced by an incongruous and unstable amalgam of

[18] Mazure, i, 409.

English, Scottish and Irish Catholics, former Whigs, dissenters and political opportunists and careerists, who formed a synthetic ruling group which was to disintegrate under the pressure of the crisis of 1688. The former Whigs, especially those who had acted as minor party agents, were efficient but untrustworthy. Most of the Catholics lacked administrative experience and political skills, and also suffered by being divided into two hostile factions. Members of the old recusant landowning families readily accepted offices from James under dispensations exempting them from taking the statutory oaths, but on long-term matters they were politically cautious, a caution based on bitter experience of the repercussions of earlier political adventurism on previous generations in the form of persecution or the severe enforcement of the penal laws. As landowners they had much to lose. Their permanent interests led them to face up to the prospect of the reign of a Protestant successor, Mary, and many of them enjoyed personal connections with William. Many Catholics had served in the Dutch army. Their knowledge that in the United Provinces Catholics enjoyed practical toleration led them to look forward with hope of some relief from their statutory disabilities, even though William might give them less than James was promising. By forming a catholic reversionary interest they would be safeguarding their future position, and they could also expect active support from William's Catholic allies in Europe, with whose diplomatic representatives in London they maintained contact, and who would become even more influential and persuasive with William if a general war should break out.[19]

In sharp contrast, the other Catholic group was closely associated with France and the French ambassador in London. Its enmity to the moderate Catholic party represented an extension of the diplomatic struggle between Louis and the allies – Spain and the Habsburg Emperor Leopold as well as William. Ever since 1672 English political alignments and developments had been influenced, and at times determined, by European forces and intervention, but formerly the division had been one between court and opposition; the fact that James's court was itself divided in this way proved to be a major weakness.

[19] PWA, 2126a, 2127a; J. Lingard, *History of England*, x, 274.

The French party were thoroughgoing extremists in terms of domestic politics. They recklessly advocated pressing on with Catholicizing measures. They used evidence of resistance and resentment to urge the determined use of royal prerogatives. In Ireland the policies which they advised were put into execution by the Earl of Tyrconnel with efficiency and some success.[20] But in terms of English politics their proposals were lunatically provocative. They had no convincing answer to the arguments of the moderates, that the prospect of Mary's succession must be accepted as imposing a limit on what could be achieved for Catholic interests without provoking a future explosion of Protestant resentment. Indeed the extremists recognized their difficulties when they played with fanciful ideas of changing the succession in favour of a Catholic heir, of intimidating Anne into conversion, of legitimizing James's bastard the Duke of Berwick or of creating a separate kingdom for him in a completely Catholic-controlled and French satellite Ireland.[21] Just as dangerous and provocative were their busy efforts, encouraged by Louis and Barrillon, to force an open breach with William as a preliminary to actual war against the Dutch. This would mean a revival of the cabal's policies; only Sunderland among the ministers realized how dangerous such a war would be in tying England entirely and irrevocably to dependence on France.

Up to the autumn of 1687 the Catholic extremists were proceeding up a blind alley with preposterous policy proposals. With the queen's pregnancy the whole situation dramatically changed. The Catholic reversionary interest collapsed. All sense of balance at court disappeared. The alacrity with which Sunderland attached himself to the queen and the extremists – Petre, Dover and Butler – was a sign that their policies were now realistic. The ascendancy of the extremist party, unshakeable after the birth of the prince, had fatal effects. It stood in the nation's eyes for popery, the French connection, continued expansion of the army (mainly with Irish officers and soldiers), and a Catholic-

[20] W. Harris, *The History of the Life and Reign of William Henry* (1749), pp. 107–12; J. G. Simms, *Jacobite Ireland, 1685–91* (1969), pp. 24–6, 35–6; Baschet, Bonrepos, 4, 22 September 1687.

[21] *HMC, VIIth Report*, App. part 1, 535; Mazure, ii, 281–2, 288.

dominated Ireland. Obviously the court became isolated and increasingly detested. Even more directly relevant for the events of the Revolution were the effects on James's remaining Protestant courtiers and servants. They were to justify their defection to William during the Revolution on general political and religious grounds, but their action should also be seen as the last act of the internal political struggle of James's court. By October the tenure of the remaining Protestant courtiers – John Churchill, Sidney Godolphin, the Earl of Bath and their associates – had become fragile and precarious, their future under James uncertain with the prospect of permanent French preponderance at court.

PARLIAMENT AND THE CONSTITUENCIES

During the civil wars and Commonwealth each successive government had interfered with electoral and parliamentary rights in violent and arbitrary fashion, so that the Restoration had been intended to be as much a restoration of parliamentary freedom as of the monarchy. After 1660 the system of representation did become stabilized, and the hostile reaction which followed Charles's grant of seats to Newark prevented its repetition, even by James. The Lords was restored, with the bishops reinstated. But although Parliament was restored in its old forms, and came to occupy a more continuously important position than ever before, the actual character of parliamentary politics was subject to continuous and fundamental change. Former royalists were technically barred from standing in the elections to the Convention of 1660, while those a year later for the Cavalier Parliament took place in the middle of a general purge of former supporters of the Commonwealth from the municipalities. After these two general elections within a year, there then ensued the eighteen years of a 'standing' Parliament, which had the effect of freezing political activities in many areas: in eleven county seats and fifty-four boroughs there were no by-elections at all, and in an additional fourteen county seats and thirty-nine boroughs there were none during the 1670s. Of the 507 original members, 245 were still sitting at the dissolution in 1679. Then this static situation was followed by rapid and successive changes during the Exclusion Crisis which, with three general elections in less than two years, demanded quite different political techniques – electoral organization, systematic propaganda and the mobilization of mass support in place of parliamentary management. However, the Oxford Parliament of 1681 was followed by four years without elections, a period in which many electoral organizations and interests withered, the Whigs were crushed by judicial repression and many of the constituencies were systematically remodelled by the court and its Tory allies. The end-product, the Tory Parliament of 1685, differed completely in composition from its predecessors, but in turn it was to experience a novel form of pressure – a series of prorogations over a period of twenty months kept it in a state of suspended animation while it was intensively pressurized by James. Finally, when this proved unsuccessful, the dissolution was followed by the entirely unprecedented and extremely menacing campaign to pack a subservient Parliament by large-scale interventions in the constituencies, and the use by the crown of all the recently developed techniques of party organization.

These structural changes in the basic conditions of politics meant a situation in which ministers, politicians and electors had to adapt themselves repeatedly and often drastically in their techniques and mental attitudes.

In the first place, the three most fundamental developments have to be examined, all of which have a direct bearing on the Revolution and the Revolution settlement: the organization of systematic parliamentary management, the rise of parties, and the establishment and use of techniques of royal control over the municipal corporations.

During the 1670s Danby constructed working majorities in both Houses of the Cavalier Parliament by the systematic and skilful use of all the patronage at his disposal, clerical as well as political. His success provoked shrill alarm that it was now practicable for a minister to set out to subvert the independence of Parliament by exploiting the human weaknesses of members and courtiers, but the constant emphasis on crude corruption in

opposition pamphlets and satires distorted the real nature of
Danby's success. He never had enough money to indulge in
indiscriminate bribery, and in making appointments for political
purposes he always ran the risk of antagonizing those whom he
could not promote, a particular danger in the case of the more
able and ambitious who pressed impossible claims and could do
considerable damage in the event of their being alienated. Danby
could rarely enforce threats of dismissing refractory servants,
and those who can be described as ministerial dependants were
never more than a nucleus in the Commons. Quite contrary to
the contemporary myth, Danby's position was not so much that
of an all-powerful minister manipulating puppet MPs but rather
of a manager constantly subjected to harassing pressures and
frequently to blatant blackmail.[22]

The reason for stressing this conclusion is that it throws light
on what James meant when he said, before the 1685 Parliament
met, that he did not propose to imitate Danby's managerial
methods.[23] This statement was more than a propaganda exercise. In reality Danby's influence had depended far more
on persuasion, on his ability to select topics and issues on which
he calculated that a majority would agree with him, than on
corrupt inducements and direct pressures on dependants.[24] It
was this deference to opinion, the acceptance of limits on ministerial action imposed by the interests and prejudices of ordinary
MPs, that James was not going to accept. Danby's working majorities were made possible by an identity of interests between
himself and those who responded to his circular letters, accepted
his parliamentary whips and directives and followed his official
spokesmen. Admittedly much organization of a very time-
consuming sort was needed to convert this support into actual
votes, but the basis of Danby's ministerial strength lay in the
acceptability of his policies. James was to fail because he did
not see this. When a majority turned against his proposed policies
he made a massive and sustained attempt at canvassing that

[22] A. Browning, *Thomas Osborne, Earl of Danby* (1944–51), i, 167–75, 191–7; iii,
44–111.
[23] Baschet; Barrillon, 30 April 1685.
[24] Browning, *Danby*, i, 147–52.

continued throughout 1686, and was extended in 1687-8 into the constituencies in the campaign to pack Parliament. The crucial difference lies in James's deliberate attempt to impose his policies, to obtain from his followers specific and binding engagements that were tantamount to a complete and permanent surrender of individual independence. James was forced by the unpopularity of his policies to rely on dictation and coercion of a sort that Danby had never envisaged employing. The resulting failure shows that techniques were not enough in themselves, that no amount of attention to detail or organizing skill could make electors, MPs or peers accept policies which they judged to be subversive of liberties, property and religion.

Insisting on the reality and importance of party in the politics of this period does not mean accepting the assumptions of such classical Whig historians as Macaulay, who uncritically attached the labels Whig and Tory to the political groupings of late Stuart England, and attributed to them many of the characteristics and principles which Victorian parties possessed. On the other hand, the tendency derived from Sir Lewis Namier's analysis of the structure of eighteenth-century politics, to deny the existence of parties in any meaningful sense and to assert the primacy of connections, interests and coalitions, has led to misinterpretations of the nature and workings of Restoration politics. It is true that connections based on family relationships and regional groupings formed a basis for politics, but after 1678 they played a subordinate role. During the Exclusion Crisis, and again in 1687-8, relatively sophisticated techniques of political organization and management of elections were employed, and the urgency of the issues at stake led to a polarization of political forces into sharply defined parties, whose centralized leadership and direction superseded more loosely linked groupings based on interests and individuals.[25] Even a brief survey of the literature of the period will show the extent to which party divisions and feelings permeated every aspect of life.[26] Although parties

[25] Jones, *First Whigs*, pp. 2-4, 18-19, 209-14.
[26] Apart from poems on affairs of state, and political satires: Otway, *Venice Preserved*; Crowne, *City Politics*; Dryden, *The Duke of Guise*.

had a less continuous existence in the years before 1688 than later, in the age of Anne, party divisions and passions were far stronger and more violent than anything experienced in the early eighteenth century.[27]

Party politics were based on local struggles between groups in the counties and municipalities, but the fundamental issues were national, and the leadership was centralized. The antecedents of the first Whigs lay in the 'country' opposition in Parliament, and the opposition factions in the municipalities, together with the general adherence of the Protestant dissenters and their conforming sympathizers. Tactically the Whigs were aggressive, harrying ministers, attacking James as Duke of York, denouncing the court, mobilizing mass support to win sweeping victories in three successive general elections, and creating a high level of political consciousness among the masses outside the ranks of the political nation by their agitation and propaganda. There can be no doubt that the first Whigs were a party. They possessed in 1679–81 a clearly defined and accepted group of leaders, headed by Shaftesbury, who made the decisions, prearranged the tactics that were to be followed in Parliament and elections, and issued orders and instructions which individual MPs and leaders in the localities accepted. Political clubs were formed to disseminate propaganda. Journalists, informers, canvassers and local organizers were employed. Strategically, however, the Whig attitude to the constitutional crisis was defensive. They believed that the nation was threatened by a design on the part of James and the ministers of Charles II to subvert the constitution, destroy political liberties, put property at the mercy of the crown, and establish and consolidate absolutism with the aid of an army and with direct support from France. Coupled with this threat was the associated menace of Catholicism. Only by carrying an Exclusion Bill to set James aside could real security be achieved. Shaftesbury, although he had no large personal connection of his own, managed to impose this policy on his followers, so that all individual interests were subordinated to the common cause of Exclusion. Concentra-

[27] G. S. Holmes, *British Politics in the Age of Anne* (1967) and G. S. Holmes and W. A. Speck, *The Divided Society* (1967).

tion on a single issue was the key to Whig effectiveness, which James was to imitate in 1687–8 in his campaign to repeal the Tests and the penal laws, and even when the prospects of success began to fade in 1681 Shaftesbury was able to hold the party together by tightening discipline and increasing the degree of central control.

The Tories came into existence as a party directly as a result of Whig successes and influence. The general elections of August 1679, when the Whigs were carrying all before them, forced their scattered and unorganized opponents to rally together, and to adopt many of the techniques and organizational features introduced by Shaftesbury, so as to check Whig influence in the constituencies and to support Charles in his declared resistance to Exclusion.[28] But it must be emphasized that the Tories, although not the creation of the ministers or the clergy, but an independent political force in the country, were less immediately effective than the first Whigs. They were defensive in both a strategical and a tactical sense. They reacted against Whig influence and demands, and against the prospect of toleration for dissenters. The danger to the nation, as they saw it, came not from absolutist-minded ministers and crypto-Catholics (although they remained often suspicious of the motives and honesty of ministers), but from incendiary demagogues, ambitious politicians and their dupes, who were pressing opposition to the point where a new series of civil wars would become inevitable.

Of course neither Whigs nor Tories admitted themselves to be a party. Both claimed to represent the nation and its interests against a corrupt and divisive section – in the Whig view, the court; for the Tories, a faction led by demagogues. Both Whigs and Tories denounced party, as meaning a confederacy of the ill-intentioned or the misled. It was a threat to unity, peace and harmony, and this common attitude explains how Whigs and Tories found it possible to combine together against James when he began to act and rule in a 'party' manner, that is

---

[28] By court, in this political context, I mean the ministers, officials and direct dependants.

by attempting to impose his personal policies and the interests of a separatist minority on the nation as a whole.

Developments during the Exclusion Crisis, and again in 1687–8, revealed the inadequacy of the court's resources to sustain effective government during a disturbed period, when issues excited popular interest and concern. General obedience to authority on the part of extensive sections of the nation could no longer be assumed, so that the crown now had to encourage and mobilize active popular support. Charles could not have routed the first Whigs without the assurance of Tory support. After his break with the Tories in 1687, James had no option but to appeal for the active collaboration of former Whigs. The Exclusion Crisis had also demonstrated the indispensability of party organization and mass propaganda. The Tories would have been helplessly ineffective royal allies if they had not imitated the Whig techniques of organization, electioneering and journalism. Similarly, James had to adopt Whig methods, as well as employing Whig collaborators, during his campaign to pack Parliament in 1687–8. Party, in the sense of centrally organized and directed political forces, was the dominant factor in the decade before the Revolution.

The Tory role during the Exclusion Crisis was that of a counter-weight to the more aggressive, better organized and more widely supported first Whigs. Admittedly the Tories rarely succeeded in reducing Whig strength in the elections of 1679 and 1681, and they were hopelessly outmanoeuvred in the Commons. But by taking on the Whigs at their own game in stimulating mass opinion against Exclusion, the Tories convinced the uncommitted of the falsity of current Whig claims to represent the wider interests of the nation against a corrupt court. Instead they painted the picture of the Whigs as a faction whose recklessness would plunge the country into civil war. Tory pledges of support to Charles impressed the waverers and uncommitted, and isolated the Whig militants when Charles began to move openly against them. By 1685 the techniques which the Tories had adopted were part of the routine of politics and James was to rely heavily upon them in the first part of his reign.

The first Tory appeals to the nation, the 'abhorrences' of

1679, lacked the genuinely popular character of the Whig petitions for Exclusion, but as early as 1681 they were organizing on as large a scale as their opponents. Counter-addresses were sponsored during the elections.[29] The dissolution of the Oxford Parliament in 1681 was greeted by addresses promising to stand by the king against the Whigs, 115 of them from parliamentary boroughs. This set a pattern. In 1681-2, sixty-eight constituencies and over a hundred other bodies addressed in condemnation of Shaftesbury's allegedly subversive intentions; for the Devon address sixteen thousand signatures were claimed. In 1683 the Rye House Plot for the murder of Charles and James was condemned by addresses which included 131 from constituencies, and James's accession in 1685 was formally hailed by 193 counties and boroughs.[30] These addresses certainly did reflect opinion, but they are perhaps more significant as evidence of the ability of the Tories to manipulate opinion. James undoubtedly appreciated their value, and continued to use addresses – they were organized after both Declarations of Indulgence and on the birth of the Prince of Wales. Fundamentally, however, such addresses made many Tories doubtful about the wisdom and propriety of making appeals to the mass of the people, and so involving them in politics.[31] They realized the price which had to be paid, in accentuating divisions, recrimination and bitterness within the nation as a whole, and inside small communities. The crisis had forced them to counterattack the Whigs, but reluctant as they were at first to adopt Whig methods they were extremely successful in doing so, and they acted as an independent force, and not as puppets or instruments of the court. James failed to realize that the Tories were partners of the crown. He regarded them as simply the representatives of those principles of unconditional obedience and blind loyalty which the Anglican clergy vociferously preached, failing to realize that the conditional nature of Tory loyalty expected him to recognize that there were clear limits to what he could do as king.

[29] *True Protestant Mercury*, 21, 22; *Loyal Protestant*, 3, 4.
[30] These addresses (and those of James's reign) were reported, and sometimes briefly described, by Luttrell; for 1681, i, 79ff; for 1682, 158ff; for 1683, 264ff.
[31] Addit., 38847, ff. 85–6; Tanner MSS, 36, f.61.

Historians of the seventeenth century, in emphasizing the importance of relations between the central government and the agents of local administration, have concentrated mainly on the Commission of the Peace, the justices who governed the Commons. After 1660, as under Charles I, this was repeatedly purged and closely supervised. The object now was rather different. It was not so much, as earlier, to ensure the enforcement of unpopular or administratively laborious laws, but for much more directly political and parliamentary purposes. Danby's appointments and dismissals of JPS formed a part of his management system. During the Exclusion Crisis all identifiable Whigs were purged, the lieutenancy was everywhere remodelled and sheriffs were carefully selected. The results were inconsiderable. The lesson of the Exclusion Crisis was clear; control over the boroughs was the prerequisite of effective control over Parliament. Consequently, municipal affairs became as central an issue in English politics as they were in the struggles for power in contemporary Holland.

The court had made a determined attempt to gain direct and permanent control over the boroughs in 1662, by means of the Corporation Act, but although its enforcement was entrusted to them, and not to officials, MPS and local gentry had recognized the danger that increasing the power of the central government might subvert the independence of the localities.[32] They insisted that the powers contained in the act should be of limited duration, so that later action was attempted only against individual boroughs. Nevertheless, the court never entirely abandoned its policy of tampering with municipal rights, and the majority in the Cavalier Parliament continued to be vigilant to check any increase in the central power of the court. It reacted strongly against the new charter issued to Newark, which incorporated a grant of parliamentary representation on a limited, corporation franchise.[33] In 1676 the administration refused to institute a *quo warranto* (a writ calling in question a charter of rights) against Nottingham, for offending its lord

[32] J. H. Sacret, 'The Restoration Government and Municipal Corporations', *English Historical Review*, 45, pp. 247–53.
[33] Grey, ii, 188–9; *CJ.*, ix, 283.

lieutenant, for fear of the parliamentary repercussions, while the use of the militia to influence voters in the Grantham election of 1678 provoked a storm of protests against 'military government'.[34] During the Exclusion Crisis the court found itself practically powerless. Whig majorities, using the committee of elections, negatived returns which official influence produced, and generally extended the franchise in cases of dispute. The boroughs demonstrated their independence by deliberately refusing to take action on the letters which the council sent out in March 1680, ordering the enforcement of the Corporation Act. Despite threats of *quo warranto,* the court did nothing, and had to replace Jeffreys as recorder because of his clumsy attempt to intimidate the independent-minded men who controlled the City of London.[35]

The other threat to municipal independence came from the local aristocratic and gentry neighbours, particularly of smaller towns. In many places these elements possessed a dominant influence, but in medium-sized and larger towns one of the main sources of Whig strength and influence derived from the efforts of a section of the townsmen to retain their independence by excluding such outside influences. Generalization is impossible, since there were such wide variations in the size and internal structure of boroughs, and in the economic and social relationship between towns and their neighbouring rural areas dominated by the landowning class. But it was clear that many Whig successes in Exclusion elections were obtained by championing and exploiting the cause of municipal independence against the predominantly Tory landowners of neighbouring rural areas. Consequently the court and the Tories had a common interest in working together to eradicate the local sources of Whig power. Many Tory addresses in the summer of 1681 called for enforcement of the Corporation Act so as to eliminate dissenters. This would have immediate effects, but in an attempt to put their control on a permanent and impregnable basis, Tory gentry

---

[34] Addit., 25124, f.87; G. Davies, 'The By-election at Grantham', *Huntington Library Quarterly,* vii, 2.

[35] *HMC, VIIth Report,* app, I, ii, 391b; *Protestant (Domestick) Intelligence,* 70, 77; Keeton, *Jeffreys and the Stuart Cause,* pp. 141–5.

and townsmen worked with the king and his legal officers in securing the surrender of charters, or in assisting actions of *quo warranto* against the charters of towns which refused to surrender them.

The legal officers were invariably certain of success in these actions against the charters, since they could always find technical breaches to justify forfeiture. Additionally, the costs of defending a charter were extremely (usually prohibitively) high – many small boroughs were crippled financially by the far lower costs of a new charter after voluntary surrender. The forfeiture of the London charter showed the futility of resistance, so most boroughs surrendered voluntarily and were given new charters. These varied in detail, but invariably the king was empowered to remove officers and veto those who were elected. Great emphasis was put on requiring all office-holders to take the oaths. Otherwise the new charters reflected local circumstances. Towns which had surrendered quickly were often rewarded by extensions of local privileges such as markets and tolls. In towns where the Tory townsmen were securely in control already, municipal autonomy was respected – particularly by careful definition of the methods by which freemen could be created. But in the more numerous places where the local balance was clearly in favour of Whig associates (Bridport and St Albans are examples) the country gentry were made eligible for election as freemen in such an easy way as to give them commanding influence within the borough.[36]

Not many towns were transformed from being Whig strongholds into Tory-controlled boroughs by the *quo warranto* itself. In most places the new charters served to consolidate the position of local Tory groups which had already been in action against their local Whig rivals. They controlled many of the places concerned; the crucial forfeiture of the London charter actually followed the seizure of political control by the Tories, while in Norwich and Bristol they had achieved power before the end of the Exclusion Crisis. The powers which the crown acquired through the new charters were consolidatory in purpose; they would be used to prevent the infiltration back

[36] *CSPD*, 1685, pp. 25, 73.

into office of Whigs and dissenters, who might otherwise regain their local influence and offices as those ejected as unreliable by the Corporation Act (1661) had done, after the expiration of the commissioners' powers in 1663. In the long term this Tory dominance of the boroughs could be expected to produce a Tory House of Commons, and it had considerable short-term advantages as well. The laws against dissenters would be more uniformly enforced. Whigs, knowing that they would be barred from office even if they gained election, would either desert politics altogether or offer to submit. But Tory control did not end factionalism in municipal politics. Divisions developed, particularly in larger cities like Norwich and Bristol, where the Tories had had to organize a mass party. A rift opened between the local oligarchs and a more extreme wing consisting of socially inferior men influenced by the 'high-flying' clergy. The tensions which resulted from oligarchical refusals to share offices and influence, the frustrations of the ejected Whigs and dissenters, and the passions which the attack on the charters aroused, were all factors which James was to exploit in 1687–8, during his campaign to pack Parliament, when the new royal powers were to be used for very different ends from those originally envisaged.

Between 1681 and Charles II's death fifty-one charters were issued; one in 1681, seven in 1682, six in 1683, thirty-three in 1684 and four in early 1685. Many were still being processed when James succeeded, so that with elections imminent forty-seven had to be rushed out in under three months. A further twenty-one followed in 1685 and 1686, thus completing the first phase.[37]

Analysis of this first phase produces interesting conclusions. First, that the progress under Charles was leisurely because he did not plan to call Parliament – which left James with little time at the beginning of his reign to do the work necessary to ensure success in the 1685 elections. Secondly, a comparison shows that Charles concentrated on large and important places, which means that for him control over recalcitrant Whig-

[37] *HMC, XIIth Report*, app. vi, 298–9.

dominated boroughs was an end in itself.[38] This left comparatively small boroughs for James's attention in 1685, many of
them in the west country, which were unable to offer serious
resistance. The speed and success with which James and Sunderland dealt with them probably led both men to underestimate
the difficulties which they were to encounter in the second
campaign of municipal remodelling and electoral preparation
in 1687-8. Thirdly, the work on the charters had impressive
electoral results, although the number of seats decided in this
way fell short of a majority. Only one definite Whig was elected
out of a total of 104 MPS returned by boroughs which had
received new charters from Charles. In the case of places recently
granted charters by James there were no more than eight
possible Whigs out of a total of ninety-one MPS. Boroughs with
new charters were also quick to mark James's accession with
addresses pledging loyalty, forty-eight of Charles's remodelling
and thirty-five of James's responding in this way.

The success of the *quo warrantos,* the collapse of all Whig
organization and the enthusiastic support which James received
from Anglicans and Tories, have led historians to emphasize
the strength of the position which Charles bequeathed to his
brother. Altogether forty-two counties and 151 boroughs sent
James addresses of support, and since they returned 365 MPS
this would seem to have guaranteed an amenable parliament.[39]
Yet it is remarkable how apprehensive contemporaries were
about these elections and the ensuing session. Despite the changes
that had occurred since 1681 they could not forget the former
Whig domination of the Commons, and feared putting the king's
position to the test. In practice this test was surmounted by the
ministers with a superb display of efficiency and tact. They supplied a firm guide for the conduct of elections, but without
attempting to override local Tory interests. The abundant
enthusiasm of loyalists was translated into electoral victories
without arousing undue fears in the localities of centralization or
dictation.

[38] They included London, Portsmouth, Derby, Nottingham, Norwich, Bristol,
Ipswich, Exeter and Lincoln.
[39] Clarendon, i, 183; Addit., 34508, f.83; J. Ralph, *History of England*, p. 848.

The ministerial achievement was remarkable. As the hurried issue of new charters shows, there had been no preparations for elections during Charles's last years; although Halifax had agitated for a Parliament he had characteristically done nothing about it. Sunderland, the minister chiefly responsible for the detailed work in 1685, had little personal experience of electoral management, but he worked hard and methodically in organizing the elections. The ministerial role was primarily one of coordination. Sunderland wrote to lords lieutenant and Tory patrons, asking them to start electoral preparations, but most of them were already corresponding among themselves, discussing candidacies and working out local bargains and arrangements. He wrote on 17 February to twenty-three leading provincial Tories asking them to reserve some of their local electoral influence, so that officials at court without strong connections with a constituency could gain election, but eventually he sponsored only twenty official candidates, no more than had been recommended during the Exclusion elections.[40] Local Tories did not expect direct help from the court. Although the new charters often facilitated their election, they certainly did not regard themselves as dependants. Lords lieutenant acted as leaders of the community, not as agents of the central administration. They relied mainly on negotiating unofficial agreements among the Tory gentry at county meetings. Such meetings of leading gentry had customarily taken place at election time since the reign of Elizabeth, but they had lapsed with the rise of party and none had been possible in the second and third Exclusion elections. Now in 1685 they were convened throughout the country, proving effective in selecting candidates for counties, and often for some of the boroughs, on whom the gentry could agree. Such candidates were usually returned without a contest. In some cases these arrangements had been concluded and all places filled before any nominations could arrive from court, but there appears to be no case where a direct clash of interest occurred between local Tories and the court; the Earl of Plymouth said that, if James did not approve those nominated by the county, he would try to elect alternative

[40] *CSPD*, 1685, pp. 21, 22, 24, 25–6, 30, 32–3, 36, 54, 63, 72, 75, 79, etc.

candidates, but his power to do so was not put to the test.[41]

In these circumstances Whig prospects were bleak. Repentant Whigs asked to participate in county meetings, and some former supporters of Exclusion were dissuaded from persisting with candidacies. There was now no Whig party as such, no coherent leadership or organization. A Whig meant a former follower of Shaftesbury who, for various local, personal or general political reasons had not submitted to the court, and had not reconciled himself with his Tory opponents. The Whigs were no more than a collection of individuals, who could expect no more than isolated successes, as in the Buckinghamshire election where Thomas Wharton defeated a protégé of Jeffreys; thanks largely to the crass, bullying tactics which the latter used, in nominating an unknown outsider, whom the local gentry were ordered to support.[42] Altogether a close analysis exactly confirms the traditional estimate that only forty former Whigs were elected. Only in a few county elections were Whig groups able to make an effective challenge, forcing the Tories to use against them such electoral tricks on the part of the sheriff as adjourning the poll, changing the place of election without notice and disallowing dissenters' votes.[43] Whigs also had to lie low during the first parliamentary session, which coincided with Monmouth's rebellion. They did not support the one serious attempt at opposition, by Edward Seymour,[44] but seem to have confined their activity to attempts to defend their electoral interests in disputed election cases.[45] In face of a harmonious partnership between James, ministers and Tories, the Whigs were not only powerless but had no future, since the new chartered powers of royal intervention could be used to prevent any revival of their grass-roots interests in the boroughs. No longer a party in any real sense, they exerted negligible influence on political affairs.

This situation, and the Tory successes in the 1685 elections,

[41] HMC, XIth Report, app, vii, 105–7; XIIth Report, app, v, 85–6; XIVth Report, app, iv, 178; CSPD, 1685, p. 55; A. Browning (ed.), Memoirs of Sir John Reresby (1936), pp. 354–6.

[42] HMC, Buccleugh, i, 341; CJ, ix, 717, 760.

[43] HMC, XIVth Report, app. ix, 484; Luttrell, i, 341.

[44] See page 60.

[45] CJ, ix, 732.

have a direct connection with James's campaign to pack Parliament in 1687–8. Crown intervention and political manipulation had transformed the whole face of politics, converting what had been a formidable, aggressive and highly organized opposition party into an impotent collection of a few individuals, so that factious and dangerous assemblies had been replaced by a loyal and respectful body. These successes of political transformation were to lead James into thinking that he could use the same techniques against the Tories, when they became obstructive, and that he could organize into existence a Parliament of new men ready to collaborate in enacting royal policies.

THREE *James and the Political Nation 1685-6*

IN ORDER TO UNDERSTAND the policies of James II that preceded and provoked the Revolution, it is first essential to have a clear picture of their chronological sequence. Only by so doing can it be seen that they contained a process of logical development. Most historians, by failing to appreciate this, and particularly by taking evidence and examples indiscriminately from what were in fact distinct and separate phases, have confused and misunderstood James's policies, minimizing their chances of success to the point where it is difficult to see why a Revolution was necessary at all.

There were five main phases. First, from his accession in February 1685 until the prorogation in November, James's objectives were immediate and practical, to consolidate the power and authority of the crown in a period of uncertainty and rebellion. He relied upon the cooperation of the Tories and Anglicans, and at first this was forthcoming. But unexpected resistance to his proposals during the second session of Parliament in November made James realize that the loyalty of these allies was conditional. Consequently in the second phase, which occupied the whole of 1686, James tried to alter the terms of his partnership with these allies to his own advantage. He tried to do so by persuasion. He was continuing to work through, and with, the traditionally loyal sections of the political nation. The one innovation was that he was trying to incorporate all Catholics within its ranks, with full enjoyment of its rights. The first essentially radical move came at the beginning of 1687, when, recognizing the failure of his attempts at persuasion, James made a direct appeal to groups that were outside the privileged ranks of the political nation. The Declaration of Indulgence in April represented a conscious bid for the cooperation of dissenters who had formerly been identified with the Whigs, but it was also concerned with advancing Catholic interests. It represented a bold departure from old patterns, and specifically from the policies of the years since 1681. Nevertheless it must be emphasized that James's objectives were still definitely limited. The limiting factor in the background during these first three phases was that James expected to be succeeded by his irrevocably Protestant daughter Mary. In practice, since she deferred in everything to her husband, William would rule after James. Certainly James's strengthening of the royal prerogative would be acceptable to him, but he refused to endorse the campaign to repeal the Test Acts, excluding Catholics from all offices, which meant that any extreme policies in favour of the Catholics would be certain to be reversed under him.

The decisive development came in November 1687, with the certainty that the queen was pregnant. The confident (and therefore suspicious) predictions that a son would be born, and a healthy one likely to live, formed the basis for the policies of the fourth phase. James could now count on a Catholic successor, under whom his policies could be continued. In order to achieve his objectives he now began to prepare for general elections, instituting a systematic regulation of the corporations which developed into an entirely unprecedented campaign to pack Parliament. This continued until as late as October 1688. It was abandoned only when James belatedly realized that William was about to invade, which led him to abandon and reverse his policies in a short final phase of concessions that were made with such obvious insincerity that they had little influence on events.

There was one crucial difference between the character of the first three and of the last two phases of the reign. During the first period James committed many errors of judgement and provoked considerable opposition, but he retained the initiative throughout. Those who feared and resented his policies could do little more than try to obstruct him, and wait for Mary's accession. William was not an active principal in politics, confining himself to wary observation of events. Despite occasional alarms, western Europe remained at peace so that James (like his father during the years of the 1630s when he governed without Parliament) could devote himself to domestic politics, largely insulated from the outside world. But at the end of 1687, coinciding with the queen's pregnancy which promised an unlimited future for the continuation and completion of his policies, these favourable conditions began to disappear, James's freedom of action became increasingly limited and, above all, events began to move on a very much faster time-scale. Faced with more complex problems and the need for quick decisions, James's judgement began to deteriorate. At home the crisis intensified, but even more important in my view were concurrent developments in Europe. The decisive decisions in 1688 were those made by William and Louis, rather than those by James, the Seven Bishops or even the seven signatories of the invitation to William. Now it was for James to react to the moves made by others. During the summer he finally became entangled in the manoeuvres of Louis from which he had previously managed to remain free, and as the pressure on him increased so his resolution crumbled.

The state of near paralysis to which the crisis of 1688 reduced James contrasted sharply with the outstanding courage and powers of leadership which he had displayed in the appallingly hard-fought naval engagements of the second Dutch war of 1665-6. But even then James had been a brave fighting admiral but a faulty strategist who threw away the fruits of hard-won victories for lack of thought and planning. As sovereign James proved similarly unable to analyse and think through complex problems, to sense and adapt himself to rapidly changing situations, or to profit from experience. James tended to simplify everything, seeing the world in clear but deceptive terms of black and white, loyalty or treachery, obedience or rebellion. In sharp contrast to his brother, James lacked the qualifications which contemporary politics demanded.[1]

In judging James's actions, decisions and mistakes we must realize that his mind worked in a very different way from that of most men today. His view of the world, of man's place within it and of his own position and duties, all need explanation. Like most of his generation he believed in the direct and regular intervention of divine providence in human affairs, small as well as great, daily and personal as well as national. Like Oliver Cromwell, although for the very different reason that he was king by divine ordinance, James thought of himself as an instrument in the hands of God. His paradoxical death-bed statement, that William was his greatest benefactor, was entirely sincere and consistent, if also staggeringly egocentric. The explanation was that William had been the 'person whom Providence had made use of, to scourge him, and humble him, in the manner he had done, in order to save his soul'.[2] By this interpretation God had not deserted James but had used the Revolution to chastise him, even though this saving of the king's soul involved changing the whole course of national history. Similarly his daughter Mary wrote in her diary: 'It has pleased God to bring things about as they are, and I must submit. We are not to be our own masters in this world.'[3] Father and daughter were deeply conscious of their two-fold burden of responsibility; they would have to give account to God for both their private sins and their conduct of public affairs. James's stewardship posed fearfully difficult problems. He felt obliged to relieve the Catholics, whatever the difficulties, because theirs was the true faith. Yet as a king with heretical heirs he was powerless to prevent the obstinate adherence of millions to false religions leading them to eternal damnation. The birth of a male heir therefore appeared as an act of divine dispensation, creating conditions in which it would be possible for James at least to

[1] For a general biography, see F. C. Turner, *James II* (1948).
[2] C. Dodd (pseudonym), *Church History of England* (1743), p. 441.
[3] Doebner, *Memoirs of Mary*, p. 19.

plan and prepare for the ultimate return of the nation to the true Church. The catastrophes which followed, and apparently testified to God's rejection of James as his agent, account for the appallingly rigorous systems of penitence which James imposed on himself in exile, and for his heart-felt relief at the end when he knew that *he* was saved, even though his unworthiness had inflicted misery on his people.

The importance of James's conversion to Catholicism cannot be overstated. It was simple, sincere and irrevocable. His new faith made James certain that he was right, giving additional meaning and intensity to his belief in divine right principles. Moreover, as James gave an unquestioning obedience to the dogmas of an infallible Church, so he expected a similar obedience from those whom God had put under him. In practical terms his religion coloured his judgement of men; only Catholics could be fully trusted, since by definition all Protestants were rebels against God, and therefore suspect in their loyalty to God's chosen servant, the king.[4] It also led him to criticise his father's martyrdom for the sake of the Church of England. This, he argued as justification for his change of attitude in 1687–8, had been a source of weakness, not of strength, to the monarchy – by sacrificing a Church that was both false and hated by most of the nation, Charles I could have saved his life and his crown.[5]

James was also critical of his brother, during the Exclusion Crisis as well as retrospectively. He disliked Charles's acceptance of conditional loyalty, his cynical tolerance of the blatant opportunism of ministers playing a double game, and his risky dependence on being able to outwit even the cleverest and most unscrupulous politicians. Unlike Charles, James would not disguise his real thoughts and feelings, tolerate dishonesty or time-servers, sacrifice loyal servants or allow innocent men to be punished. He despised Charles for having degraded the monarchy by engaging personally in politics and intrigues. Instead James relied on his authority as king by divine right and on his own integrity. In practice he was very easily deceived,

[4] John Sheffield, Earl of Mulgrave and Duke of Buckingham, *Works* (1753), ii, 70.
[5] Addit., 34512, f.84.

he had no judgement of men and he had inherited his father's obstinacy and petulance. In a fluid situation, such as that of December 1688, James was lost. Endowed with authority he could act firmly, if often mistakenly; deprived of it he became demoralized and psychologically depressed while pressure continued. He recovered his resilience and stubborn refusal to accept defeat only when he had removed himself into exile, and could no longer influence events – a pattern of behaviour repeated at the time of the defeat at the Boyne and the precipitate flight to France in 1690. James's virtues – honesty and plain speaking, the trust which he put in his servants, consistency, sincerity and openness of purpose – ill-equipped him for the political world which he inherited. Unfortunately few of his subjects could ever credit him with possessing such virtues; these were generally held to be incompatible with the principles of his Catholic religion. They attributed to James the characteristics which a century of Protestant indoctrination led them to expect: calculated faithlessness, the belief that any method was justified if it advanced the interests of Catholicism, cruelty, and a readiness to submit to dictation by the Catholic clergy.

James's abysmal collapse in the crisis of 1688 may be contrasted with his earlier success in a simpler but starker situation. During and after the Exclusion Crisis he had been sent into semi-exile in Scotland as royal representative, and had governed with marked success. He had to deal with a country whose problems and tensions were far more acute and violent than those in England, but which were also capable of solution (or at least suppression) by the crude and rough methods which had been used effectively in the past. Many of James's methods were very similar to those employed by James vi and i but, like his grandfather, James was misled by his Scottish experiences in 1681–2 into believing that his achievements there were directly relevant (and transferable) to the much more complex conditions and issues of English politics and society. But the Scottish Parliament which he dominated and controlled in 1681 lacked the cohesion of its English counterpart, and also the necessary constitutional machinery to achieve procedural independence. The Scottish episcopate, whose fervent loyalty and trust in a

Catholic prince impressed James, occupied a precarious position in comparison with the Anglican bishops, depending as it did for survival on the crown. The socially dominant nobility, for all their turbulence, could be controlled by patronage and skilful exploitation of the rancorous feuds which divided them. The towns were weak enough to be managed without difficulty. Religious and political extremism went hand in hand, necessitating the maintenance of a large standing army which was constantly in action. But it would be wrong to argue, as most historians have done, that James's record in Scotland proves that he was cruel and naturally went to extremes. Rather the situation provoked in him the kind of exasperation and frustration that prolonged guerrilla warfare has produced in many twentieth-century governments. The lesson which James drew from his experience in Scotland was the absolute necessity of strong government, in order to prevent the violent overthrow of all order and forms of duly constituted authority, and the need for government to have the backing of effective military power.

Yet despite his rigidity, inflexibility and lack of originality and intelligence, it is the thesis of this study that the policies which James followed in 1687-8 were flexible and new, representing an adoption, with certain adaptations, of the sophisticated and innovatory political techniques which had been developed by Shaftesbury, the arch-radical incendiary, Achitophel himself in the Court version of recent history during the Exclusion Crisis. How is this to be explained? It has to be admitted that we have little direct evidence on the detailed advice which James received from his ministers, but it seems to me that the answer must lie in the ascendant influence on him of one set of ministers, particularly Sunderland, Brent and (for part of the time) William Penn. All three were unorthodox in their political pasts (Sunderland and Penn had briefly supported Exclusion), none were attached to the traditional principles of loyalty, none were Anglicans. Superficially there may seem to be a resemblance with the Cabal, but James's ministers operated in a very different political situation. Instead of relying on absolutist methods to free the king from dependence on Parliament, they had no alternative but to employ the newly developed techniques that had transformed the nature of politics. James acquiesced at the time, in the hope of success, but retrospectively after their failure he bitterly regretted having done so.[6] The vehemence and consistency with which he did so in the years of exile is revealing evidence of the relation between James and his innovating ministers. When he accused Sunderland of having betrayed him, this meant far more than a charge of supplying William with intelligence. In retrospect James saw Sunderland as literally a devil, one who had tempted him into following deceitful and evil ways. Under his influence James had stooped as low as his brother, in employing strange and deplorable political methods which had turned him into a mere politician, seeking to buy the support of subjects whose loyalty and obedience were his by right. This rejection of the kind of politics which had marked the last years of his reign, and especially the campaign to pack Parliament, is seen in James's refusal in exile to give support to the compounders, the moderate ministers who were ready to purchase his restoration by a constitutional deal involving concessions at the expense of the prerogative.[7] Unrealistic as this attitude was, it should not be seen as just the product of stupidity. It was a conscious and high-minded refusal on the part of a divinely appointed king to engage in the kind of politics which had already led him to disaster.

At the time of his accession James carefully, specifically and effectively stated his intention of respecting the religion, liberties and property of his subjects. He expressed his belief in the essential interdependence of the rights of the crown with those of the nation, and he was precise and comprehensive in the assurances which he gave to the Church of England.[8] Clearly James was concerned to dispel the image that Whig propaganda had created of him as revengeful, cruel, unforgiving, a bigot and absolutist. There was obviously an element of calculation

[6] J. S. Clarke, *Life of James the Second* (1816), ii, 139.
[7] G. H. Jones, *The Main Stream of Jacobitism* (1954), pp. 25–7, 28–9, 48–9.
[8] Clarke, *James the Second*, ii, 3–5.

in his moderation, for instance in retaining Halifax as a minister, but it would be incorrect to describe James at this time as intending unconstitutional or arbitrary policies. His declarations were neither deceitful nor misleading. James made it clear that he would assert to the full what he judged to be the legitimate rights and proper dignity of the crown. He directed the continued collection of customs duties pending a vote by Parliament. He insisted on publicly attending mass. When MPs spoke of voting him supply for a limited period only, so as to ensure frequent sessions, he warned them candidly that this would be an improper and also ineffective method to use with him, but that they would find him responsive if used well.[9] When asking for money for the navy he echoed the language of Elizabeth (surely unconsciously?): 'I have a true English heart, as jealous of the Honour of the Nation as you can be.'[10]

These reassuring statements, and the approaching crisis signalled by the Earl of Argyll's invasion and Monmouth's preparations, led Parliament to respond with practical as well as verbal demonstrations of loyal cooperation. Monmouth's invasion was extraordinarily badly timed, and his propaganda proved to be counterproductive. By June 1685 James was firmly in control of all governmental functions, but he had not yet used any of them in such a way as to antagonize important sections of opinion. It was Monmouth who provoked fear and insecurity. He charged James with having poisoned Charles II, a charge which implied bringing him to trial and perhaps putting him to death. He denounced the Parliament as a pretended one, ordering its members to disperse. His initial success in establishing himself in the west country, and in organizing a surprisingly large and effective army in a matter of two weeks, raised the prospect of a long and hard-fought civil war. For most members of the political nation this was the worst of all possible prospects; the rapid and total defeat of Monmouth's forces was absolutely essential. Expiring laws were renewed, emergency legislation passed. The collection of customs was retrospectively legalized

---

[9] *CJ*, ix, 714.
[10] *Ibid.*, p. 722.

and an extremely generous financial settlement voted.[11] In combining against Monmouth in the country, and throughout the first session at Westminster, the Tories were able to retain, and act upon, their uncritical assumption that their own interests and those of the crown must necessarily, and in all probability permanently, coincide.[12] An incident at the start of the session shows how far the Tories were from realizing even the possibility of a rift with James. The committee for religion cheerfully recommended a request to James to enforce the penal laws against all dissenters; when the court managers explained that this would offend him by appearing to include Catholics, the Commons immediately modified the address.[13] With few Whigs in Parliament there was no opinionated nucleus of opposition. Only on one issue, disputed elections, did the Whigs attempt combined action and this had the effect of widening the division between them and the Tory majority. Their efforts proved totally ineffective and actually reduced the chances of success of the one aggressive attempt at opposition during the first session. Edward Seymour, former speaker and minister, raised the fundamental question of the possible effects on parliamentary independence of the remodelling of the charters. He proposed that the committee of elections should examine all returns from boroughs with new charters, and that (ostensibly to ensure its independent working, but really so as to weaken the court) all members from such boroughs should be excluded from the committee. Seymour also proposed that further pressure should be exerted on the king by the Commons withholding grants of supply until the investigation was complete. Considering James's specific warning on this point, and in view of Monmouth's impending invasion and the danger of civil war, this was reckless advice, and must have reawakened the distrust which Seymour's past political conduct generated. The consequence was that his further allegations – all to be confirmed

[11] *Ibid.*, pp. 715, 722–3, 724–6. Clarke, *James the Second*, ii, 18.
[12] Ranke (iv, 229) is entirely wrong in saying that the Tories feared that James would use the enhanced powers of the crown against them, although Barrillon reported this in his despatch of 5 March.
[13] *CJ*, ix, 721, 27 May; Addit., 34508, ff.23–4; Baschet; Barrillon, 7 June 1685.

in the second session – that James wanted amendment of *Habeas Corpus* and repeal of the Test Acts, failed to evoke any response. Seymour does not seem to have prepared opinion, and he was too obviously self-interested since his resentment stemmed from the electoral advantages which the remodelling had given to his west-country rival, Lord Bath. Seymour's failure was so abject that it misled James and the court managers into believing that they would encounter only minor resistance when James developed his policies at the beginning of the second session.[14]

James's method of proceeding during this second session, which saw the development of an open and, as time was to show, irreparable split with the Tories, was entirely in character. He dismissed Halifax before it began, knowing that he would never endorse or actively support the new policies.[15] In contrast to the tactful and reassuring generalizations of May, James's opening speech was brusque and explicit. Unlike the Tories, he did not see the total defeat of Monmouth and Argyll as ending the threat to his throne; on the contrary he stated his conclusion that these rebellions demanded a strengthening of the crown, specifically through an increase in the size of the standing army. New regiments had been raised on a temporary basis to oppose Monmouth. These were now to be continued, and men who had been pressed for the emergency would have to continue serving; this accounts for the high rate of desertions over the next three years, which necessitated the use of the constitutionally dubious provisions of martial law in order to maintain these units. Considering how potent memories of Cromwell's military rule continued to be, and given the opposition of the Cavalier Parliament to the continuance of the armies raised in 1672 and 1678, James's proposals were inevitably disquieting. Even more provocative was his admission that many Catholics had been commissioned during the crisis, combined with the statement that he was determined to retain them despite the provisions of

[14] Baschet; Barrillon, 2, 4 June; *CJ*, ix, 721; Lingard, *History*, x, 140. Only Sir John Lowther (*Memoir of the Reign of James II*, pp. 451–3), Willoughby and Sir Richard Middleton openly expressed similar views.

[15] Baschet; Barrillon, 29 October, 5 November 1685; H. C. Foxcroft, *Life and Letters of Sir George Savile* (1898), i, 448–9, 455.

the Test Act.[16] James's speech greatly strengthened the fears that he intended in the near future to ask for repeal of the Test Acts and the penal laws in their entirety so far as they concerned Catholics. In fact James intended to make such proposals later, but he was known to be about to demand repeal of the *Habeas Corpus* Amendment Act of 1679. The need to make preventive arrests at the time of the Monmouth Rebellion, and the difficulty of finding evidence to convict Whigs in areas where there had been no actual rising, proved that this act hampered the executive, and after the Revolution the same difficulties necessitated two statutory suspensions of the act.[17] But in 1685 James's proposal was interpreted as a danger to constitution and liberties because it was part of an apparent 'package' of demands, and because James's attempts to increase the powers of the crown were directly connected with his efforts to improve the position of his fellow Catholics. They did not yet go far enough to revive the old Whig thesis that Popery and abolutism necessarily went together, but inevitably there was renewed 'country' suspicion of the executive.

It is worth emphasizing that although the reaction in the Commons to James's proposals was unfavourable, it was not at any stage during this second session openly hostile or intransigent. Indeed on the last day the Commons were constructively discussing methods of raising the sum of £700,000 which they had voted earlier.[18] When an address was voted in reply to the king's speech it did not charge him with breaking the law (as he had), but merely repeated that Catholics could not hold office.[19] When a member spoke out too strongly against James's forceful reply to this address, the Commons sent him to the Tower. It deleted language from resolutions on supply that might have been construed as offensive.[20] The single division of importance related to a procedural matter, not a vote of substance – whether to give priority to a discussion of the king's speech – but the defeat of the court on this occasion by one vote (by 183 to 182)

[16] *CJ*, ix, 756; Addit., 34508, f.89.
[17] Baschet; Barrillon, 29 October 1685; Grey, ix, 136–7, 262–76.
[18] Baschet; Barrillon, 30 November 1685; *CJ*, ix, 760–61.
[19] *CJ*, ix, 758. 16 November.
[20] *CJ*, ix, 760; Baschet; Barrillon, 26 November 1685.

was disquieting.[21] It showed that the Commons was drifting towards opposition, and James rightly remained unimpressed by its repeated professions of regard for his susceptibilities. The stage of open opposition to royal policies had not been reached by the time that James prorogued, but loss of control over the Lords by the court made it only a question of time before the two Houses began to concert tactics and awaken a general response in the nation.

James was badly served in the Lords by the inexperienced Jeffreys who, after being junior peer in the first session, now became speaker *ex officio* after being appointed lord chancellor. In the summer crisis he had controlled London very successfully, but the arrogance and bullying language that had worked with aldermen only antagonized peers.[22] Four men led the attack on the court. Two of them, the Earls of Nottingham and Bridgwater, were privy councillors, but this did not prevent them from openly denouncing the appointment and retention of Catholic officers.[23] The other two opposition peers were still more outspoken, and from their attacks a vendetta was to develop with James; he was to try systematically to ruin them and they in turn were to play leading roles in the actual Revolution. The Earl of Devonshire was the only former exclusionist Whig who dared openly to attack the king. Henry Compton, the politically ambitious and self-assured Bishop of London, widened the issues in assuming the role of champion of Protestantism, foreign as well as British, in the face of the Catholic offensive. These peers outmanoeuvred the court. They began to negotiate with possible leaders of opposition in the Commons so as to coordinate moves. They mounted a clever stratagem on the issue of the Catholic officers. Making it clear that they would indemnify those who had served, they proposed that the judges should be consulted on the legality of their commissions. As Jeffreys had not had time to remodel the judiciary, they were confident of obtaining a binding statement from the judges that

[21] *CJ*, ix, 757.

[22] Mazure, ii, 65–6; *HMC, VIth Report*, app, i, 463; *Autobiography of Sir John Bramston* (1845), p. 216; Ranke, iv, 276–9.

[23] H. Horwitz, *Revolution Politicks* (1968), pp. 39–41.

the king did not possess a general prerogative power of dispensing with laws in their entirety, a severe check to James's ability to promote the interests of Catholicism.[24] It was this prospect that decided James on an emergency prorogation which was all the more unexpected because supply bills, still in their last procedural stages, now lapsed. The second session had lasted for less than two weeks, the shortest of the late seventeenth century – with the single exception of the extremist session at Oxford of the 1681 Whig Parliament, which had lasted less than a week.

James's reaction to the prospect of Parliament acting as a focus for opposition was all the stronger because of his basic misunderstanding of the real reasons for Tory refusals to accept his demands. Sincere and secure in his own faith, he never appreciated the reasons which underlaid anti-Catholicism, and especially the extent to which these were the product of fear : fear of persecution, of the organized effectiveness of the Church of Rome, of the generally accepted connection between Catholicism and absolutism – which was symbolized above all by Louis XIV, and never more clearly than in this year of 1685. For James anti-Popery was offensive, malevolent and subversive; its practitioners were insincere and aggressive. It was a brute prejudice in the ignorant but inflammable minds of the rabble or, in their educated betters, a cover for ambition and faction. James believed that all the anti-Catholic feeling and legislation of Charles's reign had really been political and not religious in its motivation. Its aim, and this applied particularly to the Test Acts, had been to reduce or even subvert monarchical authority.[25] There was certainly truth in this estimate so far as the Whigs were concerned, but it led James to distrust the loyalty of any Tory who, however faithful in political matters, refused to accept the demands being made on behalf of the Catholics. He could not understand the Tory plea that the Test Acts were purely defensive, but interpreted all opposition to his proposed repeal of the Tests as antimonarchical. In addition, he remained suspicious of all Tories who had sponsored 'limitations' in 1680–1 on the powers of a Catholic king, ostensibly

[24] Ranke, iv, 276–9.
[25] Baschet; Barrillon, 12 June 1687.

as an alternative to Exclusion but really, James thought, because they were jealous of the prerogative powers of the crown.[26]

Superficially the prorogation on 20 November can be seen as a bold, decisive move, vindicating James's prestige and giving him freedom of action. Further energetic action followed. He issued the first large batch of dispensations to Catholic officers three days afterwards, appointed Sunderland as lord president on 4 December, and ordered an expansion and reorganization of the army for completion in the summer.[27] Most of the officers and officials who had voted in Parliament against the court were dismissed.[28] James was now in process of defining his objectives, and he began systematically to develop new methods in order to achieve them. He was determined to secure repeal of the Test Acts and the penal laws by the existing Parliament. Therefore he continued the prorogations while peers and MPs were intensively canvassed, a process known as closeting, which occupied much of 1686. The generally disappointing responses showed that the next session would in all probability prove to be more refractory, not more amenable; the prorogation (repeated on 10 February and 10 May) angered opinion, closeting was resented as a form of intimidation and a breach of parliamentary privilege, and several by-elections were pending which promised defeats for the court. The previous autumn had seen a spectacular setback at Bristol (a remodelled city) where the court candidate was defeated by a man sponsored by a breakaway faction of Tories, despite the support of the lord lieutenant, the mayor and magistrates, and the bishop and clergy. The voters had rallied to the opposition Tory on the ominous grounds of hostility to the army and the need for Protestant unity in the face of the Catholic danger.[29]

Without a parliamentary session, such sentiments would lack any effective focus, and no formed opposition could exist. Nevertheless James, by these policies and methods, was in process

---

[26] *Ibid.*, 5 November 1685.
[27] Addit., 34508, ff.103, 105.
[28] Addit., 34508, f.99; Luttrell, i, 367.
[29] *HMC, Ormonde, ns,* vii, 404.

of trapping himself. He persisted with closeting long after it ceased to produce results. Pending the time when he could call a session, and this prospect was ever receding into the future, he could use his prerogative powers to achieve his objectives on an interim basis. In doing so he was achieving nothing permanent, but he was provoking the maximum alarm and distrust. The Tories had been ready to collaborate in strengthening the crown during Charles's last years only because they had been part beneficiaries, and because the exclusive rights of the Church of England had been expressly guaranteed and enforced in practice. Now James was increasing the prerogative powers at the disposal of the crown as a direct substitute for statutory methods, and using them not only to benefit the Catholics but apparently also for the purpose of subverting the rights of the Church of England. Considering that the eyes of the nation were focused on what was happening in France during these months, where absolutist governmental techniques and Catholic fervour were rapidly eradicating the Huguenots, it is not surprising that James seemed to many to be confirming the old Whig arguments that had been used to justify Exclusion.

In practice, James's religious policies through 1686 were far more limited than contemporaries thought. He was not attempting consciously to subvert Protestantism or to establish Catholicism as the religion of either the state or the nation. His central aim was to persuade the Anglican clergy and the Tories to recognize the Catholics' right to enjoy complete religious freedom and equality of political rights. Even more important, James was determined to secure these Catholic privileges on a permanent basis, in such a way that they could not easily be revoked under a Protestant successor.[30] But the amount of opposition and obstruction which James encountered forced him to intensify his pressure on the Anglicans to a point where the essential moderation of his aims was very effectively concealed. Officeholders would not agree to repeal of the Tests – partly for the reason that this would intensify competition for posts. The Rochester group was ready to concede unofficial toleration: private worship, the cessation of fines and acceptance of a work-

[30] Baschet; Barrillon, 16 April 1685; 24 April, 12 June, 9 October 1687.

ing Catholic priesthood, but not repeal of the penal laws.[31] James scornfully rejected such concessions as dishonourable and impermanent, and in any case could secure more by using his prerogative. He issued dispensations and protections on a large scale, and by judicious prompting got the judges to recognize his rights of dispensation in the case of *Godden v Hales* (June).[32] Constitutionally even this was insufficient. Only a regularly enacted statute could give absolute security to the Catholics, and even this could be repealed under his successor. James could achieve his objectives only by teaching the Anglicans to accept coexistence.

Certainly James thought that he was acting with moderation. As early as the summer of 1686 the extremist Catholic group at court began to talk wildly of emulating Louis by converting the entire nation. They spoke of compelling Princess Anne to become a Catholic and then making her heir to the throne, they advised appointing Catholic priests to Anglican bishoprics, and naturally this resulted in alarming rumours circulating widely. James was said to be on the point of issuing *quo warrantos* against cathedrals, deans and chapters, universities, colleges and schools, and of intending a general inhibition to prohibit preaching.[33] He had no intention of doing these things, but realized the damage such rumours did. Yet it was inevitable that his measures should be misinterpreted because of the steadily increasing pressure which Anglican intransigence left him no option but to employ. His methods were incompatible with his declared objectives. He was trying to force the Anglicans to renounce the use of compulsion, to compel his subjects to live peacefully and passively as neighbours of a vigorously proselytising Catholic community which he was actively favouring.

James expected acquiescence from the Anglican clergy because of their attachment to the traditional and often asserted principles of divine right, of non-resistance and passive obedience. He also relied on the divisions which existed among the Anglican

[31] Mazure, ii, 179–80.
[32] *State Trials*, xi, 1166–1315.
[33] Mazure, ii, 167; Luttrell, i, 368.

leaders, both clerical and lay. His own protégé, whom he was grooming for succession to William Sancroft at Canterbury, Francis Turner of Ely, an able and forceful clerical politician and a good churchman, entirely accepted James's sincerity and assured his clergy that while the king could be trusted, there would be reasons to fear for the Church when Mary succeeded.[34] Of the lay champions, James expected Rochester to accept his policies eventually, and throughout 1686 he was still seriously hoping for his conversion.[35] Three other self-appointed champions (Danby, Nottingham and Seymour) were unlikely to cooperate, but competition between them – reflected in divisions among the clergy – reduced their effective influence. There was only one really dangerous enemy, Compton, the ambitious Bishop of London. His opposition in the Lords led to his being dismissed in December 1685 as privy councillor and dean of the Chapel Royal. There were no serious repercussions. Compton was not popular, but James made a serious mistake when he proceeded on the assumption that further attacks could be made with impunity on such a prominent cleric in such a sensitive ecclesiastical post.[36] The offensive which he directed against Compton was intended to deter other Anglicans from obstructing his policies, but it proved to be counterproductive, converting the bishop into the symbol of Protestant resistance to the machinations of the Catholics.

The first move by James in his attempt to obtain Anglican acquiescence for his pro-Catholic policies was a private approach to the archbishops and Compton, as Bishop of London, to suppress Sunday afternoon lectures.[37] In theory these were courses on the catechism, but James believed that they were being used to inculcate anti-Catholic views. His approach was ignored. James then ordered them to issue, and take steps to enforce, Directions to Preachers. Such Directions had been issued in 1662, and also (as Anglican propagandists were quick to point out) early in Mary's reign just before the persecution of

[34] R. Beddard, 'The Commission for Ecclesiastical Promotions, 1681–84', *Historical Journal*, x, 25–30; Burnet, iii, 20.
[35] Burnet, iii, 123–5; Lingard, *History*, x, 224.
[36] Mulgrave, *Works*, ii, 68; Ranke, iv, 295.
[37] Ranke, iv, 293–4.

Protestants had begun, with the aim of preventing controversy and stopping all sermons on political subjects. Reference was made to the sad effects of polemical preaching in the 1640s, to the danger of factious clergy insinuating 'fears and jealousies to dispose people to discontent', and to the danger that arrogance and a desire for notoriety would lead the younger clergy to select the most contentious subjects. Preachers were instructed to confine themselves to doctrines actually contained in the catechism, and were to teach the people 'their bounden duty of subjection and obedience to their governors'. The doctrines and discipline of the Church could be taught, but it must be 'without bitterness, railing, jeering or other unnecessary provocation', in other words provided that there was nothing explicitly anti-Catholic.[38]

James intended the Directions to produce an atmosphere of admittedly enforced toleration, but their announcement on 5 March coincided with the beginning of a phase of intensive Catholic proselytising, and this led to their being generally interpreted as being designed to hamper the Anglican clergy in their defence of their religion in a time of peril. The Catholic clergy were now free to organize, preach and evangelize, while the Anglicans were inhibited from militant counter-action. Some tension developed as a result, particularly in larger towns. At Bristol the newly appointed bishop, Jonathan Trelawney, was forced to reprimand his most active clergy for allegedly exciting religious animosities. Writing in very submissive terms to Sunderland, he admitted that anti-Catholic feeling was difficult to control, and his view was confirmed in May when a mob attacked a priest who was publicly celebrating mass.[39] In London disturbances centred on the chapel which the elector palatine's envoy was building in Lime Street, within the city itself. Existing chapels were all situated further west, outside the city, and in April the lord mayor prohibited further building work for fear of provoking hostility in this Protestant strong-

[38] *The History of King James's Ecclesiastical Commission* (1711), p. 1; *CSPD*, 1686–7, pp. 56–8; PRO, PC 2, 71, f.300.

[39] *CSPD*, 1686–7, pp. 134–5, 185; Addit., 34508, f. 118; Baschet; Barrillon, 30 May 17 June 1686; Luttrell, i, 389.

hold. In a personal interview James rebuked him and forced him to retract. The next month a mob tried to demolish the chapel. James then ordered the lord mayor to turn out the train bands (the London militia) for its protection, threatening that if they failed in this duty troops would be sent in, so that the formerly proud and independent city would be subjected to military occupation.[40]

Although there was no evidence to establish any direct connection, Compton was held to be partly responsible for these disturbances. Jeffreys had secured political control over the city government; now it seemed to be equally important to achieve a similar control over the clergy in the capital and its surroundings – the area where the Catholic missionary effort was largely concentrated. Under Compton's leadership the Anglican clergy could be expected to use their influence to obstruct James's policies.

In the manoeuvres now directed against Compton, James was undoubtedly actuated by personal hatred against a former client who had subsequently deserted to his enemies, and worked hard to obstruct royal policies.[41] The pro-French group of ministers urged action against Compton because of his ostentatious and, so his detractors claimed, opportunistic championing of the Huguenot cause.[42] Compton was to be pilloried, to serve as an example to demonstrate what happened to anyone who actively opposed James; two Whig peers, Devonshire and Lovelace, were to suffer for the same reason later in the reign, the former being fined £30,000 for a brawl at court, the latter prosecuted for impeding the toleration of Catholics; and a humble clergyman, 'Julian' Johnson, was to be flogged, pilloried and unfrocked for publishing seditious pamphlets.[43] The occasion for the assault on Compton came with the preaching of two sermons on 2 and 9 May by one of his protégés, John Sharp, an out-

---

[40] Baschet; Barrillon, 8, 11 April, 6, 30 May, 6 June 1686; Luttrell, i, 375.

[41] Baschet; Barrillon, 11 April 1686. In addition Compton had been entrusted by Charles with the religious education of Mary and Anne.

[42] Baschet; Barrillon, 29 August 1686; E. Carpenter, *The Protestant Bishop* (1956), pp. 325–43.

[43] Baschet; Barrillon, 10 July, 30 October, 6 November 1687; 8 March 1688; Bonrepos, 7 November 1687; Mazure, ii, 176–7; PWA 2147.

standingly able cleric of the younger generation. He was rector
of St Giles in the Fields, a London parish with a high proportion
of Irish Catholic immigrants whose arrival, concentration in slum
areas, and economic competition was creating social as well as
religious tension. Their presence, and the proselytising activities
of the priests serving them, made Sharp acutely aware of the
Catholic challenge. His sermons were intended to fortify his
parishioners' faith, but in them he dealt with extremely delicate
matters, referring to James's own conversion, and to Charles's
papers in favour of Catholicism which James claimed to have
found in his brother's private cabinet, and on whose publication
he placed a good deal of (mistaken) reliance. Sharp threw doubt
on their authenticity.[44] Not unnaturally, James was incensed,
treating these sermons as a deliberate defiance of the Directions.
He ordered Compton to suspend Sharp from further preaching.[45] If he obeyed, Compton's Protestant reputation would be
shaken; if he refused proceedings could be instituted. Compton's
reply used submissive language but amounted in substance to a
refusal; Sharp could be suspended only after a full enquiry in
legal form. Sharp brought this reply to Whitehall in person, but
James would not see him or receive his justification, and he
also ignored Sharp's petition on 20 June which pleaded misrepresentation and made a very qualified apology.[46] The decision
had been made to attack and ruin Compton; the question
remained how to proceed, since Archbishop Sancroft refused to
act. Great alarm was provoked when James and his ministers
briefly considered appointing a vicar general with powers like
those which Thomas Cromwell had once exercised, but the final
decision to establish the Court of Ecclesiastical Commission was
hardly less alarming.[47]

The Ecclesiastical Commission derived its jurisdictional
authority from the king's prerogative powers over the Church.

[44] *HMC, Downshire*, I, i, 186; A. T. Hart, *Life and Times of John Sharp* (1949), pp.
92–3; *Copies of Two Papers written by the late King Charles II and one by the Duchess of
York* (1686).
[45] Carpenter, *The Protestant Bishop*, pp. 89–90; *History of King James's Ecclesiastical
Commission*, pp. 9–10.
[46] *Ibid.*, pp. 10, 11–12.
[47] Ranke, iv, 298.

But its legality was contestable, since the act of 1641 abolishing the High Commission had specifically prohibited its revival. James attempted to meet this objection in the letters-patent of 14 July which established the court, by asserting his right to do so 'by force and virtue of our Supreme Authority and Prerogative Royal'. This claim was entirely consistent with the judgement upholding the dispensing power in the case of *Godden v Hales*; for James the judgement and the commission were necessary moves if he was ever to achieve his policy objectives, measures forced on him by Tory and Anglican refusals to cooperate. To his subjects they had a very different appearance; they looked like part of a systematic plan to put the king into a position of unlimited and irresponsible power. Fears of arbitrary government were also strengthened by the extensive powers conferred on the Ecclesiastical Commission. It was to deal with all kinds of spiritual, ecclesiastical and moral cases; it could summon, try, suspend or deprive any cleric, and had the power to excommunicate anyone, cleric or layman. In addition it was to supervise and regulate universities, colleges, schools and cathedrals, with the power to investigate and revise their statutes.[48]

These powers, and the initial membership of the commission, were intended to command respect and demonstrate the futility of resistance.[49] Indeed Compton was at one stage prepared to concede defeat, offering to beg the king's pardon and make a formal retraction. This would have accomplished James's original purpose in launching the prosecution, and he committed a major political mistake in refusing to accept. Both parties in fact committed errors. At first Compton boldly denied the commission's right of jurisdiction, citing the act of 1641 and claiming that only the archbishop could try him – thus spotlighting Sancroft's obdurate refusal to serve on the commission. Had he then withdrawn his case, this argument might have influenced the judges and impressed outside opinion, but when Compton's lawyers unwisely entered into a detailed defence the essential

[48] PRO, PC 2, 71, f.300.
[49] The original members were Archbishop Sancroft (would not serve), the Bishops of Durham and Rochester, Chancellor Jeffreys, Rochester, Sunderland and Lord Chief Justice Herbert.

issues became obscured. Even the final result was inconclusive. Compton was suspended and control over the affairs of his diocese was entrusted to commissioners; this reduced his powers of obstructing royal policies at the cost of making him into a martyr.[50] On the other hand, Compton was able to retain his temporalities by threatening to defend them in an action before the lord chief justice, Edward Herbert, in the King's Bench. Herbert had been for an acquittal, so that as well as blocking James there might be an opportunity to bring into question the legality of the commission, and set the common law against the prerogative court – an old tactic going back to Coke's day. Furthermore, by a petition which carefully avoided any admission of having been in error, Compton sought to prevent any further action; by law a suspended cleric could be prosecuted with a view to deprivation if he did not submit within six months.[51] Tactically, then, the attack on Compton achieved its minimum objective of silencing him publicly and of making the clergy more subdued in their preaching. However, the long-term effects were damaging in fixing on James charges that he proposed to govern by absolutist methods and that his ultimate aim was the subversion of the Protestant religion.

Almost every Protestant made a direct mental connection between the prosecution of Compton and the freedom which the Catholics enjoyed to worship, preach, teach, publish and organize publicly and openly. When individual clergy, magistrates or town officials tried to obstruct these freedoms, James personally intervened, and guarded against any repetition by appointing Catholics as magistrates and town officers.[52] This royal protection and assistance created conditions in which the Church of Rome at last possessed an opportunity to increase its strength and appeal, but its missionary offensive depended too much on the crown. The enforcement of freedom for Catholics by prerogative means revived the old belief that Popery and absolutism were necessarily connected, and the friendship which

[50] History of King James's Ecclesiastical Commission, pp. 14–20; State Trials, xi, 1123–1166.
[51] Mazure, ii, 145.
[52] HMC, VIIth Report, app, i, 503; Luttrell, i, 398.

was known to exist between James and Louis convinced many that the developments of 1686 were only a prelude to an attempt to convert the nation by forcible means. Support from the crown helped to conceal the inherent weaknesses of the Catholic mission in England, but in doing so it helped to make anti-Popery once again a major political factor.

FOUR *The Catholic Factor*

A NTI-POPERY WAS THE strongest, most widespread and most persistent ideology in the life and thought of seventeenth-century Britain. Even the reaction against religious enthusiasm which followed the Restoration and the gradual decline of interest in theology which was apparent among the educated laity in England, did not significantly reduce its prevalence but merely modified some of the forms which it took. Fear of, and hostility to, Catholicism was to be found in every section and class and continued under each successive form of government. Constant use, abuse and exploitation of anti-Catholic sentiment did not appreciably diminish its potency, and the fact that unscrupulous politicians encouraged it for their own purposes does not mean that it lacked a real and genuine basis in national life. On the contrary, anti-Popery is explicable only when set against the social and intellectual as well as political background of Stuart England. It derived partly from historical memories, particularly those of the persecution by Mary in 1555–8 which had been depicted with such vivid and searing partisanship in John Foxe's *Book of Actes and Monuments*, and partly from the feeling of insecurity engendered by the advances which Catholicism had made, and was still making, at the expense of continental Protestantism. In addition, the Catholics were the most conspicuous deviant element in English society, with principles and practices that clearly separated them from the rest of the nation. They resisted assimilation. And they displayed many foreign or cosmopolitan characteristics derived from education in colleges abroad, and residence overseas. Although suspect, and comparatively few in numbers, they still mysteriously possessed considerable influence and were prominent at court. Consequently they occupied the same position as the Jews in twentieth-century eastern and central Europe; they were conveniently fitted into a conspiracy interpretation to explain current crises, and they were always available as scapegoats on whom attention could be directed and passions assuaged.

During the seventeenth century, in a pre-industrial society, it was considered safe to direct popular hostility, and even mass violence, against the Catholics. They were so isolated and uniquely execrated that there was little danger of such attacks getting out of hand (as they did in 1780) and turning into anti-social disturbances endangering all order and property. The reverse was true. Anti-Popery was one of the forces making for national unity; it appealed at different levels to each section of society, it could be supported by crude prejudice, traditional anti-clerical sentiment, patristic scholarship and rational argument. At times it played a crucial role, and if for short periods it was less active, nevertheless fear and hatred of Catholicism were never far below the surface of events.

After 1660 the case against Catholicism became predominantly political. Admittedly Anglican and Catholic controversialists continued the old arguments over such theological points of dispute as images and the invocation of saints, confession and purgatory, transubstantiation, the apostolic succession and clerical orders, papal authority and the nature of a true Church, but they added very little to what had already been said or written on these subjects. For the clergy, as for the laity, there was one basic issue at stake, which carried profoundly important political implications. Many Anglican divines followed Archbishop Laud's earlier example in recognizing that the Church of Rome was a true Church, even though it needed reform. Their Catholic antagonists were uncompromising and explicit in refusing any measure of reciprocal recognition. Their clear, unvarying and well-publicized statements that there was, and could be, only one true Church, and that there was no possibility of personal salvation for those who remained outside it, were effectively subversive. Confident reiteration of this claim was calculated to generate doubt in the minds of individual Protestants. More generally it was believed to imply that persecution of heretics was really a form of charitable activity. Jacques Bénigne Bossuet was currently repeating Augustine's arguments to justify the kind of forcible methods that were being used with such cruelty and effectiveness against the Huguenots; the violence and suffering involved would be as nothing compared with the pains of eternal damnation waiting for all who died unrepentant in states of schism or heresy. It was a mercy to compel all to enter the Church, all Protestant bodies were sunk irretrievably in error, and their adherents were guilty of rebellion against divine authority.

Faced by this fundamental and consistent attitude, Anglicans of all parties combined in defence of their faith, with the High Church party as resolute as any other. For Protestants in general, permanent and inveterate enmity, with the calculating employment of any methods likely to bring success, were all that could be expected from the Church of Rome, and events in France amply confirmed the belief that persecution was an intrinsic principle of Catholicism, which might be played down for tactical reasons but would never be sincerely renounced.[1]

It might be thought that the fact that the Catholics were such a tiny minority (less than 2 per cent in England) made it unthinkable for anyone to think of using the kind of forcible methods that were proving so efficacious in France.[2] But

---

[1] Even John Locke would not give toleration to Catholics: *Letter concerning Toleration* (1955, Library of Liberal Arts), pp. 50–52.

[2] The size of the Catholic minority has been a matter of speculation, with estimates going as high as 10 per cent, but in the view of contemporaries it was by this time not more than one in fifty, taking the country as a whole. Systematic demographic studies are needed on this subject.

contemporaries feared that methods and techniques existed, by which the aggressive forces of Catholicism could hope to achieve their objective of exterminating heresy throughout the British Isles. It was generally accepted (and the relative failure of Catholicism to make significant advances in 1686–8 by proselytising and missionary work confirmed this belief) that the reconversion of England and Scotland could be accomplished only if Catholics could first seize and then exploit governmental power. Earlier in the century this was only practicable if desperate methods, such as murder plots against the sovereign, or large-scale foreign intervention, were used; the result had been disaster in 1605, and the acquisition of the reputation for unscrupulousness and terrorism on which Titus Oates had capitalized in 1678. Overemphasis on Oates's blatant perjuries and fabrications in supporting his charge that the Jesuits intended to murder Charles II, has tended to obscure an important point, which was still very much in the mind of contemporaries. Real and disturbing evidence had been found, in Coleman's letters asking for French support for English Catholicism, of new and menacing ways of advancing Catholic designs.[3]

The development of absolutist methods of centralized administration, especially in France, which largely freed sovereigns and their ministers from their former dependence upon the cooperation of their subjects, opened up the possibility of a small and totally unrepresentative group of ministers and professional officials systematically using the improved machinery of the state to subvert the Protestant religion. If this was to be accomplished, they must first destroy all restrictions on their power and freedom of action imposed by the law and the constitution. This fear of a 'design' to overthrow both religion and liberties had originated with the Cabal, was apparently confirmed by the Popish Plot, and fitted in with the ever-persuasive conspiracy theory of politics. Shaftesbury based his entire policy on the essential interdependence of Popery and absolutism, describing them as sisters going hand in hand, but eventually his cynical and increasingly mechanical exploitation

---

[3] Jones, *First Whigs*, pp. 25–6. The letters were published; *CJ*, ix, 525–9, and G. Treby, *A Collection of Letters relating to the horrid Popish Plott* (1681).

of the plot had begun to produce diminishing returns. Fear of imminent civil war came to outweigh fears of Popery, but the impression left by Whig propaganda was not entirely effaced. When James succeeded, anti-Papist feeling was dormant, not dead, and Monmouth found no difficulty in raising it among the ordinary people in the west country in 1685.

English Protestants believed that they were threatened by a united, purposeful, efficient, authoritarian and confidently aggressive Catholicism. The reality was very different. The English Catholics were unready and ill-equipped to take advantage of the opportunities which James was creating for them. Serious divisions separated the component parts – the conservative, recusant aristocracy and gentry of the provinces, the fashionable and cosmopolitan court section, the exiled colleges, convents and communities overseas. Catholicism as a whole suffered as always from the jealousy of other orders for the Jesuits, which was now complicated and exacerbated by being caught up in the furious disputes raging between Louis and the Pope, and that between the Jesuits (who supported the former) and the Jansenists with their sympathizers. To further complicate matters, no sympathy or understanding existed between English and Irish Catholics, either in Britain or in Europe, and the latter were themselves divided into hostile factions.

Of all these divisions the most fundamental was that which separated court from country Catholics, a split which closely resembled the main division of English politics in its fundamental causes.[4] The country Catholics represented old, traditional attachment to the faith, while the court element included a proportion of zealous converts, some of them indiscreet and adventurist in their behaviour, many Scots and Irish, and a number of foreigners. Country Catholics usually lived in self-contained communities centering on country houses, or in remote and small market towns. Their leaders were large property owners with a place and stake in society, or retiring small gentry. Their inoffensiveness, caution and solidity have earned them

[4] Mazure, i, 404, 418; ii, 72, 125–6; Baschet; Barrillon, 12 November 1685; 21 March 1686.

the respect of Whig historians from Macaulay on, who have contrasted these qualities with the adventurism, opportunism and allegedly lax morality of the courtiers, but the fact remains that the country Catholics were inert, defensively minded, and intellectually negligible. These old Catholic families had courageously and steadfastly endured repression when it would have been easy and profitable to abjure, but they formed an essentially residual community. Social pressures were slowly but continuously weakening their numbers and influence.[5] Their leaders seldom actually tried to give a definite lead, their proprietorial attitude towards their own clergy often prevented the latter from being deployed to the best advantage, and experience had taught them that obscurity and inactivity were preferable to militancy and enthusiasm. Although James and the court Catholics were to fail abysmally, it is easy to understand the impatience which they felt at the resigned ineffectiveness of the provincial recusants.

As earlier in the century, the Catholics lacked effective leadership; apart from James himself there was no individual, cleric or layman, who commanded general respect, and the Vatican was too remote and ill-informed to give realistic guidance. The indifferent quality of those who acted as links between James and the Pope did not help matters. Cardinal Norfolk, the English representative at Rome, was an amiable aristocrat of genuine piety, good at entertaining tourists but possessing little initiative, energy or ability.[6] Adda, appointed as papal envoy and later as nuncio in London, knew little about English affairs, and was slow to learn.[7] To make matters worse James sent the mediocre and inexperienced Catholic Earl of Castlemaine as ambassador to the Vatican, with the impossible task of reconciling the Pope with Louis on what were virtually the French terms, and simultaneously asking him for help in advancing

[5] For the situation in one region, where the number of Catholics among the gentry was declining, although total numbers were slowly increasing, H. Aveling, *Northern Catholics* (1966), pp. 352–9.

[6] Dodd, *Church History*, p. 445; Lingard, *History*, x, 259; Burnet, iii, 83–5.

[7] Not formally nuncio until July 1687. Campana de Cavelli, ii, 79; Burnet, iii, 168. Transcripts of his despatches are in addit., 34502, and some are printed as an appendix in Sir J. Mackintosh, *History of the Revolution in England in 1688*.

royal policies in Britain.[8] Another Catholic disadvantage was the lack of men with administrative or political experience – a result of the operation of the Test Act. This meant that those whom James appointed as magistrates seldom emerged as local leaders, and it also accounts for the important parts and powers that had to be entrusted to the few able converts such as Hales and Sir Nicholas Butler.

Only one Catholic emerged during the reign as a figure of national importance, the much maligned and caricatured Jesuit, Father Petre, an aristocrat who had lived in France for years, who became something of a bogeyman and has been universally condemned by all historians. Petre *may* have been responsible for giving consistently bad advice, but we know far too little about him to be confident of this. What is certain is that he made the most of his advantages to build himself a position of power and influence. As a member of an aristocratic family he was socially well connected; his membership of the Jesuit order had given him a good education, invaluable European contacts particularly in France, and an excellent knowledge of political techniques. Petre seems to have possessed endless self-confidence, but he certainly had an aptitude for politics. Nothing is more revealing than the way in which Sunderland, who had originally sponsored him, came to recognize Petre as a rival.[9]

If the Catholics were an unpopular minority, if they were so weak and ineffective, it may be asked what James hoped or expected to be able to do for them. He spoke frequently of his hopes and objectives, but what he said and meant varied considerably according to the status and faith of the person who recorded the conversation or received his letter. The word which he constantly used to describe his wishes was vague and ambiguous; *établir*, to establish. This has been interpreted as meaning the establishment of Catholicism as the official, or even as the only, religion. This interpretation goes against the evidence. James was well aware of the fact that he had only a

---

[8] Mazure, ii, 241–3; Campana de Cavelli, ii, 132; *State Trials*, xii, 597–614.
[9] Very little is known about Father Petre; in general see Hay, *Enigma of James II*, pp. 154–64.

relatively short time to live and reign before the succession of his Protestant daughters changed the whole situation. He was adamant in refusing to tamper with their rights of succession, even if superficially this would seem to offer immediate advantages for the Catholic religion; the succession was not only defined by constitutional law, it was also instituted and preserved by divine ordinance. In one of his first interviews with Barrillon, James conceded the impracticability of any mass conversion of England in the foreseeable future, and in later discussions with him (and also with the Dutch ambassador) he repeatedly described his objective as that of putting the Catholics into such a state of security that they would certainly continue to enjoy toleration and civil liberties under his Protestant successors.[10]

In public James declared his wish that his subjects would voluntarily embrace Catholicism, but until his wife's pregnancy at the end of 1687 he realized that he himself could hope to achieve little beyond ensuring at least the survival of his religion. With the birth of a healthy male heir the possibilities immediately widened. Louis very significantly described the birth as making possible and practicable 'l'entier établissement' of Catholicism in Britain, meaning by this ultimately, in the long-term future.[11] This is proved by the use of the same words by Bossuet in 1693, when he was consulted on the legitimacy of the exiled James giving a guarantee to the Church of England in a proposed Declaration. Bossuet advised James to do so, since without his restoration nothing could be done to advance the interests of religion, but if he was restored there would then be a prospect of the entire re-establishment of Catholicism at some time in the future under his successors.[12] In a sense James was like King David, who prepared the way but would never see God's Temple built. His hopes and prayers were for long-term conversion, not the kind of immediate, spectacular results that Louis had recently achieved in France. With his genuine belief that there was no salvation outside the Catholic faith, and his

[10] Baschet; Barrillon, 5 March 1685; 24 April, 12 June, 9 October 1687; Bonrepos, 21 July 1687.
[11] Mazure, ii, 301.
[12] Oeuvres Complètes de Bossuet (1836), vii, 261–3.

certainty that God would intervene on its behalf, James was confident that he was initiating a movement that would lead, in the fullness of time, to the elimination of heresy throughout Britain.

By giving the Catholics equality with the Anglicans James hoped to create conditions in which the truth would have the chance of prevailing. From his accession the penal laws were not enforced against them, but priests were instructed to behave discreetly, avoiding open controversy and recrimination.[13] This line of calculated moderation continued until February 1686, giving time for the Church to mobilize its resources for a major missionary effort. This operated on the assumption that there were many individuals and groups already sympathetic to Catholicism who could now be induced to become full and open converts, and that there were large sections of the community, unacquainted with its doctrines and practices, to whom the Catholic message would come as a revelation.

James personally played a leading part in the missionary work, trying to invigorate his coreligionists into taking full advantage of the new situation. He placed particular reliance on the use of personal pressure at court and on the systematic use of his patronage powers. By making it clear that converts would be rewarded he hoped that many would follow the example of Sir Edward Hales, who was given a dispensation to enable him to retain his colonelcy after being converted; he was later given promotion and other appointments. Patronage could be used to encourage waverers and actually purchase worldly converts; James told Barrillon that its persuasive powers were likely to be greater than all the arguments of the priests.[14] From a strictly religious point of view it might be thought that such mercenary and opportunistic converts were not worth having, but it must be remembered that they were needed for what were primarily political purposes, to serve in the administration. Opportunists and careerists, malleable and unscrupulous, were precisely what James needed urgently for his immediate purposes, whereas many of the genuine religious converts unfortunately

---

[13] Ranke, iv, 219–20, 282.
[14] Baschet; Barrillon, 16 July 1685.

wished only to retire from the world and all active business, so as to concentrate on saving their souls.[15]

The court offered the most immediately profitable area for Catholic missionary effort. Its cosmopolitan inhabitants did not usually share the vulgar and insular prejudices against Catholicism of the untravelled masses. Its modish immorality represented a rejection of conventional religion; Catholic controversialists echoed Puritan preachers of an earlier generation in holding up the laxity of the court as a reproach to the Anglican clergy, as evidence of their failure and lack of influence. But when cynics and libertines began to age, or find that death was near, there were Catholic priests available to give consolation and absolution to even the most profligate and irreligious, as the cases of Charles himself and James's first wife showed. The diplomacy and sympathy of Catholic priests at court, most of them from aristocratic or gentry families, their understanding use of the confessional which served as a psychological release from the tensions of competitive life at Whitehall, were infinitely more relevant than the routine denunciations of sin in Anglican sermons, or the occasional shamefaced evasion of moral responsibility by ambitious clerical seekers after promotion. Moreover, conversions of courtiers could have far-reaching consequences; prominent men might be followed by their families – in the wide seventeenth-century sense of dependants and servants as well as relations.[16]

Throughout 1686 and 1687 James maintained regular personal pressure on all courtiers and officials who were in close daily contact with him. He arranged, and attended, confrontations between rival pairs of divines for the benefit of leading prospective converts. He attended mass in full state, both at Whitehall (where the elaborate baroque chapel was decorated by Grinling Gibbons) and during his provincial progresses. The spectacular and elaborate liturgies at court made an aesthetic appeal that contrasted with the generally plain and sometimes bleak services of the Anglican Church. The simpler celebrations of mass in provincial cities (sometimes in their cathedrals) had

[15] Dodd, *Church History*, pp. 451, 452–3.
[16] Burnet, iii, 240.

a different purpose – to dissipate, or at least diminish, the prejudices of Protestants, to demonstrate to them that there was nothing objectionable or repellent in Catholic forms of worship.[17]

The key targets for conversion belonged to James's own
family. He repeatedly urged his brother-in-law Rochester to give
serious consideration to the thought of conversion. Rochester
felt that he could not reply with an outright refusal, since this
would endanger his position as lord treasurer. By his temporiz-
ing he gave James false hopes, and also weakened his own
reputation as a champion of Anglican interests. It is possible
that he was undecided for a time, but in the last resort he
could not afford to cut himself off from his Anglican connections
and followers, who had made it plain that they did not intend
to become converts.[18] In addition, conversion would certainly
have adversely affected his relations with William and Mary,
making it impossible for him to organize and lead a reversionary
interest on their behalf, and he knew that under her husband's
influence Mary would remain a Protestant. James did attempt
her conversion from a distance, writing frequently, recommend-
ing the example of her mother, sending her books and despatch-
ing a Jesuit to the Hague for her instruction.[19] Although Mary
conclusively rejected all these advances she was, in the long run,
a less important target for conversion than her younger sister,
Anne. Mary had no children, was out of reach, and accepted
domination by her husband to whom even James did not
suggest conversion. Anne, although a victim of repeated mis-
carriages and despite the death of babies, could have heirs. She
was accessible to personal persuasion by her father and dominated her easygoing and not very intelligent husband. Already
in the first weeks of the reign Louis had emphasized how much
depended on her conversion, and in 1686 James, Barrillon and the
Pope, all on separate occasions expressed the view that permanent
advantages for Catholicism depended on her becoming a
Catholic.[20] James brought intense pressure to bear on his

---

[17] Baschet; Barrillon, 16, 20 September 1687.
[18] Mazure, ii, 179–80.
[19] Baschet; Barrillon, 26 January 1688; Tanner MSS, 29, ff. 130–32; Burnet, iii,
196–8, 199–202; J. Gutch, *Collectanea Curiosa* (1781), i, 302–6.
[20] Baschet; Barrillon, 27 June 1686, 3 April 1687; Bonrepos, 3 April 1687.

daughter, but met his match in her obstinacy. Significantly she chose as spiritual advisers precisely those Anglican clergy who were least acceptable to James, receiving guidance from Compton (who was also corresponding with Mary), who had been her tutor, and from Sharp, who was to remain her chief clerical confidant for over twenty years. Anne never wavered in her faith, but made effective demonstration of her constant attachment to Anglicanism by regular attendance at church services, in transparent *incognita*; it was from this period of her personal ordeal, during which she was sustained by the prayers of the Church, that the fervent loyalty of the Church of England of the 1700s originated.[21]

James's expectation that many prominent Anglican clergy, particularly High Church (and celibate) bishops, would become converts was also disappointed.[22] In the face of an open challenge the various parties closed their ranks. On the other hand, it is clear that it was James's personal energy, determination and optimism that stimulated and infused the whole Catholic missionary effort. With the queen he acted as a generous patron to Catholic schools and charities, and assisted the religious orders to open houses in London.[23] He was in every way the real leader and inspirer, on whom personally the impetus of the campaign for the conversion of England largely depended.

Considering the extensive experience that they had of missionary work to the heathen (which Anglicans could not equal at this time), the Catholic clergy were surprisingly ineffective. Their chapels catered primarily for existing believers; in London there was substantial over-provision. With the exception of Philip Ellis, no Catholic priest acquired such a reputation as a preacher as to attract curious congregations to fill them and so expose themselves to Catholic arguments. This was important, since the pulpit was still the most immediately effective medium for influencing mass opinion, and in the view of contemporaries Catholic priests were unsuccessful as preachers, particularly in

[21] Baschet; Barrillon, 3 April, 23 September 1687; D. Green, *Queen Anne* (1970), pp. 40–41.

[22] Mazure, i, 415.

[23] Clarke, *James the Second*, ii, 79–80; Campana de Cavelli, ii, 159, 185; Luttrell, i, 426–7; Gutch, *Collectanea Curiosa*, i, 326–8.

comparison with their liveliest competitors, the younger generation of Latitudinarian clergy. In many cases congregations found
the actual English of newly arrived priests defective, or even
incomprehensible, after long years in exile.[24]

In general, Catholic priests, and the four bishops commissioned in January 1688, could exercise adequate pastoral care,
especially in catechizing and confirming, and in ministering to
scattered congregations, but this work benefited existing
believers. Charitable provisions were sufficient for the recusant
poor, but there was no surplus to set up a fund for the purchase
of conversions on a large scale, or to support converts who might
suffer economically because of their choice of faith, as had been
done for decades in France. With the exception of the Jesuits,
the religious orders contributed little constructive. Their insistence on appearing publicly in their habits irritated Protestants,
inflaming old but strongly held prejudices. Their educational
and charitable work, and their attempts to encourage recruits,
were easily misrepresented in emotive ways, as child-stealing, the
enticement of young women, and the badgering of the sick and
dying.[25] For those of more elevated social station their appearance aroused fears that the monastic lands appropriated by
Henry VIII would have to be restored. A more serious threat was
posed by newly opened Catholic schools, especially those run by
the Jesuits, but they were denied the necessary time to make any
significant impact. These schools were open to Protestant children and were likely to prove to be extremely competitive, given
the excellent and enlightened educational techniques of the
Jesuits and the deplorable and stagnant state of many contemporary grammar schools. A testimony to their likely effectiveness
can be seen in the establishment of new Anglican charity
schools specifically to compete with them, and in the reform of
some of the older foundations.[26]

Publishing was easily the most valuable of the new freedoms
that James conferred on the Catholics. It had a much wider
range of influence than any other form of activity, having the

[24] Addit., 34512, f. 65.
[25] Addit., 34510, f. 55; Lingard, *History*, x, 220; Luttrell, i, 426.
[26] Luttrell, i, 424, 437; Addit., 34510, f. 115.

capacity to reach those who either could, or would, not enter chapels or come into contact with priests. Pamphlets, books, broadsheets, tracts and devotional manuals were published in very large quantities, and many of them were distributed free. These publications, intended for a popular readership, were designedly simple in style and presentation and direct in argument, often concentrating on getting over one or two leading ideas. Many were effective because of their brevity – for instance a translation of Bossuet's *Exposition* provided an admirably concise statement of Catholic doctrine in only forty-three pages – which was a sharp contrast with the often verbose and turgid works of the older generation of Anglican controversialists. Of course more substantial and learned works were also published, aimed at the clergy and the educated laity who could be assumed to have some familiarity with theological, intellectual and philosophical problems. Much of this literature, and the Anglican replies which it provoked, appear to be repetitious and derivative, adding little or nothing to the concepts and arguments produced by earlier generations of controversialists. Nevertheless they aroused great interest among contemporaries, and each major pamphlet was followed by refutations and reaffirmations, all eagerly bought by an expectant public. The religious controversy of 1686–8, like the pamphlet debate between Whig and Tory during the Exclusion Crisis, concentrated on issues of immediate polemical purpose, and can be appreciated and evaluated only if seen in that context.[27]

James personally assisted. His official printer, Henry Hills, produced a high proportion of the pamphlets which in this way seemed to have royal authority. James authorized publication of the essays found in Charles's cabinet, placing an exaggerated reliance on their persuasiveness.[28] Unlike James himself, most Catholic controversialists fully realized the formidable obstacle which the strength and extent of anti-Catholic feeling provided among the general public. Their main tactic was to turn this prejudice to advantage. It derived from what they regarded as decades of deliberate and malicious, deceitful and

[27] Tanner MSS, 30 f. 143; Baschet; Barrillon, 25 March 1686.
[28] *Copies of Two Papers written by the late King Charles II and one by the Duchess of York.*

emotional misrepresentation of Catholic doctrines, principles and practices by the Anglican clergy. This had produced literally *blind* prejudice throughout the nation. Their technical problem, therefore, was how to open the eyes of the people to the truth. The answer was that plain exposition (the word was constantly used by Bossuet) of the truth would be more efficacious than the old and largely futile reliance on fulminating denunciations of Protestant errors. In place of acrimonious polemics, now out of keeping with the official atmosphere of toleration which James was establishing, calm vindications were favoured. If readers could be brought to see that their Anglican mentors had deliberately deceived them, then they would become receptive to Catholic statements on the true faith.[29]

In this general approach, and in many of the detailed arguments contained in the works of Catholic apologists, one can detect the influence of Bossuet, the intellectually most powerful and persuasive of all contemporary Catholic thinkers and writers. His theses, formulated in his *Exposition de la doctrine de l'église catholique* (1671), and to be further developed in the *Histoire des variations des églises protestantes* (1688), stressed the infallibility, universality and unchanging nature of the true Church. Following him, Catholic apologists pointed to the glaring contrast between the confident claim of their Church to be the repository of infallible, divinely given authority, and the weak and anomalous basis of the Church of England. Anglicans were subject to the secular government and depended for doctrinal definition and decision, and liturgical forms, on royal initiatives and parliamentary statutes – an objection which was to play an important role in the conversion of many eminent Victorians 150 years later. Furthermore, Catholics contrasted the worldwide strength and intense missionary effort of their Church with the self-centred and provincial introspection and isolation of the Anglicans, confined to 'this one little kingdom of England'.[30] Bossuet's principal thesis was in some respects relevant to the situation in Britain. He drew a contrast between

---

[29] See *A Papist Misrepresented, and Represented* (1685). A *Second Part* was published by Henry Hills in 1686. See also *Papists protesting against Protestant-Popery* (1686).
[30] *A Papist Misrepresented*, p. 106.

the inherent constancy of the Catholic Church and doctrine
and the equally inherent divisions and splits of the Protestant
Churches, with their perpetually changing doctrinal positions
and ritual practices. This argument should be set in its context
to appreciate its potential strength; in the seventeenth century
there was no theory of progressive change, of development, still
less of evolution. The claim that the Catholic faith had never
altered, and never would, made a strong appeal to the intellectual assumptions of the time. Protestantism was represented as
something new, and therefore suspect; pamphleteers frequently
asked, 'Where was your Church before Luther?' Similarly, in
an age that assumed that religious truth was absolute, the asser-
tions of total and eternal Catholic unity were intended to be
socially as well as theologically persuasive. Some historians have
described this period as the age of the baroque, interpreting the
contemporary emphasis on form and order in art and thought
as a reflection of the social attitudes of concern for the maintenance of control and regulation of the ever-dangerous forces of
anarchy and disorder. Catholic apologists in Britain, as in
Europe, claimed that religious unity in the true faith was a
precondition for all social and political order and stability. Of
course, Anglicans made the same claim for their own Church,
and ever since the collapse of the old order during the interregnum had laid great emphasis on the principles of non-
resistance and passive obedience in inculcating obedience and
submission to divinely instituted authority. Catholic propagandists refuted these Anglican claims that the Church of England
could form an effective basis for order and stability. First, prag-
matically, it had not done so in practice; as James said in his
Declaration, the laws enacted since 1558 had not produced unity
or internal peace. This failure was represented as theoretically
inevitable. The Church of England was spurious; this was proved
by its internal divisions which generated political factionalism.
Moreover, these divisions were inevitable and irreparable –
Anglicans could have no conclusively convincing answer to
give to those who used against them the same arguments and
pretensions that had been used to justify the original schism

from Rome.[31] According to this Catholic argument, Protestantism must founder in total moral licence and intellectual anarchy, because it had to allow the validity of individual, private judgement. Without the guidance of an infallible Church the Scriptures could afford no sure revelation of God's will; Protestantism could offer only private reason, 'which when put to the Test, proves in Thousands and Thousands to be nothing better than Passion, Prejudice, Interest, Imagination, Guessing or Fancy'. The proliferation of sects, the recurrence of all the heresies of the patristic age, the bewilderment and uncertainty of the people, their restlessness due to their lack of authoritative guidance, and the dangerous excesses of enthusiasts were all evils inseparable from Protestantism.[32]

Such arguments all strongly reflect Bossuet's influence, and indeed the Catholicism of James's reign in England and Scotland (though not in Ireland) was decidedly Gallican in character. Its spearhead elements – the Jesuits in general and Father Petre in particular – were closely connected with the French Church. Ordinarily this might have been an advantage, since the Gallican privileges which were being so strongly advocated and defended at this time in France could be suggested as a model for an autonomous Catholic Church in England, which could confine its recognition of the Pope to strictly spiritual matters. But at a time when the Huguenots were suffering so severely, all connections with French Catholicism were highly damaging – in fact it would be true to say that the Revocation in itself doomed to failure the whole Catholic endeavour for the conversion of England.

Despite its eventual and total failure, which became obvious well before the actual Revolution, contemporaries for some time regarded the Catholic effort as a very real danger to Protestantism. As always, courtiers and clergy were thought to be the most vulnerable; the former because the Stuart court had always provided a milieu sympathetic to Catholicism, the latter because some of them had to familiarize themselves with

---

[31] Burnet, iii, 198.
[32] *A Papist Misrepresented*; *Second Part*, p. 58.

Catholic dogma in order to be able to refute it. This process could lead individual clergy into critical examination of their own beliefs, realization of inconsistencies and weaknesses, and so ultimately to acceptance of Catholic claims. Militant Protestants and Low churchmen feared that many High Church clergy would be attracted by the power and prestige of the Catholic clergy, which they could share if they were eligible, as celibates, for ordination after conversion. Other groups which promised converts were army officers (many of whom had served in France), the urban poor, who could be bought by charitable relief (as had happened in the reverse direction in early seventeenth-century Dutch cities), and those who would now be called intellectuals – poets, dramatists, journalists, doctors and schoolmasters.

The number of converts during the years 1686–8 does not seem to have been very much larger than in normal times, and a high proportion of those who did become Catholics were opportunists who did so primarily to advance their own careers and prospects. Contemporaries, like later historians, condemned such converts as morally contemptible, but unlike Whig historians such as Macaulay they recognized the damage that such 'political Catholics' could do. They knew that in France most of the Huguenot nobility had abjured for social and worldly reasons long before the Revocation, and by doing so had left their coreligionists exposed.[33] Bourgeois, artisans and peasants could not on their own defend themselves indefinitely against local pressure and legal chicanery on the part of *intendants* and clergy, and they had few friends to represent their case at court, when Louis himself became committed to an active campaign of persecution. Insincere converts, driven by ambition and free from scruples, were likely to prove energetic and ruthless royal instruments.

Conversion gave a few men the opportunity to rise to positions of real influence and importance, which they might otherwise have failed to reach. The best example is Sir Nicholas Butler, a former dissenter. He became a Catholic specifically so as to recover the post of customs commissioner which he had just

[33] The conversion of Marshal Turenne, in particular, had created a sensation.

lost. Subsequently, by an assumed zeal for his new religion, an aggressive and thrusting personality, and immense industry, he acquired considerable political influence and an outlet for his ambition and undoubted ability. He became a privy councillor, and a minister of the second rank with the possibility of rising higher. In normal English life such a career would have been unusual, but such men were common in the absolutist governments of Europe.[34] Under James, religious conversion was the prerequisite for such success, and there was an obvious danger of imitation. Contemporaries feared that if a few such men showed the way, then there would be a landslide of further insincere conversions. To use modern terminology, there was reason for Protestants to be apprehensive that the Catholic campaign at court and among officials might easily take off and become self-sustaining. If a significant section of office-holders became Catholics, then all their colleagues would find themselves under irresistible pressure. The administration could be used to harass or even subvert Protestant rights and interests, as in contemporary France and Hungary or in Bohemia in the first quarter of the century.

James opened the way for the conversion of officials in 1686 when, having already issued block dispensations to enable Catholics to hold offices, he consulted the judges. By a majority of 11–1 they upheld his right to do so, notwithstanding the Test Act, and in the collusive action of *Godden v Hales* confirmed the legality of the dispensing power. But Hales and Butler proved to be the only important official converts until Sunderland's conversion in 1688. Similarly, a number of conversions at the universities and among the clergy in 1686 did not initiate a trend.[35] The lack of converts prevented the Catholic missionary campaign from developing any real impetus. Opportunist converts felt vulnerable and exposed when so few followed their example. Those who were waiting to see how events would work out remained passive. Even when the prince's birth promised a perpetuation of James's policies, instead of the likelihood of

---

[34] Nottingham University Library, Phillipps MSS, 8555, iii, Blathwayt to Southwell, 20 December 1687; Luttrell, i, 400.

[35] *HMC, XIIth Report*, app. vi, 300–2, list of dispensations.

their reversal under Mary, Sunderland's example was not followed; his was a unique case in that he had particular and pressing reasons for conversion, and could rely on his complex insurance policies to extricate himself if things went badly.

The principal reason for the failure of the Catholics to reap any significant advantages from the freedoms which they now enjoyed, was that their open challenge was connected in the popular mind with the developments in France. It revitalized the Church of England, making the clergy realize that they were now on trial in an atmosphere of competition and tension. Above all, it persuaded most of them of the need for some degree of mutual charity and understanding with the Protestant dissenters. Catholics always made a point of contrasting the courage and steadfastness of their priests, as seen in such periods of active persecution as the Popish Plot, with the cases of laziness, indifference and immorality that were inevitable in the ranks of such a numerous and privileged class as the clergy of an established Church enjoying a legal monopoly. Now Anglican clergy became aware of the possibility that they in turn might have to give evidence of courage and fidelity, even to the point of martyrdom. Events in France made these fears very real. There can have been few people, even in remote areas, who were not given vivid pictures of the sufferings of the Huguenots in the sermons which were preached in every parish church throughout England, when congregations were being urged to give generously for the relief of Huguenot refugees. The well-authenticated and harrowing accounts of *dragonnades,* and the forcible separation of families, acquired a particularly sinister form when James expanded his army with Irish Catholic recruits, and when religious orders founded houses in English towns. In such an apparently threatening situation all James's disclaimers and professions of tolerance appeared to be disingenuous and unconvincing.[36]

In a situation of such danger most of the Anglican clergy seem to have made an attempt to respond to the injunctions issued by Archbishop Sancroft to live as examples to their

---

[36] Baschet; Barrillon, 4, 7 March 1686; Bonrepos, 26 January 1686.

flocks and to be assiduous in their duties.[37] There was general agreement that the younger generation of Anglican clergy had much the better of their Catholic rivals in controversies, a partisan verdict that clearly owed much to the current predisposition against the Catholics. But this is precisely the point; the onus of proof and conviction lay on the Catholics; they had formidable prejudices to overcome and so needed a clear margin of superiority if they were to have any impact. This they never looked like achieving, although their clergy were surprisingly numerous – perhaps in a proportion of as much as $1:12$, although overall there were only one or two Catholics in a hundred among the general population. The Catholic effort came fifty years too late. The intellectual climate, in the sense of the assumptions that were generally made and the modes of thought employed by most educated people, were steadily becoming less receptive to Catholicism.

In particular, the claim that Catholicism was inseparable from the maintenance of form and order was entirely unconvincing in the English context. So far from supporting the established order in society, constitution, morality and culture, Catholicism must as a preliminary subvert all existing forms which were based on error, in order to re-shape them according to its own principles. Catholic supremacy would have been entirely incompatible with the Erastianism that was the chief characteristic of every aspect of religion, from the control exercised by Parliament to that influence possessed by the patron of each parish. Its moral teachings, as well as its extensive and expensive clerical establishment would have hampered the increasingly important and self-reliant commercial and industrial classes for whom latitudinarian principles were particularly well suited. Connections with Catholic Europe, and the entry of foreign clerics, and still more of the hated and despised Irish, would arouse xenophobic passions. For the upper classes who had lived through the disruption of the old order during the interregnum there was a further objection. Ultimately Catholicism might promise to be a stabilizing factor in a more authoritarian scheme of life and thought, but this could only be achieved after a period

[37] Gutch, *Collectanea Curiosa*, i, 386–90.

of tension and crisis, of upheaval and unsettlement, that was all too likely to culminate in a new and destructive revolution, or a series of civil wars. One Anglican made the charge that this was the Catholic design, that they would welcome, or even bring about, a period of anarchy so as to bring down the existing order.[38]

On a less apocalyptic level it was argued that if Catholicism was merely inserted into the existing order, alongside the Church of England and the dissenters, this would mean the perpetuation of religious tension. Unlike the others, the Catholics could not in the long term be expected to agree to the principle of live and let live, they would never abandon their mission for the ultimate elimination of all forms of heresy. In the English context, Catholicism could never be a buttress of constitutional monarchy and law; for the conservative-minded the Anglican alternative was more familiar, intelligible and credible. In practice, it offered far more satisfactory security, despite its lack of any theological claim to infallible authority. For the less conservative, it was preferable because of its lack of infallible authority, and the Church of Rome was scornfully rejected because of its superstitiousness and irrationality.

Not all Anglicans shared the increasingly fashionable latitudinarian concern for reasonable religion. Quite the contrary. It would be facile to conclude that this was already the 'age of reason', and that the growing attractiveness of reasonable religion in itself ensured the failure of Catholicism. Although the latitudinarian group among the younger clergy was the most intellectually vigorous and formative influence within the Church of England, and was largely to determine its future character, the emphasis which they placed on reason and tolerance aroused the distrust of many traditionalists. Some, and notably the most celebrated of all converts of the time, John Dryden, were attracted to Catholicism by its attitude towards reason and its outright condemnation of the latitudinarians as being indistinguishable from deists. Dryden himself wrote: 'They who would prove religion by reason, do but weaken the cause

[38] J. Stillingfleet, *The Doctrines and Practices of the Church of Rome Truly Represented* (1686), pp. 73, 75.

they endeavour to support.' However, warmed by the controversy and seeking to undermine those who were proving to be the most effective champions of Anglicanism, many Catholic controversialists unwisely went much further. Their attacks developed into sceptical or pyrrhonist assaults on reason itself, even though this (as the Church recognized in the ban imposed on Richard Simon) was a potentially dangerous weapon to use, since it could be turned against Christianity and the possibility of any divine revelation.[39]

In practical terms, philosophical scepticism proved to be counter-productive. For some it identified Catholicism with a cynical acceptance of immorality or even irreligion as permissible if they might serve as solvent, destroying Protestant faith, so that some would then turn to the true faith. It helped to reinforce the widespread belief that Catholicism was irrational in its fundamental principles as well as in the superstitious practices of its more ignorant adherents. Latitudinarianism, with its emphasis on reason and concern for morality, was far more relevant to the mentality of the educated classes, making a far stronger appeal than either the authoritarian dogmas of Catholicism or the anti-intellectual tendencies still common among dissenters. Moreover, Anglican conservatives were largely insulated from the Catholic missionary approach; for them Papist arguments were irrelevant in face of the fact that the Church of England was the Catholic Church in England.

[39] See L. I. Bredvold, *The Intellectual Milieu of John Dryden* (1962).

FIVE *The Politics of Toleration*

J AMES'S FIRST RADICAL CHANGE of policy came at the end of 1686. During that year, by using his prerogative and patronage powers, he gave the Catholics full religious freedom and a share of offices. However, these gains could not be regarded as permanently secure unless the Test Acts and penal laws were repealed by statute, and all attempts to obtain Tory and Anglican concurrence had failed to produce significant results. Closeting had been counterproductive. Pressure through the Ecclesiastical Commission had not made the clergy more amenable. The Catholic missionary campaign was losing its impetus. This stalemate necessitated a major decision.

On the one hand, although James had provoked alarm and resentment among the Tories and Anglican clergy, a reconciliation would have been easy. But such a reconciliation would have meant James accepting terms that were virtually dictated to him by these traditional (but also conditional) allies of the crown, and for him this would have been tantamount to a surrender of royal independence. The Tests would remain. The Catholics would be assured of toleration during his lifetime, but would be utterly dependent on the goodwill of his successor and the Anglicans for its continuance afterwards. Furthermore, although this would not mean James making as dramatic and humiliating a surrender as that which Charles had made in 1673, when he abandoned the cabal and all its policies, his own power and influence as well as his prestige would inevitably be affected. As he aged, so his power would be eroded. Already Rochester was consciously preparing a reversionary interest, to use William and Mary's influence. This was why he could not afford to break with his associates by becoming a Catholic. Rochester was hoping to do a balancing act, to serve two masters, retaining influence with James while assuring its continuance under the next sovereign. His connection with William presented a further danger. Peace in western Europe was precarious. Should a general war break out, William would certainly try to involve Britain on the allied side. This would mean disaster for James. He would fall into total dependence on parliamentary grants of supply, and would have to abandon all independent royal initiatives in religious and domestic matters.

Only by a complete change of allies could James hope to remain a free agent able to continue to work for an increase in royal authority, and to place the Catholics in a fully satisfactory state of permanent security. The change of front came between November 1686 and April 1687. It entailed a sharp, and ultimately unbridgeable, break with James's former associates. Rochester was dismissed and most of his followers purged from their offices. At court this purge left the inner group of Catholic ministers, with Sunderland, in the ascendant. In the country as a whole the place of the Tories was filled by dissenters and former Whigs, old enemies whom James now proposed to transform into the instruments of royal policy and strength. The Declaration of Indulgence, on 4 April 1687, represented the formal bid for their cooperation.

The new departure was completed by the dissolution of Parliament on 2 July. This move showed that James had abandoned all hope of Tory support. It meant that a new Parliament would have to be elected to repeal the Tests and penal laws, and it was for the purpose of winning the elections that the alliance was made with the dissenters. From the first, James's policy of toleration was connected with electoral preparation, and the dissenters were soon to be involved in the campaign of manipulation, management and propaganda that was launched at the end of 1687, and was to continue until the month before William's invasion.

It is significant that virtually all the controversy and discussion created by James's policies of toleration centred on their political aspects and repercussions. At first some conservatives, especially older Anglican clergy, objected to the principle and practice of toleration itself, but their arguments met with little response. Practically all the laity welcomed the formal abandonment of any further attempt to enforce religious uniformity by coercive means, provided that the security of the Protestant religion could be assured. Toleration, which had formerly been a subject of violent controversy, was now accepted almost as a matter of course. Initially there were strong objections to Catholic worship being permitted in public, and arguments were produced that the dissenters were certain to abuse any liberties given them, but it is very rare to find pamphlets or even sermons attacking toleration on religious grounds.[1]

The attacks on James's policy of toleration were entirely political. As in 1672–3, they were concentrated on the prerogative methods by which toleration was being established, that is by the use of the suspending power, and on the hidden advantages which it was alleged that the Catholics were intended to gain. Specifically it was argued that Catholicism was incompatible with any lasting and genuine form of toleration, so that James's professions must be fraudulent. This concentration on the political aspects made the question of the Tests the central issue for all parties. For Anglicans these acts, passed in 1673 and 1678 to prevent any repetition of the cabal's policies, were indispensable safeguards against Catholic dominance.[2] For James their repeal was his first priority, a far more important task than the removal of the penal laws. He believed that the Test Acts had been the work of the politically factious who, on the pretence

---

[1] See, for example, the comments of a strongly Tory Anglican: Browning, *Memoirs of Reresby*, pp. 496–7.

[2] For the text: J. P. Kenyon, *The Stuart Constitution* (1966), pp. 461–2 (1673 Act barring Catholics from offices), 465–6 (1678 Act barring them from Parliament).

of defending Protestantism, had diminished the power of the crown by restricting the sovereign's choice of ministers and officers. Since he interpreted the Tests as an invasion of the prerogative, he could not accept the sincerity of anyone who argued that they were necessary to secure the Protestant religion.

Among those who took this view were William and Mary. In November 1686 James sent William Penn to try to persuade them to give their approval to the repeal of the Tests and the penal laws. If they had done so, James's last attempt at closeting would have been strengthened, and Rochester would have been disarmed of his objections. Penn found William and Mary ready only to promise non-enforcement of the penal laws, and not even their repeal; they were absolutely and irrevocably committed to retention of the Tests.[3] This could only strengthen the opposition to James's demands, and compelled him to seek a wider basis of support for both long- and short-term reasons. Mary's attitude held out the prospect of the Catholics losing most of their gains after her accession; they would not be strong enough by themselves to prevent a reversal of James's policies. By extending religious liberty, and granting full civil rights, to dissenters as well as to Catholics, a formidable alliance of interests would be created, strong enough in all probability to repulse any Anglican reaction under his successors.[4] In the immediate future this new alliance would enable James to dispense with Tory support. Parliament could be dissolved and a campaign launched to pack a new and reliably collaborationist Commons.

There was a clear connection between the institution of universal toleration and the lack of progress made by the Catholic missionary effort. There were insufficient Catholics to form the basis of the administration, so that James had no choice but to disregard the advice of his more extreme Catholic courtiers, who wanted to combine intensified pressure on the Anglicans with continued repression of the dissenters.[5] But universal toleration was a second best. James would have pre-

[3] Mazure, ii, 184; Burnet, iii, 140–41.
[4] Baschet; Barrillon, 16 April 1685, 24 April, 12 June, 9 October 1687; Bonrepos, 21 July 1687.
[5] D'Avaux, vi, 23; Baschet; Barrillon, 10 February 1687.

ferred to confine full religious freedom and civil rights to Catholics, Anglicans and some carefully selected and controlled groups of dissenters. This had been his attitude since the early 1670s; he had often intervened on behalf of individual dissenters and certain congregations, and he had never made any secret of his consistent dislike of the Anglican reliance on legal coercion to enforce religious uniformity.[6]

This attitude had never made more than a minor impression. Opposition and Whig propaganda had fixed in the public mind the image of James as the cruel and implacable Papist who would do anything, from commissioning the murder of his brother to re-lighting the fires of Smithfield, in order to re-establish his religion and extirpate all varieties of Protestantism. Nearly all the dissenters had preferred to follow Shaftesbury and the first Whigs, and paid for their support of Exclusion with the severe persecutions of 1681–4. In revenge the west country dissenters, with the exception of the Quakers, rallied to Monmouth in 1685. Only after yet another savage period of repression did any significant number of dissenters belatedly begin to consider the alternative option, which had been available to them for years.

James's offers of protection to dissenting groups had always been strictly conditional. First, the onus was on dissenters to approach him. Secondly, the dissenters must renounce the 'country' or Whig line of trying to obtain toleration by exerting systematic pressure on the crown. In return for protection they must promise loyalty and abstain from independent political activity. No popular agitation was to be attempted. In short, they must be entirely passive and place their trust in James's good faith, which was not such an easy thing to do in view of the prevalent notions of the faithlessness and unscrupulousness of Catholicism. But there had always been a small minority ready to accept these terms, and James never entirely lost touch with representatives of a section of the dissenters. In 1675 and 1678 a group of 'country' peers and MPs led by Lord Holles (who died in 1680) worked with him, and later, during Charles's

[6] For one example, *HMC, Portland*, iii, 348–9; Baschet; Barrillon, 10 February 1687.

last years, William Penn (the Quaker) and Sir John Baber, a Presbyterian, had acted as intermediaries. The Anglican bishops felt uneasy at their activities, but it was only at the end of 1685 that Penn's propaganda and canvassing began to evoke any kind of response in the country.[7]

Penn's efforts were strongly reinforced by James's first official moves. In April 1686 he issued circular letters to the JPS giving the Quakers effective protection from the penal laws.[8] Other dissenting bodies did not miss the significance of this, many petitioning James for similar relief, but he was not ready yet to commit himself officially. Tories and Anglican clergy watched this revival of activity on the part of the dissenters with some disquiet, but most of them were deterred from attempting to suppress it by uncertainty as to James's reaction.[9] In July dissenting expectations were raised by the grant of a large number of pardons and remissions of fines, but these covered past offences and did not commit James for the future. They were open to the interpretation of warning the Tories that if they persisted with their refusals to collaborate, James had other friends to whom he could turn. Penn organized addresses of thanks, and other dissenting bodies presented petitions, all of which could be seen as indications of the readiness and strength of the dissenters as allies of the crown.[10]

During the last months of 1686 James accompanied a last intensive effort to secure Tory and Anglican cooperation with moves designed to prepare the way for a switch of alliances should this effort fail. Vacant bishoprics were filled with clergy whose qualification was that they had publicly upheld the royal prerogative, a clear invitation for others to recommend themselves by similar statements.[11] In October the Commission of the peace was purged; many of the 257 removed, who

[7] *A Letter to Mr Penn, with his Answer* (1688); D. R. Lacey, *Dissent and Parliamentary Politics in England* (1969), pp. 95–7, 175–84.

[8] *HMC, Downshire*, I, i, 79, 95, 139; Addit., 34508, f. 110; W. C. Braithwaite, *The Second Period of Quakerism* (1961), p. 125.

[9] Tanner MSS, 30, ff. 31–2.

[10] Baschet; Barrillon, 8 July 1686; Lacey, *Dissent and Parliamentary Politics*, pp. 177–9

[11] Samuel Parker, appointed to Oxford, and Thomas Cartwright, to Chester. Their appointments were badly received; *HMC, VIIth Report*, app. i, 500.

included twenty-three MPS and two prominent clergymen in Tillotson and Sharp, were associates of Rochester. Their replacements
included many Catholics, but as yet no dissenters.[12] In November
James ordered a general investigation of the methods which had
been used in prosecutions of Catholics and dissenters. Initially this
was directed principally against informers, for whom few people
would feel any pity, and drew attention to the loathsome tactics
which they had often used, but obviously it could be extended to
cover magistrates and clergy who had employed these men and
profited from their scandalous and often illegal proceedings.[13]

James's closeting depended for success on the decision which
Rochester could not indefinitely postpone. He had been retained
as minister because of his fiscal services, but during 1686 he
was increasingly bypassed on general political matters and,
very significantly, on questions of ecclesiastical patronage. In
the end he reluctantly, but finally, refused to abjure his Anglicanism, which meant that all his associates would be confirmed in
their faith. In January 1687 he and his brother the second Earl
of Clarendon were dismissed, and James for the first time openly
turned towards the dissenters.[14] By February dissenting worship
was being held in public throughout London, and James was
openly promising an early grant of general toleration.

The first Declaration of Indulgence, issued on 4 April 1687,
and incorporated as a whole in the second Declaration of April
1688, was far more than a recapitulation of Charles II's
Declaration of 1672. Its basic thesis was the same : the need to
abandon coercion because it had not only failed to achieve its
objective of religious uniformity, but had actually perpetuated
and increased political disaffection, and inflicted serious economic
damage on the nation. James worded his Declaration in such
a way as to make it clear that this time toleration would be a
permanent feature of the constitution. This was essential if
dissenters, who remembered Charles's abandonment of toleration in 1673, were to trust him. James quoted as evidence for the

[12] PRO, PC 2, 71, ff. 325, 363–79.
[13] Luttrell, i, 387, 429; *HMC, IXth Report*, app. ii, 398; *Public Occurrences Truly
Stated*, 1. In practice the commissioners did not function until early in 1688.
[14] Baschet; Barrillon, 2, 13 January 1687.

failure of coercion not only the tensions of the past few years, but the whole experience of the nation during the last *four* reigns, that is ever since the Elizabethan settlement. He also made a point of emphasizing his intention of seeking parliamentary approval for toleration and tried to vindicate his sincerity by plain speaking, openly referring to his own Catholicism. But he did not attempt an elaborate justification of his use of the powers of the prerogative in suspending the Tests and the penal laws.

This prerogative power had been challenged by the Cavalier Parliament in 1673, and it was to be declared illegal in the Bill of Rights, the classic Whig statute of 1689, as a direct threat to the constitution. But in many ways the 1687 Declaration was a Whiggish document.[15] This is not really surprising. It was aimed at convincing those who had formerly supported Shaftesbury. Its assumptions, language and arguments, and those of the pamphlets which appeared in its support, were all Whig, and many of these pamphlets were written by former Whig journalists like Henry Care. First, while carefully and explicitly saying that God's will was the basis of his authority, James recognized the fact that he could no longer rely on universal acceptance of this divine ordinance by his subjects. They must be constructively united with their ruler 'by inclination as well as duty'. Interest must reinforce obedience. Indeed in seeking to make his rule and policies acceptable, James was going so far as to put enjoyment of property on an equal place with religion. His emphasis on the economic benefits of toleration, an old argument of the country opposition and the Whigs, was repeated and expanded by his journalist collaborators. His promises of wealth and prosperity, as well as peace and security, were designed to win not just passive acquiescence in his policies, but to enlist active support for the campaign to obtain a Parliament which would give these policies statutory form.

Since this propaganda was aimed primarily at dissenters and their sympathizers, James could not be too concerned at unfavourable reactions from Tories and Anglicans. These were predictable. However, a comparison of the security which he

[15] The text is most accessible in Kenyon, *The Stuart Constitution*, pp. 410–13.

offered to the Church of England in the 1687 Declaration with Charles's assurances in the Declaration of 1672, shows that Anglicans had very real cause for alarm and suspicion. Charles expressly confirmed the privileges of the Church of England as a corporate body, but in contrast James offered assurance only to Anglicans as individuals. This was open to interpretation as giving no more than a life interest to current occupants of ecclesiastical offices, with nothing to prevent the Church being transformed piece by piece into a branch of the Church of Rome.[16] Some royal moves tended to confirm this fear. Vacant bishoprics, deaneries and other key appointments were deliberately left unfilled. By this means James supplemented his income, and had inducements for new collaborators. His conduct in Ireland increased these suspicions; there the revenues derived from a steadily increasing number of vacant ecclesiastical offices were being transferred to a fund for the maintenance of the Catholic clergy.[17] In addition, by issuing dispensations to enable converts to retain their benefices or university fellowships he seemed to be planning another way of subverting the Church by gradual erosion of its position.[18]

Early in 1687 wild rumours spread about James's future intentions, but there were no disorders. A period of uncertainty and unpopularity was politically predictable and acceptable. James's prerogative powers, his effective control over central and local administration, and his possession of a strong and efficient army, were now sufficient to enable him to reconcile with ease and assurance the principles and practice of toleration with the maintenance of perfect public order. There was no danger of his losing control. He was confident that he would not, like his father in 1637–42, find religious divisions producing political factionalism and rebellion. Dissenters, after their experiences in the recent past, would not dare to abuse their new freedoms. In an un-

[16] The reason was that by guaranteeing the Church as such, James would be recognising what for him was a false Church. See G. H. Jones, *The Main Stream of Jacobitism*, p. 26, and *Oeuvres Complètes de Bossuet*, vii, 261–3, for post-Revolutionary discussion of this subject by James.

[17] *Parliamentum Pacificum*, p. 49; J. Hogan (ed.), *Négociations de M. d'Avaux en Irlande* (1934), pp. 57–8; J. G. Simms, *Jacobite Ireland* (1969), pp. 28, 42.

[18] *HMC, XIIth Report*, app, vi, 300–1.

expected way James's actions confirmed the fears expressed in the 1660s and 1670s by Anglican MPs, that toleration would necessitate a standing army.[19] But James discounted Tory and Anglican resentment in 1687. They would be inhibited from any form of dangerous opposition by their adherence to the often and vociferously expressed doctrines of non-resistance and passive obedience. The lack of numerous Anglican collaborators did not dismay or check James. He would be content if Anglicans remained passive while his policies enlisted active support from the dissenters.

One major question remains before James's policies become entirely explicable. What advantage did he think that he would obtain from an alliance with the dissenters, which might involve alienating the far more numerous Anglicans? According to contemporary belief, the Anglicans constituted the vast majority of the nation; an episcopal census of 1676 produced figures of 2,477,254 Anglicans to 108,676 dissenters and 13,856 Catholics.[20] Although this census certainly exaggerated Anglican predominance, yet it seems incredible that James should risk antagonizing such a large majority by allying with such a small section. His statements to Barrillon, that the sects were stronger than the established Church, would seem to be even stranger, although this view was shared by Penn, co-architect of the Declaration.[21] How can this be explained? The answer is that James and Penn thought that the dissenters were *potentially*, rather than *actually*, the more powerful. They interpreted the stubborn insistence of the Anglican clergy on continued repression as revealing evidence of weakness. Penn believed that if they lost their coercive powers the Anglicans would fail in competition with the dissenters. James expected a substantial part of the laity to desert under conditions of religious freedom, so that there might be a repetition of the collapse of the Church in the 1650s. The sects would expand. Sympathizers previously deterred by the penal laws would now openly adhere, and the

[19] Grey, i, 110.
[20] A. Browning (ed.), *English Historical Documents*, viii, 413–6.
[21] Baschet; Barrillon, 17, 31 March, 29 May 1687; *Animadversions on a. . .Letter to a Dissenter* (1687), p. 34.

dissenting Churches would proselytise energetically and successfully.

Toleration was certainly designed to weaken the Church of
England. For James it also had the wider objective of bringing
into existence conditions in which the appeal of Catholicism
would be enhanced and the flagging Catholic missionary
campaign revived. Toleration would lead to the multiplication
of the number of sects, by allowing the free operation of the
same inherent tendencies that had caused the divisions and
disputes of the interregnum. Once the pressure exerted by persecution ceased there would be no force making for unity and
harmony. Moreover, many of the smaller sects could be expected
to hold and propagate extreme and scandalous opinions and
practices. A state of licence would dismay conservatives and
discredit Protestantism itself, supporting Bossuet's theses that
division and demoralization were its inevitable consequences, and
underlining Catholic arguments that morality, order and truth
could not flourish outside the true Church.

In the outcome these forecasts, based on the experience of the
1650s, were not confirmed. Since then the character of dissent
had undergone fundamental changes. Years of repression had
turned most congregations into tight-knit, introspective bodies,
whose members were primarily concerned with mutual support
and aid. Dissenting life was now centred on isolated and small
communities, with necessarily narrow mental horizons. Nearly
all ministers had had to devote much of their energies – physical
and intellectual – to enduring persecution and pressure, and in
any case the men ejected in 1662 were a rapidly aging group,
whose successors were not only fewer in number but were
markedly less well educated, partly because of their exclusion
from the universities. These changes meant that, although
grateful for the relief that toleration brought, the dissenters did
not proselytise on a large scale, or attract such large numbers
of new adherents as to shake the established Church. Unlike
the intransigent and militantly active Scottish Presbyterians the
English dissenters were not determined to reimpose their beliefs
on the nation, or substitute their own forms of ecclesiastical
government for those restored after 1660. Although many dissen-

ters worked with James, especially in his campaign to pack Parliament, and Penn emerged as a national figure, they proved to be less useful than James had hoped when he initiated his policy of toleration.

James's first Declaration inaugurated an intense and closely followed pamphlet debate that lasted over two years, until the passing of the Toleration Act by the Convention Parliament in 1689. The preponderantly political complexion of the debate meant that few writers attempted to develop positive intellectual or theological arguments for or against toleration, but rather concentrated on the methods which James was using to introduce toleration, and the likely political and economic repercussions. As a result, the bulk of the literature produced during this controversy was polemical and ephemeral. Despite the wide interest which it aroused, and the fundamental importance of the issues that were at stake, only two pamphlets have escaped oblivion; the Earl of Halifax's *A Letter to a Dissenter* (1687) and John Locke's *A Letter concerning Toleration* (1689).[22] Perhaps their survival is justified, not only because their writers were on the 'right' side (that is, the one that triumphed), but because of their superior literary merits. However, it is also necessary to examine the arguments contained in pamphlets published on the other side, if James's purposes (and the reasons for his failure) are to be understood rather than caricatured.

Two preliminary points require attention. By issuing and enforcing the Declaration, James made toleration a *fait accompli*, forcing the Anglicans to respond to his appeal to the dissenters with promises that had to be honoured after the Revolution.[23] Effective religious toleration dates from 1687, not from the statute of 1689, which abridged the freedoms James had granted. But it must be remembered that for him toleration was only a means, not the ultimate objective. James's aim was political, repeal of the Test Acts, with repeal of the penal laws as an essen-

[22] The most accessible modern editions are: J. P. Kenyon, *Halifax, Complete Works* (Penguin, 1969), and John Locke, *A Letter Concerning Toleration* (Library of Liberal Arts, 1955).
[23] Addit., 34487, f. 11; Luttrell, i, 452.

tially subsidiary objective. Secondly, it should be noted that James's propaganda was whiggish in language and style, employing concepts and arguments that were entirely different from the principles of divine right traditionally enunciated by royal apologists and political writers.

The collaborationist journalists should not be dismissed as a group of renegades, or hacks writing for money. They were putting forward a far more plausible, attractive and rational line of argument than most historians have supposed, arguing from their eventual failure, and the collapse of their patron's position in 1688. Most contemporaries recognized it as a variation on familiar Puritan, opposition and Whig themes. The journalists claimed that religious coercion actually generated disaffection, driving dissenters to desperate disloyalty, and perpetuated tension and disunity. They repeated charges against the Anglican clergy that had been made ever since Elizabeth's reign by Puritan critics, that those who favoured coercion were often debauched men, or power addicts, or inadequate pastors and halting preachers afraid of competition. One writer commented that if the Church of England 'can no more whip People into her churches, she may perhaps modestly suspect her own virtue and ability to preach them thither'.[24] It was commonly alleged that the higher clergy were interested solely in retaining the power, privileges and income that their offices brought them. Much was made of the unscrupulous methods allegedly used by the clergy in maintaining themselves on an unwilling people : encouraging angry justices to execute the laws harshly, rigid and heartless insistence on payment of tithe and dues, excessive employment of the expensive ecclesiastical courts, and the use of informers, 'the scum of the People', 'the Pest of every Nation'.[25]

Opposition pamphleteers accused James's journalists of having abandoned their former Whig principles for money and royal favour. They replied by claiming consistency in supporting the principle of toleration and in following anyone who seriously

[24] *A Letter from a Gentleman in the Country to his Friends in London* (1687), p. 6.
[25] *A Letter from a Gentleman in the City. . . about the Odiousness of Persecution* (1687), pp. 3–4.

and sincerely attempted its introduction, and counterattacked by demonstrating the insincerity and inconsistency of Anglican clergy, whose effusive loyalty during the years of the Stuart reaction, when they had unreservedly stated their eternal attachment to the doctrines of divine right, contrasted sharply with the criticisms they were now making when James apparently threatened their privileges and monopoly.[26] The old charge made by the dissenters and Whigs, that the bishops had deliberately sabotaged Charles II's Declaration from Breda of 1660, which had promised 'ease to tender consciences', and wrecked the possibility of religious harmony, now acquired new relevance. It was used to create the impression that the Anglicans could not be trusted, when they answered James's Declarations with competitive offers of future toleration. Strenuous efforts were made to discredit the moderate latitudinarians in particular. They were constantly and eloquently asserting the need for Protestant unity in the face of the Catholic danger, and advocating mutual charity with dissenters; it was claimed that they were untypical and uninfluential, and that hot, high-flying clergy were more likely to be followed.[27]

These arguments did not prove to be as effective as James and Penn hoped. The attempt to widen, perpetuate and exploit antagonism between Anglicans and dissenters rested on a miscalculation attributable to Penn. For him the Church of England, not the Church of Rome, was in the foreseeable future the principal enemy of religious liberty. He discounted the Papist menace on the grounds that there were too few Catholics to be a danger, that the conservative laity would restrain clerical extremists, and that rash actions would provoke a reaction in the next reign. On the other hand, embittered by decades of persecution, he was reluctant to trust the Anglican clergy to continue in their new-found principles of charity and professions of toleration, if circumstances no longer forced them to do so. A Catholic presence was actually a form of security, since it would ensure a balance between the three main religions and

---

[26] *Vox Cleri pro Rege* (1688); *The Rights of the Imperial Sovereignty of the Crown of England Vindicated* (1688).

[27] For example, *Animadversions on a Letter to a Dissenter*, pp. 32–3.

prevent any single one becoming predominant.[28] Not many dissenters agreed with Penn. For them, as for most Englishmen, recent events in France demonstrated the need for Protestant unity. Penn argued that the Revocation was attributable to Louis XIV's tyranny, and not to the principles or influence of Catholicism.[29] No argument could be less convincing. Opposition writers recalled how there had been steadily mounting French clerical pressure for years, calling for the Revocation, and the paeans of congratulation after its promulgation were widely publicized in England, with particular emphasis on the suggestions made to Louis that he should now assist other sovereigns to extirpate heresy in their dominions.[30]

It would be an oversimplification to say that the Revocation, in October 1685, totally undermined James's credibility when he established toleration eighteen months later, but it certainly put him and his apologists in a predicament. Henry Care boldly took the bull by the horns in using the Revocation as an argument for trusting James. Having witnessed the suffering and economic disruption which it had caused, especially through the emigration from which England was currently benefiting, James would never sacrifice economic expansion and domestic tranquillity to religious bigotry.[31]

Unfortunately for him, James could not publicly condemn the Revocation in such a way as to quiet the fears of his Protestant subjects. His attitudes to the Huguenots were, of necessity, ambiguous. He permitted refugees to immigrate and allowed collections for their relief, although he had insisted in 1686 that relief must be conditional on conformity to the established Church. That could later be blamed on Tory ministers, but James had no alternative to censorship when books and pamphlets appeared, and sermons were preached, retailing the atrocities being committed in France. These not only reflected on a fellow sovereign, but intensified religious animosities among those whom James was ordering to live together in charity and peace. The

---

[28] Burnet, iii, 140–1.
[29] V. Buranelli, *The King and the Quaker* (1962), p. 115.
[30] Ranke, iv, 268.
[31] H. Care, *An Answer to the Letter to a Dissenter* (1687), pp. 9–10.

most celebrated case made it appear that James actually approved of French atrocities. Diplomatic pressure led James to order a ritual burning by the hangman of Jean Claude's *Les Plaintes des Protestants cruellement opprimés dans la Royaume de France* because of its denunciation of Louis XIV as a tyrant.[32]

The evidence for James's personal opinions is inconclusive. In speaking to the Dutch and Spanish ambassadors he explicitly disapproved of the violent methods such as *dragonnades* being used against Huguenots.[33] Penn clearly thought that James sincerely disapproved of all forms of coercion, and that he could be trusted never to think of using them. But there are also indications that James largely discounted the current reports of atrocities, because of their similarity to the kind of anti-Papist propaganda that had been used to justify Exclusion during the years of the Popish Plot. In private James told Barrillon that he was delighted at the virtual disappearance of heresy in France, which the French ambassador construed as approval of the Revocation itself.[34] However the decisive point is that, whatever his personal opinion, James could not publicly and explicitly condemn Louis, so that his credibility and sincerity suffered.

The repercussions of James's Irish policies were also damaging to his credit. Tyrconnel, the Catholic who became lord deputy in January 1687, reversed previous policies so as to favour the Catholic majority. Protestant townsmen lost control in the corporations, and met with discrimination in favour of Catholic competitors, while Protestant landowners began to fear a reversal of the Restoration land settlement. The result of growing insecurity was emigration to England, which began to cause economic difficulties, but repeated petitions failed to persuade James to check Tyrconnel. It seems natural to twentieth-century opinion that James should grant toleration to those who constituted a large majority of the Irish population, but by doing so he was infringing a basic principle of the period, that Ireland must be kept under rigid control by the Protestant ascendancy,

---

[32] PRO, PC 2, 71, f. 263.
[33] Addit., 34502, f.77; 34512, f.48.
[34] Baschet; Barrillon, 7 March, 1 April 1686; Bonrepos, 14 January 1686.

as a subordinate kingdom whose interests must never be allowed to conflict with those of England. Furthermore, James's failure to act on the protests which he received tended to undermine the validity of the economic arguments in favour of toleration, to which his propagandists were giving great emphasis.[35]

This emphasis given to the economic benefits of toleration is a marked indication of the progress of secular values and attitudes. Again James was taking over Whig arguments. His Declarations, and supporting pamphlets, quoted the example of Dutch prosperity, and predicted that immigration would be encouraged, emigration reduced and trade and industry expanded, and recalled James's long-standing interest in fostering commercial and industrial prosperity. The Church of England was denounced as the enemy of property, because of the fines and distraints levied on dissenters. 'Who', one journalist asked, 'dares to be industrious that would not have his Labours made the Forfeit of his Sober Conscience?' Coercion was described as the 'Destroyer of Property, the Depopulator of Kingdoms, the enemy of Humane Nature, of Kind Neighbourhood'.[36] This last point is revealing. Toleration was more than a national matter, it needs to be related to the social environment in which most dissenters lived, in relatively small communities where differences in religion were the most obvious and active divisive forces – as in the Indian subcontinent in the 1930s – far more active and visible than those divisions which we would term class differences.

Most of the communities in which dissenters lived were commercial and industrial, or semi-industrial, with comparatively few in predominantly agricultural areas. The very important consequence was that religious repression had widespread repercussions. Obstinate dissenters could be impoverished and bankrupted by relentless enforcement of the penal laws, but such action would also adversely affect business associates who did not necessarily share their beliefs – creditors, partners, employers, employees, apprentices, servants and tenants. All stood to lose by the economic disruption which religious persecution

[35] Simms, *Jacobite Ireland*, pp. 24–8, 35–6, 42.
[36] *A Letter from a Gentleman about the Odiousness of Persecution*, p. 15.

arbitrarily caused, but it should be noted that those who usually acted as the instigators and agents of such persecution would not be affected economically themselves. Informers made a living from the penal laws. The parson was secure in his benefice, compulsorily maintained by tithe and church dues, and not dependent on the goodwill of his parishioners. Tory magistrates were usually country gentlemen, or urban tradesmen dependent on their patronage. They were not directly connected with the trades which stood to lose by repression.

By holding out the prospect of ending the economically disruptive, or at least damaging, execution of the penal laws, James hoped to persuade urban and semi-urban communities (which elected a majority of MPs) to collaborate with him. Penn had already published arguments that provided a conceptual framework for this attempt. He wrote : 'Civil interest is the foundation and end of civil government ... the good of the whole must needs be the interest of the whole, and consequently the interest of the whole is the reason and end of government.'[37] Hence a wise government would refrain from persecution, which could only have the effect of preventing subjects from identifying their own interests with those of the government. One pamphlet quoted Francis Bacon, saying that when a prince's interest ran parallel with his promises, these could be trusted. As an individual Catholic, James might wish to further his own religion, but as a sovereign he would be guided by Reason of State, which would show him that any forcible effort to establish Catholicism would certainly destroy the peace and prosperity of his kingdoms.[38]

Such arguments were insufficiently persuasive to overcome the prevalent beliefs about the political characteristics of Catholicism, which led to distrust of James's sincerity and the belief that he was not a free agent. The Protestant assumption that James, like Louis and all Catholic rulers, was subject to the dictation of the Pope and his own spiritual advisers in all matters where religion might be involved was strengthened

[37] Quoted in J. A. W. Gunn, *Politics and the Public Interest in the Seventeenth Century* (1969), p. 172.
[38] H. Care, *Animadversions on a late Paper* (1687), pp. 14–15.

by the Revocation. Suspicions were created by a change of confessor in 1687, when Mansuete, a Capuchin from Lorraine, was replaced by Father Warner, a Jesuit, a protégé of Father Petre and a much more politically minded person.[39]

Reason of State afforded no real guarantees of security, indeed if applied to Ireland it must mean Catholic supremacy. To argue that the royal prerogative was now strong enough to maintain peace and order in conditions of toleration was to generate fears that it might become still stronger, to the point where governmental pressures could be used to impose Catholicism. Some form of constitutional security was needed if dissenters were to put their trust in a Catholic king, some way of ensuring that he did not put the interests of his religion before those of the nation. One proposal was for the enactment of expedients, that is a set of guarantee laws. Another more comprehensive suggestion was to embody toleration in a fundamental constitutional law, inevitably described as a Magna Carta of religion. Several versions appeared, by Penn and Care among others, all seeking to ensure the perpetuation of toleration and providing safeguards against abuse. One pamphlet spoke of: '. . . a Great Charter, Declaratory of the Ancient Constitution of our Government, whereby Liberty of Conscience may be secured on the same Foundation as our Civil Rights and Property are, and be settled among the Inalienable Rights of the Englishman. . . .' Whiggish language indeed.[40] More specifically another writer proposed an inviolable statute as the basis of universal and equal liberty of conscience. Any measure, move or action contrary to it would be punished, offenders were not to be capable of royal pardon, and its provisions were not to be subject to royal dispensation. Even Parliament was to be restricted; all peers and MPs must take an oath to respect toleration, which would then be declared a 'Natural Right of All Men' for all time.[41]

These proposals were often left vague and general, on the ground that it would be for the next Parliament to work out

[39] Mazure, ii, 218.
[40] *A Discourse for Taking off the Tests and Penal Laws* (1687), preface.
[41] *Three Letters tending to demonstrate how the Security of this Nation . . lies in the abolishment of the present Penal Laws and Tests* (1688).

the details. Some were fanciful, speculative and obviously impracticable. In contrast opposition pamphlets were able to concentrate on a single, familiar theme : Catholics could not be trusted, their religious principles could not coexist with permanent and genuine religious liberty. It must follow that James was deliberately and cynically using the dissenters for his own concealed purposes. This view was expressed clearly, concisely and tendentiously in the most influential pamphlet that appeared in 1687, Haliifax's *Letter to a Dissenter*. Halifax fully appreciated the extent to which James's offers of toleration and political alliance tempted the dissenters, and the danger that many of them would now accept the opportunity to pay off old scores against the Anglicans. To reduce the danger of their collaborating actively with James, Halifax argued the uncertainties of the alliance being proposed. He stressed the unreliability of 'new friends' who approached them only as a second best, after being repulsed by the Anglicans. More fundamentally, Halifax stressed the argument that what was being proposed, an alliance between 'Liberty and Infallibility', 'the bringing together of the two most contrary things that are in the world', could not be permanent. The Church of Rome, he argued, 'doth not only dislike the allowing liberty, but by its principles it cannot do it.'

Combined with this advice, to be cautious in dealing with James's approaches, Halifax made a veiled threat which was repeated by other writers. Dissenting activists were working for James, in his dangerous efforts to prepare general elections, with energy, enthusiasm and some success. Halifax insinuated that this was already endangering the interests and reputation of the dissenters as a whole, and threatened to provoke the resentment of the majority of the nation. The more they collaborated with James, the less likely would be the eventual establishment of full toleration by legal means. On the other hand, Halifax assured the dissenters that they could now trust the Anglican clergy, who had finally but genuinely become convinced that uniformity through coercion was both unattainable and unchristian. Characteristically, Halifax ended by saying that inaction was the course to follow; time was against James and on the side of the nation, so that the dissenters should passively enjoy all the benefits of toleration, giving as little as possible to James in return while they waited for the next reign.

This pamphlet made an immense impression. It sold in very large quantities. Halifax forced James's propagandists to devote a great deal of attention to answering his arguments, and by attempting their refutation they actually helped to publicize his case.[42] But James continued with his campaign to pack Parliament, and the proposals for a statutory guarantee of toleration and constitutional liberties were repeatedly argued, so that in 1688 Halifax published a second pamphlet, *The Anatomy of an Equivalent*.[43] This had two aims. First, he replied to the arguments that James could be trusted because toleration accorded with his interest. This he sweepingly dismissed: 'Interest is an uncertain thing, it goeth and cometh, and varieth according to times and circumstances; as good build upon a quicksand as upon a presumption that interest shall not alter.' Secondly, he demolished the idea that security could be achieved by enacting an inviolable Magna Carta of toleration. It was easy to demonstrate that this was a constitutional impracticability, since no single Parliament could bind its successors. Halifax did not even try to answer the theoretical propositions of Penn and other writers; instead he used practical arguments that were all related to the immediate situation. He represented the crux as being whether James could be trusted or not. Wisely refraining from the kind of abuse that the first Whigs had used during the Exclusion Crisis, he pointed out that any agreement between the dissenters and James would be dangerously one-sided because of the disparity in strength between the parties. James could at any time break his promises with impunity, and there could be no redress because of his control over the judiciary. Furthermore, if the dissenters helped him to the point where Parliament became entirely amenable to royal demands, they would become expendable, and subsequently as defenceless as the rest of the nation.

The blatancy with which James sought to exploit toleration in

---

[42] Care, *Animadversions on a late Paper*; Sir Roger L'estrange, *An Answer to a Letter to a Dissenter* (1687).

[43] Kenyon, *Halifax, Complete Works*, pp. 120–43.

his campaign to pack Parliament was one of two major factors which lessened his chances of success. It led many dissenters to accept Halifax's thesis that toleration was bait in a trap. In the second place, James continued to apply pressure on the Anglican Church – ostensibly to safeguard toleration by getting Anglicans to approve of his policies. Inevitably many of the clergy interpreted royal pressure as a design to ruin the Church. In turn, their defiant sermons and writings forced James to intensify his pressure, and he accompanied a second Declaration of Indulgence with an attempt to intimidate the clergy as a whole. This attempt led to the clash with the bishops in the summer of 1688, to his first decisive defeat and to greatly increased suspicion of his sincerity.

During 1687 the Anglican clergy in general reserved their political position. Few openly supported the Declaration, but the majority did nothing to actively oppose it or hamper toleration. Although they were suspicious of James's future intentions, and afraid that their rights might be invaded, they remained undisturbed. Leading divines kept up a vigorous pamphlet duel with Catholic controversialists, but in practical terms the Catholic challenge was being contained. The Anglican clergy were vigilant but there was no need for militant action, and the advice which they received, at first from such latitudinarians as Tillotson and Patrick but in early 1688 from Archbishop Sancroft also, was appropriate: they should attend conscientiously to their pastoral duties, establish the closest possible links with the leading laity, and come to an understanding with dissenters in their districts.[44]

Only in one sphere did James do anything to confirm Anglican fears. His efforts to further Catholic interests in the field of education led to a direct clash and a serious crisis. James and his Catholic advisers fully appreciated the need to challenge the Anglican monopoly in secondary and university education, and to make it possible for Catholics to be educated in England. Catholic schools were established. Dispensations were issued enabling Catholics or converts to hold fellowships at Oxford and

[44] *State Trials*, xii, 480–83.

Cambridge. These provoked opposition and official obstructionism that had to be overcome by royal pressure. This caused
considerable alarm, but the Magdalen College affair was a
much more central issue, and affected the whole future of higher
education, perhaps even the future character of the Anglican
clergy.

Following Elizabeth's example with Westminster School,
James as patron of the new Jesuit school at the Savoy planned
to institute King's Scholarships to enable pupils to proceed to
Oxford.[45] He rejected suggestions that he should found a new
Catholic college there, which might easily be sealed off and
isolated by the rest of the university, but decided instead to
plant a Catholic element in the centre of the university, which
would be able to compete directly with the Anglicans. Then, as
he said, those who teach the best will be the most followed.[46]
The opportunity to do this seemed to come with the death of
the president of Magdalen, the wealthiest of all Oxford colleges.
Unexpectedly he encountered strong and prolonged resistance
to his attempts to nominate a Catholic, and by reacting violently
to this resistance he found himself dragged into a long-drawn
struggle, which lined up against him many prominent laymen,
including the chancellor of the university (the Duke of
Ormonde) and former undergraduates, as well as almost the
entire clergy.

James crushed the opposition of the Magdalen fellows by
using the Ecclesiastical Commission against them. By doing so,
by depriving them of fellowships that were their freehold
property, and by transforming the college into a Catholic institution, James convinced Anglican opinion that he was following a
plan to subvert the Church of England. Until the university
convulsions of the late 1960s in France, it might have seemed
surprising that university affairs should provoke a serious political crisis, but contemporaries knew how much depended on the
outcome of the Magdalen case. Significantly, the first overt
Anglican move after the Restoration had been a wholesale purge
of Oxford, when almost all those who had been installed during

[45] Luttrell, i, 426.
[46] Mazure, ii, 236–7; Burnet, iii, 148–9.

the remodelling of the university by the Long Parliament were ejected. This purge of 1660 had produced quite remarkable results. The generation of graduates who entered the Church in the next twenty-five years were, with very few exceptions, reliable conformists imbued with the religious and political doctrines of orthodox Anglicanism – in sharp contrast to the situation under James I and the early years of Charles I's reign.[47] The education of the clergy was the principal function of the two universities, so that by exposing them in their formative years to Catholic influences and arguments, a lasting impression might be made even on those who did not become converts. Oxford, instead of continuing as the secure citadel of undisturbed Anglicanism, would become an arena of controversy and recriminations; there is a parallel here to the alarm which the Tractarian Movement created in the Oxford of the 1830s. Finally, the action of the Ecclesiastical Commission in depriving the fellows of their freehold, which was theirs by law, gave opposition writers an opportunity which they eagerly took, to emphasize the implied menace to property rights in general.

The Magdalen case was the one cause of active conflict between James and the Church of England during 1687, but it was enough to convince many clergy that they were entering a time of trial. Popular preachers warned their congregations to prepare for ordeals that might lie ahead, and events in France gave such apprehensions vivid reality, but there was a danger of anticlimax in arousing such fears if James did not confirm them by his actions. It was not until April 1688 that he did so, and it is worth emphasizing that the reason for a new move on his part was connected with his campaign to pack Parliament. As part of the preparations for the general elections that were planned for October, it was essential to break up the cohesion of the Anglican clergy, by bringing them under the same kind of pressure as had already been applied to office-holders, municipal officers and JPs. This was James's objective in issuing the second Declaration of Indulgence (27 April), with a text that was virtually the same as that of the first Declaration.

[47] F. J. Varley, 'The Restoration Visitation of the University of Oxford', *Camden Miscellany*, XVIII (1948).

The one innovation in 1688 was that James instructed the bishops to order all their clergy to read the Declaration from the pulpit on two successive Sundays.[48] The bishops, by transmitting these orders, and the clergy by obeying them, could be made to appear to approve James's policy. Any who refused would be identifying themselves as opponents, and could then be proceeded against by the Ecclesiastical Commission which had the power to deprive them of their benefices. The situation which James deliberately created is worth examination. Every beneficed clergyman was personally affected. His relation to royal authority and policies was no longer a matter of abstract issues and distant political questions, but something calling for personal decision. James was forcing the clergy to say whether their first loyalty was to him or to the Church. No possibility of evasion now existed. The clerical dilemma was all the more acute because most clergy were poor men, totally dependent on their stipends, and so far less able to withstand pressure than the gentry, for whom service as JPS was primarily a matter of prestige, not of livelihood. By refusing to obey the king's orders the clergy could bring ruin and suffering on their families, whereas obedience could open the way to promotion.

It was imperative that the ordinary parochial clergy should receive a firm lead. Consultations that were held at the local level were not certain to prove effective in preventing the kind of dissensions that would serve James's purpose.[49] This was the first aim of the bishops' petition to the king, in which they said that they could not distribute the Declaration. The petition had an offensive purpose as well. By challenging the validity of the suspending power the Seven Bishops were going well beyond their original aim of rallying the clergy in a united front, they were making a bid to unite the nation against what was now skilfully dramatised as a calculated and menacing attempt to ruin the Church and the Protestant religion. The bishops wrested the initiative from James for the first time and inflicted upon him a major political defeat.

[48] As the 1681 and 1683 Declarations against the Whigs had been: Lingard, *History*, x, 298.
[49] PWA, 2161, 2163, 2167.

Tactically James was outmanoeuvred at every stage. At first he and his advisers wrongly calculated that only a minority of the clergy would refuse to read the Declaration. Then the council does not seem to have obtained any accurate intelligence of the bishops' attitude, still less of their activities. James was incorrectly advised by Thomas Cartwright, his most zealous episcopal collaborator, that although unhappy the bishops would merely ask for the duty of transmitting James's orders to be transferred to their legal officers, the chancellors.[50] Cartwright did not know, being carefully excluded from the bishops' consultations, the first on 12 May with several prominent London clergymen, the second on 18 May when they decided to petition James.[51] This meant that when the petition was presented at 10 pm on the 18th, that is only thirty-six hours before the Declaration was due to be read for the first time in London churches, James had no advance notion of its contents and character. Taken by surprise, he reacted angrily, calling it a trumpet of sedition because it denied the legality of the suspending power. From the timing of its presentation he concluded that it was an act of malevolent bad faith, and this anger was increased when the petition appeared in print the same night, probably by Compton's agency. He was still further provoked by the letters which were sent out to the provincial clergy, informing them of the petition, and for a day he held up the posts in a futile attempt to stop the spread of the news.[52]

James's fury was matched by his initial hesitation as to what should be done. The council was also at first confused and uncertain, frequently changing the advice which they gave. There was no time to restore the situation in London, where very few clergy read the Declaration on 20 May, a blow to royal prestige which was bound to influence the attitude of the provincial clergy. Yet at the council on 25 May both Sunderland and Petre were against a prosecution of the bishops. Two days later a decision was made which did not commit the king to any particular course of action, but which proved to be tactically

[50] Burnet, iii, 227.
[51] PWA, 2161; Addit., 34510, f.119.
[52] PWA, 2161; Mazure, ii, 445.

disastrous. The Seven Bishops were summoned to appear before the council on 8 June. This would be too late to influence the provincial clergy. It protracted an atmosphere of uncertainty which inevitably increased popular excitement. By permitting the bishops so much time they were given ample opportunities to make thorough legal preparations and to rally lay and clerical support. They were particularly heartened when six more bishops associated themselves with the petition, and by the almost universal failure of the country clergy to read the Declaration on 3 June.[53]

Worse was to follow for James. One of his councillors, Berkeley, had assured the council that the bishops would enter into recognisances to appear at their trial if they were committed, but on 8 June they categorically refused to do so, pleading that as members of the Lords they were not obliged to do so. They also refused to answer questions, for fear that they might incriminate themselves. By these moves the Seven Bishops achieved a shatteringly effective propaganda victory. James had either to drop the case or send the bishops to the Tower.[54] By imprisoning them, James gave the bishops an aura of martyrdom. As they proceeded to the Tower they were attended by vast, anxious crowds, and once incarcerated they were visited by relays of notables, including a superbly timed deputation of dissenting ministers, symbolizing the need for Protestant unity in the face of the Popish menace.[55] Opposition writers interpreted the prosecution as part of a concerted design, connecting it with the recent consecration of two new Catholic bishops (making four in all). Sancroft was in fact seriously alarmed by the development of a rival Catholic hierarchy, and treated its recently promulgated pastoral letter as a direct and illegal invasion of his authority. Popular fears went much further, believing that the new Catholic bishops were being created so as to be ready to replace the petitioning Seven Anglican Bishops, once they had been tried and condemned.[56]

---

[53] Mazure, ii, 446, 448–9.
[54] Lingard, *History*, x, 303; PWA, 2175.
[55] PWA, 2161.
[56] Gutch, *Collectanea Curiosa*, i, 397–403; Campana de Cavelli, ii, 190–1.

In this ferment of popular excitement the ministers were divided on whether the prosecution should continue. Sunderland suggested that the birth of the prince, on 10 June, offered an opportunity to get off the hook by giving a general celebratory pardon that would include the bishops. But this God-given event had the opposite effect on James, hardening his resolution, although he does not seem to have thought through the consequences of either a successful or an unsuccessful prosecution. For him it was essential to make a demonstration of his authority, to show that disobedience by any of his subjects would meet with stern punishment. The bishops were equally determined to fight, and when they did eventually agree to enter into recognisances they had an impressive and carefully selected group of aristocratic guarantors ready.[57]

The trial of the Seven Bishops, on charges of seditious libel, was entirely dominated at every stage and in every aspect by political considerations. Westminster Hall was surrounded by excited crowds, and filled with nobles, clergy and gentry, present to encourage the defendants and their counsel, and to stiffen the jury against any pressure by the judges. The prosecution lawyers – attorney-general Thomas Powis, solicitor-general William Williams (a former Whig speaker), Serjeant Trinder (another former Whig) and Serjeant Baldock – did not falter, but the judges proved to be more impressionable. They certainly failed to keep the iron grip on proceedings which was customary in important political trials. They allowed defence counsel to bring up general political issues, so much so that the eventual publication of the proceedings made good opposition propaganda. For instance Sir Robert Sawyer attacked the whole doctrine of the suspending power. Sir Francis Pemberton was even more pointed, saying things that could not have been stated outside the courtroom: that the suspending power had been used to further the Romish religion, 'which is the very worst of all religions', that the bishops had a duty to suppress false religions, and that they would have been leading the people into error by ordering the reading of the Declaration. The prosecuting lawyers

[57] PWA, 2167; *State Trials*, xii, 464, from Tanner MSS, 28, f.76.

sensed that the trial was having exactly the opposite effect to what had been intended, but they got help only from the Catholic Alibone, who had nothing to lose. The prosecution arguments served to confirm the general suspicion that James wished to restrict constitutional liberties. Powis claimed that any reflection upon any officer of the crown was a criminal offence, and that to suggest that the king was breaking the law must be sedition. Similarly, Williams asserted that the bishops had no right to petition, except in Parliament. Both argued that it had been their duty to have acquiesced in James's orders until Parliament met in November. Williams also dismissed the parliamentary declarations of 1663 and 1673 against the suspending power as having no legal force, an opinion in sharp contrast to his own behaviour when Whig speaker. Vulnerable to charges of having sold himself in return for office, Williams behaved aggressively, and frequently clashed with the judges.[58]

Of the judges, Sir John Powell threw discretion to the winds, openly disparaging the prosecution case and specifically denying the constitutionality of the suspending power. The lord chief justice behaved more cautiously. He hoped that the fact of publication would not be proved, so that the case could be dismissed on a technicality. When publication by the bishops was proved, he and Sir Richard Holloway tried to evade responsibility by leaving the question, of whether the petition was libellous, to the jury. This was irregular. In the eighteenth century the case of the Seven Bishops was not followed as a legal precedent, the law was that the jury were judges only of *fact,* that is of publication; the question whether a publication was seditious or libellous was, as a matter of *law,* left to the judges to decide.[59] Obviously the proceedings in the bishops' case, as well as the verdict, reflected the impact of organized public opinion, and it is not surprising that only one juryman (who had considered standing as a royal candidate in the general elections) was disposed to find them guilty.

[58] *State Trials*, xii, 183–524; Addit., 34487, f.7; PWA, 2167, 2175.
[59] Until the passage of Fox's Libel Act of 1792, the jury had to decide merely on the fact of publication; the question whether the publication was libellous or not was decided exclusively by the judge or judges.

The acquittal touched off a storm of delirious enthusiasm. James lost prestige. His reaction was predictably petulant: 'So much the worse for them', he commented on hearing the news. Some of his ministers talked of continuing the prosecution by other means, by an action of *praemunire,* or in the Ecclesiastical Commission, but this was only a smokescreen to conceal a total repulse.[60] Nevertheless, James did not entirely abandon his attempts to bring the clergy under pressure. On 16 August he ordered archdeacons and chancellors to return the names of all clergy who had not read the Declaration, to the Ecclesiastical Commission. This return was not due until 6 December, a far longer period than was operationally necessary. But by then general elections would have taken place, which indicates that James hoped that this suspended threat would at least deter the clergy from open opposition to royal candidates. On the other hand, Sancroft consolidated his success by issuing new instructions to the clergy which included an injunction to preserve all the links with the leading laity that had been forged during the crisis.[61]

A final comment may be made on James's religious policies. In purely religious terms he achieved half his objectives. Catholicism did not make significant advances, but by August 1688 toleration was fully established, in a fuller form than at any time in the next 150 years. For James this meant failure. His aims were primarily political, and by converting almost everyone to toleration (Anglican bishops included) he actually reduced the political advantage which could be gained in terms of electoral preparations. Furthermore, his reputation had been seriously damaged by the unconstitutional methods which he had used in establishing it, and the blatancy with which he tried to exploit his religious policies in the campaign to pack Parliament.

[60] Addit., 34487, ff.15, 21; 34510, f.138.
[61] Luttrell, i, 455; Campana de Cavelli, ii, 241–2; Addit., 34487, ff.17, 21.

SIX *The Campaign to pack Parliament*

SUPERFICIALLY JAMES'S DISSOLUTION of Parliament in July 1687, after successive prorogations over a period of nineteen months, might be interpreted as giving him complete freedom of action and decision. But this move had been forced on him. The failure of closeting, and the refusal of Tories, Anglicans and (most important of all) William and Mary to collaborate in repealing the Tests and penal laws left him with a limited choice of allies and policies. There were advantages. Closeting, as a breach of privilege, would have given opposition leaders the opportunity to inflame the Commons at the start of a new session, but with the dissolution of Parliament no focus now existed for any legal form of opposition. Sunderland and the Catholic ministers were secure against any revival of Rochester's influence. James could continue to use prerogative powers freely. He was under no financial pressure to call a new Parliament so that, like Charles after 1681, he could safely ignore the provisions of the Triennial Act which had stipulated that a Parliament should meet every three years. Nevertheless, there was no question of James setting out, like his father in 1629, to rule without Parliament for the foreseeable future.

There was a significant difference between James's position

and objectives and those of the last years of his brother's life. Then government had been essentially static, Charles being content to retain political control for the rest of his reign. In contrast, James had necessarily to follow a dynamic policy, to change the religious laws and lift legal restrictions on the prerogative. Catholics (and dissenters from April 1687) enjoyed toleration and equality of civil rights on the insecure basis of the legally questionable exercise of the suspending power, which meant that James had no option but to try eventually to secure the election of a new Parliament that would repeal the Tests and penal laws by statute.

The magnitude, complexity and difficulty of this task need emphasis. Although there had been talk of the court 'undertaking' elections (as in 1614) no serious attempt had ever been made to do so. Danby had constructed a working majority in the Cavalier Parliament, but by keeping this parliament in being for as long as possible he had recognized the organizational and financial impracticability of managing general elections. During the Exclusion Crisis the court's own electoral interest had been virtually annihilated. Success in 1685 had depended primarily on the cooperation of precisely those Tories whom James had now alienated and discarded. How, then, could James hope for success? Most historians, from T. B. Macaulay to J. P. Kenyon, have answered by dismissing the whole attempt as unrealistic and foredoomed to failure. Certainly it did fail, but only as a result of William's invasion; it was never tested electorally.

Most historians have been so dismissive of the campaign to pack parliament that they have not attempted a serious analysis of the techniques and agents employed, or a systematic assessment of the degree of success which was achieved. This lack of a detailed examination of the campaign distorts any picture of royal policies and purposes in 1687–8, since it was in every way the centrepiece. Equally important, playing down (or ignoring) the campaign has meant grossly underestimating its repercussions, and this has often led to a series of fundamental misunderstandings of the causes and significances of the Revolution itself. Of all domestic policies, the campaign to pack Parliament was easily the most important in provoking the Revolution, more resented and feared than even the attack on the Church and its leaders.

At the level of national politics the campaign threatened to produce a subservient Parliament that would make the crown financially independent, with the result that Parliament itself might follow many European Estates into disuse. It could also be used to increase royal authority to the point of absolutism by impeccably legal means – Lord Burghley was often quoted as having predicted that England could be undone only by a Parliament. It must be added, with emphasis, that the campaign was not only a matter of central and general politics, something remote and hypothetical in its results for those who lived in the provinces. It also meant an invasion of the life and autonomy of local communities throughout the country by professional agents of the central administration. To appreciate the significance of this one should remember that in the seventeenth century the local community, or corporate body, to which the individual belonged, had the first call on his loyalties, and played a far larger part in forming his mental attitudes than is the case today. Sustained interference from the centre – Charles I's imposition of Ship Money in 1634–8, and Cromwell's handing over of local government to major-generals in 1655 – had aroused fierce, particularist resentment. James's canvassing of the gentry as well as officials, his systematic and prolonged regulation and remodelling of the corporations, represented the most deliberate, methodical and elaborate attempt that had been made at any time during the century to subordinate the localities to the centre.

The campaign was more efficient (and more resented) than previous attempts at control over local affairs by the central government, because it used paid agents, professionals who were not themselves part of the local scene, who were seldom caught up in local factions and interests, and did not belong to the political nation themselves. These agents could almost be described as electoral *intendants*, and their complete independence from local ties was essential if a centrally imposed policy was to succeed. In past instances of court intervention in the affairs of the localities, especially in dealing with the Commission of the Peace, it might be thought that the central authorities were all-powerful, with unrestricted powers of control and decision, of appointment and dismissal. But in many practical ways the court could always be manipulated by local factions and interests for their own purposes and advantage, because it was the latter who supplied the bulk of the information on which court decisions were taken, and the court had to entrust local, unpaid men with the enforcement of its directives. They could be dismissed, but the problem was how to ensure that their replacements would be more reliable. Penn, as general manager of the addresses and chief contact with the dissenters, occupied exactly such a position during the initial stages of the campaign, and intended to use his influence to see that its objectives were significantly more limited than James intended.[1] In 1688 he was superseded by the body of paid, itinerant agents controlled by Brent, and ultimately by Sunderland. It was not for these agents to initiate policy. They were executives, who followed their instructions in acting ruthlessly and systematically as regulators in the towns and electoral agents, and their efficiency was in sharp contrast with the ineffectiveness of the traditional instruments of royal policy, the lords lieutenant and their deputies.

The consequence of all the pressures that were brought to bear during the campaign was the short-lived but decisive unity of the aristocracy and gentry during the crisis of the Revolution. Pressure on them produced a sense of cohesion that united Whig and Tory, but it should be emphasized that there was no such unity and cohesion among the bourgeoisie. While James's approaches to the gentry produced meagre results, the political, social and economic structures of the towns offered his agents opportunities of which they were to take full advantage.

The dissolution in July 1687 was followed by reports that a new Parliament would meet at the end of the year, but by November it was generally expected that it would not sit until March or April. All these early forecasts greatly underestimated the amount of preparation and organization that the campaign necessitated, and also the determination of the ministers to persist with their project, despite all the difficulties. Brent was

[1] PWA, 2127a, 2141.

under no illusions. In December 1687 he accurately predicted that no Parliament could be elected before the following October, and his orderly, methodical approach to the work shows that he was well aware of the operational difficulties involved.[2]

The campaign fell into three distinct phases. The first, which began before the dissolution, centred on the presentation of addresses from dissenters, thanking James for his Declaration of Indulgence.[3] Penn acted as chief organizer. Convinced by these addresses that he had the full support of the dissenters, and of their adequacy to act as replacements for the Tories and Anglicans with whom he was on the verge of breaking, James then instituted wholesale purges of unreliable persons from all kinds of positions under the crown. In London obstruction of an address led to the removal of six aldermen in July, including the intended lord mayor, but this purge was extended into something much more systematic and extensive. In August the lieutenancy was remodelled, and in September the operationally difficult task of erasing the names of over a thousand members of city livery companies was completed. A month later systematic regulations were extended to the provinces, Sunderland writing on 25 October to instruct lords lieutenant to put three standard questions to all members of the Commission of the Peace. First, they were asked if they would agree to repeal of the Tests and penal laws, if they were elected to the next Parliament, and secondly whether they would assist the election of candidates who were willing to give such an undertaking. Finally, they were asked to support the Declaration for liberty of conscience by living peaceably with men of all religious persuasions.

The earliest replies arrived by the end of November, but most of the meetings arranged in the provinces for the putting of these three questions took place in January, and some answers were delayed until March. The purpose of the whole operation had been made clear when the *Gazette* announced on 11 December that all lists of deputy lieutenants and JPs would be revised. In the first three months of 1688 hundreds of those

[2] PWA, 2120.
[3] Luttrell, i, 400–20; they continued until November.

who gave unsatisfactory answers were dismissed. Simultaneously, even more extensive purges were being effected in the towns. A regulating committee was established in November and immediately set to work, authorizing the first major purges on the 27th. In the first months of 1688, when agents were enlisted and sent into the constituencies, the objective was explicitly to prepare for favourable parliamentary elections. By April, when the organization was complete, the campaign entered its third, most intensive and crucial phase.

During the first two phases most commentators were scornful about James's chances of success, Van Citters especially (on whom Macaulay largely relied) concluding that the whole enterprise was futile.[4] It was in the nature of the enterprise that mistakes were made, serious difficulties and setbacks encountered, but obstacles only stimulated an intensification of effort and an improvement of the techniques employed. In June a new round of purges took place, and proceedings were initiated against the charters of recalcitrant corporations. Preparations reached their climax in the late summer with further regulations of corporations, local canvassing in a high proportion of constituencies, the issuing of thirty-two new charters, the mass distribution of propaganda and, finally, the nomination of a first list of 106 royally approved candidates. At last the work was sufficiently well advanced for James to risk elections. On 24 August orders in council were made for writs (to be issued on 16 September) and for the meeting of Parliament to be fixed for 27 November. A Declaration to this effect was ordered to be published (on 21 September), but the imminence of a Dutch invasion led to the writs being recalled a week later. Finally, on 17 October the whole campaign was abandoned when a Proclamation was ordered for the restoration of all charters, starting with that of London, and James discarded the agents who had worked for him throughout the campaign.

From the point of view of organization, techniques, tactics and the personnel employed, the most novel, effective and interest-

---

[4] Addit., 34510, ff.63 (28 November 1687), 75 (6 January 1688), 87 (24 February 1688); 34512, f.77 (11 May 1688).

ing features are those connected with the regulation of the corporations, and the final phase of electoral work by James's agents which followed. Little need be said about the first phase, centering on the addresses thanking James for the Declaration of Indulgence. Apart from the fact that it was mainly dissenters who subscribed them, and Penn with a group of dissenting ministers who organized them, they were very similar to the 'loyal' addresses presented in 1681, 1683 and 1685. Ostensibly all were statements pledging support for the crown, but everyone knew that they were not spontaneous, and it was easy for critics to disparage them as the work of a small (and allegedly self-interested or intimidated) section of opinion. But addresses of this kind had been organized in preparation for the successful elections of 1685, and they now had value for James precisely because they were organized. Valuable experience was gained, and they usefully established contact between the crown and groups that had formerly adhered mainly to the opposition. Some of those who arranged addresses in 1687 qualified themselves for appointment as JPS and municipal office-holders, and helped election work in 1688. The addresses showed James that he had sufficient dissenting support for him to think of using them as allies and instruments in place of another (if socially more elevated and traditionally more loyal) minority of activists – the Tory gentry and their associates in the existing municipal governments.

It cannot be said that James was deceived in any of the three phases of the campaign as to the amount of support he could expect. On the contrary, he received far more voluminous and detailed information about the political state of the kingdom than any previous sovereign or minister.[5] Qualitatively, too, the managers and agents were candid and accurate in reporting failures and refusals of support. They made no attempt to conceal the overwhelmingly unfavourable response to the three

[5] Sir George Duckett's *Penal Laws and Test Act* is a perfect example of nineteenth-century historical antiquarianism; he edited and printed a vast mass of information from the Rawlinson MSS in the Bodleian with accuracy and precision. But the accompanying commentary is wrong on almost every point of interpretation.

questions from the gentry. Indeed, their honest and full reports were invaluable as the basis for the mass purges of JPs and deputies which James ordered. The character of these purges needs explanation. Wholesale dismissals of JPs were, of course, common during the sixteenth and seventeenth centuries, but in the past the primary aim had been administrative efficiency and dependability, to ensure readiness to execute duties which were required by the central executive. James's purges were far more directly political, their aim was avowedly electoral. The vital information which the questioning and canvassing were intended to extract related to suitability as parliamentary candidates, not as administrators. This narrowness of aim meant that James could accept generally unfavourable replies; he needed only a minority of affirmative responses in order to compile his list of approved parliamentary candidates.

In addition, it should be noted that James's wholesale and repeated purges of local government did not lead to administrative breakdown. Even if many were inexperienced and socially lightweight, the new JPs proved to be generally competent, while James's standing army freed him from dependence on the lieutenancy and the militia for both internal security duties and for defence against foreign states. The standing army was now a highly professional and efficient force, closely modelled on the French, but this was the only sector of government of which this could be said. At the centre and in the localities James's administration was defective by comparison with that in France, and it did not provide a basis for the establishment of absolutist government. It was this governmental weakness that forced James, for all his belief in monarchy as the divinely appointed form of authority, to solicit support from his subjects, to make alliances with former rebels, to act as a politician and electioneering organizer. Although he was happily free of the financial pressures that had crippled or hampered his predecessors, James was still circumscribed administratively. He could carry on day-to-day government without difficulty, but the England of his reign lacked the trained personnel and bureaucratic systems which were needed if James was to extend the range of his practical authority.

In retrospect, James concluded that he should have relied on his own powers of persuasion to influence prospective candidates.[6] He did use his 'progresses' to carry out personal canvassing, but he risked receiving refusals damaging to his royal prestige, and the work of preparing for elections was far too extensive to be undertaken by one man. Characteristically, James singled out the electoral organizers and agents as those who had failed him, when in practice they had worked effectively and devotedly. The really weak link in James's campaign proved to be the lords lieutenant, to whom the collection of answers to the three questions was delegated. This was partly because the lords lieutenant did not possess an organization in the counties that could be easily adapted for the purposes of canvassing, but far more to James's faulty choices of men to serve in office. To command respect in his county a lord lieutenant should preferably be a magnate, an aristocrat at the apex of the local social hierarchy. The loyalty and effectiveness of his deputies depended directly on his qualities of leadership and on the influence which he possessed in his own right.

Of course, there were always considerable differences in the effectiveness of lords lieutenant, but James was asking too much of his. He made eleven changes between August and November 1687, which meant that the new men had not had time to settle into their post and duties before the questioning processes began, and a further ten changes were made while the questioning was actually in progress.[7] Efficiency also suffered from the fact that by February 1688 thirteen Catholics held fifteen lord lieutenancies. It was not only a question of anti-Papist prejudices, they also lacked experience, local prestige, and the kind of detailed knowledge of family and territorial connections that would have made them better canvassers. Ten had been appointed very recently, since 1 November, and only two had held office for a year. Some of their Protestant colleagues were conscientious and hard-working, in particular the future Jacobites, Lord Preston and the Earl of Ailesbury, but two of

[6] Clarke, *James the Second*, ii, 139–40.
[7] Duckett, i, 3–17.

those holding key posts proved to be incompetent. The Duke of Newcastle, who lived in Nottinghamshire, tried to canvass Northumberland by post. His letters tended to go astray, the Clerk of the Peace sabotaged his efforts, and the local loyalists (who included the future Jacobite martyr Sir John Fenwick) made their own electoral arrangements without consulting him.[8] The Duke of Beaufort was another weak link. He was responsible for all Wales, Gloucestershire and Herefordshire, but in practice he managed to canvass barely half the gentry.[9]

In the last analysis, the administrative and personal weaknesses of the lords lieutenant were of little more than marginal effect. The crucial reason for the failure of the three questions is to be found in the social cohesion and inbuilt independence of the landowning class in the rural areas. They construed the questioning as an attempt at intimidation, and they reacted as a privileged group determined to see that their liberties were not taken away from them for the second time in forty years. By contrast, when the three questions were put to men of humbler social status who were direct dependents of the crown – such as customs and revenue officers – the results were very different, and highly satisfactory from James's point of view. Now, in a different sense, the municipalities had become dependents of the crown through the action which the crown had taken, or could still take, against their charters. James now possessed the power to remove and (more arguably) to replace their officials and governing bodies.[10] In addition, and this is a point that requires maximum emphasis, the situation in most towns was socially as well as governmentally more favourable to royal intervention, and the realization of James's objectives. The bourgeoisie showed little of the solidarity, cohesion and pride displayed by the country gentry. As a class (and as groups in individual towns) they were far more divided, and as might be expected from their humbler and more insecure social and economic position they

---

[8] *Ibid.*, 1, 129–30, 134.
[9] *Ibid.*, 1, 288.
[10] See the details of the new charters granted in 1685; *CSPD*, 1685, pp. 15, 19–20, 25, 28-9, 38, 39-40, 46, etc.

proved to be far more susceptible to various forms of persuasion and intimidation.

The systematic regulation of the corporations by James's agents during the third phase constituted the real heart and centre of his campaign to pack Parliament. Again it must be emphasized that if this was successfully completed James would be in reach of achieving his objectives. The disappointing response by the gentry to the three questions did not mean (as Van Citters thought) that the whole campaign would fail; on the contrary it led to the intensification of activity in the much more favourable territory of the towns, and this activity reached its climax only as late as September 1688. So it can be argued that James's entire policies and decisions cannot be understood unless the campaign in the towns is seen as his one realistic chance of getting the acquiescent and collaborationist Parliament which he needed.

So far from being preposterous or misconceived, James's strategy rested on a clear recognition of one of the basic political factors in late seventeenth-century England: the fact that electoral success and parliamentary majorities depended on the balance of power within the towns. James needed a parliamentary majority just as much as any eighteenth-century minister, even though the objectives which he had in mind were totally dissimilar. Having been repulsed by the Tories, the traditional representatives of the royal cause in the provinces, and having chosen to break with them, James could then achieve a majority in the Commons only by intervening directly and as an independent force in municipal politics. If this was to be done, he needed a separate royal organization to manage elections, and this would have to be constructed from nothing. Indeed James had to appropriate the electoral techniques and propaganda methods that Shaftesbury had developed and used against him during the Exclusion Crisis.

In stealing the Whigs' clothes James had some reason to expect success. The Tories and Anglicans whom he was displacing from offices in 1687–8 were intrinsically the weaker party in terms of municipal and electoral politics. They had almost everywhere been overwhelmed by Shaftesbury's Whigs in the elections of 1679 and 1681, and had subsequently gained control in the corporations mainly because they had been helped by royal action against the charters. Now royal powers would be used against them, and on behalf of those groups who had generally proved over the previous twenty years to be the strongest force in local politics, and particularly in the larger towns that sent members to Parliament.

The additional fact that by 1688 most of the aristocracy and gentry had identified themselves as opponents of James's policies was also an asset to the royal campaign to win support in the towns. Social and economic as well as political differences divided the larger towns from the landowners of the surrounding rural areas. In many places local politics had centred ever since 1640 on the struggle of the towns to keep some degree of independence, and their most dangerous enemies were those who lived in the immediate neighbourhood, rather than the central government. James's agents could therefore expect to find that townsmen would accept subordination to a relatively remote royal authority as an attractive alternative to the oppressive control of local landed oligarchs and their urban associates. If they collaborated in the effort to pass James's demands for repeal of the Tests and the penal laws, they would in return receive exclusive local power and influence. It would be a working alliance very similar to that between the same people and interests and Shaftesbury and the first Whigs.[11]

It is now possible to spell out the full implications of James's reversal of traditional royal policies and alliances in 1687. When Charles and James established control over the corporations in 1682–6, they used the country gentry as partners in consolidating their hold over towns that the Whigs had dominated during the Exclusion Crisis. The Whigs had been able to win sweeping electoral victories because they worked with those interests in

[11] On the subject of political groups and divisions in the corporations, on the part played by dissenters, and on the importance of socio-economic as well as political relations between towns and the rural gentry, I am indebted to Mr K. I. Milne, of the University of East Anglia, who is preparing a dissertation on 'The Dissenting Interest in the Corporations, with special reference to James II's campaign to pack Parliament'.

the towns who stood for municipal independence, and were often the strongest in terms of experience and power in municipal affairs. After the Declaration of Indulgence, and still more when regulating began in November 1687, this process was reversed. Tory beneficiaries of royal intervention were ejected. Whigs who had resisted royal attacks on the charters were now reinstated and given local power, in return for promises of collaboration over the penal laws and the Tests. In the psychological and social conditions of the time, Whig and dissenting acceptance of James's propositions was natural. Urban collaborators were usually men of restricted ambitions and limited mental horizons. They were absorbed in the little worlds of their own communities, and many stood to gain financially from possession of municipal office. Moreover, it should be remembered that most of them would gain personally from religious toleration and equality of civil rights.

It can be seen, then, that considerable qualifications are needed to the pattern postulated for the Revolution of 1688 by many (and especially Marxist) historians as a classic bourgeois revolution, and that the traditional interpretation of it as a Whig revolution requires revision – at the local level it was exactly the opposite. James was trying to form a working alliance with the rank and file of the former first Whigs. Of course, he was setting out to use and exploit them. They were to be instruments of royal policy, but they were not sufficiently independent or self-confident to turn into an early threat to royal authority, provided, that is, that they did not develop an independent leadership. They were not likely to prove such intractable material for the royal managers as the country gentlemen had been in 1673 and November 1685, since they lacked parliamentary experience and the kind of social cohesion and personal connections that bound together the gentry members of the seventeenth-century 'country' opposition. Under detailed and skilled managerial control they could have been as malleable, dependable and silent as the burgh members in the Scottish Parliament.

This is the general picture. A more detailed survey of the rights which corporate towns possessed by virtue of their charters, the different kinds of electoral franchise (still subject at this time to changes determined by a simple majority of the Commons), the economic and social relations between towns and rural areas, reveals a very wide variety of patterns. In particular, the balance between towns and urban oligarchies on the one hand, and the landowning classes of adjacent rural areas on the other, depended on very widely different socio-economic structures. At the simplest, many smaller towns like Gatton, Heytesbury or Aldeburgh were owned by a single proprietor, or were entirely dominated by two or three landowners. Many market towns were economically – and so politically – dependent on the patronage of the local gentry, with the mayor and alder-men particularly vulnerable as retail tradesmen. Political divisions often corresponded with different occupational groups.[12] Sometimes this reflected conflicts of interest within a town, but it was also connected with the pattern of economic relations that existed between a town and a surrounding country-side in which industry (mining, or domestic production of textiles) was largely situated; Derby and Newcastle upon Tyne are examples. Furthermore, country JPs could often determine the economic prosperity of a town through their control over roads, rivers and bridges, or by encouraging rival markets and fairs. In larger places, with a more diversified economy and a wealthier and more varied urban oligarchy, the town could aspire to play an independent role. Obviously size played an important part; a small town with a static economy was more likely to be under gentry or aristocratic influence than a larger place or one that was expanding.

Such socio-economic forces were not necessarily or universally the dominant factor. The purely mechanical political question of the type of parliamentary franchise was equally important. The Tory-dominated Commons of 1685 had favoured restric-tion of the electorate, whereas Whig majorities in 1679–81 had attempted to extend the franchise.[13] But it would not be correct

---

[12] Retail traders were vulnerable, inn-keepers intensely so, but those engaged in the textile trades and brewers were usually independent.

[13] See J. R. Jones, 'Restoration Election Petitions', *Durham University Journal*, March 1961.

to conclude that places with small electorates were dependent on the gentry, and places with popular voting necessarily independent. Norwich, with a wide franchise and a strong tradition of municipal politics, had been held by the Tories throughout the Exclusion elections. Bath, with a restricted corporation franchise, maintained a fierce independence. Some places with large electorates, like Southwark, had already gained the reputation, which they were to retain for two centuries, of being so corrupt that only wealthy men could finance a successful candidature. The intensity of competition for urban seats between townsmen and gentry also varied enormously. In some counties, like Hampshire and Nottinghamshire, townsmen could expect to be returned for the larger boroughs because gentry ambitions could be satisfied in the numerous small boroughs. But in a few heavily populated counties (Leicestershire and Derbyshire are examples) only the county town enjoyed representation and gentry competition crowded out townsmen.

Generally speaking it seems that the franchises which were most easily dominated by landowners from the countryside were those where the vote was vested in the freemen, or in the owners of certain houses or plots of land. But the whole subject is one that still requires more research work, and the same thing is true of the more general question of the political consequences of social and economic changes and development. As a hypothesis it can be suggested that society was not so rigid as it was to become in the first half of the eighteenth century, when a hardening of social divisions may have a direct connection with the growth of political stability, as Professor J. H. Plumb suggests.[14] But we do not have enough evidence at present to demonstrate any direct connection linking a trade cycle of boom and depression with the rise and subsidence of political activity and tension. The effect of particular economic developments (for instance Colbert's protective tariffs) on certain trades, industries and regions has still to be worked out in detail before any attempt can be made to estimate the political repercussions. In fact much more, and more detailed, research is

[14] See J. H. Plumb, *The Growth of Political Stability in England, 1675–1725* (1967), especially chapter 3.

needed before we can try to explain the very varied, and often highly idiosyncratic, ways in which towns behaved, and not only at this period but also earlier in the century, during the civil wars and the interregnum.[15]

Of all gaps in our present state of knowledge perhaps the most important is our relative ignorance of the social and economic structure of dissent during this period before 1688, and particularly in the towns, and of the repercussions of religious persecution or repression on dissenters and also on the communities in which they lived. They constituted a small minority in national terms, but we know that (as at Exeter and Yarmouth) they often played a major role in the economic and political life of many towns, and that this is why James selected them to be his instruments. But many unanswered questions remain. How far did dissenters form a separate, interrelated community? Were their business interests equally interconnected? Did they dominate certain distinctive economic sectors – for instance the main distributive functions in the textile trades? What were the economic effects of intermittent repression? Did neighbourly attitudes towards them change as some became prosperous and employers of labour? Did business jealousies underlie political enmities on a significant scale?

The generalizations which are all that can at present be offered on the socio-economic structure of the corporations and boroughs, and their political connections, must be treated as hypotheses, subject to verification and possible amendment in the light of further research. For the purposes of this study the outlines of the problem, and this statement of the general context, are sufficient. This is so because these questions were precisely those which James's agents were themselves engaged in asking, although unfortunately we have only a part of the material which they collected in attempting to answer them.

For almost exactly a year these agents busily concerned

15 It is unfortunate that the *History of Parliament*, acting on the assumption that connections and interests of the sort described by Namier were equally important for other periods, has taken MPs as its unit of study. Constituencies would have been far preferable, not only in giving an element of continuity in study, but in permitting extensions from political into social, economic and demographic studies.

themselves with discovering all the facts about the internal structure of towns possessing parliamentary representation, ascertaining who had local influence, what local interests needed satisfaction or conciliation. They analyzed urban factions and the relations between them and the neighbouring aristocracy and gentry, and reported on the religious composition of the population. These agents thoroughly explored all aspects of county and municipal politics, so as to be ready to take advantage of every favourable circumstance. We have summaries of their work for twenty-three counties and over 110 boroughs, and there are more indirect indications of their activities elsewhere. In all, they reached the stage of promoting royal candidates in constituencies returning over half the members of the Commons, and although we do not have the detailed correspondence between the managers and the itinerant agents and local informants, enough material has survived to reconstruct their operating methods. It is clear that they adapted their techniques to the particular circumstances which they discovered in the localities, and also that these techniques closely resembled those which had been developed and used by Shaftesbury, the architect of the first Whig party and the first organizer of systematic parliamentary opposition to the crown in the country as well as at Westminster.

This resemblance was no coincidence. Many of the professional agents employed by James had formerly worked as active Whigs.[16] Some entered royal service through Penn's recommendation, at the time when he was organizing addresses. Others had changed sides, like the journalist Henry Care, simply to earn a living. One group, of whom Nathaniel Wade was the most notorious, had entered James's service to save their necks after being captured or implicated in Monmouth's and Argyll's rebellions. By giving evidence against old comrades they had so isolated themselves that they had no alternative but to follow the king in whatever he did.

[16] Duckett, i, 432, Major Braman; ii, 218, Dr Cox, James Clarke, Benjamin Dennis, Richard Adams, Nathaniel Wade, John Jones, Richard Andrewes. Local agents, i, 197, Sir Thomas Stanley, William Farmer, Manwaring, Timothy Seymour, Richard Newton, Chris Morrall; 209, Jeffreys of Devizes.

The Treasury solicitors (first Burton and Graham, then the Trinder brothers) supervised the day-to-day work of the agents. The chief direction of the campaign was in the hands of Robert Brent, a Catholic lawyer from Gloucestershire related to Lord Carrington, who was principal successor to the ill-fated Edward Coleman as James's confidential agent in matters of domestic politics. He had bravely engaged in an extraordinarily dangerous attempt to discredit Whig informers during the Popish Plot, but simultaneously he was performing intelligence work for Danby, which on one occasion involved betraying to him confidential information on James's planned political moves. In more normal times his main work as a lawyer was as a specialist in transferring money and bequests overseas for Catholic purposes. This work gave him an extensive connection among his coreligionists, so that it was logical for James to employ him as the agent who granted dispensations in 1685. The influence which this function gave him was greatly increased when shortly afterwards he was made responsible for the distribution of secret-service money, a duty which he combined with responsibility for issuing pardons. This brought him into close contact with persons suspected or accused of complicity in the plot of 1683 and the rebellions of 1685, and it was from among them that several of his agents were recruited.[17]

Brent presided from the beginning over the detailed work involved in the regulations and purges of the corporations and the preparation of elections, and it was also to him that the lords lieutenant reported the replies of the gentry to the three questions. The only other manager who seems to have been personally active was Sir Nicholas Butler, who was credited with doing much of the work in London, but no evidence survives as to the relations, or distribution of functions, between the two men. In general they both worked under the superior authority of Sunderland and Jeffreys, but we know that the latter did not in practice participate or take any real interest, and it seems that

[17] CJ, ix, 584, 607, 612; J. W. A. Ellis, *The Ellis Correspondence* (1829), i, 215, 220, 269; J. Y. Akerman, *Secret Services of Charles II and James II* (1851), pp. 180, 196–7, 205; Grey, ix, 52–3, 65–6, 339–40; Duckett, i, 241n–2n.

Sunderland only became actively involved during the last weeks before elections were due.

The regulation of the corporations occupied a great deal of very detailed attention and work. It was a far more protracted and complex task than the procedure involved in the questioning and purging of the gentry. First, all existing members of the governing bodies of the corporations were subjected to canvassing. Agents were sent out into the provinces to carry out the interrogations, and also to collect information on who was available for appointment as replacements for men who refused to collaborate. More generally they were asked to report on every relevant detail of local politics, and the instructions which they received before setting out on their provincial tours (in December 1687, April, June, July and September 1688) deserve careful analysis.[18]

The instructions show that, so far from being a temporary expedient forced on James by unfavourable circumstances, the appointment of these agents was the first, essential step in the construction of a permanent royal electoral machine. In the first place, the agents were told to appoint correspondents in each town who were to report regularly to Brent; these men, drawn from the local residents (in some of the few instances where we know their names they were dissenting ministers) were to be rewarded with minor government posts – if they were judged to be suitable for them. The agents were also to report on the behaviour of existing revenue officers; the dismissal of those held to be unreliable would create vacancies for the appointment of correspondents. Secondly, the agents were entrusted with extraordinarily wide discretionary powers. It can be demonstrated that most major purges of corporations followed directly from the reports that they sent in, but when working in the towns they were empowered to follow their own judgement in deciding who should be dismissed or appointed – they were not restricted to the persons named by Brent and the committee. Similarly, they were given full powers to manage the actual elections. They

[18] Duckett, i, 194–9; Addit., 32523, ff.55–8.

were to organize the electors into subscribing general statements promising to return members acceptable to James or, better still, to get them to write specific letters of invitation to their intended members. The addresses sent to James in June and July 1688 contain many general promises of this kind, and by September the agents had prepared many candidacies by this method.[19] When elections were announced the agents were given additional powers and duties. They were to see that the sheriffs (who were men, it should be noted, belonging to the substantial land-owning class) attended borough as well as county elections. They were to try and baulk the candidacies of men hostile to royal policies, and to counteract the influence of the clergy, which it was assumed would be against them. In addition, they were to give general guidance to those who were elected, before they left for Westminster, and they were also to act more generally in explaining and defending royal policies (such as the prosecution of the Seven Bishops), while carefully noting and reporting all evidence of opposition activities and propaganda.

The surviving reports show how effectively the agents used all these powers, and explain the alarm and indignation which their activities provoked. There was close coordination between the agents in the provinces and the committee in Brent's chambers in the Temple. When the agents reported that a town was being obstinately resistant and unmanageable, we find that in most cases actions of *quo warranto* followed.[20] Their suggestions as to who was willing to stand, and who stood the best chance of being elected, influenced the selection of men on Sunderland's September list of royally approved candidates. In places where new charters were issued it was the agents who chose, guided and supervised the new office holders or, as at Colchester, saw to the creation of a new set of freemen who would decide the next parliamentary election.[21] They sometimes succeeded in persuading doubtful men not to stand, and recommended likely collaborationist candidates for appointment to offices in the gift of the crown. They frequently worked to

[19] Published in *A Collection of the Several Addresses* (1688).
[20] Duckett, i, 208, 210, 224; ii, 246.
[21] *Ibid.*, i, 410.

reconcile interests that were equally willing to support royal policies but were divided on local issues and by personal differences.

In boroughs where the franchise was in doubt, the agents informed Brent which would best suit the king's purposes, and they took action themselves. At Barnstaple they reported that the Tories had won in 1685 by disfranchising non-residents; now, having canvassed these people and got pledges of support from them, they would be reinstated as voters, and the agents could guarantee that they would be accepted as such by the newly regulated corporation.[22] The provisions of the new charters which were issued in September were based on the detailed suggestions of the agents as to what specific local rights could, with electoral advantage, be confirmed or extended. In some cases, by a deliberate decision, no new charter was issued after the old one was surrendered or forfeited; in Shropshire only Bishop's Castle, out of five such corporations, received a new charter. The explanation is that it was the only one in which the franchise was vested in the corporation itself, so that a new charter was needed if an election was to take place at all, and those named in it could be expected to vote for royal candidates. In the other towns the interval before a new charter was issued would mean control of municipal affairs by specially appointed temporary commissioners. As the agents reported in another case, that of Poole in Dorset, this would enable James to do as he pleased.[23]

Two factors can be seen as determining which constituencies attracted the most intense activity by the agents. First, they naturally concentrated on towns with a corporation franchise, since in such places regulation of the corporation would lead directly to control of elections. Secondly, most of the corporations which were regulated had received new charters in the years 1681–6; of sixty-five which were regulated up to the end of March, sixty fell into this category. This particularly close attention is attributable not only to the fact that these new charters had given the crown the power of removing magistrates

[22] *Ibid.*, ii, 231–2, 241; Addit., 34510, f.115; *Publick Occurrences*, No. 10.
[23] Duckett, ii, 178, 221, 242; Luttrell, i, 445.

and officers, but even more to the use which had been made of this power in 1682–5 to install Tories and Anglicans, the same men who could now be expected to try to obstruct royal policies.

Analysis of the campaign of regulation, from November 1687 to October 1688, shows that the agents' activities followed a logical pattern of development, so that by the latter stages they had become systematic and relatively standardized. The often-repeated view, that the repetition of purges was an admission of failure, and that the agents worked in confusion, without a plan, purpose or any sense of progress towards an objective, simply does not bear close examination.

Down to the end of April, during the first of the three phases, the main emphasis of the campaign was on the regulation of corporations. The first purges were made immediately after the regulating committee was established in November, and from the first the avowed purpose was to prepare for parliamentary elections. By the end of March over 1200 persons judged to be unreliable had been ejected from municipal offices, and replacements had been provided for them. In fifty-one corporations this work involved only a single purge. In fourteen other places, mainly larger towns, more than one purge was carried out, but this double purge was planned from the start, it was a deliberate move and not the result of an inefficiently planned or executed first attempt.[24]

In February the first detailed reports on the political state of parliamentary boroughs began to come in, but the bulk of this work belonged to the second phase of the campaign which began in April, when twenty agents were sent into the provinces where they continued to work throughout the summer. Included in the reports which they made from mid-April on were recommendations for further purges or, in cases where they could make no real progress, the initiation of actions of *quo warranto.* Further purges were enforced, and actions started, but now the

---

[24] The regulations and purges are listed in the register of the Privy Council: PRO PC 2, 72; Nottingham University Library, Phillipps MSS, 8555, iii. Blathwayt wrote on 19 January 1688 that the first Bristol purge would be followed by a second and more thorough, as in other corporations; in other words repeated purges *were planned*, not enforced by difficulties.

most important work for the agents was the collection of electoral information. Their reports are filled with detailed accounts of individual constituencies, listing the names and describing the interests, prospects and ascertained (or assumed) opinions of intending candidates. They discussed the reliability of prospective collaborators, and paid particular attention to the local strength and attitudes of the dissenters. Many of them were appointed as deputy lieutenants and as JPs in order to increase their local prestige and influence.

The third and last phase may be taken as beginning on 24 August, the day on which James ordered writs to be issued for parliamentary elections.[25] This initiated a short period of most intensive work. Canvassing and some purges continued, but the bulk of such work had been completed. What now happened was largely a topping-up process. There were twenty regulations of places that had already been purged; of these thirteen were for the second time, five for the third, and two for the fourth. There were also ten purges of places that had not previously been regulated. What is significant is that all but four of these purges (which affected a total of 255 persons) were on a small scale, many involving the removal of individual occupants of key posts such as town clerks. The main technical business during this last phase was issuing new charters, which represented a new development. Only two had been issued in the whole of 1687, and a further two in the first six months of 1688. Three followed in July, but in August and September no fewer than twenty-eight were rushed out at speed, following the example of February and March 1685 when grants had been made in large numbers just before the elections. Twenty of the new charters were reissues, replacing charters that had been granted in 1681–6, and of the places affected eleven were major towns with well-established urban oligarchies, where the agents needed all the help they could get.[26]

---

[25] PRO, SP Domestic, James II, Entry Book 56, p. 425. The agents had been working in the constituencies since the end of July when Sunderland asked the lords lieutenant to help them. They made their reports in return on 11 September: *Publick Occurrences*, No. 30.

[26] *HMC, XIIth Report*, app, vi, 298–9. See also R. H. George, 'The Charters granted to English Parliamentary Corporations in 1688', *English Historical Review*, 55.

During this last, pre-election phase, the agents combined final reports on constituencies with arranging matters for the actual polls. Many of their recommendations were incorporated in Sunderland's directives. In these, sent out on 13 and 15 September, he wrote to thirty-three individuals directing them to stand for named constituencies; thirteen were for places that had been regulated. In addition he wrote to lords lieutenant informing them of approved royal candidates for constituencies in their counties; eleven were for county seats, and sixty-two for boroughs (including thirty-one for regulated places).[27] The court proposed to enlist the judges, using them to supervise the arrangements, since they would be in the provinces on their autumn assizes while the elections were in progress.[28]

The total effort which James's agents and servants invested in the campaign to pack Parliament was impressive and exceptional. Only Shaftesbury's electoral activities in 1679–81 are comparable, a revealing fact in itself. Like Shaftesbury, James was concentrating all his efforts on achieving a single objective. Just as everything had been subordinated to the passing of Exclusion then, so James now aimed at repeal of the Tests and penal laws, virtually ignoring all other questions. Again like Shaftesbury when the first Whigs began to lose impetus, James had no choice in the later stages of the campaign but to rely increasingly on organization and propaganda, on manipulating every possible electoral technique and mechanism; this was particularly the case after the trial of the Seven Bishops, when spontaneous dissenting support could no longer be taken for granted. But the parallel with the first Whigs should not be pushed too far. Shaftesbury had tried to use popular support in order to force himself and his policy of Exclusion on a resistant monarch. Time and authority were against him, popularity a waning asset. In contrast, James already possessed more effective power than any of his Stuart predecessors, and the campaign represented a move to make this power complete, total and permanent. He had (or so he thought) ample time for his agents

[27] PRO, SP Domestic, James II; Entry Book 56, pp. 428–41; Addit., 34526, ff.50–54.
[28] Addit., 32523, f.54; Gutch, *Collectanea Curiosa*, i, 391–2, 393–7.

to do their work thoroughly, exploring the intricacies of the political situation in every county and borough until preparations were complete, and it was for James alone to decide on the date of the elections.

Even though the surviving reports from the agents are only summaries and incomplete, we have a wealth of information about the workings of local politics. They reveal the limited nature of the electoral influence which the court possessed in its own right – even in dockyard towns like Rochester the royal interest had to be supplemented by work by the agents.[29] The reports also show that James intended to put no reliance on crude corruption. The agents reported that several places (Eye and Stockbridge for example) were entirely mercenary and would sell their votes to the highest bidders; they did not suggest that James should enter into the competition, but proposed that they should wait until the election had taken place and then approach the successful candidates.[30] The key to success lay not in the distribution of money but in the recruitment and exploitation of sectional interests, and of these the dissenters were easily the most important.

At the simplest the agents noted that in many small towns (for instance several in Dorset) the dissenters were a majority, so that by installing them in local offices electoral success was assured. There were some areas – the whole of Wales and most of the Lincolnshire towns – where there were very few dissenters, so that a completely different approach had to be used. But in the larger towns, which possessed relatively diversified social and economic structures, and which behaved in very different ways politically, the support of the dissenting interest was recognized as being the basis for successful management; without it nothing could be achieved.[31] Again it is worth repeating how important an examination of the internal structure of municipal politics is towards any understanding of the working of late seventeenth-century politics. From the early years of the Long Parliament

[29] Duckett, i, 362–3.
[30] *Ibid.*, i, 432; ii, 228, 247.
[31] *Ibid.*, i, 146–7, 272–87, 313, 361–2, 364, 410; ii, 221–2, 231.

until at least the passage of the Triennial Act in 1694, control over the municipalities was as important as it was in contemporary Dutch politics. Political struggles within the towns, and outside attempts to gain control, were of central importance, but the patterns of alliance and enmities constantly changed over the years, as did the relative strength of the interests concerned – the crown, the clergy, the lords lieutenant, their deputies and the JPS, the country gentry, the dissenters and other urban sections, some based on certain occupational or economic connections, others on factions.

The indications are that in such large towns as Norwich, Bristol, Colchester, Coventry and Nottingham there was (and had been since 1660) a permanently unstable situation arising out of the existence of a many-sided factional struggle for municipal power and office. For most of the time there were three leading factions, of which the dissenters were perhaps in numerical terms the smallest among the office-holding classes, but also the most cohesive and united. In only one case (Abingdon) did James's agents report a division between Presbyterians and Congregationalists, but although this may have been influenced by wishful thinking, there was certainly no repetition of the formerly embittered and politically crippling sectarian feuds of the last years of the Commonwealth.[32] Moreover, by the 1680s the word dissenter needs a fairly wide interpretation, extending beyond regular attenders of nonconformist conventicles to cover occasional conformists and sympathetic conformists as well. The factor that united these sections was their common experience during the years after the Restoration and the passage of the Corporation Act in 1661.[33] This act had been intended primarily to bar all dissenters from municipal offices, but the temporary commissioners appointed to enforce it had used their powers to eject all persons whom they suspected of being politically disaffected. Inevitably they often used this opportunity to eliminate their own personal enemies,

[32] *Ibid.*, ii, 237–8. ✓ (ω13ἑω).
[33] J. H. Sacret, 'The Restoration Government and Municipal Corporations', *English Historical Review*, 45.

and the country gentry often tried to bring towns into an orbit of dependence.

The result of the ways in which the Corporation Act was enforced was that many Anglicans and conformists found themselves out of office, and that in many places the dissenters came to represent the cause of municipal independence. Consequently, the act achieved its intended effects for only a short period, and by the late 1660s the loyalist groups on whom the act had conferred a monopoly of office were losing ground. In some towns they were insufficiently strong on their own to prevent men purged in 1661 from recovering office and influence, and they did not receive regular suppport or help from the crown.[34] More often, the Anglicans were weakened as a result of dissension and divisions within their own ranks. As at court, so in the municipal governments there were never enough places available to satisfy more than a minority of aspirants. Disappointed men were therefore led to align themselves with the opposition faction which had its nucleus in the dissenting interest.

In many towns a three-sided factional struggle developed, with the group in power facing opposition from two groups who were united only for the purpose of achieving office and influence. In the 1660s this meant an Anglican oligarchy, who had been put into office by the Corporation Act, fighting a coalition of dissident Anglicans and the dissenting interest. The enforcement of the penal laws against the latter was as often and as much a part of this local political fight, as a result of genuine religious antagonism. By the mid-1670s, as at Norwich, Yarmouth and Coventry, the dissenting interest had got back into office and again dominated the corporation. Very quickly a rift developed between the leading dissenters and their former allies among the dissatisfied Anglicans, who now found themselves as effectively excluded from office as under the earlier Anglican oligarchy. In a few places, for example Norwich, a vigorous local leader took advantage of this split to launch a counter-offensive. There Lord Yarmouth reunited the two Anglican factions and led them to a series of victories in parliamentary

[34] Good examples are Coventry, Great Yarmouth ar.d Norwich.

elections during the Exclusion Crisis, quite against the general pattern, and ejected the dissenting leaders and their sympathizers. But in most places the dissenting interest provided Shaftesbury with a series of Whig electoral victories, and lost control only when the crown intervened with the writs of *quo warranto* in order to restore monopolies of office to the Anglican oligarchs.

By its nature a three-sided struggle for office and power was bound to produce perpetual instability. The Anglican oligarchs restored in 1681–3 soon began to quarrel among themselves. At Bristol an intense contest developed between one faction, which was associated with the extremist high-flying clergy, and a coterie of wealthy former magistrates, who were forced to turn to the defeated and ejected Whigs for help. In Norwich it was the popular Tory extremists who found themselves discarded by the oligarchs soon after power was regained.

Two important conclusions can be derived from this discussion. First, that when James turned against the Tories and Anglicans in 1687 there was absolutely no question of his facing anything that resembled the united front that the country gentry presented to him when they were canvassed. The vicious divisions which had existed for two decades in the towns gave his agents ample opportunity for making local deals. Secondly, and this is even more crucial, James by breaking with the Tories and turning to the Whigs and dissenters was allying with what were, in purely local terms of municipal politics, the strongest and most durable of the existing factions. In the past they had been checked only by royal intervention, but now in alliance with the crown they could be expected to consolidate a dominating position.

The dissenting allies of James were most advantageously placed in the many medium-sized towns which had been consistent in electing Whigs during the Exclusion Crisis. In a great many of these towns the Tories were extremely weak, so that both in the 1660s and again after the *quo warrantos* of 1681–3 the crown had had to rely primarily on the local country gentry for help in maintaining control. Gentlemen had been made freemen and appointed as magistrates and officials so that the towns lost all semblance of independence. In some places the country gentlemen used their influence to promote their own interests at the direct expense of the townsmen, and in most of these remodelled towns there had been a sharp increase in municipal taxation. Equally unpopular was the increased influence and freedom of action which the new charters and the appointed magistrates gave to the clergy, which led to a more continuous and effective period of repression in 1681–5 than at any time since the early 1660s.[35] Another effect of gentry control was seen in the parliamentary elections of 1685, when very few boroughs returned townsmen or even men with general commercial connections; the vast majority of MPs were country gentlemen with interests that were either remote from, or even diametrically opposed to, those of their constituents.[36]

By contrast, most of the candidates suggested by James's agents in 1688 were themselves residents of the towns. Royal propaganda attacking clerical intolerance would find a ready response. The ejection of the gentry who had triumphed over the Whig towns during the Stuart reaction of 1681–5 was a guarantee of municipal freedom as well as of religious toleration. Urban dissenters enjoyed a wider and much more secure freedom in both the religious and political spheres than was to be theirs after 1688, when they had to rely on the vulnerable practice of occasional conformity. The agents could also play on much more primitive feelings, on the innumerable personal enmities which pullulated in the enclosed life of relatively small and isolated communities, and also on the desire for revenge upon old enemies. In Bridgwater and Taunton, places which Jeffreys had savaged in 1685 during his Western Assize, and where animosities between Anglican and dissenter had already been more intense than elsewhere, bitterness led former Whigs to work with a Catholic king in order to oust and humiliate their local opponents. Similarly, James's agents found ready collaborators (as at Nottingham) among Whigs who had been victimized in 1682–4 for resisting the surrender or forfeiture of the charters.

---

[35] For instance at Chichester: CSPD, 1680–81, pp, 467, 472–3, 585; 1682, pp. 333, 345.

[36] This can be seen particularly in the impositions on trade, and on the traditional target for gentry hostility, new buildings in London: CJ, ix, 739, 742–3, 747.

James adopted another of Shaftesbury's techniques for winning support from sectional interests when his agents outlined legislation to be passed by the next Parliament, to facilitate economic development and remedy certain social grievances. At first, proposals were made to combine general toleration with an act of general naturalization (to encourage immigration), and the establishment of a register of lands for each county, but later, reform of the coinage and partial abolition of imprisonment for debt were added.[37] In an address, the clothiers of Devon and Somerset thanked James effusively for responding so quickly by appointing a commission to investigate their complaints against the export of wool. He even promised the Exeter clothiers that he would do something about the new French duties that were affecting their exports.[38] The most pointed, controversial and revealing of all proposals made in James's name was a suggestion that Parliament would finance the construction of thirty-five new warships exclusively by a land tax. In other words, the burden would fall on James's declared enemies, the landed gentry and aristocracy, a clear answer to one of the most acrimoniously debated questions of the time, the relative share of taxation to be paid by the landed and the mercantile sections of the nation.[39]

One category of constituencies was almost entirely neglected by James's agents. Boroughs by prescription were towns that sent members to Parliament but did not have a charter. This meant that they could not be regulated and their returning officers were not susceptible to direct royal pressure. There was some discussion of giving thirty-six of them charters so as to bring them under control, but nothing was done in this direction.[40] At the other extreme were the garrison towns, which were entirely subject to royal control. Officers were made freemen at Carlisle,

[37] Addit., 34510, ff.52, 113; Luttrell, i, 416–17; Nottingham University Library, Phillipps MSS, 8589, ii, Povey to Southwell, 13 October 1687.
[38] PWA, 2141; *A Collection of the Several Addresses*, p. 8.
[39] Addit., 34510, f.113.
[40] *Ibid.* f.143.

and one was named as a royal candidate at Berwick.[41] At Queenborough the two candidates were the deputy governor of Sheerness and the commander of the Nore guardship, on whose behalf the extremely drastic method of billeting of troops on the householders was seriously threatened. At a time when the *dragonnades* in France had aroused universal horror, this would have been a provocative experiment, but it was necessitated by the local strength of the Banks family interest, which had been associated with the crown in 1679–81 and 1685, but was now hostile.[42]

During the last two phases other dubious expedients were considered. There was discussion of arranging assistance (in other words frauds and malpractices) by the returning officers. A suggestion was made that the franchise should be restricted, preferably to the corporation itself, a tactic which the Tories and the court had favoured in the face of Shaftesbury's popular support, but which would now benefit the Whigs whom James had recently installed. A rumour circulated that special commissioners would be appointed to supervise individual elections, and there was a more widespread belief that James would permit Catholics to stand for election and take their seats in the Commons as well as in the Lords. Penn denied this, but certainly many Catholics in their replies to the three questions assumed that they would be eligible to serve as MPs. The position was not clarified until 21 September, when James conceded that only Protestants would be able to take seats in the Commons.[43]

None of these dubious methods became part of official policy, but that they were even considered underlines the fact that the whole campaign was inevitably a gamble. If it had produced a clear majority for the court, the tactics used by James's agents would have given a resolute minority opposition plenty of opportunities for complaints of breach of privilege and invasion

---

[41] PWA, 2161; *HMC, XIIth Report*, app, vii, 207; PRO, SP Domestic, James II, Entry Book 56, p. 441.
[42] Addit., 34512, f.77; Duckett, i, 363–4.
[43] PWA, 2110a, 2126a, 2147; Addit., 34487, f.29; 34512, f.100; PRO, PC 2, 72, p. 736.

of the freehold rights of electors, although the precedent of 1685, when Whig petitions had simply been buried in committee showed that this was a danger that could be contained. But if the court had found itself short of a working majority the practical results would have been disastrous. Petitions containing allegations of malpractices and fraud would have inflamed the House at the outset (as in the case of the Addled Parliament in 1614) and forced an early dissolution. Loss of control over the Commons, and its committee of privileges and elections, could have led to the mass expulsion of members returned through the efforts of the agents – as monopolists had been expelled in 1640.

In retrospect James regretted ever having embarked on the campaign. He had, of course, been misled into using unworthy men and methods. More convincingly, his actions at the time showed that he was aware of the risks that were involved. As part of the wholesale concessions which he made in October, on the eve of William's invasion and after the writs for elections had already been withdrawn, he wrote to the lords lieutenant ordering them to inquire into the abuses and malpractices which, he said, were alleged to have been committed during the regulations and election preparations.[44] In practical terms this meant that James was throwing his agents to the wolves. Obviously he was doing so only because of the pressure of events, so that this move did not reconcile those whom he had earlier discarded or alienated, while his collaborators naturally looked after their own interests and safety during the crisis, deserting James like everyone else. Old obligations saved Brent. When arrested he received bail, on the advice of Danby (a former employer) and Devonshire (whose pardon had passed through his hands), and was able to abscond to France.[45]

James did not have to rely entirely on the campaign. There was also a nucleus, a permanent court interest, of MPs. Forty-three of the 106 candidates on Sunderland's September list had

---

[44] Addit., 34510, f.152; PRO, SP Domestic, James II, Entry Book 56, p. 451; Clarke, *James the Second*, ii, 139.
[45] Grey, ix, 52–3, 65–70.

sat for the same constituency in 1685, and an additional four for other seats. There were also high officials who could guarantee their own return – Sir Stephen Fox at Cricklade, Henry Guy at Hedon, Richard Kent at Chippenham, and others. James also enjoyed the support of a few magnates, men of social rank who controlled interests or connections of the sort that generally formed the basis of seventeenth- and eighteenth-century politics. Such men had nothing in common with Brent's employees, and an attempt was made to prevent the latter intruding into places where James had independent and respectable support. Sir Robert Holmes, as governor, controlled three Isle of Wight towns; Bishop Nathaniel Crewe dominated Durham City and expected to dictate to the county as well.[46] The Duke of Norfolk, though there were some justifiable doubts about his reliability, was in control of Arundel, Horsham and Castle Rising.[47] Bernard Howard was responsible for Winchester and kept the agents out after a clash.[48] Jeffreys, as chancellor, expected to nominate four MPs.[49]

Only two royal servants possessed really large electoral interests. The first, that of the Duke of Beaufort, was in decline. He was expected to manage Wales and the Marches, but he gave little evidence of the vigour and skill needed for this mammoth task. His report on election prospects was so pessimistic as to indicate that he had done little or no work, and was failing to give a definite lead to his followers. In contrast the Earl of Bath really did control and oversee his geographically smaller but much more heavily represented area of Cornwall and Devon.

Bath's importance and influence depended on his longstanding leadership of the major Tory and Anglican interest in the west country. He and his family represented the outstanding example of old Cavalier principles in religion and politics; he was a man whose life was centred on service to Church and crown in the provinces rather than as a courtier in Whitehall. Indeed,

[46] Duckett, i, 115, 432; PRO, SP Domestic, James II, Entry Book 56, p. 429.
[47] Duckett, i, 314, 441.
[48] *Ibid.*, i, 431–2.
[49] *Ibid.*, ii, 216 (Camelford), 249–50 (Bletchingly).

at James's accession he lost a valuable post in the royal household, but more than made up for this by a spectacular extension of his local influence. More than any other individual he was the most active participant in, and beneficiary from, the Tory reaction of 1681–5. All but one of the eighteen Cornish corporations received new charters through his agency during these years, fifteen of them specifically in preparation for the 1685 elections. But in contrast to almost every other beneficiary of the Tory reaction, Bath retained his gains, his offices and his influence throughout James's reign. There was no action against Cornish charters. Regulations of Cornish boroughs only began in June 1688, and then on a smaller scale than in other parts of the country.[50] Bath's survival, his combination of close collaboration with James and a genuine attachment to Anglicanism, began to look increasingly anomalous after Rochester's dismissal, when Anglicans in other parts of the country were being dismissed from all offices.

Whatever their reservations towards each other, James and Bath had little choice but to work together. Each needed the other, neither could afford an open break, although Bath was becoming increasingly uneasy. James had no prominent Catholic (or dissenter) in the west country capable of replacing Bath as lord lieutenant and Governor of Plymouth. Furthermore Bath's interest was so extensive and well entrenched that if he was dismissed so much work would be needed in the way of regulations and action against charters that the date fixed for the elections might have to be put back. On his side, Bath could not afford to risk royal displeasure. Many of his relations and dependants held offices from which they could be dismissed at will. Abrogation of the charters would shatter his electoral interest. But the main tie which preserved the alliance between James and Bath was their common fear of Edward Seymour.

Seymour, arguably the most aggressive politician of the time, was Bath's rival as leader of west-country Toryism, but he had lost much of his influence during the *quo warranto* proceedings

---

[50] *Ibid.*, i, 379–81; ii, 213–17, 270–71; PRO, PC 2, 72, pp. 694, 723, 734; in June (with repeats in September), Liskeard, Lostwithiel, Bodmin, Camelford, Grampound and Bossiney; three in August, East and West Looe, Fowey.

against the charters in 1681–5. His attempt to excite the Commons on this issue during the first session of 1685, on the ground that the crown could now interfere with the freedom of elections, had met with no response at that time, but by 1688 had been confirmed in every way. He was now the natural and active head of opposition to royal policies, and in an excellent position to harass Bath. The extent of his support was revealed by the answers to the three questions; in Cornwall there was only one favourable reply, ten were absent and the fifteen refusals all followed a formula devised by Seymour. In Devon, where nine replies were favourable, all forty-nine refusals used the same formula, as did another group of eleven in Somerset whose head was a close connection of Seymour. Equally significant is the proportion of former MPS among these men, sixteen in Devon and five in Cornwall, of whom only seven had gained election in 1685.[51]

Not surprisingly, Bath was pessimistic when he reported the replies to the three questions, and he had other grounds for disquiet. Many leading Cornish families like the Trelawneys feared that they were being reduced to the level of vassals, and many ordinary gentry families had resented his imposition of relatives and more than a dozen 'foreigners' on constituencies in 1685. In the boroughs too the electors gave trouble, promising to elect his nominees only on condition that they were Cornish-men and Protestants – the first demand was awkward since (as in 1685) the court was expecting Bath to reserve some places for court officials who had no interest of their own.

To add to these troubles, Bath discovered during the summer of 1688 that 'his' territory was being invaded by Brent's agents, who had previously been kept away. Although Bath was still nominally the king's representative, the agents began to canvass independently and without consulting him, to suggest candidates for seats in his gift, and to send in reports indicating that Bath's interest was declining. The agents were clearly, if indirectly, arguing that a takeover would be necessary if royal interests were to be served in the forthcoming elections. At first they did

[51] Duckett, i. 373–6, 377–9; ii, 10–15, 25–6.

not intervene directly in borough affairs, but by the late summer the regulations were being carried out by Edward Nosworthy without reference to Bath, who bitterly complained that his position and reputation were being undermined. This intrusion also led him to maintain his correspondence with William, as a form of insurance. Nosworthy was a natural extremist, who had formerly been one of the hottest Whigs and was in personal difficulties through extravagance. He was an old enemy of Bath, who had used a *quo warranto* to get control of the family borough of St Ives. His first aim was its recovery but his general progress was such that by September he was in a position to challenge Bath, and only William's invasion prevented a trial of strength between them.[52]

William's invasion wrecked Nosworthy's interest and career. Bankrupt, he joined James in France. The other two interests fought an even battle. It is significant that Seymour was the first notable to rally to William at Exeter. By doing so he hoped to get a head start over his rival, and his sponsorship of the Western Association was intended not only to impress William but also to be an organization that would give Seymour a pre-ponderant influence in the west. Bath avoided the annihilation of his interest by switching sides at a decisive moment – he brought over Plymouth so as to free William for his advance on London. He was able to throw all the blame for the malpractices of the last few years on Nosworthy and the agents, and adroitly and effectively made use of James's restoration of the old charters in October. He presided over the reinstatement of the Tory office-holders, which consolidated his own influence, being engaged in an elaborately staged ceremony of restoration at Exeter on the very same day that William was landing in nearby Torbay.[53]

London was the other area which can be considered a separate unit during the campaign. It is a remarkable sign of changed times that James had so little trouble in the capital, which remained under firm royal control until royal authority as a

[52] Addit., 41805, f.119; PRO, SP Domestic, Entry Book 56, p. 457; PRO, 31/4, part 1, ff.106–7.
[53] Addit., 41805, f.118.

whole had begun to crumble. After all, London had been the traditional centre of political opposition to the Stuarts, and royal control had been achieved in 1681–4 as a result of a prolonged and bitter party struggle which left the city Whigs shattered. During this struggle the city Tories had developed an efficient party machine, but James was able to displace them in 1687–8 without difficulty or any noticeable repercussions. The dissenters had been hammered in 1685, and London and its suburbs had remained entirely quiet during Monmouth's rebellion. Governmentally the new charter gave James unlimited power to purge dissidents. The practice of summer camps for the army on Blackheath and Hounslow Heath contained an implied threat of military occupation, and in order to ward off the danger of troops being billeted the city authorities could be relied upon to suppress disorders.

Royal control over London was largely an end in itself, as it was not electorally important except for propaganda purposes. London was used as an example for provincial towns, being the first place to be thoroughly regulated. Those who came in for the ejected aldermen and deputy lieutenants were a mixture of Catholics, opportunists and Whigs who had been turned out in 1682–4. Some six among them feature in the lists of royal candidates for provincial constituencies, a new variation on an old theme. In addition the purge of the livery companies consolidated court control over shrieval and other municipal elections and held out the prospect of winning the prestigious elections for the city and for Middlesex. At Westminster, where there was a large, rapacious and turbulent electorate, it was proposed to cut the number of voters to a tenth of the number voting in previous elections. Finally, when James called off the whole campaign, he demonstratively restored the city charter, and offered reinstatement to those whom he had dismissed, but their cool reception of his offers defeated his object.[54]

What measure of success did the campaign achieve? Of course the question is a speculative one, since the promises of those who

were canvassed, and the predictions of James's agents (and
opponents) were never put to the test of a general election.
Circumstances had changed so completely by the time that
elections were held, in January 1689, for the Convention
Parliament – with William in control, James in exile, his
collaborators and agents abandoned, the new charters withdrawn – that they cannot be used in any way as an indication
of how elections would have gone if William had not decided
to invade.[55]

The final reports from the agents, in the second week of
September, expressed considerable optimism. They summarized
their detailed work and achievements by dividing the counties
which they had covered into three categories. In the first group
of eight counties they predicted the election of a hundred men
who would comply with James, out of a total representation of
140 MPS. In the second group (returning eighty-eight MPS) and
the third (returning eighty-four) they asserted that there would
be a similar proportion of 'right' men.[56] In sum total this
amounts to a claim that out of counties returning 312 MPS James
would be sure of 223 candidates. This would not in itself consti-
tute a majority, but it would be a very substantial contribution
towards one, and these forecasts took no account of elections
in other parts of the country, which returned a further 201 MPS.

Since the elections were never held it is impossible to say how
accurately these agents' reports reflected the situation in mid-
September, how far their judgement was justified by electoral
realities, but the surviving evidence does make it possible to
demonstrate that these claims were not entirely speculative or
wildly fanciful, that they were based on work actually done
in the constituencies during the last two phases of the campaign.
We have reports on canvassing and the preparation of
candidacies in fourteen counties and 126 boroughs which
returned a total of 279 MPS, and to this should be added the
number of seats for Wales and the Cinque Ports for which no
detailed reports have survived, but where the agents said that

[55] See J. H. Plumb, 'The Elections to the Convention Parliament of 1689',
Cambridge Historical Journal, v.
[56] Duckett, ii, 220–21.

detailed promotional work had been done. This adds another forty places. In addition, there are the seats where patrons other than the agents had prepared, and finally Sunderland's nomination lists containing the names of forty-nine candidates (forty-four if Wales and the Cinque Ports are omitted) who were to stand for places outside the scope of the surviving reports by the agents.

These figures show that the agents had certainly done enough work to permit them to make these claims, though no one can now check the validity of the claims themselves. To summarize : approximately 200 constituencies, returning 400 out of the 513 MPS, had been subjected to some kind of direct governmental intervention. A working majority must have seemed to be within reach. Certainly the agents had more reason for their optimism than had Halifax for his cursory dismissals of the entire campaign. Halifax's opinion was mainly the product of an opinionated scepticism that he used to justify the inertia that was evident in his case not only during the campaign but also during the early critical stages of William's invasion.[57] William's confidential informants were more cautious. They qualified their early forecast that the campaign would fail by adding that this was only if the agents kept to legal courses of action. If they disregarded the laws then a parliamentary majority could certainly be constructed.[58]

Most historians, when they have noticed the campaign at all, have based their dismissals of its chances of success on impressionistic comments by contemporaries. Until very recently no serious attempt had been made to analyse even the results of the putting of the three questions to the deputy lieutenants, JPS and other gentry. Now a quantitative analysis has shown that generally the results were by no means as abysmal as was thought; the surviving returns reveal three nearly equal sections. In the English counties for which returns survive, approximately 26 per cent consented to repeal of the Tests and penal laws, and 27 per cent refused; a further 28 per cent must be categorized as doubtful, either in the sense of giving ambiguous or

[57] Dalrymple, appendix, part I, 219–20.
[58] PWA, 2145.

evasive answers or because their replies are difficult to interpret. The remainder were absent. In Wales, where we have returns from all counties, the figures were 12 per cent, 37 per cent and 5 per cent, with a very high proportion of absentees – 46 per cent.[59]

These figures need some explanation. First, they do represent a satisfactory numerical sample; the total of individuals approached in the counties for which we have material is over 1500, and the number of definite replies is over 1200. If we take into account the missing counties – Lancashire, Middlesex including London, Suffolk, Surrey, Warwick and Cheshire – the total questioned must have been at least 2,000. This is a fairly high proportion of the landed gentry class, at least 15 per cent, but whether it can be described as a representative cross-section is another matter. The canvass was aimed in the first instance at all existing deputy lieutenants and JPS, but later the net was thrown wider to cover possible substitutes for the vacancies which the dismissal of those giving unsatisfactory answers would create. This can be demonstrated by the fact that although there were fewer than 400 definitely affirmative replies to the three questions, it is possible to compile a list of more than 750 collaborators by adding those who were appointed by the agents on the knowledge, or assumption, that they were 'right'. They include sixty-seven former Whig or country opposition MPS, of whom only eight appear in the lord lieutenants' returns as consenting to repeal.

There were wide variations in the replies received from different parts of the country, which reflected variations in the social and religious characteristics of individual counties. The most distinctive came from Norfolk, where dissenters were numerous and influential; half the replies (twenty-two out of forty-five) specifically agreed to repeal of the penal laws but not of the Tests, a type of reply that was uncommon elsewhere.[60] Only a handful of unrelenting Anglicans answered in the opposite way, agreeing to repeal of the Tests but not of the penal laws, or agreeing to the latter only on stringent conditions of

[59] Carswell, *Descent on England*, appendix A.
[60] Duckett, i, 300–11.

good behaviour by the dissenters. A far more common reply, and one that was encountered everywhere, indicated a readiness to agree to the questions provided that the Church of England was first given substantial security. In five English counties more than 40 per cent of those questioned gave favourable replies, but this reflected no more than the presence of a number of Catholics on the Commission of the Peace – it will be recalled that James had been making Catholics JPS for over a year. The fact that Kent gave numerically the largest number of favourable replies (fifty-six), as well as the highest percentage, was the result of having fifteen Catholics as JPS. In Herefordshire, thirteen out of twenty-one favourable replies came from Catholics, in Worcestershire twelve out of nineteen, in Northumberland five out of twelve, while in Flintshire all five were from Catholics.[61]

Other variations were the result of the different techniques used in the questioning. Personal interviews by the lord lieutenant himself reduced the number of outright refusals; face-to-face with him most gentlemen preferred to fall back on a refusal to pre-engage themselves rather than give a categorical no. In Cumberland and Westmorland twenty refused to pre-engage, nineteen of them using a prearranged formula, and the three outright refusals were all conveyed by letter.[62] Similarly in the East Riding, where no one gave an outright rejection, nineteen refused to pre-engage, all but two using a formula which clearly implies prior agreement on the response to be given.[63] In Wales, where very few JPS were questioned personally, there was a higher proportion of refusals than in England, despite the traditional loyalty of the squirearchy and the absence of any concerted opposition. James faced an additional difficulty in that he had very few substitutes available to replace men giving unfavourable replies; in the whole of Wales there were only nine Catholics and twenty dissenters, and in four of the counties there

[61] It is significant that some Catholics answered question one affirmatively, assuming that they would be eligible to sit in the Commons: Duckett, i, 71, 127.
[62] Ibid., i, 29–50.
[63] Ibid., i, 58–71.

was none in either category.[64] But this was not the case in most English counties, where the election agents were busy compiling lists of men whom they judged to be right, and suitable for employment as deputies and JPs. Many of these men were subsequently appointed, so that the whole character of the Commission of the Peace had changed by the late summer of 1688.

In trying to assess the effectiveness of the agents' work in regulating the boroughs and preparing for elections, it should be noted that nearly all the contemporary dismissive judgements date from the early phases of the campaign, from the period before July 1688, when activity was intensified. Indeed many of the earliest reports from the agents can be shown to have been facile, underestimating the difficulties which they had to overcome. Their reports show that later they recognized their mistakes, corrected their overoptimism and, when necessary, reorganized their approach and varied their operating methods. They had a whole armoury of different techniques at their disposal and sufficient time to experiment in order to find the ones that were most appropriate to local conditions and particular problems.

Above all, it must be realized that the agents were in no position to deceive their masters, to make reckless or partisan forecasts that were not in accord with the realities of the situation. They knew that their work would soon be put to the practical test of electoral success or failure. Conversely, James's opponents, who were generally scornful about his chances of success during the early phases, had become pessimistic and alarmed by September about the prospects in the forthcoming elections. For example, on 26 September William Lloyd, the Bishop of Norwich, reported anxiously to Archbishop Sancroft that in Norfolk only Norwich was certain to elect MPs loyal to the Church of England.[65] Richard Hampden, William's chief contact among the more extreme Whigs who had rejected James's approaches, feared the consequences of a 'forced'

[64] *Ibid.*, i, 272–87.
[65] Tanner MSS, 28, f. 183.

Parliament.[66] In general this prospect of a packed Parliament meeting at the end of November, ready to enact James's policies, even though opinion was hostile to them and the elections had been effected only by manipulation and fraud, gave a note of urgency to the invitation to William to invade before winter set in, and not postpone the expedition until the spring; although it must be added that the prospect of James remodelling his army during the winter was an even more relevant reason for immediate action. It is clear that counter-preparations by the opposition were not well advanced at the end of September, when they had only three to five weeks until the date of the elections.

Analysis of the agents' reports provides material to act as a direct check on the judgements, both contemporary and historical, dismissing the whole campaign as foolish and impracticable. On 21 February a secret report to William cited Reading as an example of the futility of the agents' working methods. It said that a first purge had resulted only in the installation of a new set of aldermen and burgesses who very quickly proved to be as unreliable as their predecessors, so that they had had to be purged in turn. In fact this report exaggerated the size of the purges. More significantly, it implied that additional purges would have to be carried out, but this was not the case; after 21 February only two dismissals of single aldermen were necessary.[67] Lyme Regis and Colchester provide examples of agents appreciating and correcting early errors. At the former they optimistically interpreted an address to James in April as sufficient evidence that the town was 'right'. When they realized that it was not, they carried through a new regulation and consolidated their influence with a new charter in September.[68] At Colchester they initially put too much reliance on their local correspondent, Captain Reynolds, a former Whig MP for the town. When his lack of influence was detected they altered the regulation which he was in the middle of enforcing, adopted a different candidate in his place, and got a new

[66] PWA, 2173.
[67] PWA, 2145; PRO, PC 2, 72, pp. 555, 568, 613, 661, 728.
[68] Ibid., pp. 555, 582, 639, 678; Luttrell, i, 438; Duckett, ii, 222.

charter.[69] By September the procurement of new charters as a means of consolidating control had become a familiar and easy process. Van Citters had predicted that corporations would defend their charters with determination, but this was not so and in the two cases where he expected stubborn resistance (Buckingham and Oxford) the charters fell easily into James's hands, so the new charters could be issued in September in good time for the elections.[70]

Where the agents did encounter stubborn resistance, they persisted in the face of difficulties, varying their tactics until they found the most appropriate. At Wells a formidable and well-entrenched local interest led by the gentry had to be overcome. It had used its powers under the charter issued in January 1684 to create gentlemen as freemen, and held all the key municipal offices. The agents were obliged to undertake one minor and two major regulations, and to obtain a new charter, but at the end of this struggle the opposing interest had been virtually dismantled.[71] At Reading, where they were sure of the corporation, the danger came from the 'rabble', that is from the ordinary people, who were being stirred up by Lord Lovelace, the local Whig magnate, but the dissenters were enlisted on the side of the king.[72] At Taunton, where the new charter confirmed the possession of the franchise by all residents, the ordinary people were mobilized to elect collaborationist candidates, of whom one was a very prominent Whig (and future secretary of state under William), John Trenchard, who was under obligation to James – the king having recently given him a pardon for past political activities.[73] But in some towns even continuous work did not prove to be sufficient and, as at Exeter where they testified to the electoral interest of the clergy, the agents candidly admitted in their reports that they were not likely to win the election – although in the propaganda exercise

[69] PRO, PC 2, 72, pp. 581, 608, 651; Duckett, i, 410.
[70] Addit., 34510, f.115; Luttrell, i, 445; Bodleian, Carte MSS, 109, f.327.
[71] PRO, PC 2, 72, pp. 581, 628, 667; Duckett, ii, 16, 229.
[72] PWA, 2145, 2147; Duckett, ii, 236–7.
[73] Duckett, ii, 17–18, 229, 243; Luttrell, i, 451.

of an address to James, in April, the city had promised to elect suitable MPs.[74]

As well as actually working in the constituencies, the agents also provided a stream of information for the organizers in London. We have only fragmentary and indirect evidence about the court end of the campaign, on its overall control and direction. General strategy was decided by the council, and we know that James occasionally attended meetings of the committee for regulations.[75] Day-to-day supervision of electoral preparations was carried out by Brent and Butler, but ministerial connection and interest in the campaign must be a matter of inference and elimination. Jeffreys, because of his ill-health and personal isolation, certainly did not play an active part. Penn dropped out once the campaign developed momentum as a systematic and organized business. The Catholic extremist ministers had neither aptitude nor sympathy for the campaign; Father Petre alleged that it was being spun out deliberately, with no intention of having elections and a session of Parliament, so as to keep the ministers who were sponsoring the campaign in office.[76] This attack was obviously directed against Sunderland, and he is of all the ministers the one most closely connected with the campaign and the project to get Parliament to repeal the Tests and the penal laws.

Contemporaries associated Sunderland with the campaign, but there is little documentary evidence to show the nature of the connection. He was the only minister with extensive experience of electoral preparation and parliamentary management – he had acted in both capacities with success in 1685. Certainly he emerged as the actual director of policy in September 1688, during the run-up to the elections, and James's abandonment of the campaign was connected with Sunderland's fall from power.[77] The whole campaign, and the decision to risk elections in October and November, are entirely consistent with the principles (or perhaps the contemporary word maxims is more

[74] Duckett, i, 381; ii, 231, 240; *A Collection of the Several Addresses*, p. 4.
[75] PWA, 2145.
[76] Burnet, iii, 222–3.
[77] PRO, SP Domestic, James II, Entry Book 56, pp. 425–41.

accurate) of conduct that he followed in both earlier and later phases of his career. First, the campaign was calculated to strengthen his influence with James, especially as during the first months of 1688 he was threatened by the Catholic extremists – so Father Petre was partly right. But Sunderland persisted with the campaign after he had secured himself through his public conversion to Catholicism and his new friendship with the queen. Obviously there was a risk in doing so, and his motives must be a matter for speculation, but his sponsorship of the campaign is consistent with his keeping open the maximum number of options, so that he could meet almost all possible contingencies. Only in the case of the campaign failing disastrously would Sunderland be lost. If it provided a sufficient and reliable majority, then his ministerial position would become unassailable. He would still be in business if the campaign was only partly successful – the most likely outcome – since he would be indispensable as the only minister capable (with his managers, whom he had selected in advance) of dealing with parliamentary difficulties. He would enjoy more connections and contacts than any possible rival. He would be the only politician connected with James and the court, the Catholic party of moderates, the dissenters, the former Whigs who were now prepared to collaborate, and last but not least both Louis and William. Sunderland was one of the comparatively few Englishmen who realized that a general European war was about to break out, and that inevitably England would be affected. Even if he remained neutral, James would need parliamentary grants of supply to strengthen the navy, and might have to keep it in session. Alternatively, if he went to Louis for subsidies Sunderland was the best available negotiator. In a dangerous and fluid situation, where almost anything could happen at any time both at home and abroad, it was vital for Sunderland to keep the initiative, and this he could accomplish by prompting the campaign to the point of fixing dates for elections and the session.[78]

[78] Kenyon, *Sunderland*, pp. 205–15, treats Sunderland's activity in relation to domestic politics during the months of August and September (including the preparation of the elections) as altogether marginal by comparison with foreign policy matters; it seems to me that there is too large an element of historical hindsight here.

Although clever, Sunderland's calculations in 1688 were as faulty as those which had led him to support Exclusion in 1680. He ignored the effects of the campaign in alienating all those whose support James was to need during the crisis of William's invasion. The gentry generally interpreted the three questions as a dangerous and illegal attempt to subvert the integrity of Parliament and destroy freedom of elections. The pre-engagement demanded – although there was a precedent in the instructions to elected members which Shaftesbury had organized in 1681 – would have reduced the individual MP to a permanent condition of dependence far more absolute than that of Danby's pensioners. James's agents were seen as intruders. Royal pressure gave the gentry in most counties a cohesion and solidarity that had not existed since 1660, and this unity increased during the late summer of 1688, after the trial of the bishops, when some of those who had initially promised collaboration found themselves so isolated, socially as well as politically, that they retracted their promises or began to waver. There was a clear contrast between the cohesion of rural society and the divisions in the towns which James's agents widened and exploited. The agents could not drive a wedge between the gentry and the less affluent countrymen, although Shaftesbury had done this with success in several counties, using the freeholders to overwhelm the gentry and clergy. Unlike the urban dissenters, those in the rural areas do not seem to have been effectively mobilized by the agents, perhaps because boroughs were easier to organize than county elections involving thousands of voters, perhaps because rural dissenters were more dependent on their betters socially and economically.

The unity of the gentry in the face of royal policies was translated during the crisis of the Revolution into active enmity. They rejected the king's tactical concessions with contempt. It was they who staged the provincial risings which, together with defections from court and army, shattered James's confidence. By contrast, the urban collaborators were useless once the campaign had been abandoned. They had been chosen for one purpose only, to help pack Parliament, indeed they were attractive allies because they were not likely to act independently.

James himself admitted their expendability when, in his futile effort to win back the Tories, he abandoned those whom he had installed in the boroughs by restoring the old charters.

The synthetic alliance which James constructed for the purpose of packing Parliament disintegrated even before William invaded, and disappeared forever as a force in national politics, like the equally synthetic Cromwellian establishment before it. But this was not so at the local level. The purges and regulations of 1687–8 had lasting repercussions in the corporations, where James's last-minute restoration of the charters often left the legal position very uncertain. Combinations and factions originating with the regulations and purges of 1687–8 were to persist in many corporations, contributing towards the realignment of parties which took place under William and Mary.[79]

[79] For some aspects, see Lacey, *Dissent and Parliamentary Politics*, pp. 238–42.

URING THE LATE SUMMER months of 1688 diplomats in
London were puzzled at James's apparent blindness
to the threat that was building up against him. James
was not ignorant of William's plans and preparations. He was
getting full and (as events were to show) accurate reports from
the United Provinces – most of them originating at first with
d'Avaux, the French envoy at the Hague, but later coming from
d'Albeville, the English envoy, as well.[1] In retrospect, James
and Jacobite propagandists explained away his strange behaviour
and inertia in 1688 by putting the blame on deliberate treachery
by Sunderland, but this is unconvincing. James did not want
to believe disturbing reports. He was disinclined to accept the
unpleasant fact that a major crisis was being inescapably forced
upon him, that he would have to face a major trial of strength
in the immediate future for which he had made no plans. When
James did come to terms with reality, his response can again be
described as unrealistic. He attempted to appease William, to
make offers of mediation and intervention that were entirely
meaningless and had no relevance to the harsh facts of the

[1] Addit., 41816, ff.185–6, 202, 205, 209, 212.

critical situation in Europe in the second half of the year 1688.

There is a clear and rational explanation for James's initial lack of realism about William's plans, and his failure to concentrate his attention and resources on defence against invasion. Until as late a date as the third week in September he was entirely preoccupied with the furtherance of domestic policies. James was absorbed in the campaign to pack Parliament that was about to be put to the test of a general election. The campaign had been in progress for nearly a year, and because it depended for success on organization and systematic, cumulative intervention in the constituencies, rather than on spontaneous support, any relaxation of electoral pressure would mean loss of impetus and progress. If James was forced to postpone the elections, he would have to start the whole campaign all over again. Understandably, he left the recall of the writs for parliamentary elections until the last possible moment, and kept his eyes on the affairs of the constituencies, not on the situation on the continent. In addition, James's plans to call Parliament in November meant that he could not have concluded an alliance with France, even if he had wanted to do so. Although such an alliance was being urged by his extremist Catholic ministers, who would have accepted any terms stipulated by Louis, James was not prepared to act as a subordinate, obliged to follow French policies.[2] Any French alliance, or moves that showed that one had been concluded, would have had disastrous electoral repercussions. It would have been entirely unacceptable to the dissenting allies on whom he was relying for a majority in the Commons, and James was also warned of the disaffection that naval or military cooperation with French forces would cause – not only among the people in general, but among the officers and men of the army and navy.

Ever since his accession James had based his attitude on the belief that European affairs were of only marginal importance to him. He had deliberately chosen to isolate himself from them, so as to be able to concentrate on domestic affairs. Throughout,

[2] Addit., 41823, ff.71–2; Campana de Cavelli, ii, 257–8.

The Low Countries in 1688.

James consciously tried to retain his independence, manoeuvering so as to avoid all efforts by Louis and William to draw him into their opposing camps. In this he proved successful, although it must be said that neither put much value on having James as an active ally; until 1688 it would be enough to ensure that England was not controlled by the other. In the first weeks of the reign, fearing clashes with a possibly refractory Parliament, or a prolonged and dangerous rebellion, James negotiated for a continuation of the French subsidies which Charles had received.[3] But in August 1685, having crushed Monmouth's rebellion, he asserted his independence by renewing existing treaties of alliance with the States-General, brushing aside French objections, and without realizing the resentment and lasting suspicions of his reliability which this purely formal move created in the minds of Louis and his ministers. By renewing the treaties, James most certainly did not intend to pledge active support for William's European policies, which would entail a danger of involvement in continental warfare.[4]

James did not think himself obliged to try to maintain any kind of balance in Europe, although like his brother he had rather vague notions of offering himself as a mediator. These notions became a serious basis for policy only at the last moment, in October 1688, when James offered to mediate so as to preserve the peace of Europe (as a means of saving himself), an offer so ludicrous that it failed to anger Louis or influence William, Spain or the emperor. In terms of specific British interests a policy of isolation was tenable. French policy did not threaten them at this time; some comparatively minor colonial disputes in North America were settled without difficulty, and there were no important English interests directly affected by threatened French expansion in the Rhineland. On the other hand, there were a number of issues in dispute with the Dutch which remained unsettled, causing a slow deterioration in relations.

It is significant that those questions which caused the greatest

---

[3] Baschet; Barrillon, 16 April, 17 May, 16 July 1685; Louis, 9 March, 24 April, 9 May, 15 June, 13, 26 July 1685.
[4] Baschet; Barrillon, 17 May 1685; Mazure, ii, 39–40. D'Avaux, v, 73, 86–7, 88–9.

difficulties were all directly related to James's home policies. Other issues, such as the dispute over English trade with Bantam in Java, which the Dutch were blockading, and the facilities given to Algerine pirates, which were attacking Dutch ships, in English ports, were minor irritants, but three subjects raised tension to dangerous levels: the refuge which British political exiles who fled after Monmouth's defeat were receiving in Dutch towns; subversive propaganda published in Holland where the presses were virtually free; and the affairs of the six regiments of English and Scottish subjects in Dutch service. All three questions were interrelated. It is understandable that James was alarmed at the presence in Dutch cities of groups of intransigent political refugees, Whigs associated with the rebellions of Monmouth and Argyll – both of whom had sailed from Amsterdam in 1685 – and with the alleged Rye House Murder Plot of 1683 against Charles and James. On instructions his envoys and agents gave a high priority to keeping a watch over the activities of these men, and intermittently demanded their extradition.[5] William came in for a share of the blame for the failure of the various city governments to take action, and he certainly failed to exercise the influence over them which he did possess, but he intervened to save the lives of several officers from the English regiments when they attempted to kidnap one of the leading exiles, Sir Robert Peyton, and send him back to England in a royal yacht. This kidnap attempt provoked paroxysms of fury, since it recalled the similar actions of the most hated English envoy, Sir George Downing, in the 1660s, but from James's angle these officers were among the comparatively few whom he could trust, of those holding commissions in the six regiments.[6] The other refugee against whom a kidnapping was planned was none other than Burnet, whose pamphleteering had made him personally objectionable to both James and Louis, but who was the only one of the early exiles with whom William maintained contact; the others were managed by Bentinck and Dijkvelt.

[5] Addit., 41814, ff.7–9, 22, 32, 85, 136, 206, 222–3, 229.
[6] Ibid., ff.8, 48, 52–3, 55–6, 66, 109, 115, 123, 127.

The six regiments occupied an anomalous position. Although composed of English, Scottish and Irish subjects, the units had been raised in the United Provinces and not transferred from Britain. They were under the authority of the States-General, which had not ratified a personally negotiated convention concerning their terms of service agreed upon in 1678 by William and Lord Ossory, although in 1685 there had been no difficulty when James asked for their return to oppose Monmouth. But despite William's prompt despatch of the regiments, and the dismissal of a number of Monmouth's friends, James rightly regarded the regiments as potentially dangerous. The soldiers were fully exposed to the propaganda of the exiles, and many of the officers belonged to a group associated with the opposition attitudes of their former commanding officer, Henry Sidney, of all Englishmen the man closest to William and most in his confidence. A running struggle developed over the appointment of officers. William refused to have Carlingford, an Irish Catholic, as commanding general, and he rejected a high proportion of those (mainly Scottish and Irish Catholics, and future Jacobites) whom James recommended for subordinate commissions. When the Catholic Tyrconnel began to purge Protestants from the Irish army in 1687, those dismissed moved to the United Provinces, where they formed a centre of disaffection. William saved the lives, but not the commissions, of those who attacked Peyton, and in June 1687 he took a settled decision not to appoint any Catholics in future, a move which was interpreted as a direct reply to James's appointment of Catholics in the army in England.[7]

Finally, in January 1688, James demanded the return of the six regiments from the States-General. The decision was influenced by French diplomatic intrigues, and nothing could have been more damaging for William, who was seriously concerned that the example set by James might be imitated by German princes, and that the allied forces would be dangerously inadequate in the event of a French attack either in the

[7] Addit., 41815, ff.136, 192; Mazure, ii, 317–18; *Correspondentie*, II, ii, 736.

Rhineland or on the Spanish Netherlands. When the States-General refused James's request, he tried to disintegrate the units by a Proclamation ordering the return of all his subjects on pain of being regarded as outlaws. The operation was bungled in the most inept fashion; the proclamation was issued just before (instead of after) the regiments' pay day, no assurance being given that those returning would be taken into service, and d'Albeville was given inadequate time to make the necessary logistical arrangements.[8] Consequently William was strengthened, not weakened; he agreed to let officers go if they wished, and knew that he was well rid of the (mainly Irish) officers who took up the offer. Few of the rank and file were able to go, since they would be treated as deserters if caught, but d'Albeville spent a disproportionate amount of time during the rest of the year trying to smuggle individual soldiers out of the country, and neglecting much more important business. The vacancies were easily and quickly filled, so that the regiments were able to play a vital role in William's invasion.[9]

The pamphleteering war that raged between England and the United Provinces in 1687-8 also helped to convince many people in both countries that an early war was inevitable. In fact neither James, William nor their chief advisers took the danger of war between England and the United Provinces at all seriously. Neither side tried to force a break; although the Catholic extremists wanted one, they were effectively contained by Sunderland. James knew that a war would disrupt his domestic policies. William was absorbed during the first seven months of 1688 in his urgent task of building a continental alliance against France. He assumed that he could safely concentrate on this diplomatic work, since he and his advisers were basing their entire English policy on the calculated belief that James could be discounted as a possible enemy. They had come to the conclusion that James was not prepared for an offensive war and that if he did

---

[8] Addit., 41815, ff.128-30, 134-5, 139, 142-3, 154, 159-60, 163-4, 169-70; 41823, ff.58, 62; Mazure, ii, 370-72, 384, 408, 411-12; Campana de Cavelli, ii, 171, 179.

[9] Addit., 41815, ff. 137, 145, 187, 189-90, 251.

propose one he would not get the necessary grants of financial supply from any Parliament.[10]

Similarly, Louis and his ministers left James out of their general diplomatic planning for what was certain to be a year of crisis. England had alliance-value for Louis only in the limited context of Scandinavian affairs; early in 1688 Louis negotiated for an alliance by which James would receive subsidies in return for sending ships to assist Denmark against Sweden and the Dutch. James spun out the negotiations by haggling over the amount of subsidy, but although the amount in question was relatively small what really concerned James was the prospect of being tied to France, without knowing where his commitment would take him. He was not interested in supporting Denmark, and the negotiations collapsed when danger of a northern war receded.[11] But Louis was confirmed in his view of James. Exasperation, at what Louis derided as James's pretence of independence, meant that in future French assistance would be forthcoming only when James had been reduced to a state of dependence, in which he would have no option but to accept French terms without question.

So far as foreign affairs are concerned in general, the comparatively little attention which they received from James, his ministers and the opposition, was concentrated almost exclusively on the changing patterns of relations within the triangle formed by Britain, France and the United Provinces. This was characteristic of the Restoration period. Charles II, for all his pretensions to equality, had occupied a satellite status in 1672–3 because all the diplomatic preparations for the joint attack on the Dutch had been made by France. The developments of 1688 proved again that an effective foreign policy needed foresight, money and skilled, experienced diplomatic personnel. That it could not be improvised at short notice had already been proved at the time of the second Dutch war, when England became totally isolated in Europe, and again when the move initiated

[10] *Ibid.*, f.189.
[11] Baschet; Barrillon, 22 March 1688; Mazure, ii, 403, 405–7.

by Danby and Sir William Temple for an anti-French alliance collapsed in 1680. In 1688 for all practical purposes James might as well have had no diplomatic service and no foreign policy. He did not possess an adequate network of diplomatic representatives and contacts at foreign courts. He had no reputation abroad except, quite wrongly, as a willing accomplice of French designs, a view which he tried to dispel at the very last minute by means of the d'Albeville memorial to the States-General.[12] Diplomatically James could do nothing, absolutely nothing, on his own to prevent William invading, and his bankruptcy was finally exposed after the Revolution when he could only memorialize the Catholic kings, claiming that it was now a war of religion and asking them to make peace with France so that all could devote themselves to restoring him to his lost kingdoms.[13]

James's lack of influence meant that the active diplomatic and political difficulties which William had to overcome in the various countries were of French creation. Of all European powers Spain was the most closely concerned, with its Netherlands provinces very much a part of the affairs of the triangle formed by Britain, France and the United Provinces. Although, as another gesture of independence, James had renewed the treaty of mutual assistance with Spain in 1685, it was obvious that he was no more likely to honour it than Charles in 1683–4. Ineffective attempts were made to draw James into protecting Spanish interests; a suggestion was made that a regiment should be raised in Britain for the Spanish Netherlands that would be made available for James's service in an emergency, but this was rejected as likely to irritate Louis.[14] Despite the importance of trade with Spain, actual Spanish influence in England was weak. The most influential Catholics at court were all pro-French, and the Spanish ambassador had long since lost to his French rival the role of acting as Catholic champion and protector. This had an important consequence at the time of the Revolution. In

<hr />

[12] Addit., 41816, ff.197, 216, 223; D'Avaux, vi, 221–2, 260–62.
[13] Campana de Cavelli, ii, 479, 489, 491–2, 495–8, 509, 512, 518–19; *HMC, Stuart*, i, 35–7, 60–61. H. M. Sutton (ed.), *The Lexington Papers* (1851), pp. 338, 344.
[14] Mazure, ii, 55–6, 150.

December 1688 a move was initiated to get Spain and the emperor to mediate in the affairs of England, between James and William, with the object of safeguarding the toleration and civil rights which the Catholics now enjoyed, but it did not have enough preliminary planning or preparation for negotiations to begin. The Catholics who retained contact with Ronquillo and Hoffmann were men without political influence and connections, and the whole proposal was swept aside by the speed with which events moved.[15] Later, the Spanish court was able to overcome its very real doubts about a heretic usurper and reject James's appeals for a union of Catholic sovereigns. At this time Louis was trying to build up influence at Madrid, so as to be ready for the inevitable crisis over the succession to Carlos II, and he deliberately refrained from declaring war on Spain in 1688. In fact he was attempting to encourage Spain to undertake an offensive to recover Portugal (a French ally of sorts), but the Spanish ministers knew that their own security was dependent on William's strength and diplomatic skill in constructing the widest possible anti-French alliance. French aggressions and blackmail could not be forgotten overnight. Without William the Spanish Netherlands were defenceless. In addition, naval operations in 1683–4 off the Catalan coast, and against Genoa, had shown that the French fleet now dominated the western Mediterranean. If, in the war that was about to begin, William faced an unfriendly and doubtfully neutral England, he would not be able to detach enough Dutch ships to defend Spanish maritime interests, while England as the ally of France would mean that the already dangerous threat from French and English buccaneers would be reinforced by an officially backed offensive against Spanish America.[16]

The Emperor Leopold was the key figure in all William's preparations. Imperial attention was unfortunately still concentrated on the Turkish war in the east, and the strength of Catholic influences at Vienna meant that William was bound to have difficulty in combining his planned exploitation of anti-

[15] Sutton, *Lexington Papers*, p. 330; Campana de Cavelli, ii, 262.
[16] Campana de Cavelli, ii, 583; Klopp, iv, 186–92, 452–5.

Catholic sentiment in Britain with retention of the emperor's support. Well in advance he gave careful assurances that Catholics would not suffer persecution, but that he would do all that was possible to see that liberty of conscience continued for them. Such assurances were necessary. Acting without authority in the spring of 1688, d'Avaux and d'Albeville tried to impress on Count Hohenlo, the imperial minister who put most stress on preserving Catholic interests, that William was following a specifically anti-Catholic policy, and that his negotiations with the north German princes were aimed at subverting imperial authority.[17] But even the francophile Hohenlo had to reply that the emperor could afford to act on behalf of Catholic interests only if France behaved reasonably. After the French ultimatum to the emperor and the princes, and the attack on Philippsburg, imperial policy had necessarily to be guided by reasons of state in its attitude towards William's expedition. Political interest demanded the rejection of Carlingford's appeals on behalf of James, and in London the imperial envoy Hoffmann showed quite unconcealed *schadenfreude* when Barrillon desperately urged joint intervention to save James's crumbling position.[18] The real difficulties between William and the emperor came after the Revolution settlement. By taking the English crown William went against the entirely specific pledge which he had given to Leopold on the eve of the invasion. Popular, and later legislative, attacks on the Catholics in England and Ireland outraged the imperial court (which was concurrently repressing the Hungarian Protestants), and in 1689 the absorption of William and a large part of the Dutch army in the British Isles, to the neglect of the defence of the Rhineland, led to Leopold becoming dubious about both the propriety and the value of his association.[19]

English trading connections with Baltic countries, although less important than those of the Dutch, had in the past led to active intervention in Scandinavian politics. James was in-

[17] D'Avaux, vi, 141–2. Count Hohenlo was on a visit to the Hague, where Kramprich, the imperial envoy, was hostile to William.
[18] Campana de Cavelli, ii, 309–10; Sutton, *Lexington Papers*, pp. 328, 330.
[19] Sutton, *op. cit.*, p. 337; Klopp, iv, 415–28, 443–9.

different. He had no real desire to support Denmark in 1688 as the protégé of France, a sensible attitude because no English interests were involved. Whereas earlier disputes between Denmark and Sweden had centred on control of the Sound, this one concerned a territorial dispute, Holstein-Gottorp, which did not affect England. English representatives in Copenhagen and Stockholm had few diplomatic matters to transact; their work could have been done by consuls. In the north German courts, where William, Bentinck, and Cornelis Hop were engaged in intensive negotiations vital for the success of William's plans, James had virtually no representation at all; indeed it could be said that exiles like Leven possessed more influence. Similarly, in the Italian courts English diplomatic representation was haphazard and qualitatively poor, providing no basis for the plan to use the services of Venice and the Pope as mediators in 1689. At Rome Castlemaine behaved indiscreetly, acting as a dependant of the French interest.

James, then, was a negligible figure in European affairs. Despite his possession of a strong army and navy, English influence was limited. This was not only the result of the qualitative and quantitative deficiencies of the diplomatic service, but even more of the basic reason for these deficiencies, the lack of interest in foreign affairs by the king and his ministers and a woefully uninformed public.

Like James, his English and Scottish opponents were insular in outlook and entirely absorbed during the spring and summer of 1688 by the deepening crisis in domestic politics. During this period their relative positions suddenly and dramatically changed. The birth of the prince meant that time had gone over to James's side. No longer could his opponents look forward to his death for the reversal of his policies. Now James could look forward with assurance to the long-term development and ful-filment of his policies, whereas for his opponents it was now a matter of urgency to stop James in his tracks. The acquittal of the bishops was a check, royal preparations for the elections could possibly be countered (though there was little sign of active counter-preparations), but it was now a matter of urgency to remove from James the capacity to initiate and prosecute policies inimical to English liberties and the Protestant religion. The onus was now on James's opponents to take action, and without delay.

Only by inviting foreign intervention could James's opponents alter the balance of forces within England sufficiently to be able to wreck royal policies and plans. This possibility of foreign intervention was never far from men's minds during this period; it should be realized that William's action in 1688 was not unique, even though it was so much more massive, direct and successful than the other instances of foreign intervention. The balance of forces in politics was such that both the crown and the opposition would turn to foreign powers whenever it seemed to be the only way of breaking a stalemate and achieving a decisive success, and the results had frequently been decisive. The secret treaty of Dover concluding an offensive alliance with Louis in 1670 had enabled the Cabal to attempt the establishment of absolutism; Dutch counter-intervention had effectively destroyed it in 1673. The destruction of Danby in 1678 by opposition MPs primed with secret information by the French ambassador forced the dissolution of the Cavalier Parliament, opening the way for Exclusion; the French subsidy treaty of 1681 enabled Charles to dissolve the Oxford Parliament, and finish off the first Whigs, in the process ruining an attempt by William to mediate between the court and the Whigs and turn the situation to his advantage. It should also be noted that in the past the French had on occasion worked with the opposition, exploiting fears of ministerial duplicity and absolutist ambitions just as effectively as had the Dutch agents in 1673.[20] William always possessed contacts at court as well as with opposition elements. By 1688 the situation had changed most significantly. William had extensive contacts with every section of opposition, but also possessed clandestine connections with important elements at court, as well as within the army and navy. On the other hand, all the French contacts were with the court – with the ministers, with the extreme Catholics and with

[20] Jones, *First Whigs*, pp. 28–9.

some of the collaborationist dissenters and former Whigs. Barrillon had no important correspondent or agent among those active in preparing for William's invasion, a very important factor in preserving security and secrecy.

It was natural that the leaders of the opposition in 1688 should look to William to intervene, but they were as always egocentric in their calculations. It was one of William's disadvantages, whose consequences were to be considerable after 1688, that all his English correspondents and associates thought of him almost exclusively as a force to be used for their own purposes in English politics. Since the retirement of Sir William Temple there was no prominent Englishman who fully understood the nature and complexity of the European problems with which William was primarily concerned.[21] The English opposition thought exclusively in terms of domestic politics, and in their ignorance of the situation in Europe believed far too easily that he would be free to undertake an invasion. Moreover, the existence of a strong army in England compounded the risks that William was running, risks that have been seriously underestimated by almost all English historians. Not only would an expedition late in the year face stormy weather as well as the English fleet, but William's absence in Britain might give French diplomacy an opportunity to disintegrate his alliance yet again, or at least to detach some of his less reliable allies. For William the penalties of failure would have been catastrophic in terms of the coming war with France. It would, therefore, be absurd to suppose that he was exposing himself to such considerable dangers in order to save English liberties for their own sake, or to preserve the Church of England.

William had taken an active interest in English politics since his first visit in 1670, and after his marriage in 1677 he had his wife's interest to safeguard as well, but – apart from his over-ambitious and near-disastrous attempt to solve the Exclusion Crisis in 1681 by a personal visit – he had done so from a distance, through intermediaries. William had a strong sense of

---

[21] The only Englishman fully aware of the complexities of the situation in Europe was Sunderland; this knowledge was the reason for his later employment by William.

family, and could never look into a mirror without remembering that he was a Stuart, but it is absurd to argue that he was consistently and primarily motivated by an ambition to become king of England, and that he had been laying plans for this purpose for years.[22] William's invasion of England should be seen rather as the first and arguably the only decisive phase of the nine years war. All his actions after 1688 demonstrate the fact that for William England was always a means, not an end in itself. The ultimate purpose was the containment of France, the reduction of the power which enabled Louis to dominate his neighbours. In effecting the Revolution William was acting on the belief that England was of central importance, at least in potential power, for this fight against French supremacy. Equally, Louis' conduct in 1688 (and in Ireland in 1689–91) showed that he regarded Britain as only marginally important. Effective control over English foreign policy was William's primary objective. For those who invited him, William's purpose was to rescue our 'almost lost' liberties and religion; in reality William came so as to involve Britain in the war against France, and it can be argued that all the really revolutionary consequences of 1688 were the result of this involvement in a general European war rather than of the political settlement itself.

Although in the long term William's judgement was to be proved correct, and the emergence of England as a first-class power was one of the two factors in ending the situation of French predominance that had existed since 1659, he clearly underestimated the difficulties and problems presented by his new kingdoms. As soon as he arrived triumphantly in London he was plunged into the strange and self-centred world of English politics, with their ferocious factional disputes and total instability, and he was to have to deal with two-faced politicians indifferent to the European issues which so vitally concerned him. Having eventually made himself almost a king in the

[22] Pinkham, *William III and the Respectable Revolution*, pp. 3, 38–9, 47–8, 60–61, 238–9.

United Provinces, William now found himself only *stadhouder* in England and with even less power in Scotland.

Louis, rather than James, was William's ultimate opponent in 1688. Not only did William intend to use English resources to alter the balance of forces in Europe in favour of the allies, but the major difficulties which William had first to overcome were the work of French diplomacy. In a wider sense, however, French aggression, arrogance and almost continuous examples of duplicity and bad faith, proved to be William's greatest assets. He had realized since 1672 that no state or ruler could be secure or independent until French power was curbed, but for a long time few would accept the full implications of the need to oppose Louis. Amsterdam republicans gave a higher priority to commercial affairs, English politicians to faction-fighting, German princes continued to compete for French subsidies, and the emperor concentrated on the Turkish war in the east. But in the period between his diplomatic triumph in 1684, when he extorted recognition of his new gains, and the ultimatum of September 1688, Louis persuaded them of the need for a stand by his fresh claims, and the language in which his pretensions were phrased. By blind and brutal policies – economic and religious as well as military, naval and diplomatic – Louis convinced the most timid, short-sighted and self-interested that William was right in saying that resistance must be organized, even at the cost of a general and prolonged war.

The most indispensable precondition for William's invasion of England was the miracle that Louis largely achieved for him, of uniting the United Provinces. In 1688 the States-General allowed William to leave the country with defences that were barely adequate to repulse a French military raid, and even Amsterdam republicans temporarily forgot their fears, originating in 1640, that Orangist interest in English politics was part of a plan aimed at enabling the *stadhouder* to turn himself into an absolute prince.[23] There could be no sharper contrast than

---

[23] For the general background, see P. Geyl, *Orange and Stuart* (1969), and S. B. Baxter, *William III* (1966).

that between Dutch unity in 1688, and the bitter internal differences and pathological states of suspicion that had existed in the years 1678–84. Then d'Avaux had had enormous scope to foment and exploit Dutch weaknesses. In 1678 French diplomacy, by playing on war-weariness, had persuaded the States-General to make a separate peace over William's head, and without considering the interests of the allies. William's confederation against France had thereupon disintegrated, and he was to be handicapped for years by memories of Dutch selfishness in his attempts to reconstruct it.

In 1683–4 d'Avaux prevented William from responding to desperate Spanish appeals for help against France, which would have certainly meant renewed and general war, and wrecked his attempts to re-form an effective alliance. To the commercial and financial interests who formed the republican or regent party, and were led by 'Messieurs d'Amsterdam', William meant war, high levels of taxation and major dislocations of trade. D'Avaux convinced them that his efforts to keep a large army together in time of peace were evidence both of a determination to renew hostilities at the earliest opportunity, and of an eventual intention of establishing absolute rule by force. It is easy to condemn the myopic readiness of the regents (like Barrillon's Whig contacts in England in 1678–80) to let France make use of them as part of what was an overall aggressive policy of expansion and aggrandizement, but it should be remembered that William II had done each of the things that d'Avaux alleged against his son: he had obstructed peace with Spain in 1648, he had tried to maintain the strength of the army so as to re-enter the war, he had arrested leading republicans, and he had attempted to occupy Amsterdam in 1650.[24]

Dutch commercial interests were ready to accuse William, like his father and grandfather, of following an essentially dynastic foreign policy. His intransigent hostility to France contrasted with their economic dependence on French markets and products, the latter forming the essential basis of their re-

[24] When using d'Avaux' printed despatches, it has to be remembered that they are a selection, and have an obvious apologetical purpose. I hope at a future date to publish a critical analysis of his mission.

export trade to Baltic countries. Although regent propitiation of France, under the republican regime of de Witt, had not prevented Louis from attempting their annihilation in 1672, many republicans tended to forget this and to ignore the realities of French power and the nature of French ambitions, including the attempts to cut out Dutch middlemen in the export trade. Their obsessive fears of William's absolutist ambitions were very similar to the exclusive Whig concentration on domestic politics which was to create major difficulties for him in England after 1688. In Dutch politics in the early 1680s the effects were even more damaging. Faced with continuous and systematic republican obstructionism, and links openly maintained between d'Avaux and the Amsterdam regents, William resorted to particularly ruthless political tactics and sharp practices, intimidating the regents of lesser towns, keeping the three provinces of Utrecht, Gelderland and Overijssel (which had been overrun by the French in 1672–3) out of the States-General for as long as possible, and so confirmed and inflamed suspicions.[25]

By the summer of 1684 hostility between William and the republicans had got to the point where Amsterdam expected a *coup* against the city, similar to the attempt in 1650, and d'Avaux possessed more influence in the States-General than William. At his instigation the republicans pressed for measures of retrenchment that would have made an independent foreign policy impossible. The army must be reduced to twenty-eight thousand men, the number imposed in 1648 by the republicans, which had seemed so unacceptably inadequate to William II that he subsequently attempted a *coup d'état,* and its payment decentralized so as to give each town effective control over its deployment. The Dutch diplomatic service was also to be partly dismantled, by reducing the number of representatives abroad, and by slashing the funds available for secret correspondences and intelligence. Amsterdam representatives were considering a further proposal for an investigation into the constitutional powers rightfully attached to the offices of captain-general and pensionary. Even these moves were not enough for d'Avaux. He bluntly

[25] Baxter, *William III*, pp. 108–9, 123, 195–6. See also, G. H. Kurtz, *Willem III en Amsterdam, 1683–1685* (Utrecht, 1928).

warned the republican leaders that they could not expect Louis to have real confidence in them until they got Gaspar Fagel, William's trusted associate, dismissed as pensionary. Only then might they be rewarded with an alliance between Louis and the States-General, which would enable the republicans to perpetuate William's impotence and guarantee them against any attempt to destroy their liberties, but which would also give Louis an entirely free hand in western Europe.[26]

This ascendant French influence in Dutch politics could not last long. Even in 1684 French restrictions on Dutch trade and traders were making Amsterdam merchant interests uneasy. Representations were received by d'Avaux, including one from a leading republican associate, Hop, a burgomaster of Amsterdam, and reported to Louis, but they had no effect. Gradually Louis was withdrawing commercial advantages enjoyed by the Dutch, a policy of discrimination which damaged precisely those interests that were francophile.[27] This steadily undermined d'Avaux' influence, without William having to take action. Early in 1686 a formal Amsterdam memorial to the States-General showed a serious decline in the volume and value of trade, and significantly blame for this was placed first on French policies; d'Avaux met with no response when he tried to suggest that the real responsibility lay in the imposition of higher customs duties at William's demand.[28] Later that year Louis ordered a blockade of Cadiz, so as to bring pressure on the Spanish government, a move that threatened major Amsterdam interests, especially bankers, which were concerned with the silver fleet and West Indies trade.[29]

Repeatedly d'Avaux warned Louis of the damage that was being done to French influence, and advised that only a return to observance of the clauses relating to commerce in the Nijmegen Treaty of 1678 could restore his ability to use republican suspicions of William, to the point of being able to paralyse Dutch foreign policy. Louis would not give an inch. This refusal

[26] D'Avaux, iv, 37, 47–8, 88, 197–8.
[27] *Ibid.*, iv, 6–7, 58, 346.
[28] Addit., 41814, f.119.
[29] D'Avaux, v, 241–2, 248–50, 256, 259.

was based on reasons of personal prestige rather than on economic considerations. Louis resented having had to make commercial concessions in 1678; when it had been necessary to do so for diplomatic advantage he had disregarded Colbert's protests, but now he regarded these concessions as a slur on his dignity. Legalistically he claimed that he was doing nothing contrary to the actual clauses of the 1678 treaty, but if this was technically so at first, the tactics which were used to hamper Dutch trade created furious indignation among those directly affected. Customs officers deliberately delayed clearing goods, they used any pretext to declare imported goods forfeit, and they held up the sailing of Dutch ships – all subjects on which d'Avaux received complaints to which he could give no satisfactory answer. Louis calculated that he need not answer Dutch representations, that Dutch merchants were at his mercy because of their need for French products for re-export. Consequently they must continue to buy goods in France and could not afford to take reprisals. A series of prohibitions, for instance of herrings in October 1687, were intended to reduce the level of imports into France. If exports continued at their existing level this would produce an imbalance of trade as favourable to France as that which already existed with England.

Under pressure, and receiving no satisfaction from diplomatic protests, the Dutch did eventually begin reluctantly to consider taking reprisals.[30] Characteristically, Louis used the discussions as a pretext for the application of crude intimidation. In September 1688 he ordered the seizure of all Dutch ships in French ports (some three hundred altogether) and the detention of their crews. War had not been declared, and existing treaties gave all Dutch citizens nine months to withdraw themselves and their effects even after war had broken out, so that the action was illegal. Louis loftily justified it as an internal matter of policy, lying outside the competence of foreign states, and refused to listen to Starrenburg's protests. These excesses, and the casuistical justifications which were provided for them,

[30] *Ibid.*, vi, 111, 138, 153, 195–6, 210, 224–5, 255–6, 299–300, 322; Addit., 38495, ff.9, 11, 27.

destroyed the credibility of d'Avaux, leaving him isolated and helpless, unable to sabotage or even hamper William's preparations.[31]

Even more damaging, because it affected virtually every section of Dutch society, were the effects of the campaign against the Huguenots. These were far more immediate and much stronger in Holland than in England, because trading connections between Dutch cities and Huguenot communities in French ports were closer, more extensive and longer established. As d'Avaux himself reported, there was hardly a regent family in any major Holland city that did not have some personal connections with Huguenots or with Dutch residents in France. Applications for exit permits for relatives, friends or business partners were being made to d'Avaux by the most valued of his republican contacts even before the Revocation. He could only pass these on to Louis, and make unconvincing denials of the reports of atrocities that were circulating and finding general acceptance. In reply, Louis was adamant in refusing concessions of any kind, this time on the grounds that as a matter of religion was concerned, only God could authorize changes. Under no circumstances would Louis allow any Dutchmen who had become naturalized French subjects (for business reasons) to leave the country, even though many of them were related to leading Amsterdam families, and he also deliberately held up permission for non-naturalized Dutchmen to leave. This decision was intended as a form of intimidation, since he informed d'Avaux that eventually they would be allowed to go, but the result was to raise anti-French feeling to fever pitch. Dutch citizens were involved in a series of incidents that were well publicized. Diplomatic protests had no effect. Even Dutch Catholics were alarmed, fearing reprisals that occurred on a serious scale only in ultra-Protestant Zeeland; elsewhere, for instance in Rotterdam where a proposal was made to expel priests, William intervened for fear of the repercussions in friendly Catholic countries.[32]

[31] D'Avaux, vi, 270–71, 280, 284–5, 335; Addit., 38495, ff.26–7.
[32] D'Avaux, iv, 290, 293, 308–9; v, 23, 140, 144, 146, 185–7, 191–2, 231–2, 266; vi, 14–16.

The effects of the Revocation on Dutch public opinion cannot be overstated. For a time Calvinist ministers and Amsterdam regents, usually poles apart, were united in denouncing Louis. Huguenots (especially those with capital) were readily welcomed. William did not have to give a lead, he could without effort take advantage of the new currents of opinion. One immediate benefit of great importance derived from the arrival of large numbers of Huguenot officers, whom William incorporated in the army, overcoming the objections of Count Waldeck whose clientage of German officers would now meet with increased competition.[33] William took advantage of the change in the sentiments of men who had been his bitterest enemies in domestic politics; several of them were given important missions, with William showing an unqualified trust in their fidelity. Hop, a burgomaster of Amsterdam and a former associate of d'Avaux, was sent first to Berlin and then to Vienna on diplomatic business of the greatest significance.[34] Nicholaas Witsen, an even more influential Amsterdam burgomaster, was taken into William's closest confidence. It was a measure of the change that had occurred in Dutch politics that a man who had formerly worked with d'Avaux to obstruct William should now (as early as June) be entrusted with the secret of his design against England. During the summer Witsen worked closely with the inner group of William's advisers – Fagel, Dijkvelt and Bentinck – and frequently met William himself.[35] D'Avaux had to admit that he did not know what was the purpose of these discussions, but the effects were apparent in the last critical weeks before the invasion. Witsen was able to control the few Amsterdam republicans who still tried to obstruct the preparations, and in particular to overcome objections to the new levies which were being made.

In retrospect, d'Avaux was critical of Louis' failure to listen to his advice, either to detach the republicans from William by making major trade concessions, or to intimidate the States-General by a massive show of force, or even an invasion of the

[33] *Ibid.*, v, 203, 228–9, 237.
[34] *Ibid.*, vi, 57; Addit., 38495, f.12; 41814, ff.256, 258.
[35] Japikse, ii, 237–8.

southern part of the country. In his memoirs it is clear that he was concerned to play down the unfavourable effects of the more indirect attempt at intimidation of which he was the willing agent. On 9 September d'Avaux presented two memorials to the States-General: the first warning them that any attack on his ally, James, would be treated as an act of hostility against himself, and the second threatening them with war if any intrusion was made against Fürstenberg's possession of Cologne.[36] These memorials gave William the opportunity to consolidate the unity of the nation. The statement (which was quite untrue) that an alliance existed between Louis and James – which must be a secret and therefore all the more dangerous one – raised in all men's minds memories of 1672 (*het rampjaar*, the catastrophe year), when Louis had joined with Charles in an attempt to exterminate the republic, its religion and its trade. Dijkvelt was sent at once to Amsterdam to explain the significance of the memorials.[37] Fagel addressed the states of Holland on the peril in which they stood, and pointing out the connection between the Revocation and the attempts which James was making to eradicate Protestantism from his kingdoms. D'Avaux was still trying to organize obstruction, but on 29 September the states responded to Fagel with a resolution supporting William's stand against the threat to religion and country, and Fagel (who was dying on his feet during these weeks) subsequently outlined William's intentions at a secret session.[38]

William spoke to the *secret besogne* of the States-General on 6 October, and later he addressed the deputies of the Holland towns and representatives from each of the other provincial states.[39] On each occasion he suppressed the disavowals which d'Albeville was making of the statement in the d'Avaux memorial, that there was an alliance between James and Louis, and the representations that James was making to Van Citters of his readiness to maintain the terms of the treaty of Nijmegen. William's insistence on the existence of a hostile alliance between

[36] See pp. 273–5.
[37] D'Avaux, vi, 229.
[38] Japikse, ii, 249–50.
[39] *Ibid.*, ii, 249; D'Avaux, vi, 306–7.

the Catholic sovereigns was apparently confirmed when news arrived of the French ultimatum to the emperor and the empire, followed immediately by the attack on Philippsburg. This demonstrated Louis' determination to uphold Fürstenberg, as he had said he would in the second d'Avaux memorial, but it also freed William from the fear that the United Provinces could be invaded and partially overrun while he was engaged in the English expedition. This point was immediately appreciated. There was a sudden rise in the 'actions' of the Dutch East India Company, which were not only a kind of Dow Jones index for businessmen but were widely regarded as a barometer of Dutch political confidence.[40]

The States-General approved William's expedition on 8 October, and on the day before he first set sail (28th) they issued a public declaration which was aimed primarily at reassuring opinon in other countries, and particularly the sovereigns of friendly countries.[41] It linked the alleged alliance between France and England with James's domestic policies. If the latter was able to achieve absolute power over his subjects he would then be able to join Louis in active aggression against the United Provinces. Consequently the expedition was represented as being really a defensive move; William's promises that he had no intention of removing James from his throne or tampering with the succession, and that he would not persecute the Catholics, were stated – but it should be noted that technically the States-General were not directly involved. They 'commended' his design; if it had failed catastrophically they could have disavowed him. They claimed that they were merely granting him 'for his Assistance, some Ships and Militia, as Auxiliaries', but in practice the whole fate of the republic was tied up with the success of the invasion. Finally, potential allies and existing confederates were shown what would be the result of success; England would be made able to contribute 'to the common benefit of Christendom, and to the restoring and maintaining of Peace and Tranquillity in Europe', which were other

[40] *Ibid.*, vi, 272.
[41] Addit., 38495, ff.46–7; 34512, f.7. *A Collection of Papers relating to the Present Juncture of Affairs* (1689), pp. 15–16.

words for saying that she would become an ally in the war against France.

Nothing could be in sharper contrast with the political atmosphere of 1682–4 than this declaration, and the general state of cooperation and harmony. Even in the sneering report of the intractable (but now frustrated) d'Avaux, something of the dignity and simplicity of William's final leave-taking of the States-General comes through. The whole character of the United Provinces seemed to have changed, although William himself realized that this harmony could not last long. The Polish envoy (himself in French pay) reported that the whole nation, which had formerly cared only for peace so as to advance its business and commerce, was now ardently in favour of war and the English adventure.[42] The additional customs duties, much of which went to finance the invasion, were depressing trade but there were only muted protests. Merchants were convinced by their recent experiences that they were already suffering as severely from the various forms of French economic discrimination and pressure as they would do in an open war against Louis (Jean Bart and the Dunkirker privateers were to show them in 1689–97 that they were wrong in this). For perhaps the only time in his working life, William did not reluctantly have to give first priority to domestic politics, and to the fight to preserve his authority against enemies at home. He could concentrate on the affairs, first of Germany and then of Britain.

William's Dutch biographers have described how all groups and opinions were harmoniously combined during the autumn months of 1688, when for once there was no discrepancy between national and sectional interests; religious, economic and political policies were all united in William's undertaking. For J. K. Oudendijk, William at this moment synthesized the two elements of the republic,[43] the princely and the burger, the two main strands in contemporary life, the realist and the baroque. This was the climax of the republic. For N. Japikse it was a moment

[42] Addit., 38495, ff.28–9.
[43] J. K. Oudendijk, *Willem III* (Amsterdam, 1954), pp. 208–9.

of world-historical significance – it could be added that this was the last such moment in Dutch history.[44] The anxious crowds watching on the strand at Scheveningen (d'Avaux among them, counting the ships) knew that their whole future depended on the success of William's expedition. What they could not know was that its success now depended in turn on William's English associates living up to the assurances and promises which they had given him.

In his German diplomacy, as in Dutch politics, William after 1685 had the advantage of being able to exploit growing fears of renewed French expansion and aggression. The methods of duplicity and intimidation being employed by Louis, Louvois and Colbert de Croissy were stiffening resentment and suspicions among German princes and their ministers. In the Protestant states the Revocation caused the same horror as in Holland and England, but the reaction against Louis was more generally the consequence of French military methods and the techniques being used by French diplomacy. The emperor, the princes and the cities all feared that a new wave of French expansion was imminent, which would give Louis a position of domination in western Germany.[45]

In order to preserve a balanced picture it is worth explaining what expansion and domination meant at this time. Louis was not planning large-scale territorial annexations. Rather he aimed at the permanent occupation of additional strategically valuable fortresses like those he had already seized – Luxemburg, Neuf-Breisach and Mont-Royal. With these in French hands, and re-fortified by General Vauban, Louis would have predominant influence over neighbouring German princes. General war would not be necessary nor had the French army been prepared for it in 1688; the ruthless methods by which the French army regularly maintained itself in territories whose rulers refused to be cooperative, by contributions, were enough to frighten rulers from seriously thinking of resistance. The ultimate objective was

---

[44] Japikse, ii, 250.
[45] For the general background, see O. Klopp, *Der Fall des Hauses Stuart* (Vienna, 1875–88). There is also a short dissertation: R. Wiebe, *Untersuchungen über die Hilfeleistung der deutschen Staaten für Wilhelm III* (Gottingen, 1939).

the establishment of permanent and preponderant French influence over all the princes of at least western Germany. By reducing them to a position of subordination, in which they could not follow any independent line of policy or combine to check French pretensions, Louis would be assured that the empire would remain weak in relation to France.

French arrogance, the crude bullying and threatening language commonly employed in dealing with minor and virtually defenceless states, was consistent with these general aims of French policy. It would be quite wrong to assume that German princes and their ministers would react against French intimidation, and that bullying would in fact provoke them into resisting French pressure. In the face of overwhelming French power any form of resistance was dangerous, and without effective leadership from the emperor and from William, Louis might well have succeeded in his policies. It was therefore consistent of Louis to leave the emperor to his fate during the crisis of 1683, when the Turks besieged Vienna. It should be noted that the French assumption about German politics, of a fundamental incompatibility of interests between the emperor and the princes, was still partially valid. Both William and the emperor had to overcome divisions and differences created by jealousies between princes, and between princes and the free cities. In the Diet and at every princely court, imperial and Dutch diplomats had against them French systems of influence that went back to the days of Richelieu and Father Joseph.[46] Besides the skill and experience of its personnel, French diplomacy was underpinned by power, and until the imperial victory at the Kahlenberg in 1683 it was hardly possible to do more than try to contain it.

When William did manage to construct alliances these had to be constantly maintained against determined attempts at disruption by the French, who could be relied on to use every available opportunity to exploit weaknesses such as ministerial corruption (a factor that must not be overemphasized), timidity in the face of French power, suspicion of the emperor, fears at Vienna

---

[46] G. Pagès, *Contributions à l'Histoire de la Politique Française en Allemagne sous Louis XIV* (Paris, 1905), especially pp. 66, 91-5.

that William was subverting imperial authority, and confessional differences which still existed, although not as strongly as in the first part of the century. Protestants were roused by Catholic activities in Hungary and (in their earliest phase) in the Palatinate; Catholics feared that the Protestant princes were engaged in forming an anti-imperial league on a confessional basis. It is important to keep this background of uncertainty and division in mind when estimating the risks which William's invasion of England involved. His patiently constructed and vigilantly maintained alliances did not really begin to harden until as late as the months after the death of the Elector of Cologne (on 3 June 1688) when French policy, by upholding the candidature of Fürstenberg, became openly menacing on an issue that was of general concern to all the princes. Even then it should be realized that by concentrating on the invasion of England, which must necessarily mean a prolonged personal absence from the European diplomatic scene, William was gambling on the durability of his alliances.

During the years 1679–84 Louis had made appreciable territorial advances through the *réunions,* and by skilful diplomacy had achieved a whole series of successes without precipitating a general war. His acquisitions in Alsace, where Strasbourg was occupied in October 1681, and in the bishoprics, could perhaps be represented as defensive moves consolidating France's eastern frontiers. Advances to the north and the east, culminating in the capture of Luxemburg in June 1684, were far more dangerous, since they put the entire area west of the Rhine at the mercy of France. Yet French power was so preponderant that Louis was able to extort recognition of his gains at Ratisbon in August 1684. In desperation Spain had declared war late in 1683, but no country responded to her calls for assistance, despite treaty obligations and a community of interest in preserving the Spanish Netherlands. D'Avaux reinforced the decision of the States-General to obstruct all William's efforts to go to war, thus strengthening the reputation which the Dutch had gained by their conduct in 1678 for neglecting the interests of other powers. Charles II reneged on his obligations. The emperor was unwilling to turn away from his advance into Hungary.

This French diplomatic triumph depended on what were to prove to be transient advantages. First, the victory at the Kahlenberg, one of the most decisive events in the whole seventeenth century, effectively destroyed the Turkish danger in the east. Although imperial resources were to be concentrated on the now offensive struggle against the Turks for another decade, and pay-off for the victories was to be delayed until the early 1700s in terms of power available for immediate use in Italy and the west, nevertheless imperial prestige and confidence were substantially increased. German princes did not have to fear the emperor because of his victories over the Turks, but he did become more credible as a leader against French aggression. Secondly, Louis was still exploiting the benefits of his success in 1678, when his diplomats had disintegrated the Confederation. Potential allies were wary of William's promises, fearing that he was not master in his own country and would be unable to overcome obstructiveness by the States-General. Mutual suspicions meant that Louis could negotiate with each power separately. He enjoyed almost complete freedom of manoeuvre. Louis possessed the initiative. He acted as he thought fit, and then waited for others to react. In the years 1678–84 it can be said that France was the only great power in Europe. Louis was the only ruler with a consistent, dynamic and systematic foreign policy, backed by an army and a navy ready for instant employment, which every other ruler had to take into account when considering his own policies. But there were accompanying dangers. The habits of mind which Louis, Louvois and Colbert de Croissy developed during the years of supremacy – arrogance, an unthinking disregard of the interests of others, an assumption that other powers would yield to pressure – were to lead them to commit major errors of judgement in 1688.

William's experience, by contrast, was one of repeated political and diplomatic defeats which frustrated his plans. Only his confidence that God was with him, and would aid his mission to preserve the liberties of Europe and the Protestant religion, saved William from despair. His attempts to bring together the north German princes in 1680, and his English visit in 1681, proved to be entirely fruitless. The Treaty of the Hague with Sweden in the same year was a potential liability, since it could antagonize Brandenburg as well as Denmark. The agreements concluded with Spain and the emperor in 1682 did not stand up to the test of French pressure in 1683-4. Undeterred by the humiliating failure of not being able to give the Spaniards the assistance which they depended on, William started all over again to negotiate treaties that might serve as the basis for a general alliance. The results were more impressive in appearance than in reality. They certainly failed to make Louis pause to reconsider his policies, or even vary his tactics. French diplomacy could easily nullify at any time the two treaties which the States-General ratified in 1685 : the renewal agreement with James, and the defensive treaty with Brandenburg. In fact Frederick William agreed with Louis that the latter should not infringe previous undertakings to France. The new treaty with Sweden (January 1686) was counterbalanced by Franco-Danish accord, and the agreement between Sweden and Brandenburg was extremely fragile so long as Frederick William lived and maintained links with France. The treaty between Brandenburg and the emperor, while stipulating Brandenburg support against French advances in the Rhineland, was intended primarily to obtain an auxiliary contingent for service against the Turks. But it is in the composition of the League of Augsburg (July) that we can see the most revealing evidence of the weakness of the diplomatic front which William was trying to form against Louis. He could not engage the Dutch republic. Several German princes, including Saxony and Brandenburg, did not belong.[47]

Circumstances changed in William's favour only at a slow speed, and not entirely conclusively. The first factor which helped him was an increasingly widespread, although exaggerated, belief that Louis was in general aiming at a 'Universal Monarchy'. Specifically this took the form of suggesting that Louis hoped to elect a French-sponsored candidate at the next imperial vacancy; hence the crucial importance of the four

[47] Japikse, ii, 206–10; D'Avaux, v, 134–35, 148–9.

Rhenish electorates. In fact Louis' objectives were far more limited, his main concern being to counterbalance increased imperial prestige and influence after the victories over the Turks, by exerting leverage through west German princes acting as French clients. However the longer-term objective of French foreign policy was now one that was bound to affect the interests of virtually every ruler in Europe. Informed that the health of Carlos II was deteriorating, Louis had begun to build up French influence in the Spanish court, so as to be prepared for the inevitable crisis over the succession. In 1687 he relaxed the pressure which had previously been exerted on Spain, and began to extend offers of friendship.[48]

Secondly, the dispute with the Papacy over the *régale* was now extending into foreign policy. Innocent had been alienated by Louis' cynical failure to respond to his appeals for crusading support for Leopold against the Turks. When the Cologne crisis developed, French intimidation (Avignon was occupied in October 1688) merely strengthened his hostility. It is entirely incorrect to say that Innocent favoured William's invasion, but he was certainly cool towards James, regarding his support for the French case over Cologne, and his offer to mediate in the dispute with Louis, as presumptuous. He did not condemn William's project in advance, and in 1689 responded to appeals from James with only a little financial aid. Had he thrown the influence of the Papacy on James's side with enthusiasm and without qualification (as the interests of Catholicism demanded so far as Ireland and Scotland were concerned), the effects on Vienna might have been sufficient to make Leopold take notice of French approaches for a settlement, and William might have risked losing his Catholic allies. Instead, imperial policy was divorced from religious considerations, 'reason of state' was followed and James snubbed as a French client rather than aided as a martyr for catholicism.[49]

The third and in many ways the most important change in William's favour was the death of Frederick William on 9 May 1688. This removed an element of permanent uncertainty in

[48] See A. Legrelle, *La Mission de M. de Rébenac* (Paris, 1894).
[49] *HMC, VIIth Report*, app, i, 427–8.

German politics. Although the Revocation had cooled his attitude to Louis, so that his Edict of Potsdam is often represented
as a direct reply, Frederick William had taken care not to sever
his French connections. There was always the possibility that
his insatiable appetite for subsidies (to maintain an excessively
large army) would again be exploited by Louis. So long as this
uncertainty persisted, the French alliances with Hanover and
Denmark retained real value, and the prospect of a general
northern war remained a nightmare possibility for William.

Frederick William's death clarified and stabilized the situation
in northern Germany. It meant that Brandenburg could now
be relied on not to follow a pro-French policy. William had
prudently and carefully cultivated the electoral prince for some
years, and he concentrated his best diplomatic talent on him in
the months after his accession. Bentinck and Hop were sent to
Berlin, and the former negotiated a treaty in August with
the pro-allied minister Paul Fuchs.[50] Finally, in September
William himself travelled to Minden to meet Frederick and
confided in him about his English plans. After the invasion
had been launched, Frederick came to the Hague. Nevertheless,
it is important not to overstate the results of all these meetings.
They were indirect at first. The understanding with Brandenburg helped in persuading other princes to come down off the
fence on the allied side. Frederick himself persuaded the Elector
of Saxony. Fuchs helped in winning Celle, Hanover and
Wolfenbuttel.[51] These achievements greatly reduced the possibilities of French mischief-making in Germany, and meant that
contingents of German troops were available for the 1689
campaign. By the spring of that year France had no independent
allies in Germany, and no immediate prospect existed of turning
the princes against the emperor.

Brandenburg was driven into active hostility by French
attempts at intimidation. By the agreement with William,
Brandenburg troops under Schomberg (who was then transferred into the Dutch service) occupied Cologne in September,
forestalling the French. The French responded by demanding

[50] H. L. King, *Brandenburg and the English Revolution of 1688* (1914), pp. 17–24.
[51] *Ibid.*, pp. 33–4, 36–9, 56–9.

contributions from Frederick's territories of Kleve and Julich, and by sending in marauding bands. This was a foretaste of the brutality which other areas in western Germany were soon to experience, and which culminated in the devastation of the Palatinate during the winter. French behaviour outraged the conventions of seventeenth-century warfare and united Germany in resentment. William had no reason to fear a political or military crisis in Germany when he left for England. Hoping and expecting to be able to return in time for the summer campaign of 1689, he planned to build a new alliance of greater strength, unity and durability than the one which Louis had destroyed in 1678.

EIGHT *William's English Connection*

I N ANY CONSIDERATION AND ANALYSIS of William's English connections it is essential to make a sharp differentiation between the close, but entirely legitimate, contacts which he possessed in normal times, and the clandestine and subversive activities of his agents and associates during two relatively short periods of crisis and abnormal tension. In 1672–3 William intervened in English politics so as to detach Charles from his French alliance and force him to make a separate peace.[1] Secondly the active period of intervention, which led directly to the invasion of 1688, started only with Zuylestein's visit and soundings of opinion in August 1687, and coincided almost exactly with James's campaign to pack Parliament. In the years between, William did no more than protect the reversionary interests which his wife possessed and try to influence English foreign policy.

Those contemporaries like d'Avaux, and historians like Pinkham, who depicted William as the life-long conspirator who plotted usurpation of the English crown from 1680 or even

---

[1] See K. H. D. Haley, *William of Orange and the English Opposition* (1953).

earlier, or at least from the 1686 meeting with Frederick
William, ignore the fact that a close and constant connection
existed throughout the periods of Orangist rule between the
English court and political nation and their Dutch counterparts.[2]
The contacts and connections which had flourished in the days
of Elizabeth of Bohemia were rapidly reconstituted after 1674,
with a constant stream of visitors crossing the North Sea and
many volunteers serving in the Dutch army. William's small
court was not an alternative political centre, or a threat, to the
courts of Charles and James, as were the groups of Whig exiles
at Amsterdam; it was rather an annexe or offshoot of Whitehall.
Not too much political significance should be attached to visits
to the Hague, or service in the Dutch army, although admittedly
militant Catholics or admirers of Louis xiv were not likely to
be found there, but it was not until early in 1688, when James
withdrew the British regiments and forbade visits, that attachment to William became an open declaration of opposition to
the crown.

William occupied a close but detached position in relation
to English politics. This had roughly counterbalancing advantages and disadvantages. He was not continuously involved in
everyday factional disputes, and could reserve his own judgement and opinions until a situation became clear. Friends and
associates could not easily rush him into premature decisions
and rash, unconsidered statements. As nephew and son-in-law
he had intimate connections with James, but William was under
no formal obligations to him, since Mary received no kind of
allowance from her father, an omission that reflected his original
disapproval of her marriage to William.[3]

Although usually its restrictions caused him endless frustration, William could exploit some of the peculiarities of the Dutch
constitution so as to indicate his own opinion without officially
committing himself. In 1681 he evaded responsibility for
advocating Exclusion by showing that the declaration in its
favour, which Sidney produced, originated with the States-
General and not with himself. It would have been impolitic

[2] D'Avaux, vi, 107.
[3] Burnet, iii, 133.

for William openly and publicly to commit himself in 1687 to outright opposition to James's proposals for the repeal of the Tests and penal laws; this was done very effectively by the pensionary, Fagel, in his *Letter* in which he authoritatively reported William and Mary's opposition. Again William was able to disclaim responsibility for the failure of city and provincial authorities to respond to English demands for the extradition of prominent exiles.

From the Hague William could keep a close watch on English affairs; it was a far better observation post than Hanover twenty years later. He kept up a correspondence with a large number of men who possessed very different, and often sharply conflicting, views and opinions. By this means William obtained a wide range of information. His own letters in reply did not commit him, as would have been the case had he been personally engaged in discussions in Whitehall, so that he was able to maintain correspondence for long periods and at the same time with such very different men as James, Halifax, Sunderland, Danby, Sidney, Godolphin, Rochester and Temple. However, there were serious problems posed by the differing views and conflicting advice which he received from his correspondents. Much of the information which they sent was inaccurate, biased and prejudiced. William knew that almost all his correspondents were self-interested and hoped to use him for their own (concealed) purposes. In 1680 Sunderland and Godolphin urged him to come over for the parliamentary session, ostensibly to safeguard his own and Mary's right, but in reality so as to help push through the policy of Exclusion which they had just decided to support. Had William come he would have found himself enmeshed in dangerous intrigues and manoeuvres which at the least would have ruined his reputation and influence with Charles and James.[4]

Geographical detachment enabled William to combine correspondence with Charles, James and their ministers with the maintenance of links with politicians who may be more accurately described as unofficial persons rather than active members of the

[4] Jones, *First Whigs*, pp. 128–32, 140.

opposition. Until the late summer of 1687 William did not maintain a regular correspondence, either directly or indirectly, with actual or potential rebels in England – Scotland was a very different matter. During the Exclusion Crisis he appears to have been ignored by Shaftesbury. The Whig leader's strategy was to pass the bill first, and then drive a hard bargain with William over his wife's right to the succession. Only when the fortunes of the first Whigs were in visible decline did they initiate any move to work in alliance with William, and by then he had nothing to gain from doing so. It must be emphasized that William had no long-standing connection with the Whigs as a party, he was not dependent on them at any time, and had no obligations towards them as such. Indeed he was suspicious of them, seeing them as a group similar in interest, outlook and composition to his Dutch republican opponents. Similarly, infected by Amsterdam notions, many Whigs feared William as a would-be absolutist in Holland who would assist his English uncles in their unconstitutional policies. When Shaftesbury arrived as an exile at the end of 1682, William sincerely disavowed any connection or sympathy, and it was to Amsterdam, then an enemy city for William, that Shaftesbury went.

William had no personal connection or sympathy with the rank and file Whigs who arrived in some numbers after the Rye House Plot in 1683, and they too tended to associate with his political opponents in Utrecht and Amsterdam. There was one important exception. William's attitude towards Monmouth was always ambiguous. During the Exclusion Crisis Monmouth was necessarily a direct threat to Mary's right to succeed her father or uncle, or at the very least a much better placed rival to William for the office of regent. When in 1679 he was sent abroad into temporary exile, William welcomed him because he still retained Charles's favour, but he immediately disavowed him when he returned without permission and went into active opposition.[5] William's open hospitality to Monmouth on his next visit to the Hague in 1684-5 was based on his belief that an early reconciliation was being planned between Monmouth

[5] *Ibid.*, p. 129.

and Charles. William's friendly reception would not cause resentment in Whitehall. A reconciliation would serve his interests, since earlier attempts to bring one about had shown that Charles would insist on Monmouth acknowledging his illegitimacy; this would guarantee Mary's right. In addition, the chief sponsor of the reconciliation, Halifax, intended it to be followed by the early summoning of Parliament, which held out at least the possibility of an independent English foreign policy.[6]

When all these plans were destroyed by Charles's sudden death, Monmouth left William's court. It is improbable that William had any direct or personal connection with either Monmouth's or Argyll's invasions, both of which were prepared in Amsterdam, over whose town government and admiralty college he had little influence. Indeed, the republican contacts of d'Avaux in Amsterdam hoped that by helping the rebels they were effectively wrecking the possibility of either an alliance or a good understanding between James and William, which they feared would enhance the *stadhouder's* authority and prestige. However, contacts did exist between Bentinck and Monmouth and his followers just before their embarkation. Gerbrand Zas, who had been the first secret agent despatched to England in 1672 and 1673 and was now secretary of the Rotterdam Admiralty, helped the rebels. Odijk, another prominent Orangist, was indiscreetly sympathetic. But for William himself these contacts were no more than part of an extraordinarily elaborate and extensive set of moves by which he tried to cover himself against all eventualities.[7]

The situation in England and Scotland was completely uncertain. From abroad it looked as though another prolonged rebellion and civil war were inevitable, and both William and Louis were not very confident that James could surmount his difficulties without outside support. Both went to great lengths to keep a close watch on developments. In addition to Van

---

[6] D'Avaux, iv, 211–12, 235, 240–41, 265, 271–2, 274, 283, 291, 316; v, 85.
[7] D'Avaux, v, 17, 57–8, 63. I am indebted to Mr S. Groenveld for pointing out to me the full significance of the involvement of Zas. He had been procurator for the English merchants under Cromwell, and again after 1660, as well as being employed on diplomatic missions which would indicate that he had William's confidence.

Citters, the ambassador from the States-General who was knowledgeable and had good sources at court as well as in London, he sent Bentinck and Dijkvelt on special missions to England. He also made use of the future pensionary, Antonie Heinsius, who was there on East India business, to establish contact with peers and MPS.[8] Of course the crisis was resolved far more quickly than had been expected, and Monmouth's rebellion was suppressed without the six regiments sent over by William getting into action, but he would have been far more favourably placed to influence events, if a civil war had occurred, than would the French. As it was he learnt a good deal from Monmouth's mistakes, and was to put this knowledge to good use in 1688, while the removal of a potential rival cleared the way for his own undisputed leadership of the reversionary interest.

In particular, Monmouth's disastrous experience showed William the danger of relying on the advice and intelligence provided by embittered political exiles who were out of touch with England, and claimed an influence there which they had inevitably lost while abroad. In late 1685 the survivors of the two rebellions were again gathering in Dutch cities, causing considerable but unnecessary alarm in Whitehall. Argyll's exiled supporters were more important for William's future plans, because of the lack of any real opportunities in Scotland for constitutional opposition. The English exiles, mostly radical Whigs, did not influence him in any way and were to some extent a liability. Many of their pamphlets were extreme and offensive. Some exiles returned to England to enter James's service in 1687–8, and some of those who remained acted as spies for d'Avaux and d'Albeville; the latter got his most accurate information about the invasion from a former officer in Monmouth's army. Eventually, several radical Whigs – Sir Robert Peyton, John Wildman, Robert Ferguson – accompanied William on his invasion, but it is significant that they very

[8] Japikse, ii, 217; *Correspondentie*, i, 20–29; II, ii, 702–4; D'Avaux, iv, 304, 333; v, 185. Heinsius was in England at the end of 1685, at the time of the second parliamentary session.

quickly lost the little influence which they possessed in the first days at Exeter.

Of all the exiles only Gilbert Burnet was of outstanding importance. His consistently controversial and sometimes factually incorrect writings, and his highly developed sense of his own importance, led contemporaries to sneer at him, and have led to his part in the Revolution being minimized by many modern historians. However, he did have William under an immense obligation, since it was he more than anyone else who had persuaded Mary that her duty lay in unconditional obedience to her husband, a position from which she was never to swerve or deviate.[9] Although his judgement was sometimes erratic, Burnet occupied an independent position, living at the Hague and keeping himself apart from the other exiles. He was useful as a propagandist, writing pamphlets and translating Fagel's *Letter* into English, and was consulted by Bentinck. He claimed to have drafted Dijkvelt's instructions (which have not survived) and was certainly regarded by James as his most dangerous domestic enemy. Consequently in May 1687 Burnet was summoned to surrender himself at Edinburgh on a charge of treason. To have obeyed would have meant committing suicide, as a Scottish court at this time would have made short work of him, and he faced the near certainty of interrogation under torture. William was determined to protect Burnet, and resisted demands for his extradition on the grounds that he had become a Dutch citizen by naturalization – a change of allegiance which neither English nor Scottish law would recognize as legal.[10]

After refusing to surrender himself Burnet was outlawed. Under Scottish law he could then be killed by anyone, acting on his own initiative without incurring any penalty. Two plots were organized for his assassination, one of them by Neville Paine, who was himself to be tortured as a Jacobite agent in Scotland after the Revolution. Louis expressed his hatred of Burnet by allowing it to be known that successful kidnappers would be given asylum in France. The struggle for Burnet made him more important as a symbol than as an agent of opposition to James. It was politically unwise for a Catholic sovereign to prosecute, and seek the death, of a man who was after all the foremost Protestant historian of his day, who had made a European reputation with the first two volumes of his *History of the Reformation in England*. In form William took some notice of James's protests, by telling Burnet not to appear publicly at his court, but he detailed bodyguards for his protection and Bentinck continued to consult him.[11]

William's use of special missions in 1685 was not unique. Bentinck had gone on one in 1683, and effective use was to be made of them again in 1687 and 1688. It would be simplistic to interpret these missions as conspiratorial links in a chain of plotting aimed at a usurpation of the English crown. Their primary purpose was to undertake reconnaissances. Each was sent at a time of particular disturbance and great uncertainty. Bentinck had first undertaken one at the time of the Rye House Plot, when the first Whigs were being destroyed. He accompanied Dijkvelt in the initial weeks of James's reign, when a difficult parliamentary session and dangerous rebellions seemed to lie ahead. Dijkvelt went again in February 1687, after the dismissal of Rochester, when a parliamentary session seemed possible after prorogations lasting fifteen months, and when James appeared to be moving towards an alliance with the dissenters. Zuylestein paid his first visit in August 1687, when James was initiating what was to develop into the campaign to pack Parliament; his second visit followed immediately after the momentous birth of the Prince of Wales, with the purpose of testing the resolution of William's associates now that the whole situation had been transformed, and knowing that any action would have to be undertaken during that year.

The inadequacy of English diplomatic representation at the Hague was another reason for William to use special ambassadors. He could get no insight into James's intentions and

11 PWA, 2126, 2131, 2133, 2137, 2143, 2145; Campana de Cavelli, ii, 157; D'Avaux, vi, 48–9.

thoughts from either Skelton or d'Albeville. The former became personally repugnant as well as politically antagonistic to William. D'Albeville, who arrived in January 1687, was too much of a nonentity to have to be taken seriously. His appointment was a deliberate snub, since William had let it be known that he would like a considerable person who would work to restore good relations.[12] Instead he got an elderly and petty-minded Irish Catholic with a dubious past as a spy in both French and Spanish pay. Although d'Albeville had worked with Dijkvelt in the past, and now received money from d'Avaux, he was neither a liability nor an asset for William.[13] It was James who found himself adversely affected by the appointment. D'Albeville's reports are full of questions of protocol, he had a passion for pursuing trivial issues and he showed no evidence of political judgement.[14] He does not seem to have tried seriously to penetrate William's extensive English correspondence. He entirely failed to understand the significance and purpose of Dijkvelt's and Zuylestein's special missions. In fact William realized that there were advantages for himself in James having such an innocuous minister, and was mildly alarmed early in 1688 when it was rumoured that he would be replaced. Only at the end, after being prompted by d'Avaux who kept supplying him with information, did d'Albeville's reports begin to contain the kind of information which James so urgently needed.

The information obtained by these special ambassadors was particularly valuable in corroborating, as well as supplementing, the reports being received from Van Citters and William's English correspondents and agents. As a matter of policy they saw as wide a selection of politicians as possible, even though their main interest was in a much smaller number of men who were directly connected with William. Remembering that Van Citters represented the States-General, and not William, they were used to represent William's own views and opinions. They

[12] Mazure, ii, 185.

[13] E. S. de Beer, 'The Marquis of Albeville and his Brothers', *English Historical Review*, 45. D'Avaux, v, 317–18; Addit., 38494, f.53.

[14] His despatches form Addit., 41814–41816.

could give assurances and answer questions in his name. They could make estimates of the friendliness and usefulness to William of those with whom they spoke. None of this was necessarily sinister. At least in appearance, this work was not illegitimate or an intrusion into James's sovereign affairs. All the missions, except the last, were consistent with William's position as effective head of the reversionary interest, maintaining a watching brief on Mary's behalf.

During 1686–7 William had only limited opportunities for active intervention in English politics, since there was no prospect of James allowing Parliament to meet until he had completed his preparations. The only counter-preparation that could be attempted was to try to estimate the probable balance of parties in the House of Lords, and to try to stiffen the attitude of those peers who feature as opponents of the crown on the lists that were compiled.[15] This could not achieve much, since by exercising his prerogative powers James could create unlimited new peers and swamp an opposition majority. It was impossible to attempt open canvassing at court, since this might easily be exploited by the pro-French group of Catholic extremists, and the French and Dutch diplomats in London watched each other's activities very closely. Louis also employed special missions, sending over Bonrepos on three occasions: in January 1686, June 1687 and September 1688. His instructions were very similar to those of his Dutch counterparts: to discover James's real intentions; to provide a second opinion on the political situation at times of uncertainty; and to establish a clandestine negotiation. In his case this was with Tyrconnel, to see whether in the event of James's early death Catholic interests in Ireland could be preserved, if necessary by offering to take the country under French protection.[16]

Dijkvelt's mission, from February to May 1687, is generally taken as marking the start of the process that was to lead eventu-

[15] See K. H. D. Haley, 'A List of English Peers, May 1687', *English Historical Review*, 69.
[16] Mazure, ii, 278–9, 281–2, 288. Torcy was also sent; his instructions of 12 September 1687 are in the Baschet transcripts.

ally to William's invasion. It is true that Dijkvelt laid a foundation in contacts and understandings that were to be developed later, but his mission was still essentially exploratory. It had the result of committing William only in a negative sense, the one conclusive result being to make James realize that William would not under any circumstances support repeal of the Test Acts. The background to this result needs some emphasis. The first initiative which brought William into active participation in English politics was taken by James, not by William or his English associates. James, by attempting to bring in William to support his policies – a move that if successful would certainly have cut the ground from under the feet of the opposition – forced William to declare himself. This of course strengthened his links with opposition groups, but the first move had been made by James.

This had been in November 1686, when William Penn was sent to the Hague on an unofficial mission with the object of persuading William and Mary to give their assent to repeal of the Tests and penal laws. Although William thought that he had made his refusal clear enough, James did not accept it as final but hoped to use Dijkvelt to renew the approach.[17] However, the timing of the mission, the fact that Dijkvelt arrived four days before the end of the current prorogation of Parliament, made James suspect that he had been sent to strengthen opposition to the crown. This danger was easily removed: first, Parliament was prorogued from 15 February to 28 April, and then it was made clear that there would be no prospect of an early session by a further prorogation to 22 November. French anxiety about Dijkvelt's mission took an entirely different form; d'Avaux feared that William would agree to repeal of the Tests and penal laws as the way of purchasing James's consent for a strengthening of the treaties, so that they would form the basis of an alliance to check French expansion. Yet another version was put to members of the States-General by Fagel, who told them that the main purpose was to discover whether James intended to go to war against them. In fact Dijkvelt was instruc-

---

[17] Burnet, iii, 140–41; Mazure, ii, 184–5; D'Avaux, vi, 21.

ted to try to persuade James to join in containing French aggression, and he could work for this in cooperation with Kaunitz, the imperial minister who had arrived in England a month earlier for the same purpose.[18]

Dijkvelt found James concerned almost exclusively with his domestic policies. By issuing the Declaration of Indulgence on 4 April, while Dijkvelt was still in England, James ensured that William's attitude towards the Tests and penal laws remained the central question under discussion. This move had been anticipated. According to Burnet, Dijkvelt's instructions included assurances for the Anglicans that William would remain firm to their Church interest, and explanations that he was not a 'Presbyterian'. He was also to persuade the dissenters not to collaborate with James but, equally important although not mentioned by Burnet, he was also to reassure the moderate Catholics. Dijkvelt had to make it absolutely clear to William's associates that he was irrevocably opposed to repeal of the Tests and penal laws as proposed by James, but he was to explain for the benefit of both dissenters and moderate Catholics (who were not asking for repeal of the Tests and were afraid of a Protestant reaction after James's death) that William and Mary were unalterably opposed to persecution on grounds of religious differences.[19]

At the end, in a final parting interview, Dijkvelt managed to convince James of William's opposition, but even so he was commissioned to carry a letter again asking William to agree. James instructed d'Albeville to renew pressure at the Hague. This persistence, and James's belief that Dijkvelt's attitude and refusal were the result of his having been corrupted by the disaffected persons whom he had been seeing, were characteristic of his refusal to accept unpalatable facts. Dijkvelt admitted that he had seen men of very different opinions, but naturally concealed the duty which he had performed of assuring peers

[18] *Correspondentie*, II, ii, 747–8; Klopp, iii, 285–6; D'Avaux, vi, 37, 41, 46–8; Baschet; Barrillon, 27, 30 January, 17, 20 February 1687. See also, J. Muilenburg, *The Embassy of Everaard van Weede, Lord of Dykveld to England in 1687*, University of Nebraska Studies, xx, 3, 4.

[19] Japikse, ii, 224; *Correspondentie*, II, ii, 747–50; Burnet, iii, 173–5; Baschet; Barrillon, 17, 27 March, 7 April 1687.

and MPS that William would persist in his refusal to support repeal of the Tests and penal laws. William made this known publicly, in an oblique way in June, when he announced his intention not to appoint any new Catholic officers to the English and Scottish regiments in Holland.[20]

Some of Dijkvelt's meetings had been kept secret, for instance those arranged with Lord Mordaunt's associates.[21] Colonel John Cutts, a former friend of Monmouth who had a good deal of influence with army officers, introduced him to a group of young Whigs.[22] Dijkvelt also saw Danby, and arranged for the renewal of correspondence between him and William after a break of some years.[23] When he returned he took back with him a number of letters of very varying importance. Lord Bellasis and Sunderland sent polite messages. In contrast Churchill's could not have been more informative. It contained his own personal assurances and told William authoritatively that Anne was safe and would not succumb to pressure to become a Catholic. Generally the correspondents can be divided into three categories. First, there were those like Rochester who might claim to be well-intentioned towards William, but were useless to him because they still found it possible to work with James in his policies in the hope of regaining his favour. Secondly, there were those who were already notorious as opponents of James, and were being carefully watched, so that active opposition would entail unacceptable risks. Such men as Danby, Devonshire, Compton and Halifax would have to serve as symbols rather than as agents of opposition, although they would become extremely useful if Parliament were allowed to meet. Thirdly, there were the secret friends, like Churchill, who were especially valuable because James still trusted them.[24]

After Dijkvelt's return to Holland, James made another attempt to win William's support by an approach through d'Albeville. He offered what were intended to be assurances,

---

[20] Burnet, iii, 178, D'Avaux, vi, 53–5, 66–8; Mazure, ii, 186–7, 251–4; Addit., 34502, ff. 80–81; 41814, ff. 248, 255–6, 257.

[21] *HMC, VIIIth Report*, app, iii, 559a.

[22] *Ibid.*, 560b.

[23] Dalrymple, appendix, part 1, 194–6.

[24] *Ibid.*, pp. 190–200 for the whole correspondence.

although they were all inadequate, saying that he disapproved of the Revocation of the Edict of Nantes (but his obligations to Louis prevented him from saying this in public), that he was determined to safeguard Mary's right of succession (but as it was hers by right there was no basis for bargaining here). He pleaded that he could not abandon the Catholics. William summarily rejected this approach. Reaffirming his opposition to all forms of religious persecution, he repeated his opinion that Catholics should not hold offices, and irritatingly advised James to keep to the law and cease trying to extend his prerogative powers.[25]

In August 1687 an entirely new phase began with a special mission by Zuylestein, using the pretext of conveying William's condolences on the death of the queen's mother. This visit followed James's dissolution of the prorogued Parliament in July, and coincided with the start of the campaign to pack Parliament, so that one of Zuylestein's main tasks was to learn when a new Parliament was likely to meet, and the chances of its agreeing with James. Zuylestein saw almost as many leading political figures as Dijkvelt had done, and he too carried back letters to William. Comparatively little can be learnt from the text of these letters and we have no record of his conversations or of the verbal messages which he may have reported. But by inference it would seem likely that the most important result of his mission was the establishment of an extensive clandestine system of correspondence and intelligence, which started shortly afterwards and continued uninterruptedly until he carried out a second mission, in June 1688.

This correspondence represents the first, preliminary stage of the preparations for intervention in English politics. At the Dutch end it was managed by Bentinck, helped by Dijkvelt and Zuylestein. In England the leading part was played by Henry Sidney, 'the great wheel on which the Revolution rolled', although we have only a fraction of the reports which originated with him.[26]

It is no exaggeration to say that the whole success of William's

[25] *Ibid.*, pp. 183–5; D'Avaux, vi, 66–8; Baschet; Bonrepos, 6 June 1687.
[26] Burnet, iii, 277–8; *Memoirs of the Secret Services of John Macky* (1733), p. 34.

English policies, and of the Revolution itself, depended entirely on these four men. Willem Bentinck was William's first and most intimate friend. He had accompanied him to England in 1670, was married to an Englishwoman (sister of William's mistress, Elizabeth Villiers), and was trusted by him in every matter. Reserved, cold, discreet, vastly experienced in diplomacy and intrigue, he was exceptionally well qualified to act as controller and director of an underground political organization. The others were more suited to personal negotiation and persuasion, to dealing and manipulating. They too were close personal friends of William, and influenced his private as well as his public life. They were all a little older, with personalities on which, it is to be suspected, William would like to have based his own way of life. All three were extroverts, hard drinkers, womanizers, men of the world, who combined his passion for hunting and courage in battle with a kind of assurance and suavity that William never acquired. They were *faux bonhommes,* cynical and apparently indolent, who skilfully concealed their true abilities and especially their shrewdness in judging and manipulating others. Certainly they had no difficulty in deceiving James and his ministers and in preserving almost total secrecy in their work in 1687–8.

The organizers took elaborate precautions, and the instructions for carrying on the clandestine correspondence make dramatic reading. In the earlier stages most letters were sent by the ordinary post, to genuine addresses in England and Holland, from which they were then to be forwarded. The clumsy devices which contemporaries often used, such as references to merchandise or family matters whose real meaning it was not difficult to guess, were avoided and ciphers were never used in open letters. Instead key words, or devices such as ending a postscript with an 'etc.', indicated that the blank portions of letters contained passages written in white, or invisible ink. An arrangement was also agreed to detect when letters had been opened, since it was known that Sir Nicholas Butler had been put in charge of an organization to intercept correspondence. This system worked well at first, and letters passed freely, although it was always easier to get letters out to Holland than in the other direction. The authorities never detected anything of real value to them, but as tension increased in 1688 they were able to disrupt the correspondence by the simple expedient of holding up the post as a whole. This made the alternative method of correspondence more important; letters were sent by ordinary merchant ships sailing between London and Amsterdam and Rotterdam. Outward-bound messages were often put on board below Gravesend, that is after final customs clearance. Dutch merchants had been asked to recommend trustworthy men to carry letters by this route, which was the one by which pamphlets were smuggled into England in bulk cargoes. The one disadvantage was its slowness, but the organizers were right in avoiding the regular packet boats sailing from Harwich to Helvoetsluis which, although fast and frequent, were kept under strict surveillance. Occasionally, special couriers were employed and full use was made of all Dutch diplomats travelling in either direction.[27]

In the final stages before the invasion, when speed was essential and secrecy of paramount importance, fast yachts and small vessels operated special courier services. We have tantalizingly few details, as indeed did d'Avaux and d'Albeville despite their extensive spy networks, but none of the very prominent men who joined William had any difficulty in crossing. Some made the journey in both directions. Almost certainly Zuylestein paid a secret visit to the north shortly before the invasion, and William received secret information from a small vessel after he had actually set out. None of his later letters to correspondents in England seem to have been either intercepted or delayed, and since the posts were all held up this would seem to indicate that his courier service was working right up to the end of October. Only one emissary, Captain Lenham, was arrested while carrying a large quantity of William's Declaration. Finally, quite large sums of money were safely despatched to Holland to help finance the expedition.[28]

Similarly, it has to be emphasized that there are large gaps

---

[27] PWA, 2087b, 2091, 2097a, 2120, 2137, 2167; *Correspondentie*, I, ii, 597–9.
[28] *HMC, VIIth Report*, app, i, 348, 423; D'Avaux, vi, 170–71, 199, 230, 243, 275; Addit., 34510, ff.163–4; 41816, f.160.

in our knowledge of William's underground system of support and propaganda in England. We have only a fraction of the total clandestine correspondence which can be shown to have been exchanged. We either have very few letters, or none at all, to or from several of the important correspondents who feature on Bentinck's lists – Devonshire, Henry Powle, the Earl of Carlisle, William Forrester (who had been forced to return from William's court by a privy seal letter from James) and Sir James Herbert.[29] We know that at the Hague Dr John Hutton, a Scottish physician to Mary, was the most frequently used addressee, but there is only fragmentary evidence on Mr Freeman (indeed this may be a pseudonym), whom William had employed as an agent in 1672–3, and again during the Exclusion Crisis.[30] Bentinck was apparently the only man who was actively engaged in both English and Scottish correspondence. In the latter, which was kept separate, he worked with William Carstares, forming a partnership which continued after the Revolution, when the two of them virtually controlled royal policy towards Scotland.

Most of the letters that have survived and originated in England came from Sidney, James Johnstone and James Rivers. Johnstone had been brought up in the United Provinces, where his family had gone after the execution of his father, the extreme Covenanter Archibald Johnstone of Warristoun, in 1663. The son, who was Burnet's nephew and a future secretary for Scotland, had extensive English connections, but how far in his own right and how far as William's agent it is impossible to say. Johnstone displayed great energy in collecting information and organizing contacts and correspondence, so that Burnet's statement that he did most of the actual work, and supplied the drive, while the idle, handsome aristocrat Sidney took the credit, has usually been accepted.[31] We just do not have enough evidence to substantiate, or disprove, Burnet's avuncular judgement. But it seems that Sidney consciously used his reputation

---

[29] PWA, 2087b, 2110a.
[30] D'Avaux, i, 14–15; vi, 36–37; Haley, *William of Orange and the English Opposition*, pp. 54–6.
[31] PWA, 2167.

as a man of pleasure to cover his clandestine work. Moreover, he enjoyed certain crucial personal advantages which he adroitly exploited for the furtherance of William's plans. Most important were the personal links which he retained with officers in James's army from his own years of service under Charles, and as commander of the regiments in Dutch service from 1681 to 1685. We know that he was consulted by many officers, and kept up correspondence with many of those who were to defect to William in 1688. Sidney also had the *entrée* at court, where he was to be seen as late as April, and he was related to leading men in political life, not least to Sunderland. Johnstone had close connections with the more radical Whigs and also, rather surprisingly for a Scot with his background, with many of the leading Anglican clergy.[32]

The surviving correspondence sent secretly to Bentinck and Hutton contains a good deal of general news which could have been supplied by any reasonably well-informed person in public life or on the fringes of the court: the appointment of Catholic sheriffs, the progress of the queen's pregnancy, the date on which Parliament was likely to meet, the tactics that would be used to fix elections. Far more useful for William and his advisers were the many reports giving them what we would call feedback on the propaganda originating in the United Provinces. There are many references to the popular effects of pamphlets, above all of Fagel's *Letter,* whose enormous success was emphasized. The agents also kept a close watch on the counter-effects of court replies and refutations, especially *Parliamentum Pacificum*, which boldly denied Fagel's main statement, that William and Mary were resolutely opposed to repeal of the Tests. Sidney, Johnstone and Rivers all constantly emphasized the importance of William also keeping ahead of the court in the propaganda, of retaining the initiative and so forcing the court to answer his arguments (and in the process helping to publicize them). They were afraid that the very success of Fagel's *Letter* would lead to complacency, knowing that the effects would

[32] PWA, 2163.

inevitably diminish with time. They urged the calculated maintenance of a bold, confident tone in all public statements, as well as pamphlets, so as to keep up public morale. Copies of court pamphlets were promptly sent to the Hague so that answers could be published. Finally, the vital importance of winning the battle of publications was underlined : 'In the late fermentation about the Exclusion, the Excluders never lost ground till they lost the Press.'[33]

The agents seem to have been at least partially responsible for arranging the importation and distribution of pamphlets and books published in Holland. It was not difficult to smuggle this material in bulk cargoes, but distribution presented formidable difficulties. Alarmed by the success of Fagel's *Letter* and of a commentary that appeared in February, *Reflexions on Fagel's Letter*, the administration tried to intimidate booksellers in provincial towns, interrogating them on the sources from which they had received copies of seditious pamphlets.[34] Printers were also closely watched, since some opposition pamphlets had been so popular that pirated editions had appeared to cater profitably for an insatiable demand. Quantitatively, the pamphlet controversy presents the same characteristics as the propaganda produced during the Exclusion Crisis : a very large number of ephemeral publications pouring out week after week, often in the form of answers and rejoinders, refutations and restatements. The most successful were printed in what were for the seventeenth century very large quantities; twenty thousand copies of *Parliamentum Pacificum* were produced at James's expense, and Johnstone reported that altogether the king's agents had distributed over a hundred thousand copies of books and pamphlets free of charge. William's agents had thirty thousand copies of Fagel's *Letter* to distribute (out of an initial printing of forty-five thousand) as well as a hundred thousand of *A Letter from a Jesuit at Liège*. In the anonymity of London it was not too difficult to circulate pamphlets, which were left in taverns and coffee houses and deposited in the porches of private houses, but as Butler was watching all roads and carriers it was necessary

[33] PWA, 2118a, 2126, 2147, 2159.
[34] PWA, 2159; PRO, SP Domestic, James II, Entry Book 56, pp. 407, 410–11.

to send copies for the provinces direct by sea from Holland. The disadvantage was that this made simultaneous publication (one reason for the great impact made by Halifax's *Letter to a Dissenter*) virtually impossible.[35]

Some of the confidential information contained in the letters sent by the agents must have been of the greatest value to William in preparing his moves. He received accurate and perceptive information on the complicated and constantly changing faction fighting and balance of power within James's court, and in particular on the relationship between, and relative influence of, Sunderland and Melfort.[36] Johnstone reported with intimate knowledge on the discussions that preceded the bishops' petition and the refusals of the London clergy to read the Declaration of Indulgence. He also actively assisted in the preparations that were made to mobilize members of the nobility and gentry to enter bail for them and to appear personally in the courtroom.[37] He kept a watch on the regulations of the corporations, and on the activities of James's electoral agents. But the most important subject with which the agents were actively concerned was to report the attitudes and likely behaviour of officers in the army and navy, on which the entire success of the plan to intervene in England was to depend. William's most urgent problem was how to subvert the loyalty of the army and navy, so as to reduce the risks of finding himself involved in a long and expensive military operation which would drain away resources needed for the central struggle against France. He knew that James, like Cromwell, could disregard the opinions and opposition of virtually the whole nation provided that the army and navy remained loyal to him.

There was already a marked difference between the respective places which the army and navy occupied in relation to society (and politics) in general, although it was not yet as distinct and systematized as in the eighteenth and nineteenth centuries. Despite the recent influx of Irish and Scottish Catholics who had formerly been in the French service, most army officers in

[35] PWA, 2120, 2126, 2143.
[36] PWA, 2122a, 2120, 2126, 2129, 2149, 2153, 2159, 2161, 2169, 2175.
[37] PWA, 2161, 2163.

James's army came from the English land-owning classes, from the provincial gentry as well as from the court nobility. They formed a part of upper-class society. By contrast, the navy lived a rather separate existence. Its senior officers were an uneasy mixture composed of a relatively few aristocrats, or men with good social connections, and the professional career seamen, the so-called 'tarpaulins'. The social contrast between the two services was reflected by the way in which William's methods of subversion were organized. Sidney and his colleagues dealt directly with the army officers but an entirely separate organization was used in approaching the officers in the fleet.

By the end of 1687, when James's campaign was well under way with canvassing, questioning and purges, there were rumours that the army would eventually be included.[38] There is no evidence to indicate that this was ever definitely planned, but when no action was taken before the army moved into its summer camp for exercises and training, it was too late to act in 1688. Moreover, it would seem possible that James knew that so many officers would refuse their consent to repeal of the Tests (which would facilitate the appointment of Catholic competitors) that he could not afford the disorganization which dismissals would produce. But during the summer there was further evidence of the unsatisfactory political state of many units; the soldiers in camp infuriated James by applauding the acquittal of the bishops, the rate of desertions continued to be high, and there were indications of caballing among the regimental officers. There was much more substance in the reports which now informed William of James's intention to remodel the army during the winter of 1688–9.[39] This prospect was a major factor, second in importance only to the imminence of a general European war, in convincing William that it was now or never, that the invasion must be launched in 1688 or not at all. Louis was urging James to purge his army, and the availability of larger numbers of Irish and Scottish Catholic officers and soldiers now made this a practical proposition, since

[38] PWA, 2103.
[39] PWA, 2118a, 2120, 2139, 2141 2143, 2173.

they could be used to fill the vacancies which a purge would create.

The possibility of this happening began to create tension in the army. There was already a good deal of professional jealousy between Irish officers, who usually had the advantage of service in the French army, and their less experienced English rivals. Duels, brawls and murders showed that personal relations were bad, and misconduct by recently arrived Irish soldiers was well publicized.[40] The most important development originated in the refusal by officers in Berwick's regiment, stationed at the key fortress of Portsmouth, which was valued by James as a possible place of refuge and as a link with France, to accept Irish recruits into their companies. They were court-martialled and dismissed, a bitterly resented action that was the major reason for many regimental officers defecting to William in November. Not surprisingly, many officers consulted Sidney, as William's representative, who already possessed many personal contacts among the officers. His influence should be directly related to what was perhaps the key portion of the letter of the Seven, which was sent by means of Herbert to Holland, inviting William to intervene:[41]

... many of the officers being so discontented that they continue in their service only for a subsistence (*besides that, some of their minds are known already*) and very many of the common soldiers do daily show such an aversion to the Popish religion, that there is the greatest probability imaginable of great numbers of deserters which would come from them, should there be such an occasion.[42]

James's army gave William's agents plenty of opportunity for political propaganda, exploiting these personal as well as the more general grievances.

The agents worked through several groups. One was the Rose Tavern club, a clandestine group of serving and former army officers presided over by Lord Colchester, still a serving officer

---

[40] Addit., 34510, f.161; *HMC, IXth Report*, app. v, 234; Nottingham University Library, Phillipps MSS, 8589, ii, Povey to Southwell, 26 April 1687.
[41] See pages 239–41.
[42] My italics. Dalrymple, appendix, part 1, 229. Reprinted in Williams, *Eighteenth Century Constitution*, pp. 8–10.

although a former Whig MP. Associated with him was a group of younger Whig men of fashion: Thomas Wharton, William Jephson, Charles Godfrey. Operating as an apparently separate unit were other officers who associated with General Percy Kirke, who had served at Tangier, and the young Duke of Ormonde. Two officers were particularly active, Thomas Langston, who canvassed juniors, and John Cutts, who came over from the United Provinces on a secret visit in March, but returned there to take part in the invasion together with Thomas Talmadge. Unfortunately, we have no evidence about any contacts between these groups, or about their relation either to Churchill who, as James's lieutenant-general, was to play the decisive part in disintegrating the army, or to the civilian associates of William. But personal links must have played a part, since a high proportion of the officers who were to defect were sons, relations or connections of prominent politicians who had contacts with William.[43]

William's *Letter to the English Army* was directed specifically at the officers. It cited Tyrconnel's purge of Protestants from the Irish army in 1687–8 (the source of most officers' disquiet) to demonstrate that James intended to use existing officers as instruments who would be discarded once the nation was enslaved and Protestantism ruined. The appeal made great play on the issue of religion – an indication of the likely effectiveness of this argument had been provided by Churchill's own letter to William, in which he had emphasized its paramount importance for him. Such emphasis was needed to overcome a formidable psychological barrier, not loyalty to James but rather the sense of military honour treasured by all officers. Therefore it was necessary to overcome the demands of their professional code by reminding the officers of their obligations to 'God and Religion, Country, Selves, Posterity ... of being the Instruments of serving your Country and Securing your Religion'. In this context it should be noted that James expressed his surprise to the Dutch officer escorting him to Rochester, that soldiers should have put the interests of religion before those of their honour,

---

[43] PWA, 2118a; Addit., 41805, ff.23, 68; 41815, ff.189–90, 212, 228, 232; D'Avaux, vi, 177–8.

and that Churchill should have been denigrated (by officers in the Dutch service who looked on him as a professional rival) as a deserter who had behaved dishonourably.[44]

Admiral Herbert's *Letter to all Commanders of Ships and Sea-men* laid a similar emphasis on warning them that a victory over the Dutch fleet would lead to their being enslaved and Protestantism ruined. In asking them to join William he confidently predicted that 'the major and best part of the army', as well as of the nation, would do so.[45] The navy had far fewer Catholics than the army; according to a 1687 report there were then only fifteen officers and twenty seamen, to one hundred officers and 4,220 soldiers.[46] Furthermore, there was no source from which Catholics could be recruited, since there was no large sea-going population in Ireland. On the other hand, the navy had fought its three last major wars against the Dutch. In 1672–3, when there had been little enthusiasm for the Cabal's war of aggression, officers and seamen had nevertheless done their duty in four particularly hard-fought engagements. James still had an interest among senior officers deriving from his years as lord high admiral, although he had recently dissipated some of this influence by unwisely pushing Sir Roger Strickland over the heads of other officers because he was a Catholic. Although Strickland was replaced by the respected Protestant officer, Lord Dartmouth, when invasion became imminent, he left a legacy of resentment, especially among junior captains, which others were ready to exploit. The Duke of Grafton, Charles's bastard son, had been passed over for vice-admiral and in resentment used his influence against James's policies, paying a secret visit to the fleet.[47] Consequently, when Dartmouth took over the command of the fleet he found an uneasy situation, with pamphlets and newspapers circulating among the ships' crews. With Herbert and Edward Russell already known to be disaffected and having joined William at the Hague, the threat of subver-

[44] Reprinted in *A Collection of Papers Relating to the Present Juncture of Affairs* (1689), pp. 17–18; Huygens, p. 53.
[45] Reprinted in *A Second Collection of Papers*, pp. 25–6; E. B. Powley, *English Navy in the Revolution of 1688* (1928), p. 69.
[46] Mazure, ii, 229.
[47] Powley, *op. cit.*, p. 67; *HMC, XIth Report*, app, v, 260–61.

sion of the navy was more open than in the case of the army. Herbert had clashed with Dartmouth at the time of the evacuation of Tangier, but as a brutal and inconsiderate captain he did not enjoy a good reputation with the seamen. It was debatable how far William's appointment of him to command the invasion fleet was wise from the point of encouraging inaction or desertions from James's fleet. Many officers distrusted Herbert as a 'political' officer, adept at advancing himself, but Russell had a more settled interest in the fleet, where he had earlier done some discreet canvassing.[48]

A special Declaration was composed for distribution to the fleet, which laid great emphasis on the religious issue, but this was not actually dispersed until after William had landed safely.[49] In the last analysis no one can be conclusive about the attitude of the fleet in 1688, because unlike the army it was not asked to fight. Errors of pilotage and unfavourable weather kept it away from the invasion force, and later from the Dutch covering fleet after the army had disembarked. As a direct clash never occurred, it is speculative to ask if the fleet would have fought. But there are two pieces of firm evidence in trying to establish its actual state of mind. First, although Van Citters had reported that Dartmouth doubted if all his ships would fight, William's instructions to Herbert laid emphasis on avoiding any encounter.[50] Secondly, Dartmouth behaved in an irresolute manner when he entered the channel in belated pursuit of William. Although he was assuring James of the continuing loyalty of the fleet, it did not look as if he trusted it in practice. In fact William's agents had been working for weeks. Canvassing was carried out by Matthew Aylmer, a former protégé of Buckingham, who acted on Russell's behalf. He worked in cooperation with George Byng in persuading captains not to fight if they encountered Dutch ships, and by mid-November the two agents were confident that they had won over most of the leading captains.[51] After William's successful landing,

[48] *Correspondentie*, 1, 46–7.
[49] *Ibid.*, I, 59–60; I, ii, 618–19.
[50] *Ibid.*, I, ii, 613–16, 616–17.
[51] Powley, *op. cit.*, pp. 67–8, 116–17; *HMC, XIth Report*, app, v, 260–61.

the navy was influenced by the stream of defections from the army, including Grafton, but its own decision to go over to William came late. It not only followed after the collapse of James's position ashore but it was precipitated by what was perhaps his most unwise single decision. When James sent the baby prince to Portsmouth, and then ordered Dartmouth to escort him to France, he finally alienated even those who would still have served him. Dartmouth refused categorically to obey these instructions.[52]

On more general political matters, both Sidney and Johnstone acted with virtually plenipotentiary powers. When conversing with officers or politicians they could represent William's views authoritatively. This made it vitally important that they were kept fully informed on the nature of these views, especially at times of such major developments as the prosecution of the bishops, and the birth of the prince. Other trusted correspondents could also be used occasionally in this way, for instance Compton transmitted William's assurances to the bishops at the time of the trial.[53] But Sidney and Johnstone were used on negotiations which covered a long period of time. One such was a series of interviews in the first part of 1688 with Penn, who was becoming detached from the court as he found his influence diminishing. It was worth trying to penetrate Penn's views and attitude, since his readiness to accept repeal of the penal laws, but not the Tests, might be an invaluable indication of what could happen if there was not quite enough support in the forthcoming Parliament to get James's full policy demands enacted.[54]

Another important duty for William's agents was to ascertain the intentions, and the attitudes towards William and James, of the surviving radical Whigs. From William's angle they were now a most doubtful element, because many of their rank and file supporters in the constituencies and among the dissenting

[52] Powley, *op. cit.*, pp. 125, 127–8, 129–30, 143–4, 151–2; *HMC, XIth Report*, app, v, 236.
[53] Dalrymple, appendix, part 1, 238; Tanner MSS, 28, f.76.
[54] PWA, 2127a, 2129, 2141.

clergy were collaborating with James. If they were becoming afraid of losing their basic, grass-roots support in the forthcoming elections, many radical Whigs might be tempted to come to terms with James. William had never had close connections with these radicals. He was suspicious of them, equating their leaders with the Dutch republicans who had opposed and obstructed his policies. He knew that a section of the first Whigs had worked with Barrillon, in the same damaging fashion as the republicans in the States-General had done with d'Avaux. The leaders who survived included several particularly suspect men; the younger Hampden had been engaged in some kind of intrigue in Paris in 1683, and Ralph Montagu was trying to renew his connection with Barrillon and Louis. On the other side it must be added that many Whigs distrusted William, having accepted Dutch republican arguments about his absolutist ambitions.[55]

Throughout this period William and his Dutch advisers consistently exaggerated the danger of a republic being established in England. Both in 1679–81, and again in 1687–8, they thought that this was a likely outcome of the turmoil and one that would endanger vital Dutch interests. William and Dutch opinion generally were drawing a misleading historical paralle¦ with the events that had led up to the establishment of the Commonwealth, and to its pursuit of the aggressive commercial policies that had produced the first Anglo-Dutch war. But Whig intrigues with France in 1678–81 had strengthened the fears that a republic would revive the alliance that Cromwell had concluded with Mazarin. The absolutist power of Louis, the Revocation, and Louis' continuation of Colbert's policies of economic discrimination against imports from Britain, had completely changed the whole pattern of relationships between France and England, but nevertheless it came as a relief when the elder Hampden gave a most satisfactory response to Johnstone's approach. He declared that English interests would be best served by rallying to William, on whom he urged early action, since otherwise it would be too late to shake James's

[55] Dalrymple, appendix, part 1, 78–9.

position, and declared that no one was now in favour of setting up a republic.[56]

Hampden spoke for a group of potential Whig leaders, but several individuals behaved in a less satisfactory way – there was, of course, no cohesion or party organization at this time – and were apparently ready to collaborate with James. The behaviour of John Howe, a prominent dissenting minister who had returned from the United Provinces with William's consent, was particularly alarming because it posed a threat to the personal safety of William's correspondents and agents; considerable pressure had to be applied to stop him defecting to James.[57] Another probe was made to ascertain the position of Silas Titus, a former lieutenant of Shaftesbury, whose appointment as a privy councillor, in company with Christopher Vane (also a Whig) and John Trevor (a Welsh lawyer on the make), created a minor sensation. From a distance this looked like a significant step forward by James in his preparations for parliamentary elections; it might be an indication that many Whigs were slowly coming round to support James's policies. Johnstone's investigation showed that there was no general danger; Titus explained to him that there was a personal reason for accepting office – he wanted to get into a favourable position to recover a debt of £8,000 owing to him by the crown.[58]

There was a second important reason for exploring Titus's position. Sunderland had been responsible for the appointments of Titus, Vane and Trevor, whom he hoped to use as managers in the session of Parliament planned for November. By discovering their attitudes, some light might be thrown on Sunderland's intentions. For William, his advisers and his agents in England, Sunderland's conduct and intentions were the greatest single cause of uncertainty and difficulty in trying to predict future developments. Professor Kenyon has demonstrated the absurdity of the contemporaneous Jacobite legend of Sunderland the arch-betrayer, the minister who not only gave secret information to William and suppressed information of William's plans and

[56] PWA, 2124, 2173.
[57] PWA, 2135.
[58] PWA, 2110, 2135, 2141.

preparations, but who also deliberately pushed royal policies to extremes so as to discredit his master and provoke rebellion.[59] Nevertheless, there is no doubt that Lady Sunderland did occasionally correspond with William, and that Sidney (perhaps cynically using the current gossip that she was his mistress to cover his political activities) was in regular communication with Sunderland and his wife during his period in England from late January to mid-August 1688. There had been rumours in the previous December that Sidney (then in Holland) was managing a correspondence between William and Sunderland – if so it has not survived. Much of this malicious gossip and slander originated with the Catholic ministers, led by Melfort and Petre, who had an obvious motive in wanting to disgrace their principal rival. But there was obvious plausibility in their charges, if only because of what had happened in 1680, when Sunderland had gone over to Exclusion, had tried to bring William over to support the bill, and had encouraged Sidney to get a declaration in its favour from the States-General.[60]

There is insufficient evidence to establish the actual nature of the relationship at this time between William and Sidney on the one hand, and Sunderland and his wife on the other. Sunderland's surviving letters are noncommittal, his wife's excited and confused, containing some interesting and even important items of information (sometimes in cipher), but nothing that William and Sidney could not learn from other sources.[61] But it must be added that in May 1688 d'Avaux reported that William was receiving regularly the most secret information about proceedings and decisions in James's privy council, and that this material was being conveyed in letters from Lady Sunderland. Louis took this report seriously, ordering d'Avaux to try to corroborate this information and adding significantly that he must not reveal the existence of this inquiry to Barrillon, who was allegedly under Sunderland's influence.[62] However, there is an important

[59] J. P. Kenyon, 'The Earl of Sunderland and the Revolution of 1688', *Cambridge Historical Journal*, xi, 272–96.
[60] D'Avaux, v, 110–11, 124; vi, 144, 150–52.
[61] R. W. Blencowe, *The Diary of Henry Sidney* (1843), ii, 257–62, 272–5, 275–8.
[62] D'Avaux, vi, 146.

piece of negative evidence, in Lady Sunderland's letter of 11 September to Sidney, which disproves the theory that she and her husband were engaged in William's conspiracy against James. With invasion looming ahead, Lady Sunderland began to panic, asking Sidney as a matter of urgency to give her his advice as to where Sunderland should take refuge. This was a point that would certainly have been discussed and decided much earlier, if anything resembling a betrayal of James had been arranged.[63]

The question of Sidney's own safety had already been arranged between him and Bentinck. At the end of May one of the other correspondents urged that great care should be taken not to 'sacrifice' Sidney and Johnstone, the two men who knew most about William's English correspondence.[64] He advised them to leave the country before the court could make any move towards their arrest, pointing out that if either of them was taken and interrogated there would be a risk of a general *sauve qui peut* among William's associates. Everyone who had been in contact with the agents, or had written to William or Bentinck, would be afraid for his own safety. The result might well be a general panic such as had occurred among the Whigs in 1683, when Lord Howard of Escrick and John Hampden had been arrested and had then given information about their associates. If some of William's associates revealed what they knew the whole English connection would disintegrate, and his friends would be so demoralized that he would lose all capacity to influence events. In fact Sidney did not leave England until the second week in August. He still had his most important work to do, the preparation (jointly with Russell) of Zuylestein's second visit to England, which took place at the end of June.

The main purpose of the previous special embassies of Dijkvelt and Zuylestein had been to obtain information and advice for William from his English associates. When Zuylestein came in June 1688 the position was significantly different. The birth of the prince had shattered the prospects of William's obtaining

[63] Blencowe, *op. cit.*, ii, 277.
[64] PWA, 2151, 2163.

power and influence through natural means. The reversionary interest was now irrelevant, since James's death would be followed by a Catholic regency. The queen, not William, would now be the next ruler of Britain. In fact William had already decided, at the end of April, that he would stage an invasion later in the year provided that he received definite promises of suppport. Russell and Herbert had returned from Holland with the specific task of obtaining such promises from William's leading associates, and it was Zuylestein's mission to examine these undertakings, to assist in the conclusion of a definite agreement, and to approve the preparations that were to be made to assist William.

It would be difficult to think of a more cynical cover-story than the one that was used for Zuylestein's mission : he came to convey William's congratulations on the birth of the prince. D'Albeville was fool enough to consider this a gross error on William's part, since it meant recognizing the prince as legitimate when his most fervent supporters were spreading the story that he was suppositious, smuggled into the queen's bed in the celebrated warming-pan.[65] The fatuity and inadequacy of James's security policies at this time can hardly be equalled. Zuylestein had contacted leading figures among James's opponents during his previous visit. Now he again met such marked men as Sidney, Russell, Danby and Shrewsbury. After holding meetings Herbert left secretly for the United Provinces, disguised as a seaman and despite a specific prohibition against leaving the country. He got away undetected but his arrival at the Hague, and the fact that he immediately had a long interview with Bentinck and Dijkvelt, was soon known to d'Avaux and reported to James. Yet Zuylestein was permitted to remain in the country for some time longer, no action was taken to supervise his movements, and James remained in total ignorance of what he had been doing. Certainly the court had no suspicion of the very definite arrangements which had been concluded during his visit.[66]

The outcome of Zuylestein's mission was the so-called invitation of the Seven. The word invitation is misleading, because

[65] Addit., 41816, f.146.
[66] Dalrymple, appendix, part 1, 232, 237, 239.

William had already made his decision to intervene, and the text of the invitation shows that it should more accurately be described as an association. In the letter which Herbert brought, William received certain definite assurances from Sidney, Danby, Russell, Shrewsbury, Devonshire, Lumley and Bishop Compton. It was a commitment on their part. They pledged their support, and undertook to act, when William came – at a date which was left to him. During the preceding discussions, roles were allotted to each of the signatories. Shrewsbury and Sidney were to join William. Russell was to cross to the United Provinces to assist in the preparations for the invasion. Herbert, bearer of the letter, had already been promised the command of the invasion fleet. Lumley and Danby were to organize the north country, where the invading army was expected to disembark, while Devonshire was to do the same in the north midlands. Bishop Compton, besides acting as a link with the clergy, using the contacts which had proved so useful during the prosecution of the bishops, may have been entrusted as far in advance as this with the duty of securing the safety of Princess Anne.[67]

The contents of the letter of association can best be described as assurances given in direct reply to William's questions, questions conveyed earlier by Russell as well as now by Zuylestein. First, that it was essential to act in the near future:

We have great reason to believe, we shall be every day in a worse condition than we are, and less able to defend ourselves, and therefore we do earnestly wish we might be so happy as to find a remedy before it be too late for us to contribute to our own deliverance.

William was told that nineteen out of twenty of the nation were dissatisfied with James and wanted a change, but the prerequisite for action was some form of protection against James's standing army. An effective force would have to be provided to give people cover while they were being organized and put into some sort of order. The crucial assurance related to the attitude of the officers and soldiers in the standing army. Although its existence and strength meant that William would have to intervene with a sizable force, the signatories claimed with accuracy and knowledge that many of the officers were actively disconten-ted, but events were to show that their forecast of disaffection among the ordinary soldiers was exaggerated. The facts of the situation argued for an early invasion, since the possibility that the army would be remodelled and that a packed Parliament would meet had to be taken into account, but the question of timing had necessarily to be left to William. He was to be supplied by Herbert with all the information available on the practical problems involved, such as how many arms and how much equipment should be brought over with the fleet, but the decisions were left to him.

The signatories raised one particularly important and difficult problem, which was enlarged on in Sidney's accompanying letter. The scale of William's preparations in Holland would be so large that they were bound to alarm James (although no one could have been so optimistic as to believe that he should be so slow in realizing their significance). This meant that all William's known friends and suspected associates throughout England would be in danger of being placed in preventive arrest – as had happened to potential supporters of Monmouth in 1685. The leaders did take precautions; Lumley went into hid-ing in September, and Devonshire and Compton moved about the country from place to place, but a determined and efficient administration would have had little difficulty in seizing enough of William's associates to have disrupted at least the plans for provincial risings.[68] The other obstacle was psychological, the fear that failure would lead to savage mass punishments, such as had been inflicted on Monmouth's followers. It may be objected that almost all those who had suffered in 1685 had been ordinary people, but prominent Whigs had been executed in 1683–4 after the Rye House Plot, and in 1688 William's aristo-cratic and well-off associates were uneasily aware of the fact that Catholic courtiers and officers were already anticipating the reward of a share in the confiscated estates and wealth of

[68] Browning, *Danby*, i, 394–5; *Autobiography of Sir John Bramston*, p. 318; Campana de Cavelli, ii, 306.

defeated rebels, which they confidently expected would shortly become available for distribution.

The risks which William's English associates were running, although considerable, must have left him completely unmoved. He was about to risk not only his own life and reputation, but the security of the United Provinces, and the whole future of the alliance against France. A firm believer in predestination, he was habituated to undertaking desperate and dangerous enterprises. If it was God's will he would succeed in saving the English and Scottish nations in 1688, as he had saved the Dutch in 1672. His reading of the European situation told him that he must invade England now, in the short time left before a general war broke out in full fury. With William in command there was none of the indecision and endless argument that had always prevented effective royalist action against the Commonwealth, and was to stultify Jacobite plans during William's reign, when James's adherents never overcame such problems as whether the internal rising should precede or follow an invasion, how a major port could be seized in advance to permit the French to disembark, how to verify the promises of support given to agents by ministers, generals, admirals and gentry. This is not to say that such problems did not exist in 1688, but it must be emphasized that William's decision to invade preceded their solution.

This left little time for the final arrangements to be made. William and his agents in England, and his advisers, generals and admirals in Holland, had to complete their preparations under great pressure. In this situation there could be no greater contrast than that between William, forcing his advisers and associates to early and dangerous action, and the attitude of Lord Halifax, the 'trimmer', allegedly the most sagacious of contemporary statesmen. Historians have tended to praise Halifax's political judgement and wisdom, largely because he was both articulate and by principle balanced and dispassionate. But Halifax's own contemporaries, almost without exception, distrusted him as no more than an adept intriguer who had the enviable ability of gaining the maximum credit and advantage for himself out of any situation without ever taking any risks.

This was a harsh and inaccurate judgement, since Halifax's pamphlets could have led to his being severely punished, but it is true to say that during the period of crisis his attitude so far as William was concerned was unconstructive and unhelpful.

Halifax had always consistently expressed scepticism about James achieving any of his major objectives. A shrewd and experienced observer, who had been one of the first to see that Exclusion had been doomed to defeat, he believed that James, like Shaftesbury earlier, was proposing policies which were too extensive and too complicated for him to have any chances of success. England could not be converted, there were too few Catholics and too much prejudice. He had forecast James's failure to get a majority by canvassing the Parliament elected in 1685.[69] When that had been dissolved he predicted that James would never succeed in packing a new one, and he found confirmation for this judgement in his assessment of the results of the questioning of the gentry and the regulation of the corporations. He informed William that all this activity was to absolutely no purpose, saying in April 1688:

In some particulars, to men at a distance, the engine seemeth to move fast, but by looking nearer one may see it doth not stir upon the whole matter, so that here is a rapid motion without advancing a step. . . . Every attempt turneth back upon them. They change the magistracy in the corporations, and still for the worse as to their designs. The irregular methods have spent themselves without effect; they have run so fast that they begin to be out of breath, and the exercise of extraordinary powers, both ecclesiastical and civil, is so far from fixing the right of them, that men are more united in objecting to them.[70]

Halifax persisted in this opinion about the impracticability of James's policies. As late as the end of July he again reassured William:

I find that every new attempt bringeth a fresh disadvantage upon the great design, which is exposed and disappointed by so many

[69] Dalrymple, appendix, part 1, 186–7.
[70] *Ibid.*, p. 219.

repeated mistakes; the world is so much confirmed that there is every day less danger of being overrun.[71]

There were compelling reasons why William disregarded these arguments (by which Halifax helped to persuade Nottingham not to join the letter inviting William). They were not just the product of timidity or inertia, as many contemporaries believed, but stemmed from a philosophy of life and a theory of history which William could never have accepted as his guide. This centered on the dominant role which accidental forces played in human affairs, so that the best laid human plans were always likely to be totally disrupted by chance and unpredictable events. In December 1686 Halifax advised William, largely on the strength of a serious illness from which Louis was soon to recover:

Your Highness seeth of what use it is to stand firm and quiet, neither to yield nor to give advantage by acting unseasonably. Accidents come that either relieve, or at least help to keep off the things we fear for a longer time, and that is no small matter in the affairs of this world.[72]

William should therefore wait on events, and when they had occurred try to take advantage of them: 'The great thing to be done now, is to do nothing, but wait for the good consequences of their divisions and mistakes.' Even the birth of the prince, incontestably an accident (or a miracle, according to taste), did not alter Halifax's position. For him James's projects were so complex that they would easily be upset by accident, whereas if William committed himself to an equally elaborate scheme for intervention he would be putting himself into jeopardy.

Halifax's thesis, it should be noted, developed out of the nation's recent experience. During his lifetime Cromwell, the Cabal, Shaftesbury and Monmouth had all attempted to realize ambitious policies, and all had failed miserably. But William knew that time was working against him, that a European war (the most productive source of misfortunes and accidents) was about to begin. His freedom of action would be drastically

[71] *Ibid.*, p. 235.
[72] *Ibid.*, p. 186.

restricted. Unless he could intervene in the near future his associates might cease to form a reasonably united and purposeful group. Delays would wreck morale. In any case once elections had been held, and a packed Parliament met, an entirely new political situation would come into being which would probably necessitate new discussions and new arrangements. Zuylestein's mission and meetings were therefore intended to prepare for action in the immediate future.

Comparatively little information is available on the last phase of the preparations for William's invasion. Zuylestein stayed until early in August but there is no report of his activities. D'Avaux learnt that he had taken a large sum of money with him to England but we know nothing about its distribution. Sidney kept contact with men who had been allocated their roles, for instance Churchill, who wrote on 4 August:

> Mr Sidney will let you know how I intend to behave myself; I think it is what I owe to God and my country. My honour I take leave to put into your Royal Highness's hands, in which I think it safe. If you think there is anything else that I ought to do, you have but to command me.[73]

Scattered references in correspondence between those taking part in the November provincial risings indicate that they had been prearranged in coordination with William, although the lesser gentry were only informed at the last moment for security reasons.[74] D'Avaux's spies watched in the Hague, as couriers arrived from England during the last weeks, and reported how they were immediately closeted with William, Bentinck, Fagel and Dijkvelt, but they learnt nothing of substance about the information which they brought with them.[75] On 1–11 September a junior diplomat, Van Leeuwen, arrived in London with instructions for Russell (who was about to leave) and Lumley. He was able to assure them that the design would go

[73] *Ibid.*, p. 239.
[74] Campana de Cavelli, ii, 339; *HMC, XIVth Report*, app. iv, 199–201, 205–6; Browning, *Danby*, i, 389–92.
[75] D'Avaux, vi, 172–3.

on according to plan, but he was not entrusted with the details of William's military plans.[76]

One of the last tasks was to get substantial numbers of volunteers across the North Sea, to take part in the actual invasion. Reinforcements would be useful, when Dutch defences had been reduced to danger level, but it was vital to have as many English and Scots as possible in the invading force so as to counter the appeal which James was trying to make to national sentiment against an army of foreigners.

Finally the contents of William's Declaration need careful analysis.[77] It had to be sufficiently specific in its denunciations of James's policies to arouse enthusiasm for William's cause, but it could not be overtly partisan if it was to rally the widest possible support. In particular, it must be carefully worded so as not to repel Tories and Anglicans, yet there was a danger that an anaemic declaration would fail to animate men to resistance – for instance the Whig Delamere thought that much stronger language should have been used to depict the danger in which liberties and religion stood from James's policies.[78] In authorship the Declaration ended by being a composite work. Sidney brought a draft with him, when he arrived in August, and this was discussed by him with Bentinck, Fagel and Dijkvelt. Another draft was brought over by Shrewsbury and Russell, with notes compiled by Danby. In addition, some of the radical Whig exiles were also consulted, and gave William and Bentinck a foretaste of the difficulties their essentially factional attitude was to produce after the Revolution. Wildman, a veteran Whig, and the ambitious Mordaunt, who at this time was a Whig radical, wished William to lay emphasis on the unconstitutional actions of Charles II's reign, despite the danger that this would antagonize many who were now William's secret adherents, and give the expedition the appearance of being a Whig enterprise. Whigs of course had reason to remember the last years of Charles's reign with bitterness, but Mordaunt was entirely purposeful in advocating a Whig declaration; he wished to antagonize Tories

[76] *Correspondentie*, I, ii, 607–10; Japikse, ii, 252.
[77] Text is accessible in Williams, *Eighteenth Century Constitution*, pp. 10–16.
[78] Henry Booth, Lord Delamere, *Works* (1694), p. 67.

so as to reduce the future competition for appointments, not seeing that this would jeopardize the success of the invasion itself. William was far from happy with the final form of the Declaration, complaining to Bentinck that it put him in the hands of a Parliament, but this was unavoidable; a free Parliament was a demand on which everyone could unite. It would recall Monk's declaration of 1660, indicating that the object of William's invasion was to give the nation a new opportunity to do what the makers of the Restoration Settlement had failed to achieve, to establish in durable form unity, harmony and stability.[79]

William's first and principal Declaration, dated 30 September/10 October from the Hague, listed at length the allegedly illegal actions of the past three years, which had been designed to overturn the religion, laws and liberties of the nation. However, it should be noticed that the responsibility for all these pernicious policies was placed *exclusively* on James's evil counsellors. This is in sharp contrast with the explicit statement in the Declaration of Rights, passed in Parliament after the Revolution, that:

> ... the late King James the Second, by the assistance of divers evil counsellors, judges, and ministers employed by him, did endeavour to subvert and extirpate the Protestant religion, and the laws and liberties of this kingdom.[80]

Indeed, there are only three passing references to James in the whole of William's Declaration. He was not charged with anything, all governmental activity was attributed to his ministers. 'Those evil Counsellors ... obtained a Sentence from the Judges, declaring that this Dispensing Power is a Right belonging to the Crown'; 'they' set up the Ecclesiastical Commission, invaded the privileges and seized the charters of the towns which were 'to be disposed of at the pleasure of those evil Counsellors'; 'they' had prosecuted the bishops and attempted to pack Parliament. 'They' were even charged with having, 'in order to the carrying on of their ill designs, and to the gaining to themselves the more

---

[79] *Correspondentie*, I, 49; Burnet, iii, 308–10.
[80] Williams, *op. cit.*, p. 26.

time for the effecting them, for the encouraging of their complices' published that the queen had given birth to a son. The Declaration emphasized the old 'country' opposition complaint of misrepresentation, which had always been used to explain friction between king and Parliament. This time the evil ministers were accused of having poisoned James's mind against William and Mary; 'they have endeavoured to alienate the king more and more from us, as if we had designed to disturb the happiness and quiet of the kingdom'. Consequently it was in order to protect himself from 'the violence of those evil councillors' that William found it necessary to come to England with an army.

The country opposition had always put the responsibility for unconstitutional actions on ministers and not on the king himself, and the fatal consequences for the Commonwealth of the trial and execution of Charles I made it all the more important for William to follow this convention. William could not afford any harm to James's person; in 1689–90 he gave his army and naval officers very careful instructions how to treat James if he fell into their hands. Furthermore, by putting the entire responsibility for misgovernment on evil ministers, men who were detested by everyone, from moderate Catholics to extreme Whigs, no particular form of constitutional solution was being suggested. Tories might be persuaded to forget, for long enough, that it was James, and not Petre, Brent and Jeffreys, that they were resisting. Religion was also skilfully handled in the Declaration. Religious liberty was not attacked, but emphasis was put on its political exploitation by the evil ministers, and on the divisive effects which it had been intended to have among Protestants.

By the time that the Declaration was published, James had anticipated the demands which had been included so as to permit the election of a genuinely free Parliament; the restoration of charters (especially the London charter), the reappointment of magistrates, the recognition that Catholics were ineligible for election. Consequently a supplementary statement was made, on 14 October, in the form of a postscript. This declared the concessions to be worthless because they could be revoked at any time, so that real security could be obtained only from Parliament.[81] Again, in indicating the legislative tasks of a free Parliament, William left himself freedom of action. The Test Acts were to be confirmed and made more effective, and 'other laws' passed as should be found necessary 'for the peace, honour and safety of the nation, so that they may be in no more danger of the nation's falling at any time hereafter under arbitrary government'. This was a form of wording that implied imposing restrictions on the king, but without spelling out the nature of the limitations William could hope to preserve national unity against James and his policies.

[81] Lingard, *History*, x, 331.

NINE *Policies and Decisions in 1688: James, Louis and William*

THE IDEA THAT HE might have to intervene one day in England with a major force must have occurred to William long before he received the invitation of the Seven, early in July 1688. When was William's decision to invade England made? The first specific suggestion of an invasion had come as early as 1686, from Mordaunt, who quickly withdrew it, but all the evidence supports Professor Baxter's thesis that the decision was made at a very late date, at the very end of April 1688.[1] Moreover, even this date for the decision has to be carefully related to its European context if we are to appreciate the magnitude of the problems which William still had to solve, and the risks which even the most careful planning could not reduce below a certain level. These meant that although William was putting the invasion of England on his agenda, for action later that year, it was still possible throughout the summer that developments in Europe might prevent him carrying it through.

Up to Zuylestein's mission to England in August 1687, William's attitude to English affairs was that of head of the

[1] Baxter, *William III*, pp. 224–5, 229–33.

reversionary interest. By establishing his system of clandestine contacts and correspondence during the winter of 1687–8, he was moving towards the possibility of effective intervention. But he was neither committed to taking direct action nor in a position to decide when intervention would be practicable, or necessary. The invasion was one among several contingencies. It had to be considered in conjunction with many other possibilities, especially of William finding himself involved in a war between Sweden and Denmark, or of a sudden, major French attack on western Germany or the Spanish Netherlands. By April it was possible for William to make a decision, and to give the end of September as a date for an invasion.[2] He needed the intervening five months for his naval, military and diplomatic preparations. Even more important was the consideration that it would only be in the last weeks of the summer that William would be able to weigh up the risks and dangers *in Europe* that would be involved in going ahead with the invasion of England.

The European situation was still far from clear in April, when William told Russell of his intention to invade. At least there was now no chance of a major French offensive in the early summer, like that of 1677, which could inflict really significant damage on his allies, and tie William down (in diplomatic negotiation as well as military defence) so that intervention in England would be out of the question, but there was no clear indication of the direction that French policy would take. The Palatinate question continued to simmer, as it had done since 1685, but there was no particular urgency in the situation although William believed that it would eventually provoke war. The question of Cologne would come to the boil when the elector died, but no one could predict when this would be or under what circumstances the election of a successor would take place. There was still tension between Sweden and Denmark, and the attitude of Frederick William was unpredictable. Imperial policies, prestige and strength would all depend on the

[2] *Ibid.*, pp. 224–5; *Correspondentie*, I, i, 36.

outcome of the summer's campaign in the east; the Turks had been crushed at Mohacs in 1687, but a repulse at Belgrade would mean that the west German princes could expect little material support from Vienna against French pressure. William would be expected to make up the deficiency.

Similarly, the future in England was opaque. The queen's pregnancy could produce very different political situations; as against the provocatively confident Catholic predictions of the miraculous birth of a healthy male heir, the odds were that a miscarriage, still-birth, a baby who died or was sickly and likely to die, or the birth of a girl, would reduce tension. The prosecution of the bishops still lay ahead, but there were reports that an attack was being planned against the Church of England, and this could obviously have explosive effects.[3] William felt obliged to prevent a spontaneous, premature rebellion, not only because it was likely to be suppressed by James's efficient army, but because he feared that a successful rising might result in the establishment of a republic.

The summer months of 1688 saw these uncertainties contract, and several were eliminated altogether. As each week passed it became less likely that Louis would have the time to launch a general war and overrun areas vital for Dutch security. William's preparations were such that he could switch resources; the army camp was at Nijmegen, from which units could be sent upstream to Cologne as easily as downstream to embark at Rotterdam. The fleet could be used to threaten a descent on Normandy. But even in September there was a risk that the removal of a large part of the Dutch army, on the invasion of England, would give Louis six to eight weeks' campaigning time in which substantial advances could be achieved, so that the campaign of 1689 would at the very least start with the allies at a disadvantage.

The accidents that happened in 1688 worked in exactly the opposite way to that which Halifax had predicted. They simplified the situation to William's advantage and facilitated the invasion; it can be said of William that in 1688 he had the

[3] PWA, 2122b.

essential advantage of luck on his side. Of course, this is not to say that these accidents operated as the primary factors in the march of events during that year, quite the opposite in fact. William succeeded because he was ready to take advantage of sudden changes, because he was observant and prepared for opportunist changes of policy. He was flexible and adaptable. By looking ahead, he was able to calculate the probable effects of his decisions and actions; he could preserve his freedom of action. This achievement was not an easy one, but on it his success depended. Professor Pinkham was particularly wrong when she commented that in 1688 William arranged the situation to suit his plans. The contrary was the case; William's decisions developed out of a shrewd analysis of a constantly changing situation, and his success was based on a masterly exploitation of every favourable circumstance.[4]

Nevertheless, it is important to underline the fact that William's considered decision to intervene in England *preceded* the resolution of the uncertainties and problems which he had to take into account. It preceded the two crucial accidents: the death of Frederick William on 9 May, which removed a major cause of concern, and the timing of the death of the Elector of Cologne (on 3 June), which meant that the anticipated European crisis would break out in 1688, and not in 1689 or later. This fact emphasizes the magnitude of the risks which William was prepared to run in his determination to intervene in England, although it was not until 27 September that he finally knew that it was safe for him to do so.

After the miraculous birth of the Prince of Wales, James had as much right as William to believe that God was on his side, but by contrast the little that he did in trying to help himself had the effect of considerably increasing the difficulties with which he was surrounded. James was badly advised by his ministers, and not particularly well informed. But he had only himself to blame for his myopic unwillingness to admit the danger of his situation and for his persistent concentration on domestic policies as the threat from William grew. When he did

[4] Pinkham, *William III and the Respectable Revolution*, pp. 3, 61.

realize that invasion was imminent, James took a series of hurried, unconsidered decisions, without attempting to calculate their probable results. The consequence was that for James the options available constantly narrowed, the choices before him became progressively more difficult, and the future grew steadily more frightening. It is not surprising that he finally broke under the strain, with all his confidence destroyed by a succession of major and irreversible errors of judgement.

By contrast, Louis was unruffled throughout 1688. He was at least as well informed as William, and as much in command, consulting his advisers but making all the important decisions himself. He showed himself as self-centred as James, concentrating all his attention on his own policies and designs, and barely taking into consideration the interests, opinions or possible reactions of rulers and ministers in other countries. This is how he had grown accustomed to behave. He had done so, with complete success, in 1683–4. But Louis did not appreciate either the significant changes that had occurred in Europe since then, or the simple fact that now his potential victims were forewarned against his tactics. Louis acted as if he alone had the initiative, as if the rulers of Europe still waited for him to act before coming to their decisions. Although he was fully informed of William's preparations at a fairly early stage, he evaluated this information only in relation to his own plans and immediate intentions, giving little consideration to the wider repercussions and implications of the invasion of England.

In trying to analyze the political judgements, decisions and actions of James, Louis and William in a situation that was so rapidly changing, the position is described as each of them saw it on the basis of the information which they are known to have received. The period in which their decisions are related to the options which were available to them begins on 3 June with the death of the Elector of Cologne. For James and William there are two coterminous phases: for James up to 28 September/8 October, when his Proclamation withdrawing the writs for elections was issued, for William up to 17/27 September, when he learnt of the French investment of Philippsburg, the fortress on the Rhine which was Louis's objective. The second phase lasted until William landed in Torbay on 5/15 November. In the case of Louis there are three phases: first, up to the end of August, when the crucial decision was made to attack in the Rhineland; then the interval until the attack was launched and a manifesto issued, on 24 September; and finally Louis's declaration of war against the United Provinces on 26 November which ends the period.

James's concentration on domestic politics not only diverted his attention away from the threat posed by William's preparations, it also drastically limited him in the foreign policies that he could afford to follow. So long as Parliament was planned to meet on 27 November/7 December, with elections in late October and November, it was impossible for James to conclude, or be thought to have concluded, any agreement with France. Any hint of this must have damaging electoral repercussions, and this accounts for James's fury at the wide publicity given to the untrue statement in the memorial which d'Avaux presented to the States-General on 9 September, that such an alliance did exist. Moreover James was still not a free agent after his decision, announced in the Proclamation of 28 September/8 October, to postpone the meeting of Parliament because of the threat of invasion. The concessions which he then poured out were intended to propitiate the Tories and Anglicans, and any chance of a reconciliation with them would infallibly be wrecked by any move to obtain French assistance; indeed Sir John Berry and Grafton warned James that he would be instantly deserted by the vast majority of his officers, soldiers and seamen if any French forces arrived for his service.[5] Furthermore, James's attempt to disavow the statement in the d'Avaux memorial was obliterated by the widespread belief, both in Britain and in Europe, that he was already a French puppet. Similarly in the public view, the ministers were all creatures of France, whereas in reality only the extremist group led by Petre and Melfort were for an alliance with Louis on his terms. Sunderland, and the ministers who succeeded him at the end

[5] PWA, 2141; Campana de Cavelli, ii, 331.

of October (the Earl of Middleton and Lord Preston), had to
fight the extremists, not only because they saw the lunacy of
allying with Louis but also in order to maintain their own ministerial position. It was inevitable, then, that James should move
cautiously for fear of confirming the suspicions which were so
widely held. He accompanied the offer of concessions at home
with an approach to the States-General, for joint action to check
further French advances, but it is not surprising that this was
not taken seriously and that its effect on English opinion was
minimal.

Another difficulty for James arose from the fact that most
of the information which he received about William's preparations came from French sources – from Barrillon, d'Avaux or
from Louis himself. Past experience, again significantly
confirmed by the d'Avaux memorial, convinced James that Louis
was trying to draw him into an alliance on French terms.
Participation in a major European war as the ally of France
would put him in an untenable position at home. James had
enough revenue to defray the ordinary costs of government and
maintain his army. But he fitted out each year only a part of his
fleet, so that a war against the Dutch would mean bringing a
large number of ships out of reserve, expanding the number of
men employed at the dockyards, and pressing seamen. This
could not be financed out of existing revenues, so that James
would have to go to Parliament for additional grants of supply.
This would radically alter the relationship between him and
Parliament; the campaign of electoral preparation had been
designed to give James control, so that Parliament would enact
what he demanded. If, instead, James had to go cap in hand
to ask Parliament for urgently needed money, he would find
himself in danger of becoming as much its dependant as Charles
had been in 1667 or 1673. French subsidies would never be
high enough to serve as a substitute for parliamentary grants,
and to skimp naval defences would be to incur the danger of
another Medway disaster. Indeed it was only too possible that
Parliament would be able, as in 1673, to prevent a war being
fought and simultaneously to wreck royal policies and force
the dismissal of James's ministers. Some peers and MPs could be

expected to work for William's interests, as they had done then, and to gather support in order to undermine royal authority. They would have fresh ammunition, since they would be able to quote the indiscreet revelations in the Abbé Primi's history of the 1672 war against Holland. This book, which the French censor had suppressed only after some copies had been sold, had given a partial account of the secret treaty of Dover of 1670 which mentioned a joint attack on the Dutch and spoke of Charles II becoming a Catholic.[6]

For James, a French alliance was incompatible with his principal policy of packing a compliant Parliament that would repeal the Tests and penal laws. Only after such a Parliament had done this, and increased his revenues, would he be in a position to afford an active foreign policy, and this could not be before the spring of 1689. Therefore it is not surprising that on 1/11 June, that is after news of the death of the Elector of Cologne had been received, which everyone realized would increase the danger of a general war, James rejected Louis's offers to send ships if they were needed to repulse a Dutch invasion.[7] Although made so many months before William's invasion, this rejection was to prove to be a crucial decision. It led Louis to decide to retain fully manned ships only in the Mediterranean, and to reduce those sent to Brest to a care and maintenance basis. This meant that it was impossible for Louis to give James direct assistance when it became certain that William's preparations were directed against England.[8]

James suffered seriously from the inadequacies of his envoys in the two key posts. Bevil Skelton at Paris was not only virtually a dependent of the French Foreign Ministry, but used his position to help the extremist ministers advance their influence in Whitehall; it was he who first suggested the move that culminated in the presentation of the d'Avaux memorial. D'Albeville's despatches from the Hague were uninformative until a late date. They were filled with trivia about consular disputes, and the

[6] *The Twelfth and Last Collection of Papers* (1689), p. 1.

[7] Mazure, ii, 452.

[8] P. Clement, *L'Italie en 1671* (Paris, 1867), p. 336; C. Rousset, *Histoire de Louvois* (Paris, 1879), iv, 101.

boycott by Hagenaar society of his celebrations of the birth of the Prince of Wales. He entirely failed to guess the purpose of Zuylestein's mission. When he learnt that Herbert and Burnet were meeting regularly, this rated only a casual mention. On 6 August he reported his opinion that William was preparing a descent on France.[9] Very foolishly, he was then permitted to return on leave for most of August, when James received virtually no information from Holland. This absence meant that on his return he found himself largely dependent on d'Avaux for intelligence information, which was fed to him with arguments that no time should be lost in transmitting evidence of William's design to England. D'Albeville was still hesitant before accepting this information from d'Avaux at its face value, as well he might be considering the difficulties which the d'Avaux memorial were creating. His despatches of 21 and 24 September reported the extent of William's preparations, but he commented that they could be aimed at either France or Britain.[10] It was the despatch of 30 September, which he actually sent express, and one of 1 October, which finally contained specific information proving that William intended to invade England.[11]

These two despatches finally awoke James and his ministers to the dangers of the situation. Received in Whitehall about 24 September/4 October, they led to the Proclamation of the 28/8th which called off the parliamentary elections.[12] Until this late date James had persisted with wishful thinking. He had thought that William's visit to Minden for discussions with Frederick on 30 August/9 September indicated that Dutch preparations were intended against France after all. When news arrived of the French ultimatum of 14/24 September to the emperor, and of the simultaneous attack on Philippsburg, James for a short time hoped that this development would prevent William launching an invasion, but Sunderland immediately realized that on the contrary he would now be freed from anxiety

[9] Addit., 41816, ff.106–9, 116, 123, 124, 140.
[10] *Ibid.*, ff.185–6, 191–3.
[11] *Ibid.*, ff.205, 209.
[12] Campana de Cavelli, ii, 270–71.

about the security of the Spanish Netherlands and the United Provinces.[13]

D'Avaux wrote scornfully to Louis about the long sleep of James and his ministers and d'Albeville's obstinate refusal to accept his interpretation of William's preparations. Consequently he carried on a supplementary correspondence with Barrillon, who was to pass on warnings to James personally, thus bypassing ministers whom d'Avaux suspected of suppressing information. On 9, 14 and 18 September he reported having given d'Albeville full (and, events were to show, very accurate) information on William's plans, but these had been treated with no sense of urgency, one of the warnings actually being forwarded by ordinary post to England. The last was sent by one of d'Albeville's secretaries, but in order to ensure attention being given to this material d'Avaux asked Louis to continue writing himself to James.[14] Letters from Louis in fact made little impact on James, who replied noncommittally to the warnings which he received. This attitude astonished the French, who were to fall back for an explanation on a simple, but entirely fallacious, belief that James's apparent blindness was due to the malignant influence of Sunderland, the arch-traitor.

To appreciate the reasons for James's reluctance to accept these warnings from Louis, d'Avaux and Barrillon, it is necessary to rid one's mind of the knowledge that comes from historical hindsight, to try to put oneself into the situation as it was in September 1688, without taking into consideration what we know was about to happen. James resented having been declared a protégé of France in the d'Avaux memorial of 9 September, but it looked as though it had had a definite purpose, of pressurizing him into accepting an alliance on French terms which Bonrepos (who arrived as an additional or special ambassador at Windsor on 26 August/5 September) would offer.[15] Seignelay, the French naval minister, had told Bonrepos that no French ships would be provided unless a treaty was signed by James committing him to France, but in the event

[13] *Ibid.*, ii, 356; Mazure, iii, 76–7.
[14] D'Avaux, vi, 218–19, 231–3, 250–51.
[15] Addit., 41823, ff.71–2; Campana de Cavelli, ii, 257–8.

(because of a momentary decision by Louis that William was not intending to attack England) no pressure was applied. Only an excessively vague agreement for French naval aid was initialled on 3/13 September, which left blank the number of ships and the time at which they were to be provided.[16]

Secondly, James had reason to be suspicious about the strong warnings which he received from French sources about the treachery of some of his ministers. D'Avaux had repeatedly reported that the most secret proceedings and decisions of James's council were quickly known to William. He was particularly suspicious of Godolphin, and believed that a regular correspondence existed between Sunderland and Sidney. In addition, he claimed that William had an extensive network of contacts among officers in James's army. He passed none of this information to d'Albeville, but sent it to Barrillon for transmission to James personally, or reported it to Louis for inclusion in his letters to James.[17] So the warnings about treachery came exclusively from French sources. This was too convenient for James to take them at their face value. Barrillon was working in notoriously close conjunction with the group of extremist Catholic ministers led by Melfort; all those whom he was describing as secret correspondents of William were obstacles to the political ascendancy of this francophile group. Similarly, if James purged the army as a result of the warnings he was being given, the vacancies would have to be filled with Irish and Scottish Catholics, most of whom had formerly served in France. Although the events of November were to show that James's ministers and officers were every bit as unreliable as d'Avaux reported, James cannot be blamed for hesitating before handing himself over to the power of a ministerial and military group which was tied to a policy of dependence on France.

Because we know what happened in 1688, it is easy to overlook the incredible nature of William's behaviour. James can hardly be blamed for finding it difficult to believe that his kingdom would be invaded by his son-in-law, with his daughter's

[16] Mazure, iii, 61–3; Campana de Cavelli, ii, 255, 268–9, 300.
[17] D'Avaux, vi, 198.

approval. Secondly, although the Dutch had frequently contested English supremacy at sea, not even at the height of their success in 1667 had they attempted more than coastal landings. It was out of character for the States-General to allow William to take off with him the best part of their army. James, as an experienced naval commander, was aware of the hazards of an invasion attempt so late in the year and in the face of an unbeaten English fleet.[18]

James actually began to take precautionary measures before he was certain that William intended to invade. D'Albeville pressed the Dutch on their reasons for making such extensive preparations so late in the year. His representations were badly prepared, but they had no chance of making any impact on Dutch opinion because of their unfortunate coincidence in time with d'Avaux' threatening memorial. This enabled Fagel to reply with counter-protests against the alleged alliance between James and Louis, so that the States-General delayed an answer until the next month.[19] Van Citters evaded James's questions in the same way. On 21/31 August a scout ship sailed for the Dutch coast, and orders were sent to the Navy Board to fit out additional vessels 'for life and death'. On 22 August/1 September instructions issued to Vice-Admiral Strickland made it clear that his primary task was to stop a Dutch invasion. East-coast garrisons were alerted. By the end of September sixteen major warships had been fitted out, and twenty-one more were preparing – almost exactly the same strength as the Dutch. Pressing was authorized on 23 September/3 October, so that Dartmouth, who was appointed admiral the next day, had the capacity to execute his instructions, issued on 1/11 October, to meet 'a great and sudden Invasion from Holland, with an Armed Force of Foreigners and Strangers'.[20] James was also expediting the arrival of Irish recruits and, appreciating correctly that the

---

[18] On the other hand, James specifically warned Dartmouth of the danger of being caught behind the shoals, a warning which a complacent Dartmouth ignored: *HMC, XIth Report*, v, 144, 152, 261–2.

[19] Addit., 41816, ff.192–3, 197, 212, 216, 223; Klopp, iv, 126.

[20] Powley, *English Navy in the Revolution*, pp. 16, 18–21, 28–9, 46–52, 60, 63–4.

decision would be reached in England, sent orders for the despatch south of virtually all units in Scotland.

Acting against the advice of Louis, James made a sudden and complete change of both domestic and diplomatic policies early in October. At home he entirely reversed his policy towards the Tories and the Church of England. In foreign policy James proposed to the Dutch cooperation for the maintenance of the Nijmegen treaty and the twenty-year truce, if necessary by military action.

How far were these new policies genuine? Without doubt the diplomatic approach to the Dutch was completely bogus. James's real object was to gain time. A delay of even a few days would create difficulties for William, and James was also hoping to revive differences of opinion between him and the republicans. But the impression made by the d'Avaux memorial prevented his approach having any success, and James had actually been threatening republican Amsterdam earlier in the year during disputes over consular rights and the activities of English exiles.[21] William, Fagel and Dijkvelt relied on the statements in d'Avaux' memorial to convince the States-General, the provincial states, town representatives and magistrates that the country faced an alliance of the two Catholic sovereigns determined to achieve in 1689 what they had narrowly failed to accomplish in 1672. William knew that in fact no formal alliance existed between James and Louis, but he was right in concluding that James would never freely follow an anti-French policy; at this moment James was assuring Barrillon that he would never willingly go to war against France and was making approaches to William for propaganda purposes.[22]

James's domestic concessions represent a much more complex and difficult subject for historical judgement. Unlike the change in foreign policy, they were not a matter of words or gestures; James was discarding most of the agents, and dismantling all the policies, that he had been employing since the break with the Tories in 1687. Some of his Catholic confidants claimed

[21] Addit., 41815, ff.114, 149; 41816, f.183.
[22] A.A.E., CPA 166; Barrillon, 3 October 1688.

that he was merely withdrawing under pressure from temporarily untenable positions, and that the policies would be revived later, but it is difficult to see how James could have done this within the foreseeable future.

The first indication of concessions came on 21 September/ 1 October, when a Declaration was authorized, stating that Catholics would not be eligible to sit in the Commons and promising to accompany the enactment of religious toleration with a confirmation of the Acts of Uniformity, so as to ensure the Church of England.[23] Seven days later the writs for elections were withdrawn and a Proclamation was issued announcing the imminence of invasion.[24] This was described as an attempt at conquest by a foreign power, 'although some false Pretences relating to Liberty, Property and Religion, contrived or worded with Art and Subtlety may be given out'. This anticipated William's Declaration, but James relied more on concrete concessions. On 5/15 October the Ecclesiastical Commission was abolished, the next day the Charter of London was restored, on 11/21 the Bishop of Winchester was authorized to restore the old Fellows to Magdalen, and on the 17/27th corporations where the deeds of surrender had not been enrolled, or judgements entered on record, recovered their former charters, liberties, rights and franchises. Promises of restoration were also made in the case of places where deeds of surrender had been enrolled (twenty-eight parliamentary boroughs) or judgements had been recorded (six corporations), and this was done in the cases of Chester, York, Winchester and Exeter. Orders were given to dismiss all mayors, sheriffs, aldermen, etc. who held office by virtue of charters granted since 1679. The lieutenancy was also changed in most counties, with Catholics usually being omitted. The electoral agents and regulators had already been thrown overboard, with letters going out instructing lords lieutenant to investigate complaints against their alleged irregularities. Offers of reinstatement were also made in several counties to those who had been purged from the commission

[23] PRO, PC 2, 72, p. 736.
[24] *Ibid.*, p. 738.

of the peace, with some lords lieutenant given discretion as to who should be reappointed.[25]

By making these concessions James was abandoning, not just suspending, the campaign to pack Parliament, and it is difficult to see how he could have reactivated it. James was turning back to the traditional Tory and Anglican supporters of the crown, but their marked reluctance to accept his offers showed that the partnership, if it was to be re-established, would be one whose terms and conditions would be dictated to him. Some bishops, whom James summoned to meet him on 3/13 October, gave an indication of this; they demanded that the dispensing power (the joker in the prerogative pack) should be left to Parliament to determine, that toleration should not be accompanied by equality of civil rights, and that Catholic schools and ecclesiastical organization should be prohibited.[26] Furthermore, remembering how James had disregarded the promises which he had made at his accession, any Parliament could be expected to try to ensure that these concessions would not be withdrawn once the crisis was over.

Some ministers at least affected to believe that the concessions would defeat William's designs against James, by depriving him of grievances to exploit.[27] In addition, the concessions were intended to open up divisions between Tories and Whigs, to win the former so as to leave William with only partisan support of an extreme sort. But there was not sufficient time for this to happen; James had delayed his change of front until far too late. Those who benefited gave him no thanks for what were clearly enforced, not voluntary, concessions, and the effect on James's Catholic followers was demoralizing. James got the worst of both worlds. The concessions were generally treated as insincere, they severely damaged James's reputation for determination and constancy by showing that he would give way in the face of danger; obviously if the pressures on him were further intensified then more concessions could be extracted.

[25] *Ibid.*, pp. 745, 749, 751, 752, 785–6; SP Domestic, James II, Entry Book 56, p. 451; 31/4, part 2, f.142.
[26] Gutch, *Collectanea Curiosa*, i, 410–13.
[27] Addit., 41823, ff.77, 78.

James's change of policy produced a split within the court. The Catholic ministers, now led by Melfort, naturally opposed them, arguing that James could rely on his army and on French assistance. Moreover, the effect of the concessions was reduced by the fact that they were the work of Sunderland and, to a greater extent, of Jeffreys, who now became a major influence for a short time after being in virtual eclipse for over a year. Jeffreys had been trying to reconstitute an Anglican interest linked to the court as early as July, but his presidency of the Ecclesiastical Commission had ensured a cool response. Similarly, when he pressed for the restoration of the London Charter, his past record of intimidation and manipulation in the city meant that he got no thanks for his advocacy. Jeffreys' greatest weakness lay in his lack of insurance policies, which was to lead to his being saddled with the role of universal scapegoat after the Revolution. The role of protector of Anglicanism was preempted. The Catholic group of ministers hated him. He had no contacts with William. His own fellow-countrymen, Williams and Trevor, were waiting for an opportunity to destroy him. Sunderland, owing to his recent conversion to Catholicism, was equally incredible as the champion of a constitutionalist and Anglican policy, and was to lack the time in which to utilize the concessions for his purpose of mediating between James and William.[28]

It is doubtful whether James, in his anxiety about the invasion, realized how far the concessions would restrict his freedom of action. By dismantling the campaign of electoral preparations James made it inevitable that elections would now produce an uncontrollable Commons, so that he could not agree to them except as a last resort. William's Declaration – framed in conjunction with his English associates – indicated the lines that a dominant opposition was likely to take. Ministers would be impeached, even though James had given them pardons. The prince's birth would be investigated, the suspending power declared illegal and Catholic Church organization destroyed. In effect James would be left with little more than the title of king.

[28] Lingard, *History*, x, 327–8.

More restrictive in a practical sense, the concessions made it impossible for James to take adequate security measures in the provinces. Militarily he could crush risings and hope to repulse William by using the standing army. But because of his reliance on the army he had allowed the militia to fall into almost total decay throughout England. In most counties it had not been embodied since 1685, and when former Tory officers and deputies were offered their commissions back, most either refused or delayed their half-hearted acceptance until nearly the end of the month.[29] This made it impossible for James to repeat the mass preventive arrests that had so effectively deprived Monmouth of gentry support and diversionary risings in 1685. As Sunderland realized, mass preventive arrests (which meant holding men in custody by demanding impossibly high recognizances – there was no need to prefer charges) were incompatible with the concessions. Many suspects were themselves Tories, and their friends could not be expected to rally to James if they were being taken into custody. The militia was not only politically unreliable, but organizationally incapable of carrying out large-scale arrests; it failed to execute the orders that were issued for the arrest of a few suspects – Lumley, Sir John Guise, the Charltons.[30] On the other hand, nothing would be more inflammatory than to use men of the standing army – often badly disciplined – to round up suspects.

The confusion which the concessions caused in local administration, with James's collaborators ousted and the Tories reluctant to take their places, had further damaging effects after William landed. JPS and deputies were more than executives of the central government, they also acted as the natural leaders to whom the counties looked for guidance. The upheavals which James had caused had destroyed all respect for those in office, and there was too little time and insufficient spirit of cooperation for the old links to be re-established. This opened up opportunities which William's associates were to exploit when they

[29] Addit., 41805, ff.72, 85; PRO, 31/4, part 1, ff.79, 81, 101; Entry Book 56, pp. 444, 446, 447, 450.

[30] Addit., 41805, f. 59; PRO, 31/4, part 1, f.110; part 2, f.191; *HMC, VIIth Report*, app, i, 348, 413.

gathered in provincial centres declaring for a free Parliament. The success of these provincial risings was a direct consequence of James's faulty policies towards local government.

In the last three weeks before the invasion there was little that James could do but wait. The fleet and army dispositions had been made. William's propaganda was still circulating, despite intensive attempts to stop its import. Sunderland was dismissed, but this came far too late to reassure those who distrusted James, and it left his successor, Preston, with insufficient time to make any mark. Like most of his subjects, James knew that as in 1588 the wind was now the crucial factor.

The key to Louis's faulty conduct of policy in 1688 lies, first, in the fact that his attention was concentrated almost exclusively on the implementation of French designs for an offensive in the Rhineland. Secondly it should be realized that he planned, and confidently expected, to achieve his objectives (as in 1683–4) without precipitating a general war. Instead he precipitated the nine years war, a war of attrition, but nothing could have been further from his mind when he made his crucial decisions in August 1688. The major assumptions on which these decisions were based proved to be incorrect. Louis thought that France could easily intimidate and divide the emperor and the German princes; instead, they defied his blackmailing policies from the start. Louis calculated that by exerting commercial and diplomatic pressure he could increase the timidity and passivity of the States-General. By thus ignoring repeated warnings from d'Avaux, Louis found himself surprised by the readiness of the Dutch republicans to support William.[31] Louis did not expect James's position to crumble as quickly as it did, but even after William was securely established he still grossly underestimated the effects of England's enmity.

These mistakes were not due to lack of information. The French diplomatic system was still unrivalled in quality and size. Louis was the best-informed man in Europe, and he had experienced and able advisers. Nevertheless, Louis and his

[31] D'Avaux, vi, 147, 189, 191–2, 213, 237–8.

ministers, perhaps because of the ease and magnitude of their previous diplomatic victories, made surprisingly little use of the material with which they were supplied, particularly if (as with warnings from d'Avaux) it did not fit into preconceived patterns. All decisions were made by Louis himself, and there was no way of ensuring that he first took into account all the relevant information that his diplomats had supplied. This meant that frequently French policy was based directly on Louis's illusions – for instance his ineffective attempts to prise apart the emperor and the princes were based on an instinctive and historical (but for the 1680s and 1690s quite erroneous) belief that their interests were necessarily and fundamentally incompatible.[32]

Moreover, when he sought to repeat his earlier diplomatic triumphs Louis did not take into account the changes in the European situation that had occurred since 1684, although these had been reported to him. He relied on tactics which had worked on an earlier occasion, apparently without appreciating the point that now his opponents and potential victims were forewarned and would discount his professions of peace because they had heard them before.

Louis's professions of respect for the peace of Europe were in sharp contrast with the brutal and crude methods of intimidation which he was using, and the arrogance of the language in which his declarations and diplomatic notes were phrased. Genoa and Geneva had been bullied. The Pope was being currently threatened. When the States-General began to consider commercial reprisals, Louis seized Dutch ships. German tourists in Paris were detained as hostages in September, and soon west German territories were being ravaged or forced to pay contributions.[33] In the event these acts of arrogance stimulated opposition, but it is even more pertinent to note that they reflected an unthinking assumption of predominant strength, an excessive confidence in his own influence, that were now no longer entirely justified by the realities of European power. Consequently, Louis rejected advice from d'Avaux that commer-

[32] A. Lossky, 'Maxims of State in Louis XIV's Foreign Policy' in R. Hatton and J. S. Bromley (eds.), *William III and Louis XIV* (1968), p. 11.
[33] Rousset, *Histoire de Louvois*, iv, 112–13.

cial concessions would be wise, since they would enable the Dutch republicans to renew their opposition to William's foreign policies. Concessions were not in keeping with the greatness of France.[34] Overconfidence led to a serious setback in September. Louis had verbally extended his protection to Fürstenberg in Cologne, with violent threats to anyone who dared to invade the territory. But nothing was done militarily, which allowed General Schomberg to move in, occupy the city of Cologne, and subsequently to oust Fürstenberg's other garrisons.[35]

The contrast between Louis's behaviour in 1688 and in 1700–1, the two great crises of the second part of his reign, is revealing. In 1700–1 he had to make agonizingly difficult decisions on the question of the Spanish Succession. Whatever course he chose involved great difficulties and foreseeable disadvantages. Overshadowing him was the fearful prospect of a new war that might be as damaging and expensive as the nine years war had proved to be. Sudden developments, like the deaths of the electoral prince and James II, and the will of Carlos II, demanded rethinking and new decisions. Under almost intolerable strains Louis committed serious errors of judgement, even though it may be rather too extreme a judgement to say that his nerve broke.[36] But in 1688 Louis simply was not aware of the difficulties that were in fact closing in on him and restricting his freedom of action and decision. He did not see that serious dilemmas had to be resolved, he did not pause to take into account the likely consequences of alternative courses of action. It is not accurate to say that he chose to go ahead in the Rhineland, rather than save James – for Louis the question of having to choose did not occur. He never seriously considered the possibility of turning aside from his own clearly thought-out line of policy.

In general French policy was continuing to follow the same line of direction as in 1679–84, when the exceedingly successful *réunions* had brought substantial gains in territory without precipitating a general war. But Louis had additional reasons

[34] D'Avaux, vi, 299–300.
[35] *Ibid.*, vi, 257.
[36] M. Thomson, 'Louis XIV and the Origins of the War of the Spanish Succession', Hatton and Bromley (eds.), *William III and Louis XIV*, pp. 140–61.

for asserting himself and following a forward policy in 1688. He had to offset the increased influence and prestige which Leopold would be able to use after his victories in the east; indeed, it was now important to prevent the Turks from concluding a peace which would free the emperor and this could be done by renewing pressure on the empire in the Rhineland. Louis had also committed himself to Fürstenberg's candidature for the electorship of Cologne, and could not abandon him without a major loss of prestige. The territory was of immense strategic value, and the electoral vote would be a valuable asset in French intervention in German politics, but above all Louis planned to use the Cologne issue as a means of smashing the League of Augsburg.

When the chapter met to elect a new archbishop-elector, on 19 July, the result was a deadlock. Fürstenberg had a simple majority, but not the two-thirds vote that he needed; his chief rival, Josef-Clement, who was backed by Bavaria and Leopold, lacked the simple majority that he needed. News of this setback came to Louis on 23 July, and he at once made it clear that he would not give way.[37] He made a suggestion for a compromise that would give him all that he wanted: Fürstenberg should have the electorship, with Josef-Clement being given the valueless compensation of a coadjutorship. Louis proceeded to put pressure on the Pope, to whom the case was now referred, but having already embarked on a campaign of intimidation against Innocent (which had failed to make any impression) he could hardly expect the Vatican to decide in favour of his candidate. In fact on 16 August the College of Cardinals made a recommendation in favour of Josef-Clement.

This decision called for an even more important decision on Louis's part. During the last week in August he decided to persist in his support of Fürstenberg, and to destroy the League of Augsburg by launching a military offensive against Philippsburg, the last key fortress on the middle Rhine in unfriendly hands, and to occupy the Palatinate.[38] It is important to emphasize the fact that when he made this decision Louis had received the despatch of 21 August, sent by special courier, in

[37] Klopp, iv, 88–99.
[38] Rousset, *Histoire de Louvois*, iv, 110.

which d'Avaux reported completely convincing evidence that
William's preparations were directed against England. In other
words, when Louis ordered an offensive on the Rhine he was
well aware that by doing so he was creating a situation in which
it would not be possible to do anything that would keep William
in Holland and prevent him intervening in England. D'Avaux
reinforced this warning with further despatches, containing a
great deal of convincing detail, about William's plans for
invasion, on 9, 14, 16 and 18 September, all of which arrived
before Louis published his manifesto on 24 September and
ordered the attack on Philippsburg.[39] He knew from d'Avaux
that the defences of Maastricht were incomplete.[40] Marshal
d'Humières had just reported on the virtually defenceless state
of the Spanish Netherlands.[41] Louis took no notice of all this
information. He ignored advice from d'Avaux that the invasion
of England could be prevented by a bold (and militarily
impracticable) attack on the badly maintained fortress of
Bergen-op-Zoom.[42] Louis's eyes were on the Rhineland and
Germany. He was not interested in wrecking William's invasion
plans. His aims would be satisfied by neutralizing Spain and the
United Provinces. He had at this time no intention of making
any move against them that would lead to war, and he assumed
that they in turn would remain inactive towards France.

The piece of information which Louis found relevant in
d'Avaux' despatches was his comment that, although the Dutch
were concerned about Cologne, they had not got the resources
both to invade England and to defend Cologne effectively, and
that if faced with a choice it was the former that would get
priority.[43] This was exactly what Louis wanted to hear. The
Dutch were not members of the League of Augsburg, and by
going ahead with the invasion of England at a time of major
crisis in Germany, they would be confirming the reputation for
selfishness that their conduct in 1678 had fixed on them. Once

[39] D'Avaux, vi, 218–21, 226–30, 231–5, 239–43, 248–51.
[40] *Ibid.*, vi, 213, 257.
[41] Oudendijk, *Willem III*, p. 207.
[42] D'Avaux, vi, 252–3.
[43] *Ibid.*, vi, 239–40.

the princes realized that they could expect no assistance from William, the offer of a settlement with France would become irresistibly attractive. There would be no reason to reject the French offer to turn the existing twenty-year truce into a permanent peace, even though this might allow Louis to make new advances in other areas.

By August 1688 Louis had already decided on the subject that would become his main concern once his Rhineland policies had been successfully completed: the Spanish Succession. Reports from Madrid indicated that Carlos ii's health was deteriorating, and the able French diplomat, Rébenac, was now working to create a pro-French party in the Spanish court. Louis had no intention of handicapping his work by using force against the Spanish Netherlands, or forcibly crossing its territory to attack Maastricht or Bergen-op-Zoom. Spain had suffered disastrously in the war 1674–8, and the short war of 1683–4 when she had been left alone to face France had demonstrated her helplessness. The French navy now dominated the western Mediterranean. As a result it could be expected that Spanish ministers would appreciate the inadvisability of taking any action that would provoke French resentment, which they knew they were helpless to resist.

Louis's policies stretched in front of him in a logical progression. First secure the Rhine, break up the League of Augsburg, and reconstruct a group of client princes. Then, having counterbalanced the increase in imperial power and ensured a continuation of the Turkish war, Louis would be well placed to determine the Spanish Succession and further French interests. Leopold would not be in a position to intervene effectively. The impending clash between James and William would prevent the maritime powers intervening. So the immediate gains which Louis hoped to achieve in 1688 would open the way for further, major advances.

Louis made his decision to invade the Rhineland in the last days of August. Military preparations had already been made in the usual form of a summer camp and manoeuvres, and with the frontier towns well stocked, only three weeks passed before the French armies crossed the frontier. During this period Belgrade fell (6 September), but this could not affect the immediate situation since it was too late in the year for Leopold to transfer forces to the west. The one important development was the presentation on 9 September by d'Avaux of two memorials to the States-General.[44] This move originated with Skelton, James's envoy in Paris, who hoped that it would push his master towards concluding a French alliance. For Louis the primary purpose was to intimidate the States-General so as to prevent Dutch intervention in Cologne. He hoped that by exploiting the concern for personal and sectional interests, inherent in a system of government which depended on representative institutions, he would succeed in repeating his diplomatic triumphs of 1678 and 1684. He calculated that republican obstruction or inaction would again paralyze Dutch foreign policy, so that many German princes would see no alternative to safeguarding their own interests by coming to terms with France.

The memorials are an excellent example of the way in which Louis employed diplomatic pressure as an alternative or supplement to military force. While the French army invaded western Germany, Louis relied on diplomatic threats to keep the Dutch passive. The memorials also demonstrate very clearly the single-minded and self-centred character of French policy. Louis did not care that his assertion of the existence of an alliance with England would compromise James with his subjects. This was all the more cynical because Louis had no intention of backing up his threats to the States-General, either by an invasion of Dutch territory that would divert William from invading England, or by giving James any significant aid. In this context it should be noted that the memorial could not be expected to prevent William's invasion. As d'Avaux had indicated in his despatches, this could be undertaken with the resources already at William's disposal. But the cooperation of the States-General was essential for any intervention in Germany; it was this that

[44] *Ibid.*, vi, 215–16, 220–21; PRO, SP Domestic, 31/4, part 1, f.75. D'Avaux believed (vi, 118) that only the threat of French intervention against a rebellion kept the English loyal to James; this may be the origin of the idea of the memorandum.

both memorials were intended to prevent. James was being used as a pawn on one side of the board, while the real moves were to be made in Germany.

The arrogant, menacing language of the memorials shows that Louis was using the method of 1683–4, crude pressure, and not the concessions that had been used to win the republicans in 1678. Consciously rejecting d'Avaux' advice, Louis had decided not to attempt to detach the republicans from William by commercial concessions. Like any aggressor, Louis began by emphasizing his concern to preserve peace and disinterestedly advised the Dutch to follow the same principles of prudence that characterized his own conduct of affairs. He claimed to find it difficult to believe that the States-General would imperil European peace, but could only conclude from the scale of their preparations that this was so. Seeing that these preparations must be intended against England, d'Avaux declared that he was authorized to state that the existing 'bonds of Friendship and *Alliance* between him and the King of Great Britain' would oblige Louis to assist James. Of course no such alliance existed, but his lack of any preparations to assist James did not prevent Louis warning the Dutch that any act of hostility against England would be regarded as a 'manifest rupture of the Peace, and an open breach with his Crown'.

D'Avaux then presented a second memorial warning the Dutch against any interference with what were described as Fürstenberg's rights in Cologne. They were warned of Louis's determination to uphold these rights, with the threat that any intrusion would mean war. Although it made less impression at the time in the United Provinces, where all eyes were now on England, this second memorial was the more important, because Cologne was the main objective of French policy. But it should be noted that Louis mistakenly failed to follow up his threats on the subject of Cologne with action, although it was within his power to have done so. D'Avaux repeatedly warned that only commercial concessions would persuade the republicans to try to obstruct any part of William's policies, so that if the States-General disregarded his second memorial some move in the Rhineland could be expected, and on 14 September he listed the support obtained from German princes that would enable William to act. Louis did not react. No reinforcements were sent to aid the garrisons in small towns like Bonn that acknowledged Fürstenberg, and as a result Schomberg's troops were able to get into Cologne first. By the time that Philippsburg fell, on 29 October, there were sufficient forces on the right bank of the Rhine, north of the Main, to check a further French advance, and during the winter most of Fürstenberg's garrisons surrendered.

Absorbed in what was virtually a personal vendetta against William, d'Avaux expected that Louis would carry out the threat in the memorials and declare war against the Dutch as soon as any move was made against either Cologne or England.[45] But although the threat had not prevented Schomberg moving into Cologne, Louis's plans did not include an actual declaration, or an invasion of Dutch territory. D'Avaux advised a bold attack on Bergen-op-Zoom, but it was absolutely impossible to switch the French offensive to an objective 200 miles north of Philippsburg at such short notice. Even more important, a declaration of war would wreck his entire diplomatic strategy; it would give the emperor and the princes the assurance of Dutch support, and force the States-General to join the League of Augsburg, and by doing so stiffen the resolution of those German princes whom Louis hoped to intimidate into accepting a settlement. Louis did not want a general war. His manifesto addressed to the emperor and the princes on 24 September represented an attempt to secure a general settlement of all problems and disputes, admittedly on French terms, so as to establish peace in western Europe.

This manifesto on 24 September is a key document to understanding Louis's attitudes and decisions in 1688.[46] Its language was very similar to that of the d'Avaux memorials, with Louis emphasizing his own moderation and concern for peace. At

---

[45] It is significant that d'Avaux failed to realise the general direction of Louis' policy in 1688; his assumption that William was the enemy to be isolated and attacked led Louis (who was concerned to neutralise William while French interests in Germany were advanced) to underestimate, or fail to grasp the significance of, the information he despatched.

[46] Klopp, iv, 192–5; E. Lavisse, *Histoire de France*, viii (1), 16.

least the Dutch were making large-scale military and naval preparations, but the evidence which Louis could produce of German hostility and belligerence was much more tenuous – the formation of the League of Augsburg and refusals to turn the twenty-year truce into a permanent peace. Since Louis insisted on formal recognition of all the gains made by him through the *réunions,* as a condition of such a peace treaty, the princes were no more likely to be persuaded now. Persuasion was not the method which Louis proposed to use; military intimidation was to be used to force the princes to accept his terms. This reliance on pressure and force was transparently disguised by his offer to hand back Philippsburg (to a French puppet, the Bishop of Speyer) and Freiburg, if their defences were dismantled, and to withdraw all French forces from the territory of Cologne if the Pope would recognize Fürstenberg, and withdraw his decision in favour of Josef-Clement. The emperor would also have to recognize Fürstenberg, and had he done so Louis would have been well placed to exploit the resentment which the Elector of Bavaria would have felt for the abandonment of his candidate. This kind of moderation was not very convincing, since it would give Louis all that he wanted. French troops would be capable of moving into the Rhineland whenever Louis wanted to put pressure on the princes.

The manifesto actually did coincide with the forward movement of a French army, to attack Philippsburg. But this does not mean that Louis's professions of peace were meaningless. He intended to use force on a limited scale only. Nothing was further from his mind than launching a general war, for which his army was not fully prepared. The attack on Philippsburg was planned as a demonstration of French strength. It was intended to bring the emperor and the princes to negotiate; the manifesto contained a three-month time-limit within which they could agree to do this. If the offer met with no response, then Louis reserved his freedom of action from 1 January 1689. By then he hoped to have brought the Pope to a more compliant attitude, through the occupation of Avignon, and William would be fully engaged in England in what could prove to be a prolonged struggle.

Louis had used the same technique with success three times in the recent past – in October 1682, November 1683 and April 1684 – but this very fact reduced the chances of his succeeding a fourth time. On each occasion he had made explicit demands, setting a time-limit for negotiations before force would be employed. With great tactical skill he had readily extended the original time-limits, with the purpose of prolonging tension and uncertainty, and creating divisions among those who might combine against him. He had offered deliberately deceptive bargains, proposing to return places already occupied in exchange for territories which did not concern those with whom he was negotiating; for instance, Louis had suggested to the Dutch republicans that he would renounce gains in Flanders in return for annexations in Catalonia. Spain had been isolated and then systematically intimidated, while diplomatic action had kept the other European powers inactive.[47]

This time the snare was being set in front of men who could recognize at once what Louis intended. Secondly, Louis and Louvois, his war minister, made the mistake of using excessive intimidation from the start and so seriously reduced their later freedom of manoeuvre. They started by trying to terrify the German princes by methods of frightfulness, so that when circumstances changed, their sudden switch to methods of persuasion proved to be ineffective. When, during the first phase, a French general, Chamlay, represented the danger that extreme measures would disprove Louis's sincerity in wanting peace, and drive the princes into enmity, Louvois snapped back: 'Dismiss from your mind the idea that you have anything to gain from the Germans by friendship or moderation. Plenty of guns, and fortresses in their country, will reduce them, and there is no better course of action to follow than this.' When General Boufflers found the Elector of Trier inclined to resist, he threatened to burn down his palace. The application of methods of terror, that were to culminate in the devastation of the Palatinate during the winter, was already apparent in the period before Louis's time-limit expired.[48]

[47] Klopp, ii, 380–83, 427–40; Baxter, *William III*, pp. 182–92.
[48] Rousset, *Histoire de Louvois*, iv, 132, 133.

The French declaration of war on the States-General on 26 November represented a major change in Louis's strategy; it was an action that he had not originally planned to take. It was forced on Louis by the unexpectedly firm resistance that he was now facing in Germany, by the refusal of the emperor and the princes to negotiate or make concessions. Furthermore the States-General, by accepting William's policies, and voting money, made it certain that Waldeck would be able to assemble an adequate army to fight the campaign of 1689. Louis now had a major war on his hands. The Pope was unimpressed by the occupation of Avignon. The governor of the Spanish Netherlands had been prepared to give William indirect assistance. D'Avaux confirmed, in reply to a direct question from Louis, that republican obstruction of William's policies could not become effective again in the foreseeable future.[49]

It should be emphasized that the major change of policy represented by the declaration of war on the Dutch had nothing to do with the events in England. On 26 November (the 16th in England) William was still at Exeter gathering his forces before advancing towards James. The first of the defections which were to shatter James's strength and confidence had just happened, but Louis did not know this. It was not developments in England but the situation in Germany that led Louis to declare war. He was not belatedly trying to save James, the precariousness of whose position he did not yet realize. On the contrary, James still featured in his plans as someone whom he could use. It was important that James should be prevented from trying to save himself by coming to terms with William, as his approaches to the States-General in October might indicate that he would try to do, if only to gain time. Louis tried to bring about an irreparable breach between William and James so as to prevent any possibility of a settlement which would certainly include an alliance against France. On 1 November he advised James to act firmly by arresting all potential supporters of William and, even more revealing, to declare war on the United Provinces – without undertaking to do the same himself.

[49] D'Avaux, vi, 319–22.

This advice was repeated on occasions during the next two weeks by Barrillon, and on 18 November Louis again urged James to declare war. Had James taken this advice, there would then have been no need for Louis to do the same.[50]

The declaration of war against the Dutch formed a part of a new diplomatic policy which circumstances now forced Louis to adopt. By the end of November it had already become apparent that the emperor and the princes were not going to respond to the manifesto in the way Louis had hoped. There was a danger that Spain, where Rébenac was having some success in building a pro-French party, would nevertheless become an active member of the expanded alliance that was forming against Louis. This was disquieting, because in the event of Carlos II's early death this would virtually eliminate French pretensions to a share in determining the succession.

It was only at this stage that William became central to the calculations on which French foreign policy was based. The new French line was aimed at persuading the emperor, the Pope, Spain and the Catholic princes of Germany that William, by attacking James, was initiating a war of religion. His successful negotiations in north Germany, and the meeting of princes at Magdeburg, were depicted as moves in the formation of a Protestant league. Later this argument was reinforced by the arrival of James as an exile in France, and by William's usurpation of the English throne, which showed that the principles of legitimate monarchy were also threatened by this new Cromwell. Again it should be noted that James remained a pawn in the French game; it was better for Louis that James should be a homeless exile suffering for his religion than for him to remain in England, keeping at least the title of king, because in that case he would be an instrument at William's, not Louis's disposal.[51]

The arrogant policies of intimidation and terror that Louis had been using since 1678 ensured the failure of this new French line of policy in the short term, but by 1691 it was beginning to create serious diplomatic difficulties for William. So long as

[50] AAE, CPA, 167; Barrillon, 22 November 1688; Mazure, iii, 166–8, 176–7.
[51] Sutton, *Lexington Papers*, pp. 335, 336, 338; Huygens, p. 68; Klopp, iv, 199–206.

France presented an immediate and overwhelming threat to all neighbouring states, self-preservation and self-interest dictated a policy of alliance, but once the threat began to recede other considerations became operative. The emperor began to develop scruples over Catholic interests in Britain and William's dispossession of a legitimate sovereign. The Dutch republicans again began to declare that William's control of foreign policy meant perpetual war. Now that he no longer occupied a position of unrivalled power, but found himself engaged in a difficult, defensive war of attrition, Louis's policy acquired a flexibility, resourcefulness and realism that it had not possessed in 1688.

In considering William's relentless pursuit of his objectives in 1688, it should be remembered that he had been in a very similar situation before, in 1672. Then he had been on the receiving end, improvizing resistance and stiffening morale as the world fell to pieces around him. Inexperienced and young, he had worked largely by intuition. Now, in 1688, he was the aggressor, working methodically according to plan, ready to take advantage of every favourable circumstance. He knew what he wanted, effective control over English policy. While Mary would have preferred William to become regent, rather than have to become queen herself as his co-sovereign, William was indifferent to forms.[52] What mattered was which solution would give him the most efficient control over British foreign policy, and her naval and military forces. In purely institutional terms sole occupancy of the throne might be the obvious answer, but this had to be decided later under circumstances which it was impossible to predict. William was not committed, either in public or in private, to any particular solution before the invasion began, or indeed until after James's first attempt to escape from England.

On the other hand, it is important to realize that William took his decision to invade England before the risks involved could be estimated. But once he had made the decision, William did not hesitate or falter in his determination or preparations,

[52] Doebner, *Memoirs of Mary*, p. 11.

although he admitted the burden of the difficulties and uncertainties that surrounded him in a letter to his intimate,
Bentinck, as late as 4 September.[53] He could not be deflected
from his purpose, but was upheld by his belief in predestination,
in his own role as defender of the liberties of Europe and the
Protestant religion against the tyranny and malice of Louis XIV.

Judged by rational standards William's determination to go
ahead with the invasion was preposterously rash. It was not
until 27 September, when he got the news of the French attack
on Philippsburg, that he could be confident that the United
Provinces would be safe in his absence.[54] Even then other major
uncertainties remained. The invasion was being launched
dangerously late in the year, and it was nearly wrecked by
gales on the first attempt. Yet William insisted on sailing again
as soon as possible. The place at which his army disembarked
was determined entirely by the wind; the first sailing had
Yorkshire as its destination, and but for a lucky change in the
direction of the wind late on 4/14 November he would have
over-shot Torbay, so that the landing would have been in the
far more remote Cornish peninsula, where it is possible that his
army would have been contained throughout the winter. Finally,
and by far the greatest risk of all, William was relying on the
ability and (still more questionable a quality at that time)
the good faith of his English associates and correspondents. The
assurances which they had given him were the whole basis of
his plans, for otherwise his army was grossly inferior in numbers
to James's, but there was no way of verifying these assurances
until he was ashore.

There were some dangers that William could eliminate in
advance. It was a vitally important achievement to ensure the
benevolent understanding of the emperor. William's letter of
26 October was skilfully phrased to reassure him and anticipate
the objections that would be raised by the group of francophile
and clerically-influenced ministers at Vienna.[55] William ex-

[53] *Correspondentie*, I, 54–6.
[54] D'Avaux, vi, 267–8.
[55] Dalrymple, appendix, part 1, 254–5; Sutton, *Lexington Papers*, pp. 328–9, 331, 354–5.

plained that his intervention was a result of internal crisis in England, and at the invitation of peers and other considerable persons, with the expedition played down as a kind of personal escort for himself against menaces from the evil ministers. William was entirely specific in assuring Leopold that he had no intention of harming or deposing James, or (more ambiguously) of interfering with those who had a right to the succession, and that there was no intention of exterminating or extirpating the Catholic religion. These were undertakings that were to require some explaining away in and after 1689, but William's arguments were decisively reinforced by his promise of future benefits from a free Parliament. In addition to settling domestic issues, this Parliament would establish such a union of the nation that England would be able to contribute strongly to the public good – in other words go to war against France. This alluring prospect, which as early as 1689 led many to ask when English subsidies would be forthcoming, was also held out to the German princes. It was this consideration that enabled Hop to satisfy Leopold's growing doubts about the propriety of William's conduct in England, which were making him listen to the new approaches made by French diplomats from December 1688 onwards.

William also gave similar assurances to Gastañaga, the governor of the Spanish Netherlands, that he would not harm the Catholics or depose James. In the case of Spain there was a danger that Gastañaga and Ronquillo, ambassador in London, would attempt mediation between James, his subjects and William. This would waste precious time, deprive William of the initiative, and give French diplomacy ample opportunities for intrigue.[56] It was in order to prevent this attempt making headway that William was so determined to sail for England at the earliest opportunity. In fact the attempt never even got started, and the presentation of a threatening memorial from Louis at Brussels helped William. This and the d'Avaux memorials were ruthlessly exploited. The German princes were made to realize that their subsidies would have to be reduced

[56] Sutton, *Lexington Papers*, pp. 327–8, 330; *Correspondentie*, II, iii, 49–50; Huygens, p. 10.

if Holland had to fight a naval war against England as well as a land war against France. The Dutch were faced with the spectre of a hostile alliance between Louis and James recreating the crisis of 1672, *het rampjaar*. Consequently the States-General in its declaration of 28 October spoke of the two kings who 'out of Interest of State, and Hatred and Zeal against the Protestant religion, would endeavour to bring this State to confusion, and if possible quite to subject it'. Without appearing to be unreasonable, William could reject all James's approaches, and when he got to England reject negotiations until he had achieved a position of supremacy.

Militarily the diversion of a considerable proportion of the best troops for the invasion army meant that there were some dangers that could not be excluded. It is generally said that if Louis had attacked Maastricht in September, William would not have been able to embark, but the evidence does not bear this out. William's instructions to Waldeck were to organize defences on the line Zwolle-Nijmegen-Grave-Den Bosch, with Maastricht (which is seventy miles due south of Nijmegen) as an outlier.[57] D'Avaux, who urged an attack on Maastricht, was even more in favour of an attack on Bergen-op-Zoom, thinking that only such a deep penetration of Dutch territory would make sufficient impression. He reported William's iron determination to go ahead with the invasion, adding that even the bombardment or capture of Brussels would not deflect him. William had said that he would be ready to accept the loss of most of the Spanish Netherlands, provided that the two great fortresses of Namur and Mons, and the port of Ostend, were retained.[58]

Of all the dangers with which William was surrounded none was more acute than the threat from espionage to the security of his political connections in England, on which the success of the whole enterprise depended. Large-scale preparations of the kind that were being made in Dutch ports and arsenals could not be concealed for long, so that it was inevitable that

---

[57] Oudendijk, *Willem III*, p. 210.
[58] D'Avaux, vi, 276-7.

some general idea of their purpose should get out.[59] But knowledge of William's underground contacts and connections in England would have been quite a different matter. With historical hindsight it can be said that, apart from a force-nine gale, the only way in which the Revolution could have ended in catastrophic failure would have been through the exposure of William's English connection. The mass arrests of prominent men, their interrogation (in Scotland by torture), trial, condemnation, execution and confiscation of their property, would have spread panic and demoralization – as in 1683, after the discovery of the Rye House Plot. Informers and perjurers would have enjoyed a new harvest, the spirit of resistance would have been at least cowed, and William would have had to attempt a conquest if he was to act at all.

There was a very real danger of this happening, not through action in England but through the extensive and efficient espionage system which d'Avaux maintained in Holland. At the English end, William's associates were comparatively safe. Butler would appear to have been lax and inactive. Sunderland was preoccupied, first with elections, and then with the concessions, and it is doubtful whether he would have favoured drastic action – he opposed preventive arrests because of the upheaval they would create, and also characteristically because they were advocated by Melfort, his rival. Even so, many of William's leading associates took precautions. Devonshire travelled about constantly, Lumley went into hiding, Bishop Compton alternated between London and the country, and diplomats noticed that few of the aristocracy came up to court from their country estates in October.[60] But even negligent or equivocal ministers would have had no option but to take action, if they had been supplied with full details of William's contacts at court, in the army and navy, and in the provinces.

William and his ministers had to take stringent precautions against d'Avaux' spies. Like Downing before him, d'Avaux had been able to discover virtually all the state secrets of the United

Provinces. In 1685 he had sent Louis all the secret letters from the Dutch ambassadors in England, as well as Dijkvelt's private correspondence. He regularly obtained full reports of the discussions of the *secret besogne* of the States-General and its recommendations.[61] By 1688, despite his loss of political influence, the intelligence system was still working well. Agents watched the arsenals at Delft and Dordrecht, following the barges to Rotterdam, noting their contents (planks and sand for disembarking horses and artillery) which indicated that England was their destination. An Amsterdam contact arranged for a master-carpenter to take one of Seignelay's *commis* around the arsenal there, although he came to the erroneous conclusion that the state of the fleet was such that no invasion would be attempted in 1688. A real *coup* was achieved when another contact got Mary's treasurer drunk, and then extracted from him information about the money which Zuylestein had taken to England.[62] More humble servants at William's court were more often valuable. D'Avaux learnt valuable information from a footman who remembered what he heard when William read out a letter in his closet.[63] A Catholic *valet de chambre* of William's picked up details about the coming invasion and, thinking that they might endanger the interests of his religion, mentioned them in his confession to a Carmelite monk, who immediately passed them on to d'Avaux.[64] A close watch was kept on all visitors to William at the Hague and (with more difficulty) at his country seat, het Loo. In March d'Avaux penetrated the negotiations with the Brandenburg General Spaen; in September he obtained advance notice of William's journey to meet Frederick at Minden, and of the amount of money that was being provided for troops supplied by Luneberg. On 14 September he was able to report full and accurate information about the contingents which the German princes were to provide, and he gave Louis warning of Dutch plans to move into Cologne.[65]

[61] D'Avaux, iv, 355; v, 100–1.
[62] *Ibid.*, vi, 126–7, 135, 187–8, 202, 213, 231.
[63] *Ibid.*, iv, 287–8.
[64] Mazure, iii, 56.
[65] D'Avaux, vi, 234–5, 257.

It was of the first importance that d'Avaux never learnt anything of major significance about the English connection. The valet's information came nearest to being so. He spoke in general about William having contacts in James's army and navy, and of assurances having been received that the latter would not fight, but he named Captain Cornwall as a leading agent in the army. More general information came from a former officer in Monmouth's army, who had been offered a commission by William; he accurately revealed that William would command in person, that it had been decided to increase the size of the invading army to 14,000 men, and that there was disagreement among the exiles over the Declaration which was to be drafted. However, he was wrong in saying that the landing would be in the Thames estuary or on the coast of East Anglia.[66] D'Avaux discovered that William was being kept well informed of the proceedings of James's council, but he was unable to find out how this was being done. He failed to obtain any incriminating information to substantiate his suspicions about connections between Sunderland, Godolphin and Sidney. He did not manage to intercept any of the vital correspondence that was being exchanged between Holland and England. This was partly because, after June, Van Citters wrote direct to Fagel on all important matters rather than to the States-General, and the letters in reply were personally written by Fagel's brother.[67] In July Van Citters returned, bringing important despatches, but d'Avaux could not learn their contents, and he also failed to discover anything of significance about Zuylestein's mission. William's all-important achievement in preserving the security of his English connection was made possible by the fact that vital knowledge was shared, and decisions made, by a tiny group of entirely reliable advisers – Bentinck, Fagel, Dijkvelt, Zuylestein and (after their arrival from England) Sidney and Shrewsbury.

The other crucial factor on which William's plans depended was time, and in this case William cut things very fine indeed. Originally the invasion was planned for late September, then

[66] Ibid., vi, 248–50.
[67] Ibid., vi, 152.

for mid-October, but the fleet eventually sailed on 29 October, only to be driven back by a gale which started on the 30th. Although only the horse transports were seriously affected (because they were badly stowed), and no ships were lost, bad weather set in, keeping the ships in harbour. Some advisers began to falter, suggesting that the transports should remain until the warships had carried out a sweep towards the English coast, but William would not sanction any delay.[68] When the Catholic west wind gave way to the Protestant east wind the fleet sailed again on 1/11 November.

[68] Huygens, p. 12; Powley, *English Navy in the Revolution*, pp. 45–6, Burnet, iii, 324.

TEN *The Invasion*

WILLIAM'S ARMY BEGAN TO disembark in Torbay on the most appropriate possible date, the Protestant day of 5 November, and by the evening of the 7th over 12,000 men out of a total force of 15,000 were safely ashore without any interference. The ease with which the invasion was carried out is often taken for granted, but after all, William did make the only successful large-scale landing that has occurred in England since 1485, and although the French were to make many plans, during the series of wars that began in 1689, for an invasion of England, none of them ever materialized. Moreover, it should be noted that William launched his invasion without any assurance of naval supremacy. His fleet of transports was as large, and almost as unwieldy, as the Armada in 1588, or Tromp's convoy which Blake had mauled in the channel fight of 1653. How, then, is William's success to be explained? It was more than a matter of luck with the winds, or of mistakes by Dartmouth. The crucial difference lay in the fact that William came from the east, whereas the Armada, Tromp and French fleets based on Brest, all approached Britain through the western channel, where geographical and meteorological factors favoured the British.

The British fleet possessed well-sited bases against any threat from the west. In 1690 the French found Plymouth too heavily defended for an attack, but a defending fleet was usually based on Portsmouth and the Solent and Spithead, the anchorages behind the Isle of Wight. These were difficult to attack and (with two entrances and four tides a day) impossible to blockade or even to reconnoitre. An enemy fleet would have to watch widely separated entrances, and being divided in strength would be inferior to the force coming out, as well as being attacked in the rear by ships coming from Plymouth or the Downs. This meant that if the British did not choose to fight it was impossible to secure naval supremacy for long enough to allow an army to disembark. There were no sheltered points on the coast east of Portsmouth where a landing on a large scale would be safe, and there were no large harbours on the French side of the channel in which ships could take refuge from weather or enemies (as the French discovered in 1692). This maximized the penalties of failure. Any force that was committed to the channel would find it almost impossible to retreat if plans began to go wrong. Like the Armada it would have no option but to proceed east, with the British astern and with no friendly base of adequate size ahead. Only if Antwerp and the Scheldt were in friendly hands would it be safe to risk such a venture.

Napoleon understood these strategic considerations when he described Antwerp as 'a pistol pointed at the heart of England'. Britain was much more vulnerable to an invasion from the east than from the west. Since Portsmouth was far too distant, harbours in the Thames estuary provided the only bases for the fleet, and this meant that the Yorkshire coast (the objective of William's first abortive invasion attempt) could not be effectively covered. Prolonged close blockades of Dutch bases were logistically difficult to maintain at any time, but in the kind of weather to be expected in October and November the risk of being driven on to a lee shore prohibited any attempt. This meant that with a steady east wind the channel route was open to an invading fleet, but it must be emphasized that by taking this route and landing in the west country William was deliberately cutting himself off from the possibility of receiving any major reinforcements from the United Provinces, a point which deserves attention since it underlines the conclusion that his success depended on his English associates fulfilling their undertakings. On the other hand, there were plenty of safe harbours where the Dutch warships and transports could lie up once the army was ashore.

The 'Protestant' east wind that enabled William to sail on 1/11 November kept Dartmouth's fleet blockaded, as it were, in his anchorage in the Gunfleet, with insufficient sea-room for getting out beyond the shoals by beating against the wind or using the tides. He had chosen the Gunfleet because it gave him shelter; a more open anchorage – for instance off the Nore – would have led to risk of damage from gales, and he would still have taken some time before starting a pursuit of the Dutch. As it was he saw some stragglers sailing south on the 2/12th, but it was not until the 4/14th that his fleet got under way, and then a shift of the wind to the west prevented him from making up any of the time lost.[1] Once William got through the straits of Dover (on the 3/13th) he had a wide choice of landing places before him, all protected against gales from the west: Poole, Weymouth, Torbay, Dartmouth and Falmouth. Portsmouth and Plymouth were too strongly fortified and Lyme Bay, where Monmouth had landed in 1685, would not be a morale-boosting choice.

During the night of the 4/14th–5/15th the wind changed to the west, a change that was widely interpreted as another example of divine intervention, since William's pilots had overshot the mark, and the west wind enabled them to bring the fleet back into Torbay, besides first impeding Dartmouth (then off Beachy Head) and eventually driving him back into the Downs. Consequently William was under no pressure while his army landed. By the 9th he was in Exeter, and his army of 15,000 men was dispersed in surrounding villages recuperating after three weeks on shipboard, well out of reach of a sudden onslaught by James's numerically superior forces of 40,000 men.[2]

In the situation created by the invasion James had an advant-

[1] Powley, *English Navy in the Revolution,* pp. 88–92, 95.
[2] *Correspondentie,* I, ii, 635–8.

age in that he had faced and overcome similar problems in
1685. Some of his decisions and moves were clearly influenced
by this earlier experience. Politically, James's position had been
far stronger in 1685. Then he had received enthusiastic and
expeditious cooperation from Parliament, and from the Tories
who monopolized local government offices, whereas in 1688 the
court was ostentatiously boycotted, and offers of reinstatement
were refused by those whom James had antagonized.[3] In 1685
James had been able to identify, isolate and disarm his opponents
– the radical section of the first Whigs. Large-scale preventive
arrests effectively stopped Monmouth receiving adherents from
outside a limited area, and no diversionary risings took place.
The London Whigs were held in subjection by their victorious
Tory opponents.

In 1688 James knew, or suspected, in general terms that
William had secret friends at court, in the army and navy, in
London and the provinces, but he did not have enough reliable
evidence, or absolutely reliable agents, for him to venture on
stern precautionary action, although he certainly could have
tried to detain known enemies. Monmouth had contributed to
his own failure by issuing ill-judged and inflammatory declarations that alarmed all but partisan Whigs, whereas William's
statement that a free Parliament would be called to solve the
crisis had a universal and unifying appeal. William's leadership
provided a guarantee that the invasion would not plunge the
country into anarchy and confusion, and the fear of another
civil war – which Charles had exploited in order to defeat
Shaftesbury and James had repeated against Monmouth – was
now overlaid by the prospect that James would succeed in his
existing policies, which were thought to be on the point of
establishing absolutism and popery. Finally, there was a crucial
difference between the reserve resources on which James could
call in the two crises; in 1685 William and the regiments in
Dutch service were an effective and politically acceptable last
line of defence. In 1688 James depended on reinforcements from
Ireland. Most of the men who arrived were half-trained. All,
as Catholics, were loathed and feared, but the hostile reaction

[3] Campana de Cavelli, ii, 278.

which they provoked would have been nothing in comparison with the explosion that the arrival of French troops would have caused.

James's political weaknesses meant that during the crisis he had to rely entirely on his standing army. Ever since the clash with Parliament in November 1685, when he had refused to dismiss its newly appointed Catholic officers, James recognized that the army was the basis of his authority, but by November 1688 he had no other form of support. The concessions had not appeased his opponents – as the demonstrative failure of the bishops to respond to his suggestion that they condemn William's invasion and declaration had shown – but they had destroyed his reputation for firmness and gave the impression that more could be extracted from him by pressure. (Moreover, there were justifiable doubts as to his sincerity in making such extensive concessions.) Nevertheless, despite his political failures, James's military position was incomparably stronger than it had been in 1685. He controlled a larger, more efficient and better disciplined army than any previous English king. This military strength enabled James, like Cromwell, to rule without reference to the opinions and interests of the vast majority of the nation. Its existence and dispositions created serious problems for William. But this reliance on the army meant that James would find himself in an impossible position if the sword ever broke in his hand. Once he had lost authority within the army, once the crisis ceased to be a military one and became political in character (as it did with the Proclamation of 30 November) James was lost and finished.

One of the most difficult questions before James was whether to stay in London (as he had done in 1685) or join the field army. Against the advice of Louis and Petre, who quoted the irrelevant example of Charles I's withdrawal in 1642, James rightly decided to go to Salisbury, where the *rendezvous* had been arranged, but he wasted precious time in doing so without gaining any advantage from prolonging his stay in London, which remained passive, overawed by the strongly-held Tower and by the reserve force of some 8,000 men in the district. James hoped that by personally accompanying the army he would be able to inspire the generals into taking the offensive against William; a set-piece attack was perhaps James's one remaining chance of success. He was also doubtful about the reliability of some units, particularly Guards regiments, but his delay in leaving London meant that he arrived at Salisbury too late, on the 19th, when defections of officers had already begun to demoralize the entire army.

In addition to the field army, James also possessed strong garrisons in several major strategic centres. Three key fortresses – Plymouth, Portsmouth and Hull – were securely held, with Catholic commanding officers and many Irish among the troops. Militia officers and units were expressly excluded from these places, and the restive civilian populations were dominated by citadels built on the continental model.[4] Secondary garrisons were maintained at Carlisle and Berwick, guarding the roads along which reinforcements from Scotland were moving south; at Chester, where reinforcements from Ireland could land; at Tynemouth, Scarborough, Yarmouth and Dover, guarding the east coast; and at Sheerness, Gravesend and Landguard on the coast of the Thames estuary.

These fortresses, and the superiority in cavalry of James's army, compelled William to land at a relatively remote place so as to have time for consolidation; it had to be north of the Humber or west of the Isle of Wight. This remoteness had disadvantages. Communications were difficult with associates in other parts of the country, such as Danby in Yorkshire. William would have to take the initiative so as to encourage the diversionary risings planned for other areas, but his cavalry had suffered severely in the gale of October and he was short of draught animals. This meant that he had to leave both his baggage train and his heavy artillery at Exeter, when his advance began. The roads surprised the Dutch officers by their badness, and with winter setting in their condition could only deteriorate. Some units were enfeebled by dysentry.[5]

William's chances of a quick success depended entirely on being able to disintegrate James's army by means of the defec-

[4] *HMC, VIIth Report*, app, i, 348.
[5] Campana de Cavelli, ii, 322–3; Huygens, pp. 27, 29.

tions that had been arranged. Otherwise it would have been hazardous to have advanced so soon against an apparently superior army. William also depended on receiving voluntary support from as wide a spectrum of politicians as possible, but while this would give him overwhelming advantages once political negotiations opened, it was first necessary to force James to agree to negotiations, and this could be accomplished only by stripping him of his last source of strength, the army and the garrisons.

William entered Exeter on the 9th. The bishop had fled (to get as an unmerited reward the archbishopric of York – he was a supporter of William within four months). The city magistrates were hostile, which is not surprising since they had been reinstated by the Earl of Bath at an elaborate Tory-Anglican ceremony at the cathedral only four days before, and now rightly feared that they would be ejected again.[6] The ordinary citizens gave William a tumultuous welcome. He freed Captain Hicks, a determined Whig and son of a martyr of 1685, who had tried to list troops for him on the 7th. Recruits flocked in for the new regiments (Peyton's, Guise's, Mordaunt's, Waller's) for which arms had been brought over.[7] The often-repeated statement that William and Bentinck were so disheartened by their reception and isolation at Exeter that, after a week, they seriously considered re-embarkation (which would have been physically and strategically impracticable anyhow, with the English fleet between them and Holland) has no real basis in fact. Seven days after his entry, William wrote to Waldeck that he was confident of success, since he found that the state of affairs in England was as it had been represented to him before he set sail.[8] If there was a danger in the first days, it was that William was surrounded by Whigs, so that the enterprise might appear to be a party venture. William was particularly concerned not to appear to be a Whig leader, since he was anxious to learn

[6] Addit., 41805, ff.118–19; PRO, 31/4, part 1, ff. 106–7; 'The Expedition of the Prince of Orange', *A Third Collection of Papers*, pp. 5–6.

[7] *Ibid.*, p. 7.

[8] Müller, *Wilhelm III von Oranien und Georg Friedrich von Waldeck*, ii, 118. Campana de Cavelli, ii, 445.

whether James's concessions had affected the undertakings which he had earlier received from Tories and churchmen.

The pattern of adherences and defections from James also shows that there was never any danger of William having to abandon the invasion. The first man to come in, Captain Burrington of Crediton, arrived on the 12th. He was followed the next day by Lord Colchester, Thomas Wharton and Charles Godfrey. All were leading Whigs but they had wider connections, outside the party. Colchester was a leader of the military conspiracy. Wharton, perhaps the ablest young Whig, had large personal as well as political connections. Godfrey was married to John Churchill's sister Arabella (James's cast-off mistress). They were followed by officers from the Plymouth garrison. On the 16th the deluge began, with the first arrival of substantial bodies of officers and men from James's main army which was only just assembling at Salisbury. Lieutenant-Colonel Langston brought over most of the St Alban's regiment with him; he was the key figure among William's military contacts and was immediately rewarded with command of the regiment. Lord Cornbury's defection was militarily disappointing, since most of his soldiers returned to James's service once they realized where they were being led, but it created a political sensation. As Clarendon's son, and James's nephew, he came from what had been thought to be the most loyal of all Anglican families. Officers also came in from Oxford's regiment, but here again they were not followed by all their men; the loyalty of the common soldiers (who on closer examination may turn out to have been Irish or Scottish Catholics) was the only unexpected asset that James gained during the crisis, but the loss of officers, and the general air of suspicion and treachery which the defections created, prevented it from having any effect on events.[9]

Simultaneously with the defections, most of the gentry of the west country rallied to William. Edward Seymour, who came in on the 17th and was followed by most of his associates, was a key figure. His adherence and that of his followers ensured that William would not be the prisoner of the Whigs. With

[9] *HMC, VIIth Report*, app, i, 416–17; Addit., 41805, f.200; *Correspondentie*, I, ii, 626–7.

shrewd political sense and initiative, and seeing a way to expand his own political influence, Seymour organized an association pledging support for William and a free Parliament and threatening to revenge William's death on the Papists. This association was signed by adherents as they came in, giving the rather heterogeneous group with William an organizational unity.[10] On the 19th William received important assurances from Seymour's rival, Bath, pledging support and undertaking to seize Plymouth from its Catholic commanding officer, and to rally the Cornish gentry. This assured William that his rear was safe as he advanced towards London.[11]

When William set out from Exeter on the 21st he was only three days behind his original plan. By now he had an organized revenue system, a council of English advisers and an efficient intelligence system. He sent Shrewsbury and Guise to take Bristol. By this time James was at Salisbury, where he arrived on the 19th; during the seven days that he stayed there the decisive collapse occurred. He found the army becoming demoralized by defections, with everyone wondering who would be the next to go, but with no way apparent of preventing further desertions. After holding a review of his army, James suddenly broke down. In London he had been bombarded with conflicting advice. On reaching the army he found the atmosphere just as murky and confused. His officers were divided on whether he should advance and seek a battle or retreat to cover London. Ten years before, James, like Richard III, would have had no hesitation but would have advanced into an all-out attack, even though there were many candidates for the role of Stanley among his senior officers. Instead he hesitated and collapsed both physically and psychologically. A succession of what seem to have been psychosomatic nose-bleeds disabled him. He could not sleep. A council of war was held on the 23rd, at which most of his officers advocated an offensive, but James agreed with his cautious commanding general, the Earl of Feversham (who had commanded incompetently against Monmouth at Sedgemoor in 1685), in ordering a retreat. At this time William's army, it

10 *Correspondentie*, I, ii, 628; Huygens, p. 22; Burnet, iii, 337.
11 *Correspondentie*, II, iii, 67, 69–70, 71–2; Dalrymple, appendix, part 1, 335.

should be noted, was over sixty miles away and only two days on its march from Exeter. Later James was to rationalize this pitiful behaviour by claiming that his order for a retreat, and his own return to London, foiled an attempt by Churchill and other officers to kidnap him and hand him over to William.[12]

The order for a retreat marked the beginning of the end. Churchill and the Earl of Berkeley defected on the night of the 23rd, to be followed shortly by Prince George, Ormonde and other senior officers. During the next week whole units began to go over, one regiment being taken over by its NCOs, and the local population began to attack groups of Irish stragglers.[13] William arrived at Sherborne on the 27th, where he was greeted by the Earl of Bristol, the lord lieutenant, and most of the Dorset gentry, but he did not reach Salisbury until the 4th. James was further demoralized on his return to London, where he arrived on the 26th, by the news that even his daughter Anne had deserted him, going off under the escort of Bishop Compton. Considering the earlier talk by Catholic extremists of converting her to Catholicism by force, there had been some fears that Anne would be abducted to France as a political hostage, but her disappearance must have strengthened James's fears for the safety of the prince.[14] In addition, his authority had received another severe blow from the series of provincial risings which he was quite powerless to suppress.

Originally the provincial risings had been planned to break out as William advanced on London, but favourable circumstances were created for them sooner than expected, largely by the very speed and completeness with which James concentrated his army at Salisbury, leaving the provinces stripped of mobile forces; in very few counties had any militia forces been embodied, and in any case they were not now reliable. The first rising, staged by Lord Delamere in Cheshire, actually started on the 15th, nearly a week before William left Exeter, but there were exceptional reasons for this. Delamere, the only Whig leader who tried to organize a diversionary rising in 1685 and son of

[12] Clarendon, ii, 206–7; Clarke, *James the Second*, ii, 222–4.
[13] *HMC, VIIth Report*, app, i, 418.
[14] *HMC, XIth Report*, app. v, 214; D. Green, *Queen Anne*, pp. 45–8.

the leader of the 1659 rising, was prepared to take risks. He also deliberately jumped the gun, rising sooner than had been arranged so as to outmanoeuvre his temporary ally but local rival and future competitor for offices and influence, the Earl of Derby.[15] On 21 November another Whig, the Earl of Devonshire, seized Nottingham, and on the next day a bloodless *coup* gave Danby and a strong group of his associates control over York. In the next ten days other risings, or latterly assemblies of gentry, followed, with declarations of support for William and calls for a free Parliament. With Northampton, Leicester, Carlisle, Newcastle, Gloucester, Norwich, King's Lynn and Derby all in the hands of William's friends, James's crumbling authority was limited to a contracting area of south-east England.[16]

In a military sense these provincial risings were not very formidable, although the gentry could have provided William with much-needed cavalry, and especially remount horses, had there been a battle against James. They met with no resistance. This was because James's remaining provincial forces were static, immobilized in heavily defended fortresses. The amateur, improvised forces of the provincial magnates could not have reduced these places by siege operations, but political negotiation quickly did the work. Danby, in approaching the Hull garrisons, laid emphasis on religion so as to exploit the differences between English and Irish soldiers.[17] Only Portsmouth, with a Catholic commanding officer and a high proportion of Irish troops, remained loyal to James, but it could not hold out as a place of refuge for his adherents because it had not been properly provisioned and could be easily blockaded by the fleet.

Politically the risings were of great significance. They completed James's isolation and demoralization. They provided an example of Englishmen helping themselves, so that they could claim that not everything had been done by William. Their calls for a free Parliament recalled the petitions that had greeted

[15] Addit., 41805, f.275; 38695, f.86; Campana de Cavelli, ii, 339.
[16] *HMC, XIth Report*, app, v, 228, 230–31, 234, 282–3; vii, 28–9.
[17] *HMC, XIVth Report*, app, ix, 449–51; Browning, *Danby*, ii, 149–52; Campana de Cavelli, ii, 352–3.

Monk in 1660. In general the declarations which were published and subscribed tried to avoid narrowly partisan statements, and reveal in particular a concern for Tory and Anglican reservations about the propriety of resisting even such an unconstitutional king as James. The Nottingham declaration said : 'We will not be bugbeared with the opprobrious Terms of Rebels, by which they would fright us, to become perfect slaves to their tyrannical Insolencies and Usurpations.' It also took considerable care to disparage James's concessions, which were described as being intended 'to still the People, like Plums to children, by deceiving them for a while'. As in William's Declaration, the weight of the attacks was directed against the evil ministers who had infringed liberties and religion.[18]

Delamere's call for support was much more thoroughgoing. His bluntness in stating unashamedly Whig principles provides an exception to the otherwise moderately phrased declarations on which all could agree. After referring to the dangers of Popery and slavery, he made no effort to disguise his Whig belief in the necessity and legitimacy of resistance : 'I see all lies at stake, I am to choose whether I will be a Slave and a Papist, or a Protestant and a free man and therefore ... I shall think myself false to my country, if I sit still at this time. I am of Opinion that when the Nation is delivered it must be by Force or Miracle.'[19]

Although James still had large forces at his disposal, since only about 3,000 men had deserted to William by the end of November, and William's army was still far away, James's return to London on 26 November was immediately followed by what was tantamount to an act of capitulation. On the 17th, before setting out for Salisbury, he had abruptly rejected a petition from a group of peers and bishops calling for a compromise settlement, to be achieved by calling a free Parliament.[20] He had even made fierce noises that he would regard anyone who suggested negotiating with William as a traitor. Now James belatedly fell back on these proposals, which he had rejected when he thought he was in a position to do so – not a situation

[18] *A Second Collection of Papers*, pp. 29–31.
[19] *A Collection of Papers*, pp. 23–5.
[20] Clarendon, ii, 201–5.

in which his sincerity was likely to be accepted. In fact his only purpose now was to try and gain time, although he had no idea of what to do with any time gained – apart from saving himself and his family. The day after his return he called a meeting of peers and bishops, of whom about forty attended, and referred them to the petition which he had rejected on the 17th. On the next day, the 28th, he informed the privy council that he was going to issue a Proclamation for a Parliament, which was to meet on 15 January. He also promised a general pardon, which would make William's adherents eligible to sit and be elected, security for the Church of England, and the early opening of negotiations with William.[21]

The Proclamation was published on 30 November.[22] It was an admission of total defeat. In effect James was now appealing to the Tories for the second time in two months, having in the interim attempted to defeat William without their aid or consent. Few could accept his sincerity. William had no intention of allowing the offer of negotiations to slow his advance or of relaxing his pressure on James. The Proclamation of 30 November was decisive in one important respect. It created a new situation, one in which the dominant forces were political rather than military. This faced William with an entirely new set of problems. He had to retain the initiative, and this meant that he had to prevent the Tories, and especially the bishops, interposing themselves as mediators. The effects on James were shattering. He was now lost, both politically and mentally, with only the idea of saving the queen and the baby prince from the malice of his enemies. As for himself, he was not prepared to rely on the Tories to save something for him. Like his father, Charles I, who had fled to the Scots at Newcastle (and later to the Isle of Wight), he thought that by distancing himself from his opponents and subjects (almost the same thing by now) he would be able to use his royal title as a bargaining weapon and wait for his enemies to start quarrelling among themselves. But with his nerve gone, and his father's fate before him, real security could apparently be found only in France. There he

[21] Ibid., ii, 208–11.
[22] PRO, PC 2, 72, f.798.

would wait for the poison instilled into the nation to work itself out, and for his deluded subjects to come to their senses – although this was hardly consistent with the state of anarchy which he deliberately tried to leave behind him, and which fixed on him the charge that he had deserted the kingdom.

The danger that James's collapse of authority would lead to raging and widespread disorders, or that it would create a vacuum that would give opportunities for spontaneous political action in which religious and political radicals could assume leadership, was substantially reduced by the provincial risings. These were a conclusive demonstration of the social cohesion and (admittedly temporary) political unity of the land-owning classes, who had an obvious interest in preserving order. Moreover, the wealthier inhabitants of the towns, on whose antagonism for the gentry James had tried to play, now readily accepted their leadership, since it was in the larger towns that there was a considerable danger of violent disorders. Riots had occurred before William's invasion in London and some provincial towns, ostensibly directed against Catholic schools, chapels and small religious communities – the visible and provocative signs of the attempt at urban proselytising. As James's authority weakened riots occurred in Newcastle, Norwich and Lincoln, and tension mounted elsewhere.[23] The disuse into which the militia had fallen in virtually every county, the weakness of the Commission of the Peace after so many changes, and above all the confusion which regulations and restorations had created in the corporations, meant that local government was particularly weak at the time of maximum danger. There was a danger that attacks on Catholic houses could develop into a general attack on the property of the wealthy, but the assertion of control by the nobility and gentry re-established order and stability in time.

They did so only just in time. In the first days of December a nationwide panic developed, remarkably similar to the *Grande Peur* of July 1789 which pushed France towards revolution. This panic, the Irish Alarms, had been started deliberately by Hugh Speke, but it assumed an existence of its own, spreading spontaneously and rapidly across the country. Speke was an

[23] PRO, 31/4, part 1, f.68; Luttrell, i, 467, 472, 474, 483.

extreme Whig, whose father and one brother had been exclusionist MPS, and who had had another brother executed for aiding
Monmouth in 1685. In 1688 he was acting as a double agent,
sending reports to James from Exeter, but in reality working
against him and misleading him. He fabricated a Declaration,
supposedly issued by William at Sherborne on 28 November,
which had the specific aim of heightening tension and terrifying
James's remaining supporters.[24] It succeeded only too well.
Speaking in William's name it expressed the hope that a free
Parliament could be obtained without spilling blood, but it
specifically excluded from its hopes 'those execrable Criminals
who have justly forfeited their Lives for betraying the Religion,
and subverting the Laws of their Native Country'. This threat
reinforced the fears of mob violence which led many of James's
Catholic advisers to flee the country even before he tried to get
away. The general references to the Catholics were equally
menacing. Those who stayed quietly at home were not to be
molested, but any found in possession of arms or who continued
to serve in offices (military or civil) in defiance of the law were
to be killed out of hand, and the same threat was made against
any obeying orders from them. This was intended to disintegrate
James's remaining army units, a high proportion of whose
loyalist officers were Catholics.

Finally, the most inflammatory section of the spurious
Declaration drew an alarming picture of the Papist threat to
London. It alleged that native Catholics, Irish and a force of
French troops procured from Louis by a sinister Jesuit intrigue,
were assembling in and around London and Westminster. The
staunchly Protestant capital stood in danger of another fire (it
was a firm part of Protestant mythology at this time that
Papists had deliberately started the Great Fire of 1666), or of a
massacre of Protestants resembling the massacres of 1572 in
Paris and of 1641 in Ireland.

In the provinces the presence first of detachments of Irish
troops and then of vagrant bands of disbanded Irish soldiers
greatly increased the impact of the spurious Declaration. During
the second week of December town after town experienced the

24 *A Collection of Papers*, pp. 31–4; Luttrell, i, 485.

Irish Alarms. Rumours spread that a neighbouring town had been plundered and burnt by marauding Irish, who were now on their way to repeat their atrocities.[25] The militia were called out, although they were still in a disorganized state, under their old officers so that the Irish Alarms, instead of liberating and crystallizing popular, radical forces, helped to consolidate the leadership of the traditional local ruling class in the provinces. By Christmas the situation was so much back to normal that the gentry were entirely absorbed in electioneering, and magnates like Danby and Seymour were occupied in the double task of re-establishing their local influence and arranging parliamentary candidatures, and in staking their claim to high office in whatever new administration was about to be formed.

William's deliberate march on London gave time for all opposition to him to crumble. At Hindon on 1 December he received a message from Feversham asking for passports for James's commissioners. On the 3rd he was joined by Clarendon, and learnt from Van Citters (who had left London with James's permission) of the French declaration of war against the United Provinces on 16/26 November.[26] On the 7th he arrived at Hungerford, where he met James's three commissioners the next day. William welcomed Halifax, Godolphin and Nottingham politely, but they received such a cool reception from his adherents, and particularly from those who had come over with William from Holland, that he thought it expedient not to see them in private.[27]

This hostility had nothing to do with the fact that the commissioners had been sent by James. It was because both Halifax and Nottingham had at a late stage drawn back from the invitation sent to William; they had declined to run risks by participating in the Revolution but were now apparently hoping to gain advantages for themselves. Halifax in particular aroused the greatest suspicion among all the competitors for high office;

[25] Addit., 34487, f.50; 38695, f.103; Browning, *Danby*, i, 413–14; *Hatton Correspondence*, ii, 122, 124, 125; *HMC, XIth Report*, app, vii, 28; *XIIth Report*, app, ix, 92; XVth Report, app, i, 135.
[26] Huygens, p. 35; Clarendon, ii, 213–15.
[27] Foxcroft, *Life of Sir George Savile*, ii, 24–6; Clarendon, ii, 216–17, 219–22.

Danby, isolated and out of touch in the north, was acutely afraid
that Halifax would have an advantage over himself, despite all
that he had done for William.[28] But the general point about
the Hungerford negotiations is that they showed that the struggle
against James, his ministers and his policies was already being
superseded by the faction-fighting characteristic of politics since
the Restoration. This can be seen in the important controversy
that developed there over the writs for parliamentary elections
that had been issued on James's authority, after his Proclamation of 30 November. William's Tory adherents, with Clarendon
particularly concerned, wanted elections to proceed on the
basis of these writs.[29] First, this was in the interests of constitutional legality and the Parliament that assembled would not be
irregular or dependent on William. But there was a self-interested
motive as well: the local Tory gentry were well ahead of their
Whig rivals, and of those who had accompanied William, in
canvassing and preparations for elections. For this reason
William's companions demanded the withdrawal of the writs;
they wanted a free Parliament, but not yet. They must continue
with William on his advance, and only at a later stage would
they have opportunities for electioneering. Those who had been
in exile would need some considerable time to revive their
interest, and all were afraid that a Tory-dominated Parliament
would be able to mediate between James and William, substantially reducing their own opportunities for power, influence and
offices. William himself disagreed with them, insisting twice that
he would not demand the recall of the writs. This is an important
piece of evidence for the task of trying to establish his intentions
at this time; it shows that he had not committed himself to
depriving James of sovereign powers, that he was not hostile in
principle to a free Parliament being one that owed its election
to James's authority. However, the demands which the commissioners were to take back to James show that William was determined to apply pressure; all Catholics were to be dismissed,
James's army was to withdraw from London and its neighbour-

[28] Browning, *Danby*, ii, 160; *HMC, XIVth Report*, app, ix, 449, 452, 453, 455, 456.
[29] Clarendon, ii, 219, 222; Lingard, *History*, x, 363-4.

hood, and precautions were to be taken that would prevent the French coming to his assistance.[30]

In fact these demands, and the Hungerford negotiations, were rendered irrelevant by James's sudden and secret departure from London early on 11 December. The idea of fleeing the country had been in his mind since the privy council meeting of 28 November. On the next day he had authorized Dover to arrange for the prince to be taken to France via Portsmouth, but the refusal of Dartmouth to cooperate led to the baby being returned to London. On the 8th he and his mother were secretly got away, under the protection of the French adventurer, Count Lauzun, a move whose significance was appreciated much more clearly abroad than in England.[31] At home the departure of the prince, perhaps because so many people regarded him as supposititious, attracted little attention, but it was at once realized abroad that by giving hostages to Louis James had still further reduced his freedom of action. Now the crisis could end only with him as a dependant, either of Louis or of William. At court James successfully concealed his intention of following his family. On the 10th he adjourned until the next day a meeting of peers who were discussing William's proposals, but by the next morning he had left for Kent where he planned to pick up a yacht for France.[32]

Before he left London James deliberately set out to create a governmental vacuum. The writs which had not been issued for parliamentary elections were destroyed, the Great Seal dropped into the Thames and orders given for disbanding (but not disarming) the remains of the army. In general William was already assuming the direction of government in the counties which were in his hands, or those of his adherents, but James's abdication of authority created an extremely dangerous situation in London, where the risks of anarchy were greatest at any time. Disorders occurred on a large scale immediately after it was known that James had fled. Particularly on the 13th, the day

[30] Foxcroft, *op. cit.*, ii, 29–30.

[31] Powley, *English Navy in the Revolution*, pp. 134–6, 137, 141; *HMC, XIth Report*, app, v, 220, 223, 226, 276.

[32] *HMC, XIth Report*, app, v, 226; Addit., 34510, f.198.

of the Irish Alarm, crowds attacked Catholic chapels and the houses of known Catholics, pillaging the residence of the Spanish ambassador. Great alarm was aroused by the depredations of what Hoffmann, the imperial envoy, called this 'detestable populace'. Lord Mulgrave, in describing the consternation of the city magistrates (who had only been reinstated in their offices very recently), commented that 'indeed the rabble were the masters, if the beasts had known their own strength'. Yet the fact remains that the disturbances did not last long and quickly subsided (rather than being suppressed) before William's troops moved in.[33]

It would be entirely incorrect to describe late seventeenth-century London as a potential centre of revolution. At no time during the century was there a popular outbreak on the scale of the Gordon Riots of 1780, still less of anything resembling events in Paris in 1789–92. Radicals could organize mass demonstrations for particular purposes, as John Pym had done in 1640–1, and John Lilburne later, but the London masses were not capable of independent and sustained political action. As a hypothesis, it may be suggested that the periods during which radicals were able to mobilize popular support were ones in which there was a good deal of dislocation to trade, resulting in a shortage of employment and high prices for food and fuel. This was certainly the case in 1640–2, 1647–9 and perhaps also in 1678–9. In 1688 many Londoners must have been affected by the embargo which James had placed on all east-coast ports in October, but there is no evidence of a prolonged depression having caused economic distress. A period of high corn prices and acute social tension came later, in 1693–5.[34]

The absence of a revolutionary movement or potential for popular radicalism, the lack of any revolutionary tradition, has to be related to the capital's social, demographic and economic structure, on which comparatively little has been published and where there is still a great deal of research to be done. London, of course, was the one significantly large urban centre in Britain,

[33] Campana de Cavelli, ii, 418, 421–3; Mulgrave, Works, ii, 74; Correspondentie, II, iii, 84–5.
[34] Luttrell, i, 476; Addit., 41805, f.110.

whose huge and growing population contained a dense concentration of the most miserably poor and destitute. A high proportion of the population formed a mass lumpenproletariat, people with no settled occupation or skills, for whose labour there was very varying demand during the seasons of the year and who lived in monstrously congested and unhealthy areas. The tip of this iceberg, known to all students of the period, was the large, picturesque but vicious criminal world which was to be found in certain quarters.

The extreme misery and poverty of the vast majority of the inhabitants is probably, if at first sight paradoxically, the main reason why London was not a potential centre of revolution. The very poor had no natural, functional leaders as the Roman plebs had in their tribunes, or the Paris population of the days of the Catholic *Ligue* had in members of the religious (and especially the mendicant) orders.[35] Most Londoners' energies were entirely absorbed by the struggle to survive. The actual population was constantly and rapidly changing; London resembled a bath with the taps full on and the plug open. It had a constant surplus of deaths over births, and the rise in the total population indicates that the deficit was more than compensated by large-scale immigration from the provinces. Newcomers must have had to fight ferociously to establish themselves at all in a brutally competitive labour market. They lived in crowded tenements or in lodgings which they frequently changed. London lacked any sense of neighbourhood. The once popular city companies which had given some slight degree of social cohesion, and a sense of belonging even to journeymen in some trades, had become oligarchical, ornamental and exclusive. Finally, it may be suggested that after the Great Fire there was a marked tendency towards residential segregation, with the wealthy moving out of the city itself. The development of the West End as a fashionable residential area reduced social tension; there the upper classes lived surrounded by a dependent

[35] The only possible exceptions may be under-officers in the city administration, several of whom (Richard Nelthrop and Richard Goodenough are examples) acted as Whig organisers under Sir Thomas Player and Sir Robert Clayton.

population of servants and tradesmen who represented no threat to the established order of things.[36]

Although there was this momentary danger of anarchy in London, nothing could have been more convenient from William's point of view than James's voluntary abdication of authority. William had not had to apply direct pressure. It was particularly gratifying because James had deserted the Tories and Church leaders, while they were still trying to mediate between him and William, when they still hoped to preserve for him at least his royal title and possibly the succession of the Prince of Wales provided that he was brought up as an Anglican. William could have gained effective power without breaking the unity that had been demonstrated during the Revolution, and James would have ruined his reputation with every section of the nation. Nothing, therefore, could have been more inconvenient to William than James's unfortunate detention by Kentish fishermen, who recognized his travelling companion and man-handled the king before they realized who he was. Zuylestein was immediately sent to tell James not to return to London, but he was too late to prevent this.[37] Ominously, James received a favourable reception from large crowds when he arrived back in London on the 16th. This was partly due to sympathy for him, after the maltreatment and humiliation he had experienced, partly to a mistaken belief that he had voluntarily returned to grant his subjects' wishes, but perhaps mainly to the disorders that had happened during his absence.

James's return revived the hopes of all those Tories and churchmen who were concerned above all with the preserva-tion of James' title. These men were beginning to fear that William was now aiming at the crown for himself. Two of their leaders, Rochester and Turner, the Bishop of Ely, had convoked a meeting at the Guildhall on the 11th, immediately after James's departure, which more than thirty peers and bishops had

---

[36] It was suggested that a royal citadel should be built to dominate the West End, as the Tower dominated the city; the site would have been on the former royal mews, where the National Gallery is today: *HMC, VIIth Report*, app, i, 501.

[37] *HMC, XIVth Report*, app, ix, p. 453; Campana de Cavelli, ii, 441.

attended. This assembly had been intended to secure public order and to ensure an early meeting of Parliament – a sufficient number of writs issued by James still existed for partial elections to be held; the members at their first meeting could then have authorized the filling of vacancies. This would have favoured Tory candidates, and facilitated the achievement of Turner's and Rochester's plan, which was to limit William to the position of regent.[38]

The assembly did not prove to be successful. Serious differences of opinion developed among those present, which indicated that it would be difficult to present an effectively united front against William's supporters. More ominously, neither these peers nor the city authorities were able to do much to cope with disorders in London; they seemed to occupy a position uncomfortably reminiscent of the *parlementaires* in Paris during the Frondes. There could be no suggestion of keeping William's troops out of the capital while a settlement was worked out. James's unexpected return on the 16th seemed to offer the high Tories a final opportunity to mediate a strictly constitutional settlement. James himself disappointed their hopes by remaining totally inactive during the forty-eight hours he stayed in Whitehall. He did nothing to rally support or give a lead. Observers noted that he was attended almost exclusively by Catholics. He undertook no governmental functions, but he was clearly only waiting for a new opportunity to leave the country. On the other hand, William's actions showed just as clearly that he did not want James to act as sovereign and that he would be relieved if James did leave again. Feversham was arrested. William refused to meet James. The Dutch Guard were moved into Whitehall, and English troops withdrawn at his demand. Peremptory orders were sent to James to leave London, but William's acceptance of James's request that he should go to Rochester, and not up-river to Ham House, showed that both men were thinking of easing a second flight to France.[39]

After these moves the polite fiction that James acted volun-

[38] R. Beddard, 'The Loyalist Opposition in the Interregnum', *Bulletin of the Institute of Historical Research*, XL, 101–9.
[39] Huygens, p. 48; Campana de Cavelli, ii, 438, 441.

tarily, as a free agent, in leaving for France (for which he embarked on the 22nd), plausible in relation to his first attempt at escape, could not be sustained. But even at this late stage the high Tories sent a delegation to follow James to Rochester, with the futile task of trying to persuade him to come back a second time. Their pressure seems to have embarrassed James, who deliberately deceived them. After saying that he would give them an answer the next day, he slipped away during the night.[40] This was soon forgotten. For many Tories, as well as those who were to become outright Jacobites, the sequence of events after 16 December proved that William had deliberately driven James out of England, so that he could become master of the kingdom himself and then usurp the throne.

William had in practice been exercising *de facto* authority ever since he established himself at Exeter. All royal revenues within his power had been paid to his treasurer and army paymaster. William had promised rewards and pardons, and threatened penalties and impeachments. He formed a council of advisers. These were actions necessitated by the army's requirements, they did not (as Pinkham claimed) pre-empt any decision on the permanent form of government.[41] Only one (little-noticed) order by William did commit the country to a future policy of great importance. On 10/20 December, *that is before James had left London for France,* William sent explicit orders to Herbert, whose commission as admiral was a Dutch not an English one, to use the English flag in attacks on French ships.[42] This move was clearly intended to force a rupture between England and France – the basic object of the entire invasion. It was followed by orders sent to Barrillon to leave London without delay; he left on the 24th. Louis played into William's hands by his orders to seize English ships and their crews, so that by the beginning of 1689 an open war had become inevitable.

[40] Huygens, p. 53; Campana de Cavelli, ii, 442–45, 456–57.
[41] Huygens, pp. 18, 19; Pinkham, *William III and the Respectable Revolution*, pp. 169–71.
[42] *Correspondentie*, II, iii, 78–9, 81.

ELEVEN *The Revolution Settlement*

WILLIAM'S POSSESSION OF APPARENTLY predominant power on his entry into London proved to be almost as short-lived and deceptive as his enthusiastic popular reception. Similarly, the cooperation which he received during the weeks of the interregnum, ending on 13 February, was not an accurate pointer to the real state and character of English politics. It was only during this initial period, when decisions had to be made (and quickly) on matters of urgent and major importance, that politicians and political groups showed themselves ready to face realities and accept compromises.

The first stage in the Revolution Settlement consisted of the calling of a representative assembly. The Lords, consisting of some sixty peers including many who came over with William, met on 21 December. On the 24th they agreed to an address, asking him to take on the administration and to issue circular letters for parliamentary elections. This was presented on the next day by six peers of very dissimilar political views and affiliations – Nottingham, Bishop Compton, Bishop Turner, Wharton, Delamere and Culpeper. The Commons, who had taken longer to assemble, concurred with this address and thanked William for his great services; their debates occurred on the 26th, and

27th and 28th. The composition of this Lower House (with about 300 present) gave a first indication of the tactical ascendancy which the Whigs were to hold during the coming months; it consisted of members of any of Charles II's Parliaments, plus the lord mayor, aldermen and common councilmen of the City of London.[1] This exclusion of men who had sat only in the 1685 Parliament was the first instance of a thesis which was to be developed later by the Whigs: that the process of subverting the constitutional rights and liberties of the nation had begun in 1681, with the dissolution of the Whig Oxford Parliament, and not with James's accession.

Circular letters were issued on 28–9 December and the Convention Parliament met on 22 January, about as soon as was electorally possible. Considering the excitement and upheavals of the last few weeks, and the major political changes of the past decade, the elections were remarkably peaceful and orderly, with William setting an important precedent by ordering soldiers out of towns while the polls were in progress. The Convention faced a daunting set of fundamental issues – the succession, the powers of the crown, the preservation of parliamentary independence and electoral freedom, the rights of the judiciary and juries, martial law, the position of the established Church and of the dissenters. In addition it should be remembered that those who had to tackle these questions had behind them a succession of attempted settlements that had all failed lamentably, in 1640–2, 1646–8, 1654–6 and 1660–1. The immediate past was one of crises, convulsions and tension. Practically all peers and MPs in the Convention had belonged to bitterly antagonistic parties and court groups. Personal and political vendettas proliferated.

Two further important factors need to be considered when attempting to appreciate the promptitude with which these questions were tackled. First, James's disappearance made it necessary to fill every office and place, both at the centre and in the localities, within a few weeks of decisions on the form which government should take. In anticipation, the most intense

[1] For William's attitude at this time: Müller, *Wilhelm III von Oranien und Georg Friedrich von Waldeck*, ii, 126.

manoeuvring and lobbying took place; as in 1660 every working politician was frantically involved, with major figures under pressure from relatives, friends and clients. This time there was an added complication in that until the succession was determined, and the system of government settled, no one could be certain how, and by whom, patronage would be dispensed; would it be by an all-powerful council acting nominally on behalf of a reinstated James, by Regent William or King William, by Queen Mary, or by William and Mary? In 1660 Monk had temporarily dominated the scene; would Bentinck, Schomberg, Zuylestein, Halifax, Danby or Mordaunt now occupy his place? Secondly, the rapidity with which events had moved, and issues changed, meant that political alignments were extraordinarily fluid and uncertain. The months of crisis, from October until February, acted as a kind of political pressure-cooker, accentuating all the forces of instability and change.

James's synthetic political alliance had disintegrated when he reversed his policies by granting concessions in October. His flight eliminated the Catholics. The groupings that formed during William's invasion were obsolete by the time the Convention met; the few, like Preston, who remained loyal to James could not influence events; those who had hoped to mediate between William and James had to reconsider their attitude. William quickly dispensed with the radical Whig exiles, whom he had never trusted, and some exiles (William Harbord and Sir Rowland Gwynne) who had acted as his advisers in Holland diminished in stature and usefulness as prominent politicians joined William.[2] The division between those who had accompanied William, or joined him early on, those who staged the risings in the provinces, and those who remained in London, ceased to be relevant once the Assembly met.

The main division in the Convention concerned the succession. The most scrupulous were those few loyalists who followed Sancroft in refusing to take any part in public life while James was prevented from exercising his sovereign rights. Next were those who still wanted the recall of James on conditions, but he had already made it clear that he would not accept limitations

[2] Huygens, pp. 72, 116.

on his powers as the price of restoration. More important and realistic was the large group (initially almost a majority in the Lords) who advocated the establishment of a regency, either as a temporary expedient, which would strengthen Parliament's hand in bargaining with James for his return on stringent conditions, or as a permanent solution which would give William effective power, while safeguarding the law of the succession and constitutional legality. After the regency proposals were defeated in the Lords many (but not all) found it possible to follow Danby, switching to the nomination of Mary as sole queen, assuming that the prince was either supposititious or barred by his religion and future upbringing in France. This would not have prevented William from exercising effective governmental powers under her nominal authority. These groups contained practically all Tories, many of whom moved uneasily from one to another, and all became reluctantly aware that fundamental (and irregular) changes in the succession were unavoidable, not least because of William's own attitude. With some alarm they began to realize that although Tories had been the main sufferers from James's unconstitutional policies in 1687–8, and despite William's particular eagerness to secure Tory assistance for his invasion, the Whigs were now aggressively and confidently advancing their own claims and arguments.

It is not surprising that the Whigs were more united and determined on the question of the succession. After all, it was their original *raison d'être*. Whigs who had voted for Exclusion in 1679 and 1680 were not going to be worried now by fears that the monarchy would become an elective institution, or by deviating from the strict line of hereditary succession. The Whigs necessarily enjoyed an advantage in that they had made up their minds on the issue long ago, and could quote the arguments of 1679–81 against new proposals for regency or that limitations would make it safe to recall James. Basic Whig principles justified resistance to a tyrant. Belief in the contractual basis of authority entitled them to remove an unjust ruler who disregarded the law of the constitution. In contrast, the element of resistance involved in the Revolution, and the principles of the Settlement, were to plunge the Tories into ideological difficulties when the succession question again became a central issue during the last years of Anne's reign.

However, in 1689 comparatively few Tories refused to acknowledge the new joint sovereigns; the non-jurors were a predominantly clerical group with little political significance. Most Tories realized that there was no practical alternative and that the dangers threatening in Ireland and Scotland, and from France, necessitated the immediate establishment of an effective government. Tory leaders like Danby, Bath and Seymour had an additional motive – the need to share in the distribution of offices. It would be facile to dismiss these politicians as careerists or cynical opportunists, since without the prospect of office and of being able to dispense some patronage they would not be able to satisfy their followers, on whom they in turn depended for support in Parliament, and in county and municipal politics.

In the Commons the Whigs held the initiative on the succession issue. They argued that James had violated his coronation oath to respect the laws, and that consequently he had broken the original contract. They claimed that events had proved the case which they had put forward for Exclusion, that a Popish king was incompatible with both the Protestant religion and the liberties of the people. They were in a position to assert that James had abdicated, that the throne was therefore vacant, and that it should be filled by Parliament. The Lords, where on 29 January there was a majority of only two against a regency, could not at first agree that the throne was vacant, and preferred the word 'deserted' to 'abdicated', besides rejecting any explicit reference to the original contract. A deadlock ensued between the Houses, which could have produced the delays, confusion, divisions and animosities on which James had calculated, and which were being confidently expected at Versailles.[3] Ominously, some radical Whigs, instigated by Mordaunt and Lovelace, were working up popular pressure by organizing a mass petition from London and Westminster, calling for the crowning of William and Mary. Superficially this resembled the monster petitions which Shaftesbury had organized in favour of

[3] G. J. Cosnac and E. Pontal (eds.), *Mémoires du Marquis de Sourches* (Paris, 1883), III, 11, 30, 40.

Exclusion, but whereas they had been aimed at impressing the king, these new petitions were an attempt to pressurize a freely elected Parliament.[4]

On 2 February, after a debate dominated by Whig speakers, the Commons rejected the Lords' amendments. A committee restated the reasons for the original resolutions, and these were put to a conference between the two Houses on 5 February. No agreement was reached. Later, by a majority of 282–151, the Commons decided to uphold its rejection of the Lords' amendments, and on 6 February another conference failed to reach an agreement. In the face of this stand by the Commons, the Lords gave way. The word 'abdicated' was accepted. By a majority of 62–47 it was agreed that the throne was vacant, in the full knowledge now that this would mean offering the crown to William and Mary; a clause to this effect was accepted immediately afterwards without a division.[5] Clarendon thought that about forty peers would have voted against this offer of the crown, but by this stage such opposition would have been no more than a gesture.[6] The decisive factor in producing this result was the knowledge that William would not accept a position of even nominal subordination to his wife.

As well as determining the succession, Parliament was simultaneously discussing how best to safeguard constitutional liberties. A committee of the Commons reported heads of a declaration on 2 February, combined with a statement of general grievances. These finally passed through both Houses on 12 February, but several points that had been included originally – especially on religion and reforms of the law – were omitted because they posed too many problems of detail to be included in a general act. On the next day the Declaration of Rights was presented to William and Mary in a formal ceremony, at which they were offered the crown. With their acceptance the interregnum came to an end.

The Declaration of Rights contains the essence of the Revolu-

---

[4] Grey, ix, 45; Huygens, p. 80; Luttrell, i, 499.
[5] Grey, ix, 7–25, 26–37, 46–65, 70–83; Clarendon, ii, 255–61.
[6] Clarendon, ii, 261.

tion.[7] It is centrally relevant in a way in which the pamphlets of the time, and John Locke's writings, are not. The voluminous controversial pamphlets of the period, although they aroused immense interest and excitement among contemporaries, have all fallen into oblivion. In terms of their contribution to political theory this is easily explained, since these pamphlets were as devoted to immediate issues as the equally ephemeral mass of pamphlets published at the time of the Exclusion Crisis. Theoretically they are defective and not very interesting. They were nearly all based on faulty historical assumptions and partisan Whig scholarship about the origins of Parliament and the constitutional liberties which were being claimed as the property of Englishmen. Like Locke, many of the writers were primarily concerned to refute the claims to absolute authority being made by James's apologists, with the corollary that it was unlawful to take up arms against the king on any pretence whatever. Instead the pamphlets claimed that both the exercise of authority and the duty of obedience were conditional since men were free-born and had instituted government for their own purposes. Perhaps the only major point of interest was the common injunction of the writers to the Convention, to remember that it was a trustee for posterity, that it should ensure the renewal of government on its original bases (in one pamphlet on the 'primitive and immortal Foundation of Liberty and Property') so that succeeding generations would be secure from Popery and slavery.[8] The theme throughout was one of restoration and renewal, of protecting existing (or assumed) rights, not of establishing new ones.

The speed with which the Convention made its major decisions meant that there was no real opportunity for an exhaustive political debate. The few proposals that were made for new and experimental constitutional forms – such as a Governing Senate of twenty peers and twenty MPs, half serving for life, half elected biennially – were in any case concerned with means not with ends.[9] In this spirit the Declaration of Rights was

---

[7] Most accessible in Williams, *Eighteenth Century Constitution*, pp. 26–33.

[8] 'Popish Treaties not to be relied on', *A Third Collection of Papers*, p. 37.

[9] 'A Modest Proposal', *A Sixth Collection of Papers*, pp. 24–5.

intended primarily to restore and perpetuate liberties and rights that were unquestionably assumed to belong to the nation. Its purpose was to repair the damage which James had done in a long list of allegedly illegal actions. The thirteen points in the Declaration were not just statements of the true nature of the law of the constitution, they were also intended to provide a guideline for the future conduct of government, so that any departure from legality would be instantly signalled, and remedial action could be taken.

The Declaration (subsequently enacted in a statute) subordinated the royal prerogative to the common law. Its one novel clause was to apply the principles of the Test Acts, which James had tried so strenuously to repeal, to the monarchy itself; any Catholic, or anyone married to a Catholic, was barred from the crown. The suspending power was abolished. The dispensing power could not legally be used in a wholesale fashion, as James had used it to render statutes entirely ineffective. Prerogative courts, like the Ecclesiastical Commission, were declared illegal. The exercise of martial law and collection of revenue were illegal unless they had parliamentary consent. A stop was put to the various devices which James had used to manipulate the law – demanding excessive bail, inflicting unusual punishments and packing juries. The campaign to pack Parliament resulted in the clause that Parliaments ought to be free, and the statement that they should also be frequent was followed up shortly afterwards by a bill, to remove the crippling amendments enacted by the court in 1664, which had deprived the 1641 Triennial Act of its effectiveness.[10]

The enthronement of William and Mary as joint sovereigns was in itself a break with strict constitutional law. So too was the further determination of the succession, first to the survivor and to any children born to them, then to Anne (who had a prior claim to William), then to her children, and finally to William's children by a second marriage. During the Exclusion Crisis the Tories had denied Parliament's right to decide the succession, but their acceptance of this Settlement was eased by requiring only a simplified oath, with no mention of the

[10] *HMC, XIIth Report*, app, vi, 343–4, 364–8.

legitimacy of their title: 'I A.B. do sincerely promise and swear, That I will be faithful, and bear true allegiance, to their Majesties, King William and Queen Mary.' But in general the Bill of Rights was to prove a most effective barrier to the restoration of James and his son. As in 1660 their restoration would automatically have invalidated all legislation enacted under a usurped authority. Consequently, all the constitutional safeguards contained in the bill, especially the invalidation of the suspending power, would immediately lapse. James would be free to employ all the powers whose exercise had provoked the Revolution, whereas in contrast Charles had been restored in 1660 without the prerogative courts and powers, whose provocative employment by his father in 1629–40 had caused the mid-century English Revolution. A restored James would have to be taken on trust, with no legal security against him abusing his powers.

The disagreements between the Lords and Commons had not prevented the questions of the succession and constitutional liberties being settled in three working weeks – about as quickly as could be expected. However, this significant achievement was followed by a dismal return to all the worst and most negative political practices of the time, as politicians became engrossed in faction-fighting, patronage questions and personal and party recriminations about issues of the past. Even a cursory examination of the debates in the Convention will show how legislation was held up, particularly the Indemnity Bill, which had been intended to promote reconciliation.[11] The religious settlement, such as it was, was almost entirely negative. A comprehension bill, to widen the basis of the Church by making concessions that would allow dissenters (mainly Presbyterians) to enter it, failed largely because of the lack of positive interest in Parliament. The so-called Toleration Act was as grudging as possible; it merely exempted dissenters (except those who rejected the doctrine of the Trinity) from the penal laws, and William provoked an explosion when he suggested that they should be made capable of holding offices. Continuing Whig hostility to

11 The bill was still being discussed when the Convention was prorogued and dissolved.

the High Church clergy led to their insisting that all must take the new oaths; this led to the deprivation of Sancroft and several hundred clergy, whose withdrawal to form the non-juring Church weakened the establishment.[12]

The behaviour of the Convention disillusioned William. His suspicions about English politicians in general, and Whigs in particular, were quickly confirmed. In Holland William knew exactly where he stood. Although members of the regent class might work with him for a time as valuable collaborators, like Witsen and Hop in 1688-9, William never trusted the class as a whole. His ministers and chief advisers had to be literally his own men, like Saxon house-carls, from whom he demanded unswerving loyalty and obedience, and who in return could depend on effective protection from him, however unpopular they might become. In England such a clear relationship could not exist, a fact that deterred most of his Dutch advisers from ever venturing into English politics. As Zuylestein explained : 'He did not claim any part in discussing important matters, that it was the custom in England for favourites and councillors to be accused and punished, although the king had given them pardons.'[13] From William's point of view this meant that he could never expect steady loyalty from ministers, because they either had to protect themselves or they were concentrating on advancing their own interests at the expense of colleagues or superiors. William thought Guise's conduct outrageous when as a junior minister he joined in 'country' attacks on other ministers. He had to reconcile himself to ministerial corruption, to bitter factionalism between ministers, and to the fact that many of the most indispensable ministers were reinsuring themselves with James.

For over a year William found himself unexpectedly enmeshed in the details of English politics, so that he could not concentrate even on the reconquest of Ireland, let alone turn to European problems and the war against France. In his absence, and with Fagel dead, serious problems arose in the United Provinces.

[12] *HMC, XIIth Report*, app, vi, 49-52; G. V. Bennett, 'King William III and the Episcopate', in Bennett and Walsh (eds), *Essays in Modern Church History* (1966); Lacey, *Dissent and Parliamentary Politics*, pp. 225-7, 232-9.
[13] Huygens, p. 70.

There are glimpses of William's frusration in Constantijn Huygens' journal: his longing to be back at the Hague, his anxiety about military operations, his complaints about the inconstancy of the English. He had only contempt for the 'foolish old Popish ceremony' of the coronation, for which Mary prepared herself by prayer and prolonged heart-searching.[14] Unfortunately, William's response to the uncertainties and confusion of English politics materially increased his problems. His taciturnity, brusqueness and lack of personal warmth were all personal (and family) characteristics which he could not easily discard, but his coldness was also a deliberate response to the pressures of English life, and especially the instability, ambiguities and selfishness of the strange political world which he had not yet learnt how to control.

Ultimately William's greatest difficulties were to centre on finance, but his first major problems concerned his use of the power of patronage, which was still reserved entirely for the crown. Initially, because of his obligations, William had to distribute offices to both Tories and Whigs. The rough balance which this established (often praised as a wise compromise) satisfied nobody. Danby as lord president and Halifax as lord privy seal loathed and opposed each other. The Earl of Shrewsbury had an ill-matched fellow secretary in Nottingham, who had drawn back from the Revolution, and voted for regency. The Treasury commission was strongly Whig, but this did not make the Commons any readier to vote supply, and only Godolphin possessed any real fiscal ability and experience. Mordaunt, first commissioner, used his office to push his claims for higher office. Delamere's experience speedily convinced him that the Revolution meant only a change of persons, not of governmental principles and methods, so he resigned. Sir Henry Capel was more malleable since he hoped for (and got) higher office. John Hampden's mind was beginning to give way. Even more immediately damaging in their results were the appointments to the Admiralty commission. Admiral Herbert lacked administrative ability but had a large retinue of corrupt dependants.

<hr />

[14] *Ibid.*, pp. 122, 132, 147, 157, 171, 193; Japikse, ii, 277; Doebner, *Memoirs of Mary*, pp. 11–13.

William Sacheverel was being rewarded for his part in promoting Exclusion in 1678-9. Sir Thomas Lee was even less well qualified since he had belonged to the lamentable Commission concocted in 1679 for similarly political purposes, and to whose gross inefficiency most of the current weaknesses of the navy could be traced.[15]

William's balanced appointments were reminiscent of the 1679 reconstruction of the Privy Council, when Charles included both ministers and opposition members. But that had been a clever stratagem, to divide and rule. The appointments of 1689 accentuated divisions and stimulated animosities to a point where government was impeded. The main divisive issue concerned the punishment of those held to be responsible for the unconstitutional policies that had led to the Revolution. James's evil ministers presented a disappointingly small target. The Catholics had fled. Jeffreys and lord chief justice Sir Robert Wright, cast as scapegoats, disobligingly died. Sunderland and Godolphin were out of reach – the former in Holland, the latter secure in William's favour. The scarcity of targets facilitated the Whig offensive against those who had served Charles in 1680-5, the men who had defeated Exclusion and then strengthened royal authority by allegedly illegal methods. The Whigs traced back to the royal reaction of 1681-5 the start of the 'design' to destroy the nation's liberties, and hoped to use the Convention to drive their most prominent opponents out of political life.

Among the ministers this meant Halifax, who was still active and influential, not Rochester who was temporarily unimportant. Halifax's real crime was his contribution to the defeat of Exclusion, and the fact that he was now influential as William's confidential adviser – although he had not played an active part in the Revolution – infuriated them. Technically Halifax was vulnerable, because as privy seal he had participated in the proceedings against the charters. His arch-rival, Danby, the pioneer political manager and manipulator, was regarded by the Whigs as an equally undesirable minister, particularly because he was once again constructing an extensive parliamentary

[15] W. A. Aiken, 'The Admiralty in Conflict and Commission', in Aiken and Henning (eds.), *Conflict in Stuart England* (1960).

interest. But the main Whig attack was directed against their opponents in the localities. They attempted to use a bill for the restoration of the corporations as the means of establishing a monopoly of local office for their own adherents, and so build up the basis of a permanent parliamentary majority. In fact they were trying to do in reverse what the court had attempted in 1661–2, 1681–5 and 1687–8.

The bill, which lapsed later, would have invalidated all forfeitures and surrenders of charters (of certain colonies as well as corporations).[16] Sacheverel introduced a clause which would bar from municipal office for seven years anyone who had assisted in the surrender of the charters. This would affect those who had collaborated with the court in 1681–6: that is Tories. It would not touch those who had taken part in, and benefited from, the regulations of corporations by Brent and his agents in 1687–8, when the powers conferred on the king by the new charters of 1681–6 had been used. Now of course those who had collaborated then with James would resume voting for orthodox Whigs. Technically, there was a strong set of arguments in favour of the proposal. With the important exception of Holt, the judges had ruled that voluntary surrenders of charters were not legal. As Nicholas Lechmere commented: 'There is no direct authority for surrender, but several against it. To my understanding, all corporations that send members to Parliament cannot waive it and destroy it. Out at this leak may run all the Government of England.'[17] Constitutionally the clause was defended as necessary to preserve parliamentary independence. As John Somers said: 'To destroy Corporations, and to make Parliaments at the pleasure of the Crown, this is the thing, and these persons are complained of for it.'[18] But the danger was not likely to recur in the seven years of the proposed disqualification, and the object was clearly to annihilate Tory support in the corporations.

The Tory tactic in the debates was to emphasize the social as well as the political consequences. Heneage Finch claimed that men of wealth and estates would be put out, and replaced by

[16] *HMC, XIIth Report*, app. vi, 422–32.
[17] *Ibid.*, pp. 429, 431.
[18] Grey, ix, 516–17.

'men of little or no fortune, and some call them the Mobile.'
More generally, Tory debaters rightly stressed the disruptive and
divisive effects. The clause would mean the ejection of thousands
of men who had already been turned out by James, but who
would now be tempted to turn to him. They would be replaced
by unreliable men who had succumbed to the temptations of
collaboration; even if they would now vote for the Whigs,
could they be trusted? This was certainly not the 'way to make
friends for the King (and) the Government'. It might promise
the Whigs a majority as large as the Tory one in 1685, but it
would give James substantial support at a time when he was
still firmly entrenched in Ireland.[19]

The division on 10 January 1690, when the clause was
defeated by eleven votes, was the last round of the battle that
had begun with the introduction of Exclusion of 1679. So long
as issues from the past were being discussed, the Whigs remained
united, but the price of this was the alienation of William. He
took no notice of the appeal directed to him in December 1689,
by Thomas Wharton, to trust the Whigs as his only friends, and
not to listen to those evilly disposed ministers who were advising
a dissolution.[20] The image which the Whigs had of themselves
as disinterested patriots did not correspond with their behaviour.
Many Whigs acted corruptly in office; William Jephson and
William Harbord were particularly bad examples. Few Whig
ministers proved to be as good administrators as the men like
Godolphin whom they attacked. By remaining deaf to repeated
entreaties from William, on the need for money for the expedition to Ireland and for foreign allies, by delaying the Indemnity
Bill, and finally by preparing an address calling on him to abandon his plans to go to Ireland in person, the Whigs convinced
William that they were practising political blackmail. On the other
hand, the Whigs genuinely believed that William's mind was
being poisoned against them by evil ministers, who would proceed
to subvert liberties unless they were checked in time. If the
agents of unconstitutional policies under Charles and James
escaped punishment after a major political upheaval, what

[19] *Ibid.*, pp. 511, 519, 520.
[20] Addit., 4107, ff.78–91. Reprinted in Dalrymple, appendix, part 2, 84–95.

chance would there be in the future of bringing such men to justice or of deterring ministers from unconstitutional methods?

William's disillusionment with the Whigs left him with no alternative but to turn to Danby and the Tories. His own preference was for ministers who were not attached to political parties, but would make service to him their first priority. Initially William hoped that Halifax would fill this role, but after acting as royal confidant for most of 1689 he buckled under the strain, resigning in February 1690, and then abandoning political activity of a constructive kind.[21] Infinitely tougher, and driven by ambition, Bentinck took on all the most thankless tasks (for instance Scottish affairs), working with devotion and tireless industry. It would be no exaggeration to describe him as the mainstay of William's government in its first five years, and apart from Puisars, Betty Villiers' brother-in-law, he was the only foreigner who from the start plunged into English politics. By comparison with Bentinck, Sidney failed to measure up to the duties assigned to him, although he was still invaluable as a confidant. Of William's English ministers only Sunderland, later, as 'minister behind the curtain' approached Bentinck in usefulness.[22]

The dissolution of the Convention, William's turn towards the Tories, and the rewards given to Bentinck, outraged Whig opinion. By February 1690 an active, if ineffective, Jacobite underground was operating. Serious army mutinies had occurred. A high rate of desertions testified to low morale. Soldiers in the new regiments sent to Ireland with Schomberg were dying in their thousands during the winter of 1689–90, as a direct result of the incompetence and dishonesty of their officers and the commissary departments. French privateers were ravaging merchant shipping; all trade with the Mediterranean was paralyzed. Governmental duties were generally being executed in a corrupt or slovenly fashion. The fleet was defeated at Beachy Head, so that in 1690 England was more open to invasion than at any other time during the French wars. This is the background to the failure of the Convention to rise above

[21] Foxcroft, *Life of Sir George Savile*, ii, 65 ff, and 201 ff.
[22] Kenyon, *Sunderland*, pp. 252–300.

issues and feuds arising from the past, and the all-absorbing competition for places. It cannot be emphasized too strongly that the immediate aftermath of the Revolution was a period of weakness, confusion and something like demoralization. Had James been restored by the French in 1690 historians would have had no difficulty in explaining the inevitability of this happening, and could have drawn illuminating parallels with the months of strife and confusion that preceded the Restoration of 1660.

In fact the new regime did more than survive. It supported a war that imposed greater burdens and presented more complex problems than any in previous English history. Important consti-tutional changes – such as the Triennial Act – were enacted. The reform of the fiscal system was carried out while the war was in progress. But even more surprising was the fact that after such an unpromising start a basis was laid for political stability and internal peace.

Why did the Revolution Settlement succeed, when all previous attempts had failed? The first reason is that the only alternative now was absolutism on the French model. The situation was entirely dissimilar to that of the 1650s, when Clarendon had succeeded in promoting the image of the monarchy as one of Protestantism, constitutionalism, reconciliation and indepen-dence of all foreign states and obligations. In contrast, James's acceptance of legislation passed by the Jacobite Dublin Parlia-ment, particularly its mass attainders and property confiscations, created a picture of vindictiveness that no later Declarations could efface. Catholic domination of the exiled court at St-Germain contradicted James's promises to respect the Church of England's rights, and guarantee religious liberty; no Protestant worship of any kind was permitted, Protestants were under constant pressure to convert, and royal declarations were first submitted to priests before being issued.[23] Melfort's influence created distrust, but it was James's dependence on France that most seriously damaged his cause. He had struggled hard, but unsuccessfully, in Ireland to escape French direction and control. Back in France, he depended on Louis's charity for everything

[23] *Memoirs of the Secret Services of John Macky* (1733), xxxviii–xxxix, xli–xlvii, l–lii.

after 1690. He could be restored only by a French invasion, which meant that, although legitimate king, he would have to conquer his subjects. This meant that even if he was sincere in promising to respect the religion and liberties of the nation, and send his French army back, it must be doubtful whether his patron would allow him to do so.

French exploitation of James gave English foreign policy a vital relevance; the survival of the Revolution Settlement and later the Protestant succession depended on the alliances formed against France. But in general the success of the Settlement was due to the fact that it confirmed, protected and perpetuated existing rights and liberties. There was an essential difference between the situation after 1688 and that of 1648–60. James repeated the claim which had been made by his father, that the destruction of the rights of the crown must necessarily be followed by the invasion and subversion of the individual rights of every subject and corporate body.[24] The arbitrary actions of the Rump and the Protectorate, their dependence on military force and coercion in ordinary acts of government, had confirmed Charles I's prediction. But after 1688, while James's right suffered, the existing rights of the nation were strengthened and confirmed.

Of course these rights were for the most part possessed by only a minority, although every section of society had a common interest in abolishing the methods which Charles II and James had used to manipulate the law, and the position of all classes and sections of society was incomparably freer than that of their counterparts under Louis XIV. But it is significant that former Whig proposals for the reform of popular grievances were abandoned. One of the reasons for its success was the conscious preoccupation with the need to preserve the constitution from change which influenced the framers of the Settlement. Change of any kind, however well-intentioned, could lead to dangerous instability.[25] This conservative caution, which of course benefited those whose position within the existing order was relatively

---

[24] *HMC, XIIth Report*, app, vi, 148–54.
[25] See, for instance, the very revealing debate on disfranchising the admittedly corrupt borough of Stockbridge, Grey, ix, 423–5.

favourable, makes most modern historians deny to the events of 1688–9 the title of a real revolution. Admittedly some of its features were purely negative, reactions against James's dynamic but unsuccessful policies. The Settlement represented a victory for decentralization in local government. The Church of England was permitted to squander a last opportunity for governmental reform. Parliamentary privilege was allowed to turn increasingly into a device for furthering the interests of MPs at the expense of the public and even of the electors.

So it can be seen that most of those who rallied to William against James were conservative, or conservationist, in their aims. They had been led to resist James because of the kind of changes he was trying to introduce; now the Revolution represented an opportunity to repair the damage which he had inflicted on the constitution, and to take measures which would prevent any future repetition of his actions. Old rights were to be preserved, there could be no question of attempting to establish new ones. The underlying theoretical reasons for this deliberate and conscious limitation of constitutional action in 1688–9 need emphasis. The success of the Revolution entailed the victory of an unhistorical but potent myth about the nature and origins of the English constitution. Whig theory triumphed.[26] All the constitutional and legal rights and liberties which were now confirmed, were believed to have originated before the Norman Conquest. They were a form of property, inherited from ancestors in the remote past, not a series of rights based on abstract reason or theory. Consequently their extent and nature must necessarily be fixed and defined, and each generation had the duty of ensuring their transmission intact to posterity.

It followed that there could be no question of one group of men using the power which they possessed in 1689 to establish new rights, or impose new institutional forms. This would have been as arbitrary an action on their part as anything that James had attempted; it was this recognition of the entirely theoretical limitations on their power by the men of 1688 that aroused Edmund Burke's admiration and praise a century later, in his

[26] This thesis is developed by J. G. A. Pocock, *The Ancient Constitution and the Feudal Law* (1967).

Reflections on the Revolution in France. For Burke, as for the Whigs of the years of stability after 1714, the Revolution had been entirely conclusive and effective. It had achieved all that a constitutional revolution could ever be expected to achieve. Its success as a final and once-for-all measure, firmly and permanently re-establishing the constitution, meant that later generations were left only with the task of defending and preserving its achievements – there was no call or scope for further action on their part.

Of course Burke was creating a new historical myth, in the face of what he recognized was a very different kind of revolution in France. It would be a gross oversimplification to suppose that the Revolution of 1688 produced a totally secure state or stable society. The immediate aftermath was one of war and depression, of unprecedentedly high levels of taxation and of civil wars in Scotland and Ireland. The confidence and unity of the nation, the efficiency of every section of government, were all subjected to the most intense strains during the war against France which began in 1689. The demands created by this prolonged war were to have revolutionary repercussions on government, particularly in the area of finance. Few of those who had taken part in the Revolution had expected or intended such a result. But the exploitation of English resources for the struggle against France had all along been William's primary objective. Power and position in Britain were only a means towards this end; in 1688 he had set as his minimum aim an English declaration of war against France, and William was clearly right in believing that only active English participation could enable him to contain French power and check French policies. In order to achieve this William was prepared to force the subordination of the Dutch to the English in naval matters, something that he accomplished as early as May 1689 in the little-known agreement about fleet commands, which was to lead to the rapid decline of Dutch naval power, and was in fact the first stage in their abdication of great power status.[27]

[27] J. C. M. Warnsinck, *De Vloot van den Koning-Stadhouder 1689–1690* (1934), pp. 14–23. On the general effects on foreign policy see G. C. Gibbs, 'The Revolution in Foreign Policy', in Geoffrey Holmes (ed), *Britain after the Glorious Revolution* (1969).

William was not interested in administrative problems as such, but the unprecedented demands which he made had the effect of forcing revolutionary changes in the financial aspects of government. English politicians were confronted with new and complex problems, but the 'country' Whigs and Tories refused to recognize them as real and urgent. Their parsimony, isolationism, xenophobia and instinctive hostility to the executive greatly hampered the prosecution of the war. William never overcame their obstructionism, as the failure of his turn to the Tories in 1690 proved. In the short term the key to the success of the Revolution can be found in the readiness of the younger generation of Whig office-holders to accept tuition from William, so that his foreign policies could be adequately supported despite their mounting cost and unpopularity.

One final question needs to be put. Where does the Revolution of 1688 fit, in the broader perspective of the history of revolutions in the modern world? It would be difficult to substantiate the claim that it had a very direct influence on either the American or the French Revolutions – except, perhaps, through the general influence of Locke's thought and writings. The Revolution of 1688 was neither a 'national' nor a bourgeois revolution. Its significance lies primarily in the fact that it delivered the first decisive blow to what may rather generally be described as the principles and institutions of the *ancien régime* – legitimate monarchy, divine right, an authority demanding unconditional obedience in every sphere of life. True, these had already been challenged and overthrown in one corner of Europe, by the Dutch war of independence against Spain, but if Dutch commercial society was distinctively modern in some respects (at least in Holland), forms of government in the United Provinces were most emphatically not. They may have been appropriate to certain local conditions and traditions, but even so they functioned effectively for only a relatively short period. The English forms of government which were safeguarded by the Revolution – Parliament, the common law, the jury system, local government by the justices and corporations – may also appear to be distinctively local to one country, and largely medieval in origin. But there was a vital difference between the record of government in these two cases. Foreigners were amazed at the cumbersome nature of the Dutch constitution, and often quick to exploit its many and obvious weaknesses. By contrast, English government in the decades after 1688 functioned, and was seen by contemporaries throughout Europe to be functioning, far more efficiently and equitably than any other. Specifically its solvency, as well as its successes in war after 1702, proved its superiority over the absolutism of Louis XIV. Limited, or mixed, government was shown to be capable of respecting liberties at home while waging successful war abroad. Such an achievement would have been impossible before 1688, and Montesquieu and Voltaire would have found few of the characteristics which they admired in early eighteenth-century England if they had come during the reigns of Charles II or James II.

Obviously the Revolution of 1688 is most closely related to the 'English Revolution' of the mid-seventeenth century. The thesis of this study has been to controvert the prevalent view that 1688 was a mere postscript, and that the future trend of English political development had already been determined by the defeat of Charles I. It has tried to show that on the contrary the establishment of absolutism was a much more practicable proposition in the decades after 1660 than in the years before 1640. It is true that the Revolution of 1688 was a very rapidly concluded process, which gave no time or opportunity for the kind of development and fermentation of ideas, experimentation with constitutional forms (abortive and sterile though they were), and intellectual and religious controversies, which have attracted most historians of the seventeenth century to the middle years, to the 'English Revolution'. The Revolution of 1688 lacks the rich and varied detail of the earlier period, but it was far more conclusive and decisive in its results, both for later development in Britain itself and for the emergence of Britain as a power in Europe.

Bibliography

Abbreviations Used in Bibliographical Essay

AAE, CPA,   Archives du Ministère des Affaires étran-
           gères, Paris; Correspondence politique,
           Angleterre.
Addit.,   Additional Manuscripts, British Museum.
Baschet,   Baschet transcripts, Public Records Office.
           The dates of the despatches are New Style.
Burnet,   J. Routh (ed.), *Bishop Burnet's History of
           my own Time* (6 vols, 1833).
CSPD,   Calendar of State Papers, Domestic.
Campana de Cavelli,   Marquise Campana de Cavelli, *Les
           Derniers Stuarts à Saint-Germain en Laye*
           (2 vols, 1871).
Clarendon,   S. W. Singer (ed.), *The Correspondence of
           Henry Hyde, Earl of Clarendon . . . with
           the Diary* (2 vols, 1828).
CJ,   *Commons Journals.*
Correspondentie,   N. Japikse (ed.), *Correspondentie van
           Willem III en van Hans Willem Bentinck*,
           I (1927), I, ii (1928), II, ii (1935), II, iii
           (1937).

Dalrymple,   Sir J. Dalrymple, *Memoirs of Great Britain and Ireland*, vol. 2 (1773).

D'Avaux,   E. Mallet (ed.), *Négociations de Monsieur le Comte d'Avaux en Hollande depuis 1679* (6 vols, 1752–53).

Grey,   A. Grey, *Debates of the House of Commons* (10 vols, 1759).

HMC,   Historical Manuscripts Commission.

Huygens,   Constantijn Huygens the younger, *Journaal van 21 October 1688 tot 2 September 1696* (1876).

Japikse,   N. Japikse, *Prins Willem III, de Stadhouder-Koning* (2 vols, 1933).

Luttrell,   N. Luttrell, *A Brief Historical Relation of State Affairs* (6 vols, 1857).

Mazure,   F. A. J. Mazure, *Histoire de la Révolution de 1688* (3 vols, 1825).

PC,   Privy Council.

PRO,   Public Records Office.

PWA,   Nottingham University Library, Portland Manuscripts, Intelligence out of England.

Ranke,   L. von Ranke, *A History of England* (6 vols, 1875).

SP,   State Papers.

State Trials,   T. B. Howell (ed.), *A Complete Collection of State Trials* (vols xi and xii, 1812).

Tanner MSS,   Bodleian, Tanner Manuscripts.

This bibliographical essay is not intended to be all-inclusive, nor is it an historiographical survey; for a discussion of the classic works on the Glorious Revolution and changing historical interpretations, the reader is referred to the opening pages of the introduction. The main purpose of this essay is to survey mainly the more recent writings on the Glorious Revolution, its background and long-term consequences, and on topics associated with it. In addition, since it has been emphasized that this is an underworked field, some indication is given of topics on which further research is needed, and of the kind of questions which could be asked.

The best general, factual background study is that by David Ogg, *England in the Reigns of James II and William III* (1955), a continuation of his earlier and equally excellent *England in the Reign of Charles II* (revised edition, 1956, 1962). In addition to Macaulay's *History of England from the accession of James II* (the best edition is C. H. Firth's, six volumes, 1913–15), L. von Ranke's *History of England, principally in the seventeenth century* (six volumes, 1875) is the one probably best worth reading. Some of Ranke's judgements, based on the material provided by German diplomats in late Stuart Whitehall, have to be discounted. After all such men, as foreigners in a very strange land, were often wrong in their assessment of the workings of the constitution and of English ways of life and thought. The same caution has to be used in reading F. A. J. Mazure, *Histoire de la révolution de 1688 en Angleterre* (three volumes, 1825), which was the first study based on the French diplomatic archives.

Of modern general studies, *The Growth of Political Stability in England, 1675–1725* by J. H. Plumb is required reading, with a clearly presented and convincingly argued thesis on the reasons why England escaped from the chronic instability, unsettlement and disunity that produced the Glorious Revolution. Of studies on the Revolution itself John Carswell's *The Descent on England* (1969) has the merit of fully describing the European context of William's invasion. *The Glorious Revolution of 1688* by Maurice Ashley (1966) provides a straightforward factual narrative. Apart from perhaps the chapter on Scotland, *The English Revolution, 1688–1689* (1938) by G. M. Trevelyan is now obsolete. Finally, as has been said repeatedly in the course of this study, it is my contention that Lucille Pinkham's *William III and the Respectable Revolution* (1954) is uncritical, unhistorical and defective in interpretation throughout. Perhaps this sweeping and unreserved condemnation ought to provoke readers into checking on such a dismissive judgement, either in the original, or in the extract printed with others by late seventeenth-century and modern writers in the collection edited by G. M. Straka, *The Revolution of 1688, Whig Triumph or Palace Revolution?* (1963).

Four biographies of leading actors in the Revolution are essential reading. The oldest, F. C. Turner's *James II* (1948) is thoroughly adequate, but it now requires revision to take into account work completed since its publication. J. B. Wolf, in his *Louis XIV* (1968), performs the feat of achieving comprehensive treatment of all aspects of developments in France, and of the French impact on Europe, in a single, lucid and manageable volume. An equally important subject, *William III*, has at last received the treatment he deserved in the biography by S. B. Baxter (1966). The most informative and directly relevant life for the study of the Revolution is the exceptionally good biography of Sunderland by J. P. Kenyon, *Robert Spencer, Earl of Sunderland* (1958). By comparison, the same author's *The Stuarts* (1958), while vigorously and entertainingly written, is rather general, and his *The Nobility in the Revolution of 1688* (1963) remains an exploratory essay. Other biographies of statesmen concerned in the Revolution vary considerably in value. A. Browning, *Thomas Osborne, Earl of Danby* (three volumes, 1944–51), H. Horwitz, *Revolution Politicks: the career of Daniel Finch* (1968) and G. H. Jones, *Charles Middleton: the life and times of a Restoration politician* (1967), all provide important material on the workings and character of politics and government at this period, as well as on the events leading up to the Revolution. G. W. Keeton has important things to say about the law, and the administration of justice in the courts, but his attempted rehabilitation of the most celebrated judge and universal scapegoat of the time, *Lord Chancellor Jeffreys and the Stuart Course* (1965), is not entirely convincing. A new biography is needed to replace the primly pedantic biographies of Halifax by H. C. Foxcroft, *A Character of the Trimmer* (1946) and *The Life and Letters of Sir George Savile, Marquis of Halifax* (two volumes, 1898), which was useful because it contained his writings. However, the pamphlets and essays are now far more easily accessible in the Penguin edition by J. P. Kenyon, *Halifax, Complete Works* (1969). W. S.

Churchill's magisterial *Marlborough: his life and times* (two volumes, 1958–63) is also becoming dated; its partisanship and endlessly eloquent and highly-coloured language tend to become monotonous. Sir Tresham Lever has little to say about James II's reign in *Godolphin: his life and times* (1952). Finally M. V. Hay exposed many of the inconsistencies in the traditional view of James, but his own attempt to supply an alternative interpretation in *The Enigma of James II* (1938) cannot be described as convincing. Sir K. G. Feiling's pioneering study, *A History of the Tory Party, 1640–1714* (1959), is still very useful.

The long-term consequences of the Revolution have been examined in the last few years in some important studies. The best introduction is the generally excellent collection of essays edited by G. Holmes, *Britain after the Glorious Revolution* (1969); the best are those on foreign policy (by G. C. Gibbs), the structure of parliamentary politics (by H. Horwitz), conflict in society (W. A. Speck) and in the Church (G. V. Bennett). D. Rubini has examined the effects on parties in *Court and Country, 1688–1702* (1968), while Sir Charles Petrie's older study, *The Jacobite Movement, the First Phase, 1688–1716* (1938), has now been largely superseded by *The Mainstream of Jacobitism* by G. H. Jones (1954). P. G. M. Dickinson has dealt clearly and authoritatively in *The Financial Revolution in England* (1967) with the central financial problems of government finances after 1688. A study of these problems during the reigns of Charles II and James II is the subject of C. D. Chandaman's long-awaited study of the public revenue, 1660–88, but this has yet to be published at the time of writing.

Another important study is awaited in the field of Church history. Robert Beddard has been engaged in a biographical study of Archbishop Sancroft, but this has yet to be published. An article by him, 'The Committee for Ecclesiastical Promotions, 1681–84' (*Historical Journal*, X, 1967) arouses expectations of the valuable contribution his book may make. G. M. Straka has explored the trials of conscience which the Revolution created for many Anglican clergymen in his *Anglican Reaction to the Revolution of 1688* (1962). Relations between the clergy and James form the subject of a useful short chapter by Godfrey Davies, *Essays on the later Stuarts* (1958), and V. Buranelli in *The King and the Quaker* (1962) explains the partnership of James with William Penn, and pleads for their common sincerity. There are biographies of several leading clergy who were concerned in the Revolution, many of whom achieved bishoprics or prominence as latitudinarian divines afterwards. E. F. Carpenter published biographies of *Thomas Tenison* (1948) and Henry Compton, *The Protestant Bishop* (1956), while A. T. Hart wrote *The Life and Times of John Sharp* (1949) and *William Lloyd, 1627–1717* (1952). Overall the best surveys of Church history and of relations between Church and state are those by Norman Sykes: *Church and State in the eighteenth century* (1962) and *From Sheldon to Secker, aspects of English church history, 1660–1768* (1959). G. R. Cragg's *From Puritanism to the Age of Reason* (1950) is particularly illuminating on the changes in the intellectual climate, and can be profitably read in conjunction with the stimulating monograph by R. S. Westfall, *Science and Religion in Seventeenth-Century England* (1958).

Two subjects which need much more detailed research are military history and the connections between business and politics. On the first the only recent book is a general study by Correlli Barnett, *Britain and her army, 1509–1970* (1970). There is also some relevant material in J. R. Western, *The English militia in the Eighteenth Century* (1965). On business, banking and commerce we have little beyond the pioneering biography of D. C. Coleman, *Sir John Banks, baronet and businessman* (1963), and a brief introductory essay by W. Letwin, *Sir Josiah Child, merchant economist* (1959).

The most useful collections of documents on political affairs and constitutional matters are by J. P. Kenyon, *The Stuart Constitution* (1966) and E. N. Williams, *The Eighteenth Century Constitution* (1960). Reference can also be made to the more detailed volume (VIII) edited by Andrew Browning in the *English Historical Documents* series (1966). The most important contemporary political texts are those by John Locke : *Two Treatises of Government* is best read in the accessible edition by Peter Laslett (1967), and *A Letter Concerning Toleration* in the (1955) edition by Patrick Romanell. Of the enormous literature on Locke the reader can be advised to begin by reading the collection of essays edited by J. W. Yolton, *John Locke, Problems and Perspectives* (1969).

Three bibliographies refer directly to this period. Mary Keeler has produced a new (1970) edition of the standard *Bibliography of British history, Stuart period, 1603–1714*. W. L. Sachse covers the shorter period of 1660–88 in *Restoration England* (1971). Robert Walcott in *The Tudor–Stuart Period of English History: a Review of Changing Interpretations* (1964) uses an approach and makes assumptions (derived from those employed by Sir Lewis Namier for the study of later eighteenth-century politics) which most specialists in late-seventeenth-century political and social history have rejected as invalid and inappropriate.

Of all the subjects which need research perhaps the most important is to establish the connections between business and politics, and in particular to examine mercantilist policies, principles and interests. The tensions within the East India Company, and the careers of Sir Josiah Child and Sir John Friend, would repay attention. Secondly, the court of Charles II and James II would seem to provide ample ground for analysis. Some of its leading figures – Rochester, Godolphin, Melfort and Halifax – need new biographies. The politics of the army are an important subject about which we know little. There is room for a systematic study of the pamphlet literature of years before 1688. At the local level we need to know more about the functioning of the Commission of the Peace after James II's wholesale purges, and the effect of royal policies on the corporations is a subject of first rate importance. Finally James himself is due for a new biography.

Index